OXFORD RESEARCH STUDIES IN GEOGRAPHY

General Editors

J. Gottman   *J. A. Steers*
F. V. Emery   *C. D. Harris*

Rural Conservation in Inter-War Britain

John Sheail

CLARENDON PRESS · OXFORD
1981

Oxford University Press, Walton Street, Oxford OX2 6DP
London   Glasgow   New York   Toronto
Delhi   Bombay   Calcutta   Madras   Karachi
Kuala Lumpur   Singapore   Hong Kong   Tokyo
Nairobi   Dar Es Salaam   Cape Town
Melbourne   Wellington

and associate companies in
Beirut   Berlin   Ibadan   Mexico City

Published in the United States
by Oxford University Press, New York

British Library Cataloguing in Publication Data

Sheail, John
Rural conservation in inter-war Britain. – (Oxford research studies in geography).
1. Land use, Rural – Planning – Great Britain – History
I. Title   II. Series
333.7'6'0941   HD598   80–40975

ISBN 0–19–823236–5

Photoset in Great Britain by
Rowland Phototypesetting Limited, Bury St Edmunds, Suffolk
and Printed in Great Britain
at the University Press, Oxford
by Eric Buckley.
Printer to the University

For
KAREN

ACKNOWLEDGEMENTS

A very great number of people have helped me in the preparation of this book. My greatest debt is to Gillian, my wife, without whose constant encouragement and advice the book would never have been written and completed.

I am grateful for the support given me by Professor J. A. Steers, who first suggested that I might write a book, Professor G. E. Cherry and Mr F. B. Gillie, who commented on early drafts of the manuscript, and the late Mr A. J. P. Gore and other members of the Monks Wood Experimental Station (Institute of Terrestrial Ecology). Mrs Pauline Dower very kindly gave me access to, and permission to quote from, her late husband's papers. It is a pleasure to record all the help given me by the many record offices, and in particular the staff of the East Sussex and Surrey Record Offices.

Hilton,
1980

JOHN SHEAIL

EDITORIAL PREFACE

JOHN SHEAIL after taking his doctorate at University College, London, in 1967 was appointed to the Monks Wood Experimental Station of the Nature Conservancy as an historical geographer – a post which was, and still is, unique in that context. After the changes in 1973, made as a result of Lord Rothschild's recommendations, he was transferred from the Nature Conservancy to the Institute of Terrestrial Ecology, a change which made no difference to the work he was doing.

In 1976 his book, *Nature in Trust, The History of Conservation in Britain*, was published. In it he demonstrated how the present-day interest in conservation originated in the nineteenth century when nature lovers, amateur and scientific, emphasized the necessity of preserving wild animals and plants. These ideas expanded greatly in the first half of this century, and after the War of 1939–45 the early and valuable work of, e.g. the National Trust and the S.P.N.R. was strengthened by the formation of many county trusts, the Nature Conservancy and the National Parks Commission. Despite later changes of titles the work of these bodies still continues, although at the present time it is often handicapped by lack of finance.

In this book the author is concerned with the planning and conservation of the countryside. His work is based on a wide and intimate knowledge of the natural landscape, and also on the study of numerous files and reports preserved in record offices. He also draws attention to the great mass of material in archives, national and local, which has yet to be investigated in detail. In spite of the fact that papers in the Public Record Office are closed to the public for 30 years, so that much recent work cannot be consulted, the available sources afford an abundance of data not only for the material used in this book, but also for a corresponding one on the urban environment.

The author has already established himself as an authority on the history of conservation, and in this book he seeks to encourage his readers to take a new look at this formative period in the development of our environment.

November 1980   ALFRED STEERS

CONTENTS

LIST OF ILLUSTRATIONS

FIGURES

TABLES

PLATES

(between pages 12–13)

by suburban development (*courtesy of The Commons, Open Spaces and Footpaths Preservation Society, Henley-on-Thames*).

2. The type of development in Great Bookham that caused the Surrey County Council to seek planning powers in its Bill of 1931. The photograph of a rutted road and ill-assorted development was one of many specially commissioned by the County Council in 1930 (*courtesy of the Surrey Record Office*).

3. The Ancient Monuments Act of 1931 was designed to preserve the rural setting of Hadrian's Wall and other outstanding ancient monuments from building, quarrying and other forms of development (*courtesy of Aerofilms Ltd.*).

4. Avebury and Silbury Hill were the subject of the first statutory planning scheme intended to help preserve the rural setting of an ancient monument (*courtesy of the Allen Collection, Ashmolean Museum, Oxford*).

5. The northern by-pass around Headington, Oxford, was one of many built to relieve urban congestion, but threatened by ribbon development. Roadside-planting schemes were often encouraged as a way of blending the new road with the countryside (*courtesy of the Allen Collection, Ashmolean Museum, Oxford*).

6. An example of the hill-and-dale topography that threatened to devastate the Northamptonshire countryside around the iron-works of Corby (*courtesy of Aerofilms Ltd.*).

CHAPTER I

Inter-War Britain

Planning means taking stock of the present and preparing for the future. Why then look at the past? Surely the aspirations, challenges and circumstances of the past were very different from those of today. This may well be so, but, as John Dower told a group of students in the late 1930s, 'our humanity, our basic needs, are largely the same'. The physical make-up of Britain has hardly changed. History provides us with an essential perspective for the things we do. If we understand the reasons for the existing state of town and country planning, we shall, in the words of Dower, obtain 'a better, clearer and deeper judgment of their value, their limits, their defects'.[1]

This book has a twofold objective in looking at the Britain which John Dower knew in the 1920s and 1930s. First, the inter-war years are worth studying for their own intrinsic fascination and, secondly, the skills and experiences gained during that period still influence the concepts of planning today. The inter-war years were not a discrete period: the generation of the 1920s and 1930s drew on the experience of earlier years, and many of the issues were further developed and brought more tangible results in the 1940s. Indeed, the inter-war period was so critical and innovative that precedents can be found for almost every aspect of rural planning and conservation today. A study of the period helps to place our present-day anxieties and activities in a better context.

This book will indicate some of the ways in which that generation strove to use and manage the rural environment to the optimum. Evidence will be drawn from the books, reports, and papers of the period, which throw light on the issues which exercised the minds of central and local government, professional and voluntary bodies, landowners and users, residents and visitors to the countryside. The fact that there is almost unrestricted access to the official papers of the period, held in the Public Record Office and county record offices, means that it is possible to obtain a well-rounded and intimate view of how decisions were made and of how concepts and concern for the countryside were translated into executive action.

Rural planning did not occur in a vacuum. Town and country were closely integrated and, although the emphasis of this book will be on the countryside, many of its themes impinged on town and country alike. They were in turn part of a wider response to the complex changes taking place in Britain during the inter-war period. In the early 1920s the key words were Reconstruction, Restoration, and Recovery: there was a conscious attempt to recreate the conditions of the pre-war period. By the 1930s Planning had become a key word, both in the economic and social sectors of life. Eyes were fixed on some utopian point in the future. Meanwhile, account had to be taken of more immediate goals, especially when the boom of 1919/20 turned into a slump, and when the modest progress of the later 1920s was followed by the still greater economic crash of 1929–31.[2]

The inter-war years have been generally regarded as a time of failure and missed opportunities. They have been described as the wasted years or the 'long week-end' of the twentieth century. No matter what steps were taken to sustain the peace abroad and prosperity at home, wars broke out and industries failed. Over 10 per cent of the insured work-force was out of work in any year between 1921 and 1938. Almost 3,000,000 people were unemployed in January 1933, and the figure remained at over 2,000,000 until the summer of 1935. Some unemployment was only to be expected as industries underwent reorganization and modernization, but the long dole queues were evidence of a more deep-seated problem. As late as 1936, 250,000 men were classified as long-term unemployed. When old industries collapsed, there was often nothing to take their place and men were left to 'rot'. This was seen in its most extreme form in Brynmawr and Jarrow, where 74 and 68 per cent respectively of the insured work-force were unemployed in 1934.

The economic and social malaise of the inter-war years has been variously attributed to the ineptness of governments, industry, and workers. This does not, however, explain the reasons for their lack of understanding and in-adequate response to the problems of the period. To dwell on the personal inadequacies of politicians, employers, and unionists is often to overlook the complex and rapid changes taking place. There was such a conflict of evidence. British economic life was heavily dependent on the prosperity of a few export-oriented industries at a time when world trade was stagnating and Britain's share of that trade was falling. Output in the cotton and shipbuilding industries declined in absolute terms. Despite this, the national economy was growing at 'an historically respectable rate', and a new industrial structure was evolving. In the manufacture of electrical components, motor cars, and aircraft, Britain's performance compared well with that of other countries, whether measured in terms of technical innovation, professional management, or capital investment, and each of these products was to have a fundamental effect on economic and social life.[3]

Many were baffled by this apparent contradiction in economic performance. Should they try to revive old industries or concentrate on promoting the new enterprises? How much attention should they give to the traditional export markets? Detailed investigations tended to lead to even greater confusion. The coal-mines of Nottinghamshire and south Yorkshire, and the steel plant of Lincolnshire, were relatively prosperous, and there were fears that any financial aid given to the coal and steel industries might benefit the more vigorous parts and leave the remainder untouched. In the new industries, there was little room for complacency. Far from achieving economies of scale and standardization among products, the new industries tended to be small scale and of great variety. In the electrical industry, for example, this led to the manufacture of twenty-three different types of plug for electric fires!

Everything seemed topsy-turvy. Far from depending on exports, the new industries looked to the home market. Less than 10 per cent of vehicles, electrical goods, and artificial fibres were exported. Instead, these new industries appeared to flourish in spite of the depression in the staple industries and consequently high unemployment and static wage rates. The paradox was achieved because the cost of imports of food and raw materials had fallen to a much greater extent than the value of Britain's exports of manufactured goods. As Taylor explains, 'the terms of trade turned strikingly in Great Britain's favour. Taking 1938 as 100, 142 units of exports were needed before the war to buy 100 units of imports; in the twenties only 115 units of exports. Great Britain could, as it were, afford both higher unemployment and a higher standard of living at the same time'.[4]

Real wage rates for a full week's work rose slowly with the fall in prices until 1932, when further growth was checked until the worst of the slump and cuts in salaries were over. Wages rose again between 1935 and the outbreak of war. These improvements, albeit modest, were sufficient to ensure the prosperity of those industries contributing to the amenities of life, producing, for example, electric irons and vacuum cleaners. Employment in hotels, restaurants and places of entertainment actually rose during the Depression, providing clear evidence that at least a significant proportion of the population could, and wanted to, enjoy the opportunities now within their economic grasp.[5]

These opportunities might include a new house, a motor car and longer holidays. Over 4,000,000 houses were built between the wars; new houses had never been so cheap or widely available as in the mid-thirties. The number of private cars rose from 110,000 to 2,300,000. Perhaps of greater significance, especially in the 1920s, was the contribution of the motor bus and coach. One contemporary observer described their introduction as little short of a revolution, and 'infinitely more swift than that of the railways' in the nineteenth century. The number of ordinary stage-bus operators rose from 331 during the war to 3,962 in 1930, so that almost every village became linked into an intricate urban–rural communications network. By 1932 buses carried more passengers than did trams. A major constraint on suburban and rural building development was removed. Helped by the general reduction in the length of the working day, the town-dweller could now live further from his place of work, and many families accordingly moved into a semi-detached house on the outskirts of town, helped by the building society, hire-purchase, and the season ticket. It became easier to visit the coast and venture into the countryside for relaxation and exercise.[6]

There was a poignant aspect to this new-found affluence. There were not only 1,000,000 motor cars in 1930, but also over 1,000,000 men unemployed. As Stevenson has written, the improvements in the standard of living for the majority served only 'to highlight the inequalities in opportunity and expectation amongst different sections of the population'. For the lower 30 per cent, Glynn and Oxborrow have described how 'drabness was universal, mal-nourishment common'. Particularly in times of cyclical depression, well over 10 per cent suffered severe hardship and poverty. Striking inequalities in wealth were experienced not only within, but also between, communities and regions. Mathias has written of how a car journey in 1930 between Slough and South Wales would have passed from almost the boom conditions of industrial ex-pansion, rising consumption standards, and social innovation, to a region of depression, economic stagnation, and social apathy. National averages were more than usually deceptive during this period. Everything depended on whether one spoke of Slough or Merthyr Tydfil, Oxford or Jarrow, Coventry or Greenock.[7]

The economic and social tragedy of the inter-war years arose out of the extreme concentration of employment on the large-scale, ailing industries. In 1920 over half the work-force was in the mines or manufacturing, and of these 9,000,000 persons, 2,600,000 were in metal manufacturing and engineering, 1,500,000 in mining and quarrying, and 1,300,000 in textiles. These had been the staples of the Industrial Revolution, and had made Britain the 'Workshop of the World'. Their role as an employer had even increased in the decades immediately before the war. For historical reasons, they were concentrated on the coalfields, and two-thirds of their employees were north of the Trent. The remainder were largely in the Midlands and South Wales. Worse still, each of these areas tended to specialize in some aspect of the staple industries. Thus, Clydeside was the centre of shipbuilding and heavy engineering, and the West Riding of coal and woollens. Their vulnerability was most graphically high-lighted by the plight of Jarrow, where the demise of one industry and even one firm ruined a community. Even if some alternative employment was available, it could hardly absorb many of the displaced and unemployed. Various remedies were proposed—moving the unemployed to more prosperous parts of the country, and the movement of new industries to the depressed areas. None was a panacea, and all involved immense practical difficulties.[8]

The disparities in regional wealth showed every sign of increasing. During the inter-war period the Home Counties, and the East and West Midlands, increased their share of the population, whereas the population of Glamorgan and Monmouth fell by 9 per cent. Whilst the population of Greater London rose by nearly 500,000, the population of South Wales declined by 115,000 and that of Northumberland and Durham by 39,000 between 1931 and 1938. These changes reflected the shift in prosperity away from those areas associated with the typical nineteenth-century type of development toward the far more heterogeneous kinds of industrial growth characterized by the Home Counties. Significant numbers of miners, and workers in heavy engineering and textiles, moved southward, where they took up new skills and mastered the new tech-niques required for the mass production of cars and other consumer goods. In doing so they began to reverse the 150-year-old trend of migration to the north.

In this respect, the inter-war years marked a new phase in the Industrial Revolution. It was the young and vigorous who found it easiest to leave the depressed regions, leaving behind 'the middle-aged, sick and elderly, who became a greater burden on local relief, social and medical services'. According to Perkin 'it further reduced spending in the local shops and left empty houses and lower property values in the old areas, reducing rent and rate income and the capacity of the local authorities to support social and other services'. Depressed areas became more depressed 'in a vicious downward spiral of decay'.[9]

In a recent study of the period Glynn and Oxborrow have warned against exaggerating the impact of unemployment on economic and political development. Helped by the essentially local nature of high unemployment, the problem proved to be both limited and containable, especially when compared with the experiences of some continental countries. It was possible 'for the majority of the population to accept unemployment as an inevitable misery which had to be tolerated by an unfortunate minority'. Whilst the truth of these observations is not to be doubted, a mixture of conscience and fear ensured that poverty and unemployment remained sources of considerable anxiety on the part of some of the more thoughtful and influential members of society. Direct action in the form of hunger marches not only kept 'the other Britain' before the public eye, but it was a warning of what might occur if remedies were not found. Confronted with Fascism and Communism, British democracy had to be especially vigorous in fighting these economic and social evils. Writers warned that 'the democratic system of government is on trial. It will only survive if it can produce a policy equal to the problems of our time and a leadership capable of evoking the co-operation and enthusiasm necessary to carry it through'.[10]

In this context Marwick has drawn attention to the 'agreement' aspect of the 1930s, whereby people from a wide range of political and professional backgrounds felt they had a special responsibility to pool their expertise and experiences in discussion and the production of broadsheets on the most pressing fundamental issues of the day. The PEP (Political and Economic Planning), founded in 1931, was the most famous of these spontaneous groups. A year earlier, the influential *Political Quarterly* was launched as a channel for 'injecting new ideas, new proposals, new ways of looking at the problems confronting the nation, the Empire and the world'. In 1935 another group, called the Next Five Years' Group, published a five-year programme of action in the fields of economic policy and international relations. Over 8,000 copies of the programme, subtitled 'an essay in political agreement', were sold. By adopting a philosophic and scientific approach, it was hoped to replace ignorance, prejudice, and dogma with a more rational plan for the use of the nation's resources.[11]

Whilst promoting a fresh approach to the governance of Britain, such groups as PEP and the Pilgrim and Rowntree Trusts were continuing the tradition of voluntary work in public life. This work might take the form of serving on district or county councils, or of helping to promote one of the many societies devoted to such activities as the protection of children or animals, ancient buildings or rural amenities. Some societies were long established; others were new. The Council for the Preservation of Rural England (CPRE) was a product of the inter-war period, founded in 1926 and actively supported by persons from all parties and professions, and residents of town and country. Far from becoming redundant, voluntary activities continued to play an important role in the life of Britain.

The reasons for voluntary work were many, but nearly all were related in some way to the improvement of human society. Those voluntary bodies and their supporters dedicated to the protection of the rural landscape were motivated not only by a love of the countryside but also by the certain knowledge that they were improving the quality of life in inter-war Britain. Their efforts were playing a part in reducing the scale of personal and corporate thoughtlessness and selfishness, of which the despoliation of the countryside was a symptom. Rural protection was part of a larger battle to create a more responsible human society, in which the individual was prepared to sacrifice personal gain or advance where this was in the interests of the larger community.

It is in this context that reference may be made to the eminent social historian, G. M. Trevelyan, both as an example of how public figures could be drawn into voluntary work and for the cogent reasons which he put forward for protecting rural England. As a boy, Trevelyan had taken up long-distance walking over the grouse moors of the family's estates and, from this, had developed his passion for natural beauty in the landscape of Northumberland and elsewhere. When living in Hertfordshire, he had helped to organize an appeal for funds to buy and save the beautiful Ashridge estate from the speculative builder. In later years, he used his inherited wealth to purchase farms specifically to preserve their open, natural appearance. Thus, by inclination and by deeds, Trevelyan became involved in the voluntary movement, taking up the honorary posts of chairman of the estates committee of the National Trust, president of the Youth Hostels Association, and a trustee of the British Museum.[12]

In his view there were both material and spiritual reasons for protecting natural beauty. Tourism brought much needed revenue to many parts of Britain. If the charm of the countryside and coast were destroyed, the visitors would cease to come. If a man built an ugly building that marred the landscape, everyone would suffer. Changes in the appearance of the landscape were a matter of common concern. But above all, natural beauty was one of the most creative forces in the British national character. The happiness and spiritual health of the whole people depended in large part on their having ready access to natural beauty.

This concept of the role of natural beauty was widely shared by scientists of his generation. The countryside was regarded as more than a repository of food and shelter. J. S. Huxley wrote of how man did not live by bread alone. Some men at least required 'the beauty of nature, the interest of nature, even the wilderness of nature, the contact with wild animals living their own lives in their own surroundings'. R. G. Stapledon was a leading agronomist and the last person to harbour fanciful notions about the countryside. And yet he believed every human being had a deep-seated love of nature. The land was an essential source of inspiration and recreation. The beauty and variety of scenery were no mere luxury or ornament of pleasant living: their protection was of fundamental importance to the spiritual welfare of the nation.[13]

The appeal of Nature was perhaps threefold. First, there was its aesthetic value—the beauty of its form and colour; secondly, natural life was always being renewed, season by season, and year after year; thirdly, there was a natural bond between Man and Nature for both were products of the Earth. Far from diminishing, Trevelyan believed these feelings for Nature were becoming stronger, with more and more people seeking out 'the wildness and greatness of untamed, aboriginal nature', and venturing into even the most mountainous parts of upland Britain and Europe.

This keener sense of awareness reflected the fact that natural beauty could no longer be taken for granted. Through the science, machinery and organization of the Industrial Revolution, Man had transformed extensive areas of country-side into something quite different. The lowlands had become so 'de-naturalized' that it was often only in upland areas that Nature could be found natural and unadulterated. It was only here that one could escape the vulgarity of man's triumphs over Nature, and get 'back to old beginnings, to nature as God made her, as first she arose from the deep of time'.

This desire to get 'back to old beginnings' was particularly strong as ideals and aspirations crashed one on top of another in the wake of the Great War, slumps, and depression. The appeal of natural beauty was strong because it was completely free of new argument, dogma, and doctrine. It represented no change in fashion but 'something far older yet far more fresh'. Like the universe and life itself, natural beauty was a mystery and, as a mystery, it made 'a common appeal to the sectaries of all our religious and scientific creeds, to the lovers of all our different schools of poetry and art, ancient and modern, and to many more beside'. According to Trevelyan, natural beauty was the highest common denominator in the spiritual life of contemporary Britain. Why then destroy the remaining, unblemished parts of the countryside and coast? Why 'rob unborn millions of their delight in life'? In the same way as it was unthinkable to burn the treasures of the National Gallery or British Museum, it was equally reprehensible to allow the Lake District or Cornish coastline to be spoiled piecemeal by the exploiter.

The generation of the inter-war years faced a critical choice, namely whether to protect this heritage of natural beauty or to allow it to be dissipated and lost. In former times, natural beauty 'needed no conservation. Man was camped in the midst of it and could not get outside it, still less destroy it.' Science and technology had brought that age to an end: the inter-war generation now had to make a conscious choice whether to conserve that heritage. It was the role of the voluntary bodies to emphasize the magnitude of the choice. Unless the present rate of destruction was arrested and reversed, the future social, economic, and political life of Britain was likely to be 'brutish and shorn of spiritual value'.

CHAPTER II

The Urban Attack

The boundary between town and countryside has never been well defined, and the distinction became even more blurred during the inter-war period. According to Taylor, 'all England became suburban except for the slums at one extreme and the Pennine moors at the other'.[1] This chapter will describe this suburbanizing trend and look in greater detail at the way in which one part of the country, Surrey, tried to ensure that as many people as possible enjoyed an urban way of life within a still rural setting.

It was the scale, rather than the direction, of change that was so breathtaking during the 1920s and 1930s. As early as 1811 an American visitor described how London extended 'its great polypus-arms' over the neighbouring countryside. Prosperous citizens lived 'in the outskirts of the town in better air—larger houses—and at a smaller rent'. The city centre became 'a mere counting-house, or place of business'. The trend continued and, by the 1860s, a writer described how the rich 'outbid one another for suburban dwellings, until all fields and meadows for miles become covered with houses, more or less closely built, and the fresh air of the open land is further and further removed from the heart and centre of the town'. When an amateur naturalist returned to his old collecting grounds north of Marble Arch in 1859, the hedges and songbirds had gone. 'The sharp click of the bricklayer's trowel was now the prevalent sound. The grass-field was turned into a square, laid out with flower-beds and fenced with an iron railing.'[2]

By the turn of the century, ambitious schemes were being proposed for the suburban development of London and other cities, including a Lakeside Suburb for London around the Brent reservoir. After the First World War, development took off at an unprecedented rate, especially in the 1930s. Over 4,000,000 houses were built in Britain, equal to about a third of the housing stock by 1939. Whereas the nineteenth century had been the century of the private landlord, the twentieth became that of the owner-occupier and the council tenant. The boom in privately built houses in England and Wales reached a peak of 293,000 units in 1934–5, and continued at a high level until the war, when perhaps a quarter of all families lived in their own home.[3]

No precise record was kept of the amount of land converted to residential use. Best has estimated that, between 1927–8 and 1933–4, about 38,000 acres of land were developed for housing each year, which rose to an average of 50,000 acres per annum between 1934–5 and 1938–9. A report on north Middlesex described how 'the shadow of urbanisation hangs over it like a cloud ready, on the slightest encouragement, to precipitate a rain of bricks and mortar'. London was spreading and 'absorbing town after town, and village after village, on its outskirts; obliterating boundaries in a solid mass of buildings'. Often the developer's only concern was to find cheap land suitable to provide the foundations of his houses. As a consequence, some of the finest market-gardens disappeared during this period, as their well-drained soils, sitting astride good communications, were bought up and developed for housing.[4]

No matter how great were the delights of suburban life, many dreamed of an idyllic home set in the very heart of the countryside, away from it all. For an increasing number, the dream became a practical proposition. In his book, *Wild England*, C. J. Cornish described in 1895 how the 'pine and heather country' of the Surrey hills and Hampshire commons was being parcelled out and covered with substantial houses. 'The villas follow the line of the sand as closely as collieries follow the line of the coal.' Cornish warned that the area of pine and heather was finite, and that soon the buildings would destroy the scenery and sense of remoteness that had originally attracted the house-owners to the area.[5]

The coast was similarly threatened. Fields on top of cliffs and overlooking bays were acquired by speculators, and plots were sold for individual building development. The most famous example was Peacehaven, a completely new settlement of over 2,000 houses that grew up in the inter-war years on the South Downs coast. The official guide described how the land was once 'just a bare stretch of downland, terminating abruptly to the south in 100-feet high, white chalk cliffs'. It made a perfect 'haven of peace for the retired city man, and yet so easily accessible that a half-hour's bus run westward would bring the resident to Brighton or two miles eastwards to Newhaven affording two easy routes to London'. Vaughan Cornish estimated that there were 500 miles of cliffed coastline in England: the average frontage of a modern villa was 22 yards, so that 40,000 villas could be built along the top of the cliffs. He noted that 160,000 houses were built in England in the half-year ending 31 March 1935. It was not a question of protecting the countryside and coast from vandals, but of preserving them from the very people who wanted to enjoy their amenity and atmosphere more fully.[6]

What caused this comparatively sudden and dramatic acceleration in the development of the countryside and coast? It did not arise from any substantial increase in the nation's population. On the contrary, the (crude) birth rate had fallen from 35.4 per 1,000 population in the period 1871–5 to 14.7 per 1,000 in 1933, when the trend was arrested and a small rise took place. The Registrar-General warned that unless a significant improvement in fertility took place, the population would rise by one or two millions to 47,500,000 in the decade 1951–61, and then fall in absolute terms. Biological 'forces' might, of course, prevent this happening, but clearly no dramatic increase in population was taking place and none was expected.

The physical demands being made on the countryside and coast arose from profound changes taking place in the economic and social outlook of an essentially stable population. According to the distinguished architect and planner,

Patrick Abercrombie, the countryside was under attack from the towns, and rural life was disintegrating from within. At the same time as towns were overspilling into the countryside and their citizens were ransacking even the remotest areas, agriculture was depressed and many craft industries were disappearing. These trends could not be entirely explained in terms of cheaper houses and the advent of the motor car. House mortgages and the Ford Eight, or Austin Seven, only facilitated a social movement which was already gathering momentum. In the words of Abercrombie, there was a growing desire to escape from 'the respectable rows of suburban houses built under the sanitary bye-laws' of the Victorian and Edwardian periods for a new, more rural, environment.[7]

The largest element in this outward movement was the white-collar worker. The inter-war period was marked by an expansion in the service or tertiary industries, leading to a proportionate rise in the number of personnel in managerial, administrative, and clerical posts. According to Burnett, 'here was a great army . . . keenly anxious to demonstrate their arrival by the adoption of a life style which separated them from the respectable poverty from which many had risen'. For many, this was achieved by moving to a new suburb and into a detached or semi-detached villa, which was owned rather than rented. The suburb represented a kind of utopian ideal, made up of single-family houses-and-gardens providing a better life for the family, away from 'the racket, smell and din of the town' amid 'the quiet and peace of rural surroundings'. The tragedy was that in many instances the suburb destroyed many of the attributes so widely admired in the countryside without any commensurate improvement in conditions nearer the city centres.[8]

THE SURREY COUNTRYSIDE

In order to appreciate the ramifications of suburban and rural development, it may be helpful to look in more detail at events in one part of the country, namely the county of Surrey. This was not only the most prosperous county in Britain, but also one of the most seriously threatened by urban development. The main roads between London and the South Coast made it easy to reach the Surrey heaths, woods, and river valleys. A growing number of Londoners visited Surrey for picnics and other forms of recreation, and some took up permanent residence. The county's population rose from 845,578 in 1911 to 1,180,878 in 1931. With the electrification of the Southern Railway, commuting became possible from many hitherto remote parts of the county.

In welcoming these trends, the Surrey County Council stressed the equally important tasks of safeguarding the interests of the existing residents and 'the great heritage' of the Surrey countryside. In evidence to a parliamentary committee in 1931 the Council described how 'large numbers of broken down vans, railway wagons, tramcars and other objectionable vehicles are constantly being brought into the County, and dumped down in some of its most beautiful parts' for use as permanent or holiday homes. However, the most serious threat to the Surrey countryside was from the speculative builder. During the 1920s, several large estates had been sold to speculators, who were described by the Council as 'the modern equivalent of the slum landlord'. They did little more than subdivide the previously open land into building plots, without proper provision of roads, sewers, and other essential services. Because the plots were often sold to persons with little capital, many years might elapse before every plot was developed. The scattered development paid no regard 'to the amenities of the District nor to the effect of this type of development on adjoining properties'. The lack of any maintenance meant that the roads were often impassable in wet weather, and the Epsom Rural District Council warned of the risk of the water supplies being contaminated by sewage. The scattered nature of development made the cost of installing mains sewerage prohibitive. In the interests of both amenity and public health, some degree of regulation over building was needed.[9]

For the County Council, matters came to a head in 1929 when the beauty spot of Norbury Park in the Vale of Mickleham was threatened. Not only did the park include the famous yew woods of the Druid's Grove, but it was also overlooked by Box Hill, which had been given by the previous owner of Norbury Park to the National Trust and was visited by many thousands of holiday-makers each year. The owner had also intended to give the Park to the Trust, but had died before the conveyance was expedited. Now there were rumours of a speculator making 'a very effective bid for this estate of 1,340 acres' in order to extend the housing development which the Council claimed had already ruined the amenity of nearby Fetcham, Great and Little Bookham, and Effingham.[10]

In order to forestall the speculator, a member of the County Council bought Norbury Park in a personal capacity for £85,310. Soon afterwards the owner of the adjoining Fredley estate died, giving rise to fears lest that area might be developed to the detriment of Norbury Park. The same member of the Council thereupon bought the Fredley estate for £11,350 and in both cases the County Council met the cost and assumed responsibility for managing the properties.[11]

The Council wanted to keep the main and most beautiful parts 'in a state of natural preservation' for the public enjoyment. Everything depended, however, on the level of contributions toward the cost of buying the estates. The County Council, although taking temporary custody, vouchsafed only £20,000. The response of the district councils was disappointing, and a public appeal for funds was postponed until the general economic climate improved. Accordingly, a flexible management programme was required, and a report commissioned by the Council in 1930 recommended that up to 270 acres of peripheral land should be sold for building development in order to help meet the cost of buying and preserving the remainder of the land. The impact of the buildings on the rest of the Park would be kept to the minimum. In accepting these recommendations, the Council realized that it lacked the necessary statutory powers to carry them out. Although it could contribute to the purchase of property under

1. Norbury Park, Surrey, overlooking the Vale of Mickleham in 1931. It was one of the objectives of the Surrey County Council Act of 1930 to help preserve such views which were threatened by suburban development (courtesy of The Commons, Open Spaces and Footpaths Preservation Society, Henley-on-Thames).

2.   The type of development in Great Bookham that caused the Surrey County Council to seek planning powers in its Bill of 1931. The photograph of a rutted road and ill-assorted development was one of many specially commissioned by the County Council in 1930 (courtesy of the Surrey Record Office).

3.   The Ancient Monuments Act of 1931 was designed to preserve the rural setting of Hadrian's Wall and other outstanding ancient monuments from building, quarrying, and other forms of development (courtesy of Aerofilms Ltd.).

4.   Avebury and Silbury Hill were the subject of the first statutory planning scheme intended to help preserve the rural setting of an ancient monument (courtesy of the Allen Collection, Ashmolean Museum, Oxford).

5.   The northern by-pass around Headington, Oxford, was one of many built to relieve urban congestion, but threatened by ribbon development. Roadside-planting schemes were often encouraged as a way of blending the new road with the countryside (courtesy of the Allen Collection, Ashmolean Museum, Oxford).

6. An example of the hill-and-dale topography that threatened to devastate the Northamptonshire countryside around the iron works of Corby (courtesy of Aerofilms Ltd.).

the Open Spaces Act of 1906, the development of the estates for building and other purposes would require a Local Act of Parliament.[12]

The example of Norbury Park provided the Council with first-hand experience of the difficulties of buying and thereby saving tracts of countryside, outstanding for their scenery or recreational value. Especially in districts with a low rateable income, it was virtually impossible to raise sufficient funds to acquire and manage land. There had to be additional forms of protection. Although extremely reluctant to interfere in the sale and management of land, the Council concluded that it was reasonable to impose 'protective clauses' when previously open land was sold for building purposes. In order to prevent 'the wholesale destruction of the countryside', no development should take place until roads were built and steps taken to preserve amenity and public health.[13]

Meanwhile the Council received encouragement from those individuals and voluntary bodies advocating the preservation of the countryside. An article written by J. C. Squire in the *Observer* in 1929 was particularly important. Squire had already played an important role in 'battles' waged by voluntary societies for the preservation of Stonehenge (see p. 52) and Waterloo Bridge. In his article Squire cited the case of Friday Street in Surrey, where a hamlet and hammer-pond stood in the bottom of a secluded, well-wooded valley. An 'enlightened' landowner protected most of the pinewoods and heathland, but about sixty acres had been offered for sale. The development was only likely to take the form of a few brick villas, set within well-wooded gardens, but Squire argued that this would be enough to change the character of this famous beauty spot. In view of the development of 'district after district in the London neighbourhood' surely there was a case for preventing this spot from being 'built over and uglified'.[14]

The article caught the attention of James Chuter Ede, a member of the County Council and Labour Member of Parliament for South Shields. He was particularly impressed by Squire's realistic attitude toward development, and he especially commended the following part of the article:

development there must be; the population is expanding, and family for family, it is demanding more space and more fresh air; the development of the motor-car has made it possible for multitudes of people to 'live in the country' who never thought of doing so before. The business of those who desire to preserve our inheritance of landscape beauty as nearly as possible intact . . . is to reconcile themselves to these facts and to think about how expansion should best be governed, in what direction it should be set, and under what conditions. If Friday Street should not be overrun by small houses, where can the small houses be built, and, when we have decided where they can most suitably be built, how are they to be arranged in such a manner as to interfere as little as possible with existing amenities

In bringing the article to the attention of the County Council, Chuter Ede emphasized how the Local Government Act of 1929 had, among other measures, made the County Council responsible for the upkeep of rural roads. Because road improvements increased the accessibility and therefore the building value of the countryside, the Council had become even more intimately involved in land-use issues. They had a clear responsibility to help in finding ways of accommodating more people in the countryside without destroying the essential beauty of that countryside.[15]

The Council's statutory powers were very weak, but if a Local Bill could be successfully promoted, the County Council would be in a uniquely strong position to save the countryside. Chuter Ede described how the sums of money collected by the voluntary bodies to protect the countryside were ludicrously inadequate, especially where 'rapacious agents' behaved in a manner 'little short of blackmail'. In contrast, Surrey had the highest rateable income *per capita* of any county: a penny rate produced £35,000, on which a capital value of £500,000 could be financed. If the Council could obtain powers to pursue a carefully formulated purchasing policy, within a statutory framework of rural planning, a worthwhile contribution to the preservation of the countryside could be made. In the cases where land had to be purchased, the cost could be made a public charge, and 'every citizen high and low could contribute on a fair basis'.

THE SURREY COUNTY COUNCIL ACT

Chuter Ede was the county councillor for Epsom, and it was the Epsom and Guildford Rural District Councils that set the precedents for action. In 1930 the district councils successfully supplemented their ordinary powers by promoting separate, but identical, Local Bills, which allowed them to regulate building development more rigorously. The councils could introduce planning schemes for land which was developed or in the course of development, and could buy land in order to improve or develop frontages on streets and roads being built or widened. The Local Bills also improved controls over the erection of outdoor advertisements, location of petrol stations, and felling of trees over 30 feet in height or a specified girth.[16]

From the experience at Friday Street, the County Council realized that every council would seek additional statutory powers by promoting a Local Bill. In order to make this unnecessary, and to meet its own requirements at Norbury Park, the County Council decided to intervene. Even before the Royal Assent had been given to the Epsom and Guildford Bills, the Council started to promote a Surrey County Council Bill, which would convey similar powers to all district councils in Surrey under the aegis of a joint planning committee, on which the County Council would be represented. The Bill would make it possible to include all types of land in a planning scheme and grant extra powers to check ribbon development, protect beauty spots and vantage points, and facilitate the management of Norbury Park.[17]

In his article Squire had condemned the ribbon development taking place along many major roads. Even if the new houses were well designed and the builders made considerable savings by making use of existing roads and utilities, it was wrong to cut off the countryside from the roads by a thin ribbon of development. All building should be channelled into existing or new settlements. The County Council believed it was fully justified in asking for unprecedented powers to control this kind of development in view of the heavy costs which local authorities had incurred in road construction. Some years earlier £463,000 had been spent on a bypass for Kingston-upon-Thames. The results were 'extremely disappointing' because the new, quick through route was soon aligned by 'all manner of premises each with its own individual access to the road'. Cars and the carts of bakers and milkmen were parked outside, thereby turning the bypass into another 'ordinary town street'.

The Council argued that because it had provided landowners with a new road frontage and had paid compensation for the severance of their land, the Council should be given powers to regulate access to the new roads in the public interest. Under the Bill, the Council wanted powers to regulate the construction of access ways and building development up to 200 feet from any new road, or from any of the 'main thoroughfares' in the county. Any person adversely affected by the regulations could claim compensation. In addition, powers were sought to purchase land up to 220 yards from the centre of the roads in order to preserve amenities of the locality. By these means, the Council hoped not only to improve the flow of traffic along these expensive highways, but also to provide unprecedented opportunities for landscaping the highways. They would 'bring within the scope of practical politics ideas which have been discussed in town planning circles in England for some years'.[18]

The Surrey County Council Bill was given the Royal Assent in July 1931. As expected, it served as a precedent for Bills promoted for other parts of the country and for more general legislation, namely the Town and Country Planning Act of 1932 (see p. 70) and the Restriction of Ribbon Development Act of 1935 (p. 133). Although soon 'overtaken' by these general statutes, Surrey continued to pursue a vigorous policy of its own. As a local authority, it had both the will and, equally significantly, the resources to do so. The Local Act of 1931 had given the county a valuable headstart and insight into the regulation of road and building development. A Surrey Joint Planning Committee was in existence by the end of 1932 and, by mid-1934, steps were being taken to regulate the use of land adjoining fourteen roads, with an aggregate length of 62 miles.[19]

The Joint Planning Committee soon discovered widely differing attitudes toward building development. The Bagshot Rural District Council claimed that there was little danger to the 5,400 acres of open space in its district, and the expense of preparing a planning scheme and of meeting the consequent claims for compensation was not worth while. In contrast, the Dorking and Horley Rural District Council was seriously concerned at the risk of development on parts of Leith Hill, which would impair the scenic value of over 5,000 acres of wood and heath land. As an alternative to building development, the owner of a wood had agreed, after long negotiations, to sell his property for £6,000, promising £200 as a contribution toward its preservation. An adjacent owner offered £4,000 if the wood was conveyed to him as an open space, and the Dorking council appealed to the County Council to contribute the remaining £1,800 as the first stage in a Leith Hill Preservation Scheme. The Council agreed and was thereafter responsible for the drafting of the Scheme, which limited development to private dwellings at an average density of one to seventy-five acres, with a minimum curtilage of one to five acres. The drafting of the Scheme took a considerable time because the Council wanted to obtain the voluntary agreement of the landowners in order to obviate future opposition and heavy claims for compensation. In the event, 80 per cent of the landowners approved the final scheme, which was submitted to the Ministry of Health for statutory approval in 1938. War prevented further consideration.[20]

Similar steps were taken to preserve a nine-mile length of the North Downs, comprising 5,000 acres of scarpland between Merrow Downs and Ranmore Common. The County Council agreed to incur the costs of the planning scheme 'in order to secure for the public the full and permanent enjoyment of this at present unspoilt country'. Footpaths already gave 'the public free access over the most beautiful parts': the aim was to preserve from building all those parts visible from the Vale of Holmesdale and to limit development in and around Netley Heath to one house per seventy-five acres.[21]

One of the more remarkable aspects of these schemes was the way in which almost every landowner voluntarily accepted the restrictions imposed on building development. In 1934 the County Council was therefore asked to provide 'a specific example' of their own support for preservation schemes by abandoning the sale of the outer parts of Norbury Park for development. Already eleven plots of an acre each had been auctioned, and a house built. At first the Council decided that 'a complete reversal of policy could not be justified unless substantial contributions were received from outside sources to enable the County Council's liability to be reduced'. Local authorities had contributed only £3,000 and the Council 'felt badly let down'. It was only after heated exchanges, and the offer of £10,000 by the Leatherhead Urban District Council, that the County Council finally dropped plans for further development in 1936.[22]

SURREY AND THE GREEN BELT

The County Council believed a profound change was taking place in the public attitude toward the countryside. People were no longer just interested in town parks and recreation grounds; they also wanted access to the countryside for informal enjoyment and relaxation. It was because of this perceived shift in public taste that the Council decided to preserve as much of Norbury Park as possible in its 'natural' state, rather than turn it into 'stereotyped playing fields or recreation grounds'. The Council became increasingly interested in the future of all open spaces, beauty spots and commonland in the county.[23]

The Council had learned through experience that land should be acquired *before* it fell into the hands of speculators and, accordingly, a long-term strategy had to be worked out as to the type and location of open spaces to be preserved from building development. One of the objectives of the Local Bill in 1931 was to concert the efforts of the individual local authorities and thereby enable the county to participate in any regional schemes for the Home Counties. It was decided, however, to stay outside a scheme proposed in 1934, whereby members of the Greater London Regional Planning Committee would pool their contributions for the purchase of open spaces within the Committee's proposed Green Girdle around London. The Council noted that Surrey intended to spend up to £10,000 per annum on preserving areas of its choice. The County Council would be 'in a distinct minority' in the proposed scheme and, furthermore, the County Council was equally interested in preserving areas outside the Green Girdle.[24]

The Council was much more enthusiastic toward the Green Belt Scheme launched by the London County Council in 1935, which offered up to half the cost of acquiring and preserving open spaces and farmland in neighbouring counties. Instead of being one of a committee, the County Council was able to enter under this scheme into direct negotiations with the London County Council. Between July 1935 and November 1936, five properties with an aggregate of 1,440 acres were acquired in Surrey for £224,270, ranging from Ockham Common of 347 acres to Buccleuch House in Richmond. Ockham Common was so accessible from London and popular with visitors that the London County Council contributed about £7,000 to the purchase price of £24,000. Guildford Rural District Council gave £2,000 and adjacent landowners £3,400. The County Council realized that the cost of paying compensation in order to prevent ribbon development through the area would be so high that they decided it was cheaper to contribute the remainder of the purchase money and ensure that no building development could take place. Nonsuch Park was acquired for its scenic and historic value: the London County Council contributed 40 per cent of the purchase price of £118,000, and the County Council and two local councils contributed £23,616 each. Shabden Park was acquired following the death of its owner. The County Council was especially interested in safeguarding an area of West Horsley called the Sheepleas, where the 263 acres of land provided 'a natural approach' to the area preserved under the Council's North Downs Preservation Scheme. Following disagreement over the purchase price, the County Council issued a compulsory purchase order under the Local Act of 1931, but agreement was eventually reached and grants were obtained from the London County Council and rural district council.[25]

By the time the green belt scheme was extended and given statutory effect under the Green Belt (London and Home Counties) Act of 1938, a further twelve properties had been acquired. The scheme in Surrey had cost £500,000, of which the County Council contributed £200,000, the London County Council gave £150,000, and the local authorities £125,000. In addition, the County Council had approved the expenditure of £40,000 in acquiring or assisting in the preservation of 240 acres outside the scheme.[26]

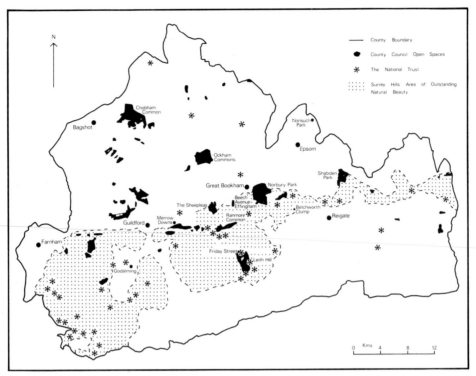

Fig. 1. The open spaces of Surrey in 1975

AMENITY AND LOCAL GOVERNMENT

Although Surrey was one of the first areas to register a keen interest in the protection of the countryside, the response was at first muted. Voluntary effort was frustrated by a lack of resources and local authorities by their lack of statutory powers. As J. C. Squire wrote, 'everybody grumbles and nothing is done'. It is in this context that the initiatives taken by members of the Surrey County Council had a considerable significance, on both a regional and national scale.

Chuter Ede and his fellow councillors wanted the best of both worlds, whereby more houses were built in the Surrey countryside and the beauty and recreational potential of the countryside could be preserved. For them, Squire's article was a breakthrough in that it suggested how a policy of planning control and land acquisition might not only avert conflicts in land use but might also provide opportunities for improving and enhancing the amenities of the countryside. By introducing this positive aspect to land-use controls, it became politically possible for Chuter Ede to stimulate Surrey into action. His task was made considerably easier by the fact that the County Council was a very prosperous authority and had already obtained considerable experience in promoting legislation.

Surrey exploited the scope for autonomy in local government to the full, and retained a reputation for independent action throughout the 1930s. The value of its headstart in rural conservation became even more obvious in the post-war years. By 1975 the public had rights of access to 6 per cent of the land area of the county. The fact that Surrey was so well provided with open spaces made it easier to withstand the enormous recreational and other pressures exerted by the nearby urban populations (figure 1). There were not only 1,000,000 people resident in Surrey, but a further 7,000,000 living in nearby Greater London.

The Surrey experience had a wider, national role in highlighting the important part which local authorities could play, if they chose, in deciding the future use and management of land. So far, planning historians have tended to give short shrift to the activities of individual local authorities. They have instead devoted a lot of attention to the writings of Ebenezer Howard and his fellow advocates of the garden city movement. They have recited how these pioneer thinkers tried to combine the attributes of urban and rural life by planning garden cities, equipped with a choice of employment and the other advantages of urban residence, set within an essentially rural environment. The concept was widely discussed, and two ventures started—Letchworth Garden City in 1903 and Welwyn Garden City in 1920 (see p. 125). They were intended as working models of what could be achieved on a larger scale.

Despite a vigorous propagandist lobby and the obvious interest aroused in the garden city movement, historians have emphasized how modest was the response of the inter-war generation to the ideal. They have attributed this to the lack of insight and initiative shown by that generation and, on a more practical level, to the apathy shown toward non-profiteering ventures. Events in Surrey may suggest a further and more positive reason why the garden city movement did not take off in the way expected by its followers. There was an alternative course of action, that appeared to many in local and central government to be more practical and in greater accord with the capacity of private and public enterprise at that time. The Surrey experience drew attention not only to the damaging consequences of uncontrolled building development, but also to the possibilities of regulating such development through a formula of statutory planning and land acquisition. Instead of resorting to radical remedies and new forms of *ad hoc* administration, the existing pattern of local government could be extended and adapted. With leadership, foresight, and resources, it might be possible to check urban sprawl without resort to such devices as the garden city. The Surrey method was incremental, and perhaps more in tune with the British temperament.

So far the planning historian has tended to concentrate on the literature of such voluntary bodies as the Garden Cities and Town Planning Association, and on the proceedings of the various professional bodies. The Surrey example may suggest that the time has come to quarry further into the archives of local and central government in order to gain new perspectives on the activities of the voluntary, professional, and official bodies, as well as on such well-worked themes as the garden city. Record Offices exist for nearly all counties, and they contain not only the minute-books of the local authority committees concerned with early planning issues, but they have often preserved files of associated correspondence and memoranda. From these sources, it is possible to trace the growing involvement of local government in environmental issues, and it may eventually be possible to obtain a more balanced view of the quest in the inter-war years for a new way of life, which sought the merits of town and country, without the attendant defects of both.

CHAPTER III

Rural Disintegration

According to Patrick Abercrombie the 'urban attaque' was encouraged and made more devastating by the increasing disintegration of rural life. He wrote in 1930 that 'if the country had remained in the hands of the same families who have done so much to create its typical English beauty of park, farm, village, lane, copse, and hedgerow trees, there would have been an unchanged landscape, except for a few new roads and the electric pylons of the main grid'. It would have been easier to concentrate development into well-defined areas, with 'the bulk of normal country remaining unchanged'.[1]

Instead, personal factors and the growing burden of death and estate duties encouraged the sale of large areas of land. Even when the estates remained intact, the rapport that had existed between the local inhabitants and the previous owners had been destroyed. The traditional feeling of being jointly responsible for preserving local amenities had gone. In many cases, estates were broken up and sold to farmers in small lots, particularly in the years just after the war. The proportion of farmland in owner-occupation rose from 11 per cent in 1913 to 20 per cent in 1921, and 36 per cent by 1927. It represented the largest change in landownership since the sale of monastic lands in the sixteenth century. In prosperous times, the new owner-occupiers might have been tempted to sell a few plots for building purposes but, with the dramatic fall in agricultural prices in the 1920s and 1930s, the heavily mortgaged farmers had no scruples in selling as much land as possible.

The disfigurement of the countryside was therefore symptomatic of a deeper-seated malaise. Any search for remedies had to take account of the fact that the rural population was in a distinct minority. Only 6.7 per cent of the national workforce were engaged in agriculture, compared with 30 per cent in Germany and 38 per cent in France. Out of a population of 41,000,000 only 3,500,000 to 4,000,000 lived in agricultural villages, and fewer than 2,500,000 in the open countryside of England and Wales. Not surprisingly, most people looked upon their town or city as 'the real England—or Wales'. Although the countryside covered 33,000,000 acres, it was regarded functionally as little more than an adjunct of the towns and cities, which occupied little more than 4,000,000 acres.

Rural policies tended to be conceived from an urban standpoint. In a lecture of 1932 Lord Phillimore distinguished four strands in the townsman's perception of the countryside. First, rural areas were required for accommodating such urban prerequisites as sewage farms and refuse tips. Secondly, the countryside provided sites for golf courses and playing-fields, and thirdly areas for new housing developments. The fourth claim was less well defined, but no less important. Because so few people actually worked in the countryside and their contribution to national wealth appeared to be so small, there was a tendency to look upon rural areas as 'a vast park or pleasure ground for the townsman, where he should be able to recuperate from his efforts, and be solaced by its natural beauties'.[2]

AGRICULTURE

The townsman's ambivalent attitude toward the countryside was demonstrated by the fortunes of agriculture. The countryside of the inter-war period displayed all the classic features of a one-industry town, in so far as the whole way of life was centred on the dominant occupation. The pre-eminence of agriculture had become particularly striking following the obsolescence and disappearance of so many craft-industries. The ramifications of any change in the fortunes of agriculture were therefore widely felt but, whereas the economic and social misery caused by the demise of a one-industry town was concentrated and easy to comprehend, the effects of agricultural decline and failure were much more dispersed and therefore harder for the townsman to grasp.

During the food crisis of the latter part of the First World War, farmers were encouraged and indeed compelled to increase food production by means of improvements in land husbandry and by the extension of the arable area. In order to achieve these changes in the minimum of time, the government safeguarded investment through a system of price guarantees, which the Agriculture Act of 1920 was intended to continue for at least a further four years. Soon afterwards, however, market prices fell and the Exchequer was required, for the first time, to provide heavy subsidies to farmers. The risk of famine had long since ended, and the public demanded cuts in the tax burden: in the political reassessment which followed, the townsman abandoned farming. The Act of 1920 was repealed in 1921 and all price support and controls were scrapped.[3]

During the Depression of 1929–33 the price of wheat fell by a further 50 per cent, and barley by a quarter. Once again, farmers reduced their arable acreage and abandoned more marginal land in order to reduce labour costs and make other economies. According to one estimate the conversion of 1,000 acres of arable to grass could lead to a reduction of up to forty workers. In a brief to a Cabinet Committee in 1930 the Ministry of Agriculture described the bleak prospects for those farmers who were unable to switch from grain to a more remunerative crop. The Eastern Counties and parts of Hampshire, Oxfordshire, and Berkshire were hardest hit. The long-term nature of their plight was underlined by a further confidential report, prepared in 1938, which drew attention to areas containing a large proportion of sub-marginal land, where the output had fallen substantially since 1918. Once again, the areas of light sand and gravels, limestone, and heavy clay soils figured prominently (figure 2).[4]

During the inter-war years, the international pattern of free trade gave way to a search for economic self-sufficiency through protectionism on the part of an

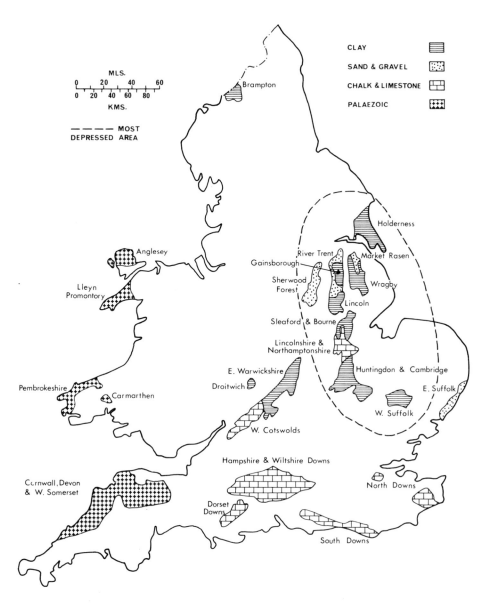

Fig. 2. Areas containing a relatively high proportion of sub-marginal land, as identified for the
Ministry of Agriculture in 1938

increasing number of nations. Despite considerable debate as to the repercussions of tariff barriers and other expressions of nationalism on land use,
the effects were scarcely significant in Britain by 1939. The arable area fell by
4,000,000 acres to 11,900,000 acres between 1918 and 1939. Although livestock
numbers remained high, up to a quarter of the annual output of animal

products depended on the import of 8,750,000 tons of imported feeding-stuffs. About 70 per cent of the wholesale value of annual peacetime food requirements for the British population continued to be imported. It took the threat of another war to reverse the trend significantly. At first incidentally, and then more openly, steps were taken to safeguard food supplies in the event of another war by raising home food production.[5]

Once again, submarine warfare threatened the import of food supplies and therefore military defeat through starvation. In addition, the centres of many towns and cities were devastated or threatened by bombing, so that by 1941 the countryside had become the scene of not only a desperate attempt to raise food production but also the venue of many war industries, dispersed from the towns into the comparative safety of the countryside. It was in order to assess the long-term significance of these two disparate trends that the government appointed a 'Committee on land utilisation in rural areas', under the chairmanship of Lord Justice Scott. The vice-chairman was the geographer, L. Dudley Stamp, and members included S. R. Dennison, Professor of Economics in the University of Wales. At about the same time, the Institute of Agricultural Economics at Oxford made an in-depth study of a sample area of 15,000 acres of rural Berkshire. Although both inquiries dealt with post-war reconstruction, they drew heavily on pre-war experiences, and their findings provide a convenient forum for introducing discussion on the status and character of farming and rural life in the inter-war period, in the larger context of industrial development and rural amenity.[6]

Both studies painted a very gloomy picture of rural life. 'In none of the country's major activities was the need for reconstruction likely to be greater than in rural industry.' The countryside had lagged far behind the towns in both economic and social progress. 'Both in his purchasing power and in the physical and social conditions of his life—housing, the public services, education, leisure and the opportunities for using it—the countryman was at a disadvantage compared with almost any urban dweller.'

Most commentators attributed this ever-increasing disparity between urban and rural standards of living to the depressed state of agriculture. There had been little or no scope for raising the comparatively low farm wages, providing opportunities for promotion and advancement, improving housing conditions, or supplying piped water, sewerage, or electricity. Almost half the parishes of England and Wales lacked a sewerage system, and a third had no piped water (figure 3). Electricity had reached less than one in twelve farms by 1938 (figure 4). Some families left the countryside as a result of redundancy, but many more moved voluntarily because of the lack of opportunities and amenities. Between 1921–4 and 1938, the number of men and women employed in agriculture fell by over a quarter. The Scott committee found it significant that the number of males under 21 years, employed in farming, had fallen by 44 per cent, compared with a fall of 19 per cent among those over 21 years.

Not only had the depression encouraged the depopulation of the countryside,

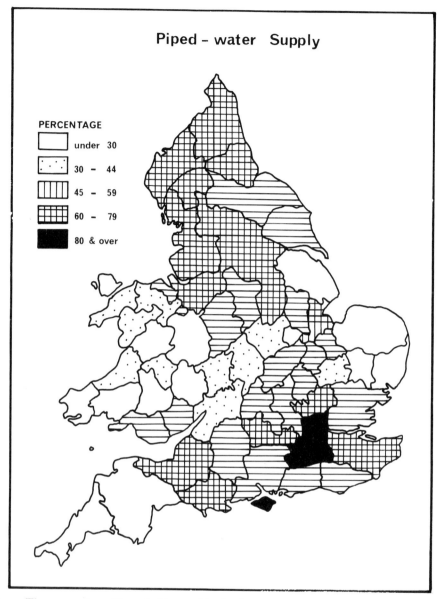

Piped – water   Supply

PERCENTAGE

☐ under 30

⬚ 30 – 44

▥ 45 – 59

▦ 60 – 79

■ 80 & over

Fig. 3. The proportion of farm holdings with piped water, as indicated by the National Farm
Survey of 1941–3

but it had accelerated the rate of urban encroachment. Between 1919 and 1939, about 862,500 houses had been erected in rural districts, of which 700,000 were built by private developers. Although urban expansion was to be expected in an essentially industrialized nation, the weakness of agriculture had accelerated the trend. Almost any land suitable for building could be sold, irrespective of its

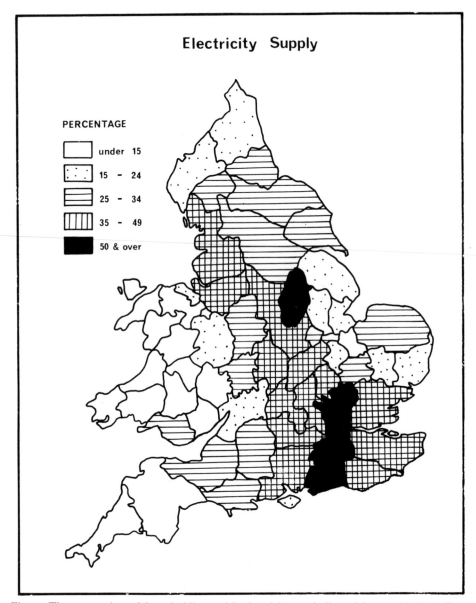

Fig. 4. The proportion of farm holdings with electricity, as indicated by the National Farm Survey

agricultural quality and usage. As the Scott committee stressed, it was 'often the best agricultural land—level, well-drained stretches of good soil—which was most suitable and the least expensive from the building point of view'. Most development occurred around the fringes of towns, where land was frequently intensively managed for such purposes as market-gardening. Housing estates and roads broke up farm units, isolating fields from the main parts of the farm, and the incidence of trespassing, vandalism, and pollution increased.

To most observers, this trend towards rural depopulation and urban encroachment could only be allayed by turning agriculture once more into a prosperous industry. The disagreement arose in deciding how this long-term prosperity could be achieved. Eleven of the twelve members of the Scott committee believed the only way was to preserve the farming industry at its present size, halt the drift of labour from the land, and revive or sustain the 'traditional mixed character of British farming'. Because developers could always purchase land for higher prices than farmers, the members of the committee called for new powers which would enable the farming industry to 'fight its battles on terms of greater equality'. They put forward a proposal which had been discussed for some years, whereby no one should be allowed to alienate farm or forest land without first proving that it was in the national interest that the change should take place. By placing the onus of proof on the potential developer, it would be easier to safeguard good agricultural land.[7]

These assumptions and recommendations were described by a leader in *The Economist* as an unusually fine specimen of vague, romantic flubdub: the kind of muddle-headedness that was the curse of well-meaning planners and the vice of vested interests. What was really wanted from a committee was not a hotchpotch of vague and benign recommendations, but rather an authoritative inquiry into what extent, under what conditions, and by what products, British farming could be made as productive as other industries. One member of the Scott committee, Professor Dennison, shared these misgivings, and he accordingly produced a Minority Report which was published with the Majority Report in August 1942.[8]

Far from regarding the existing area of farmland and the size of the labour force as essential to prosperity, Dennison believed that they were major impediments. Whilst it was sensible to ensure that development should take place on inferior, as opposed to good, farmland, if this did not entirely offset the benefits of development, there was no case for granting agriculture a greater priority over other forms of land use. On the contrary, where a developer was prepared to purchase a piece of land, the onus should be on the agricultural interests to prove why the change in use should not take place. It should be the role of those interests to identify equally suitable sites for development on poorer farmland.

In Dennison's view, the only way to increase profits and wages, and thereby enhance rural prosperity, was to increase productivity. Wealth depended on efficiency rather than size. His views were supported by the report of the Institute of Agricultural Economics at Oxford, which asserted that agriculture was suffering not so much from a withdrawal of land from farming as from the archaic layout and organization of farm units and from their frequently out-of-date, poorly maintained equipment. Urgent attention also had to be given to the marketing of agricultural produce. In the words of the agriculturalist, Sir

Daniel Hall, 'our methods of trading grew up at a time when producers brought their wares into a neighbouring market and sold them directly to consumers. Nowadays they have to cater for a world market, or at least a national market, in which as an individual the farmer has no control over the prices'. The over-riding need was for greater efficiency. Mechanization had already provided one way of reducing costs in relation to output on the farm, and the experience of the inter-war years suggested that specialization would be much more effective than the traditional mixed farm in raising output per capita still further.[9]

These were not simply the views of a minority of academics. They closely reflected those put forward by the Economics Intelligence Division of the Ministry of Agriculture in a confidential report of 1938. That report dis-tinguished two types of sub-marginal land, where output had fallen substan-tially during the inter-war period. First, the decline might arise out of negli-gence, ineptness or lack of resources on the part of landowners and farmers, and clearly there was a responsibility to bring this land back into intensive use as quickly as possible. In other instances, the expansion of sub-marginal land was a sign not so much of decadence as of the more effective use of labour and resources, which had been switched to inherently more productive lands. It was much better for farmers to allow their worse fields to become sub-marginal than to continue wasting money on cultivating them.[10]

Up to the outbreak of war, the Ministry of Agriculture was against any long-term policy which strove to maintain the existing extent and levels of management of farmland. On the contrary, the Ministry expected to see instances of land improvement and land deterioration taking place simul-taneously. Improvements in the quality of pastures, the introduction of new seed mixtures, and extension of artificial drainage, would be complemented by an increasing area of abandoned land or land farmed well below its capacity. The report of 1938 believed that, for the most part, this sub-marginal land should be converted to forest through a programme of afforestation promoted by the Forestry Commission.

In order to achieve the greater productivity which the economists both within and outside the Ministry regarded as essential for prosperity, farmers would have to increase their output or reduce their labour force. The Majority Report of the Scott committee called for an increase in output in order to sustain the existing labour force and prevent 'the pre-war prevalence of malnutritional diseases'. Dennison challenged this by pointing out that improved nutrition depended not so much on the quantity but the availability of the right kind of food—namely vegetables, milk, and other 'protective' foods. These were most easily produced by specialized farming and, from the point of view of nutrition, it was irrelevant whether the food came from British or foreign producers.

In their programme for economic revival, published in 1935 (see p. 5), the Next Five Years Group had emphasized that it was cheaper to buy many foodstuffs from abroad out of the proceeds of industrial exports than to devote the same amount of labour and capital to producing the food at home.

Throughout the 1920s and 1930s, there had been no difficulty in purchasing cheap food from abroad. Indeed, foodstuffs became so plentiful and cheap that Britain did not need to export so many manufactured articles in order to pay for all the food required. In the opinion of the Next Five Years Group, this was one reason for the depression in the export trades. In 1927 a consignment of imported food could be bought at 7/8ths of the volume of exports that would have been required in 1913. By 1934 the proportion had fallen to 7/10.[11]

In view of the fact that Britain could buy all the food required, and that the number of unemployed workers in the export industries exceeded the total labour force in agriculture, it was impossible to protect or boost home agriculture through the imposition of tariffs on imported food. The Board of Trade strenuously opposed such a course of action during Cabinet discussions of 1934/5 and, when a deputation from the National Farmers' Union demanded this kind of support in 1936, a draft letter prepared by the Ministry of Agriculture for the use of the Prime Minister, Stanley Baldwin, commented:

The United Kingdom is to-day predominantly an industrial and commercial country and industrial prosperity must always be an essential foundation for the well-being of home agriculture. Our overseas trade consists in the main of the exchange of industrial goods for food and raw materials from Empire and foreign sources, and considerable importations of agricultural produce are inevitable if Trade Agreements are to be concluded that will keep open the channels of our international trade, improve the demand in overseas countries for our industrial goods and thereby increase purchasing power at home.[12]

Not only would tariffs invite retaliation and further damage to the exporting industries, but they might lead to higher food prices and consequently greater social deprivation or increased wage demands on hard-pressed industries, and all for the sake of the minority of less than 10 per cent of the population dependent on agriculture for their income. It was difficult to exaggerate the benefits of cheap food, which had helped to give the urban working class the highest standard of living in Europe. Cheap food meant that a higher proportion of incomes could be spent on manufactured products, and thereby contributed to the prosperity of a wide range of new, light industries producing domestic products.

In the words of the Next Five Years Group, 'our aim should be to maintain and foster the productivity and standards of living of workers on the soil without impairing the standard of living of the towns'. The government tried to achieve this in four ways. One method was to encourage self-help and reorganization through improving credit facilities and setting up marketing boards. The Agricultural Marketing Act of 1931 greatly enhanced credit facilities, and by 1939 seventeen boards or associations had been established, the most famous of which was the Milk Marketing Board. The second, by regulating imports, was introduced in only a modest way and provided some help to farmers. The third method was to subsidize output and, more significantly, guarantee wholesale prices if output failed to reach agreed levels. Finally, there were measures to improve efficiency. Initially, these were confined to promoting agricultural education and research, but the Agricultural Act of 1937 extended them to include grants for drainage schemes, soil improvement, and the ploughing-up of old grasslands.

These various devices could not, in themselves, guarantee a sustained or expanding demand for home-grown food, and Dennison advocated the alternative strategy of reducing the size of the agricultural labour force. The Majority Report had rejected this, claiming that there 'is an innate love of nature deeply implanted in the heart of man and that the "drift" from the land had been occasioned in large measure by economic inequalities between town and country rather than by any deep love of supposed urban joys'. According to Dennison, these 'inequalities' could never be eliminated until the labour force had been reduced.

By Dennison's strategy, the drift of labour to more attractive and productive forms of employment should be encouraged. As the labour force shrank, the families who remained dependent on the land would become increasingly more prosperous as they began to enjoy the fruits of higher productivity. The easiest way of minimizing the personal upheavals caused by the search for new employment was to provide farm-labourers with a wide range of alternative work through the introduction of new industries to the countryside.

RURAL INDUSTRY

Any assessment of the advantages of industrial development in the countryside had to take account of the many interests and aspirations within the rural population itself. In addition to the rural work-force, there were those who lived in the countryside but worked in towns, and others who had retired to the countryside. Not surprisingly, their attitudes towards existing and potential industrial development varied from that of the farm-labourers and rural craftsmen. In many respects, these residents had closer affinities with the outlook of the townsman, who ventured into the countryside for recreation and relaxation. Instead of perceiving the countryside as primarily a source of livelihood, they were much more interested in scenic beauty and access for leisure pursuits.

These differences in approach between town and country-dwellers, and between the various occupants of the countryside, could lead to conflict. As the Institute of Agricultural Economics conceded in its report, many country lovers opposed developments because of the changes which might result from loss of amenity and recreational use. Whilst housing represented the most ubiquitous form of change, factories and mineral extraction could have a more devastating local effect. It was often very difficult to impose controls or close these activities down because of the number of workers employed, the capital investment involved, and the potential profitability of industrial and mineral development.

There were now unprecedented opportunities for establishing new rural industries. A survey published in 1933 showed that almost half the industries established in the north-western sector of Greater London since 1914 had migrated from London itself, attracted by the greater space for expansion and much lower land values. Raw materials and finished goods could be efficiently transported by lorry, often over new arterial roads. The industries depended mainly on electricity for power, and this became more widely available as the national grid was extended.[13]

The rural setting of these new industries should not, however, be exaggerated. Figure 5 indicates that they usually occupied 'waste land' near railways, rivers or canals, or wedges of land between residential areas. Many were concentrated along main roads, around established towns, and on derelict munitions and military sites. A number of factories had already been developed at Welwyn Garden City. Far from seeking out secluded and remote country districts, the overriding consideration was easy access to urban markets and facilities. When Imperial Chemical Industries was asked why it had built a factory at Welwyn, it cited 'the advantages of nearness to customers, government departments and three large University centres'.[14]

There was no doubt that the decentralization of factories into relatively rural areas greatly improved the lot of the town-worker. The erection of modern hygienic factories with their sports grounds and other amenities would 'herald the abandonment of slum life in London and the sordid environment in which so many have been condemned to spend their lives'. It was much more difficult to assess the impact of these new industries on rural life. This may be illustrated by the conflict of evidence received by the Scott committee.

Witnesses told the committee of how 'a judicious mixture of town and country' would revitalize rural life and bring prosperity back to the countryside. The introduction of selected industries would provide employment for women, who might otherwise remain unemployed, and for the young people who might leave. Not only would this lead to a fuller and more prosperous family life, but the facilities required by industry in the form of electricity, piped water, sewerage, and better transport facilities could be exploited for agriculture and domestic use. Other witnesses developed the opposite viewpoint, warning of how the higher wages, shorter working hours and more congenial working conditions would encourage a drift from the land and cause resentment among those farm workers who remained. Many industries would bring their own workers from other areas, who would increase the competition for local accommodation.

The Majority of the Scott committee was afraid that the industrial ventures would soon overwhelm rural life. Even the smallest factories would need fifty employees, and several factories would be needed to avoid the dangers of an area becoming too dependent on one type of industry. This meant establishing four or five factories with a minimum of 200 employees, with perhaps 1,000 dependants. Villages would soon take on the dimensions of a small town. In adopting this view, the committee may have overlooked the way in which the new industries attracted employees from a very large area. By the late 1930s 28 per cent of those employed in Welwyn lived elsewhere, about 40 per cent of

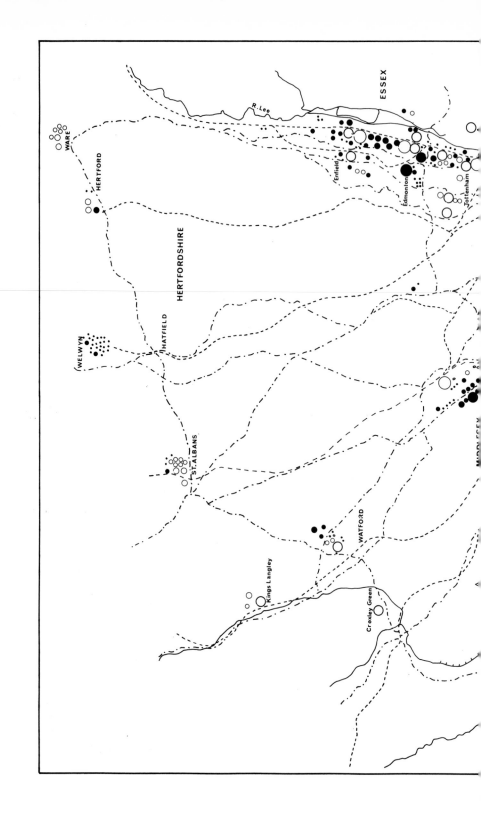

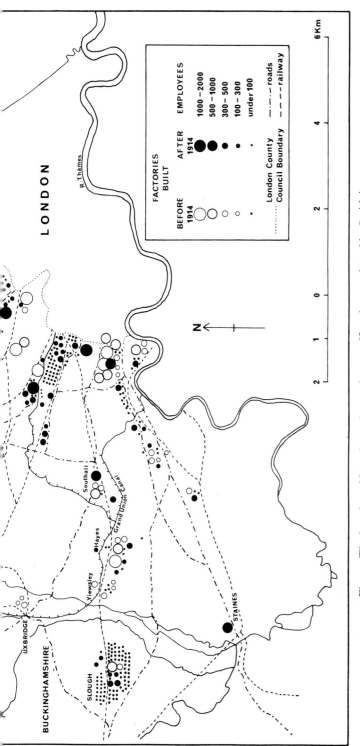

Fig. 5. The location of factories to the north-west of London, as plotted by Smith in 1933

them in small villages. Many were unskilled and would have been otherwise unemployed. The impact of the new industries was often thinly spread over a very large 'catchment' area and, in some instances, helped to sustain rather than erode rural life.[15]

Rural life might be adversely affected in more subtle ways. This was suggested in a survey of industries in Wales, published in 1927, which described how a factory had been established in a rural area, employing 100 girls and producing frocks and pinafores for the ready-made clothing trade. The girls came from a wide area and especially from the small towns. Although commending the venture, the survey stressed how the industry made very different demands from those of the traditional rural craft industries. The new enterprises depended for their prosperity on 'specialised machinery and . . . a minute division of labour'. They called for a considerable readjustment in the rural temperament. They introduced the routine and boredom more usually associated with urban occupations.[16]

On balance, the Majority Report of the Scott committee concluded that industry caused more harm than good, whether in the form of urban expansion or through the creation of industrial nuclei in the heart of the countryside. Once again, the Minority Report by S. R. Dennison took the opposite view. Far from isolating rural communities from these ventures, a much higher priority should be given to the promotion of industries in the countryside. The Institute of Agricultural Economics agreed. It was a fallacy to imagine that the revival of agriculture would automatically resuscitate rural life. The primacy of agriculture would never sustain the living standards expected by most people. Instead, the solution was to be found by restoring industry to the countryside. In the sample area of Berkshire, studied by the Institute of Agriculture, this industrial element had virtually disappeared: the number of blacksmiths had fallen over forty years from twenty-two to six; nearly all the water-mills were derelict, and the plush-making factory had closed. The result was a series of small, impoverished and ill-balanced communities. In the sample area, the average population of the three larger parishes was 1,150: the thirteen smaller parishes had an average of 216 inhabitants. The Institute believed that a population of only a few hundred people was unhealthy, both in an economic and social sense.

The Institute argued that the most effective way of countering these weaknesses and of reducing the disparity between urban and rural living standards was to introduce greater and more diversified opportunities for employment. Recognizing that it was impossible to revive the traditional craft industries and that no new industry could survive based entirely on rural markets, the Institute advocated the introduction of industries previously associated with the towns. At a time when ways were being sought for relieving congestion in urban and industrial areas, surely there was a formula for positively encouraging industries into the countryside to the mutual advantage of both town and country. Through the close collaboration of government, local authorities, and industry, it should be possible to provide the necessary facilities without 'the more obvious mistakes of unplanned commercial enterprise'.

The kind of dilemma which could arise was demonstrated in an extreme form by correspondence between the Town Clerk of Sheffield and Miss Evelyn Sharp, a member of the Ministry of Health in 1938. A Portland cement works, covering 250 acres and costing £1,000,000 had been established in the Peak District during the late 1920s. The tall chimneys and buildings were a terrible eyesore and large quantities of dust were emitted until filters and collectors were installed. The Town Clerk castigated the company for building the works in open country, instead of carrying the clay and limestone to some of the hundreds of sites in the West Riding of Yorkshire where the land was already 'spoiled by industrial processes'. On behalf of the Ministry, Miss Sharp admitted that the introduction of industry into the countryside was a contentious issue. The industry would, however, provide much needed local employment, and the transport of raw materials over long distances to the industrial plant would have greatly increased costs, and 'we are still, after all, primarily an industrial country'. Furthermore, the cement works would have been equally unsuitable in a town location. There was 'something to be said for blasting an area of countryside in preference to blasting a place where people have to live'.[17]

Almost every large-scale industrial development promoted this kind of debate, and this Chapter will conclude by examining two major confrontations between industrial development and rural preservation. First, it will trace efforts to close down an industry and rehabilitate the countryside. This will take the form of a case study of the closure of the quarries in the Malvern Hills, based on the reports of a parliamentary Select Committee, press reports and local authority papers. The second major confrontation took the form of opposition to hydro-electric development of the previously unspoilt Highlands of Scotland. This case study will be based on government papers and the parliamentary debates of the 1930s and early 1940s.

THE MALVERN HILLS

There were two reasons why rural preservationists might decide to close down an existing industry. The scale of devastation might become intolerable, or there might be a marked increase of concern for rural amenity on the part of the local population or wider community. In the Malvern Hills both factors were subtly interwoven and influenced a campaign to close down the quarries, culminating in a Bill promoted by the Malvern Hills Conservators in 1924. This measure became an important precedent for rural protection from quarrying and other forms of industrial development in the inter-war years.[18]

The Malvern Hills form a long, narrow ridge of ancient rock, rising from the Severn Plain to a height of over 1,000 feet on the borders of Herefordshire and Worcestershire. Under an Act of 1664 the forest or chase of Malvern was subdivided, with a third granted to the king in severalty and the remainder held as commonland. During the late nineteenth century, the Lords of the Manor, commoners and outsiders attempted to make encroachments. After a series of disputes and threats of litigation, a general settlement was reached, and incorporated in an Act of Parliament of 1884, which vested the control and management of the Hills in a body called the Malvern Hills Conservators, who were elected by the vestries of the surrounding parishes and nominated by the Lords of the Manor. Their expenses were met by a precept on three local parishes. Control of manorial and mineral rights was excluded.

The fact that the Hills were now protected as a public open space did not prevent their being threatened by 'disfigurement and vulgarisation'. A large quarry was opened on the west side of the Hills, and the National Trust warned, in its Annual Report of 1907, that only wholehearted opposition from the local population would prevent further damage to 'the wild and picturesque beauty of the hills'. By the 1900s the Malvern district had become an important health resort and educational centre. Further prosperity was derived from the increasing number of visitors from the industrial Midlands and South Wales, who liked to roam the hills. The local economy had become so dependent on income from these sources that there was considerable alarm when further quarries were opened. Traditionally, the market for stone had been confined by the distance a horse could pull a cart in a day: the small quarries had caused little damage. Once traction engines and lorries could carry the stone much further afield, and markets began to expand, the quarries quickly grew in size and number. When the backwall of one quarry reached 1,000 feet, there were fears that the skyline would soon be broken. The vicinity of the quarries was often disfigured by dumps of stone, strewn over 'the greensward which had taken hundreds of years to form'. The quarry buildings and machinery were unsightly, and the engines and lorries damaged the local roads.

Soon there were reports of houses remaining empty and unlet because of the 'traction engine traffic which passed their doors', and even the Worcestershire County Council became concerned – Malvern was the 'one spot in South Worcestershire where they looked for an increase in rateable value'. In 1908 the Malvern Urban District Council asked the County Council for help in preserving the Hills 'so far as possible in their natural state, and in preventing the damage which was being done to the county by the quarrying, and the conveyance of stone over the roads'.

The councils would have preferred a new body to manage the Hills, but it was soon decided to take the easier course of extending the powers of the Malvern Hills Conservators, who had already begun to promote a Bill for this purpose in 1909. The Bill gave the reconstituted Board of Conservators powers to manage the Hills 'as a Park', but fierce local and parliamentary opposition prevented their being given powers to acquire the manorial and mineral rights compulsorily. The precept was, however, raised, and this helped the Conservators to acquire some of the rights voluntarily and to meet claims for compensation where controls over quarrying were agreed. By 1924 the manorial rights of about 890 acres out of a total area of 1,513 acres had been acquired. Meanwhile, the expansion of the quarrying industry had been curtailed by the discovery that stone from the Clee Hills and elsewhere was superior to Malvern stone for repairing roads.

Conflict once again arose when trials indicated that Malvern chippings were ideal as a road dressing, when mixed with tar. Soon the fortunes of the quarries revived, and alarmed by the prospect of further damage to the amenity of the Hills, the Conservators once again successfully promoted a Bill in 1924, with the support of the local authorities and four-fifths of the landowners. In order to 'preserve the natural aspect of the Malvern Hills', the Bill granted powers of compulsory purchase for a period of five years. The quarry owners and licensees could claim compensation, where adversely affected. To help offset costs, the precept on the local rates was raised once again.

The Bill was considered by a committee of the House of Lords, with Lord Islington in the chair. Members heard how in one instance the Conservators and local authorities had managed to persuade a quarry company to 'withdraw' from the higher slopes in exchange for a grant of a quarry on the lower ground where the damage would be less obtrusive. Lord Islington intervened by suggesting that the same kind of agreement should be negotiated for other quarries 'climbing up the side of the Hills' because 'we are all very anxious to see the main object of the Bill carried out, which is to remove such disfigurement and to do so with the least possible loss as regards public convenience and on the most economic lines to all the ratepayers and public authorities concerned'.

Lord Islington reminded the contending parties that negotiations could be conducted during adjournments outside the committee rooms, and, in one such adjournment, the largest quarry company proposed a compromise, whereby it would 'withdraw' from 62 acres of higher ground, where the manorial rights had been acquired by the Malvern Urban District Council in 1920. The company would not claim compensation if two conditions were met. First, the company should be given the use of a small quarry on the lower ground, previously worked by the Council for local road-stone, together with 21.5 acres of lower land for further excavation. Secondly, the company's licences should be extended for twenty-five years (later reduced to eleven years) so as to compensate for the necessarily slower rate of extraction from the lower quarry faces. The Conservators readily agreed to the compromise, which removed all opposition to their Bill.

The agreement could not, however, be implemented without the consent of the Urban District Council, which had taken the precaution of lodging a petition against any amendments to the original Bill. This was a device to ensure that the Council exerted the maximum influence over the contents of the eventual Act. The Council contended that the amendment created a new kind of Bill. Quarrying would continue and expand. Whereas the Council's quarry had operated on a modest scale, the new, commercial quarry would be free of constraints. The Conservators replied that the amendment was the only way of safeguarding the higher ground at reasonable cost. Eventually, the Council was persuaded to agree to the transference of the land, but utterly rejected any extension of the present licences, claiming that the Conservators or Council would have to pay a much higher price for the enhanced concession if they chose to buy out the company in the intervening period. In order to meet this eventuality, the company gave the Conservators an option to purchase the company's undertakings as a going concern: the price would be assessed by an arbiter and would exclude any consideration of the extension of the licence. Under pressure, the company also gave an undertaking that all quarrying in the Council's former quarry would be restricted to the base of the quarry for at least the first five years after the Royal Assent to the Bill.

The Malvern District Council was now satisfied, the Select Committee recommended the Bill to parliament, and the measure was enacted without further debate. The Conservators decided that it would be foolish to buy out the existing quarries until steps had been taken to prevent new quarries being opened. Their first priority was to acquire 'those very large tracts of hill land which so far had not been spoilt by quarrying operations'. These were, however, negative successes, and critics focused their attention on the small, but unsightly, areas of quarrying that remained. In a letter to *The Times*, George Bernard Shaw warned that the Malvern Hills would soon become a row of jagged teeth and ultimately the Malvern Flats. The Conservators retorted that they had already raised £34,000 by way of loans to buy out mineral and manorial rights. In their Annual Report of 1929 they described the Malvern Hills as 'a national asset' and a national appeal was launched for the £100,000 required to buy out the last quarry. Notices were served on the quarry company before the five-year period allowed for compulsory purchase lapsed under the 1924 Act. By 1931 the level of compensation had been fixed and approval was given for a further rise in the local rate to cover the cost of the necessary loan.

Far from being greeted with universal acclaim, the closure of the last quarry aroused considerable disquiet. Fifty men were likely to be thrown out of work, at a time when the level of unemployment in the Malvern district was three times above normal. The Malvern Development Association vigorously protested. The Lord President and leader of the Conservative Party, Stanley Baldwin, was not only Member of Parliament for the area but President of the Development Association. He had 'always made it his practice to stand aside from local matters concerning Malvern', but he decided to intervene in order to keep the quarry in use until the labourers could be found alternative employment. He met with little success. The Ministry of Health reminded him that parliament had decided in principle that the quarries should be closed, and the Conservators had adopted the most economical way of carrying out the decision of Parliament'.

When it was proposed at a meeting of Conservators that closure might be delayed, the chairman pointed out that one of the highest and most beautiful parts of the Hills was threatened with irreparable damage. If quarrying continued, 'there would be an enormous amount of depreciation in the rateable value of the area'. It would, therefore, be wrong to put the interests of fifty quarrymen before those of 20,000 residents and many more visitors. For the sake of these larger economic interests, dependent on the amenity of the Hills, it was agreed to close the last quarry forthwith.

In passing the Bill of 1924, parliament gave notice that it was prepared to grant exceptional powers for protecting areas of outstanding beauty and recreational value from obvious and immediate danger. The successful promotion and implementation of the Act owed much to the fact that the Malvern Hills were so famous. Nevertheless, their preservation highlighted the scope for conflict between those who wanted to sustain and increase industrial employment in the countryside and those who rated the protection of rural amenities as more important. The debate was confused by the fact that rural preservation could also be justified on economic grounds. Attractive scenery would encourage holiday-makers and even permanent residents to an area. Rather than a battle between 'industry and no-industry', the conflict became one of a search for optimal forms of rural industry. This involved making long-term projections, affecting every facet of rural life. During the debates over hydroelectric development in the Highlands of Scotland, these projections had to be made on a regional and even national basis.

HYDRO-ELECTRIC POWER

In the Malvern Hills obtrusive developments were allowed to take place before remedial or regulatory action was taken. In the Highlands, efforts were made to stop harmful changes before they happened. Prevention was better than cure.

Hydro-electric power was still a relatively new concept in the inter-war period. The first projects were modest in scale and devoted almost entirely to generating power for electro-metallurgical industries. It was not until 1926 that the Clyde Valley Company provided the first public supplies of electricity generated by hydro-electric power. Under an Act of 1922, the Grampian Electricity Company had also obtained statutory powers, but nothing was achieved until 1927, when the company was taken over and the Rannoch and Tummel schemes were completed in 1930 and 1933 respectively. In the southwest of Scotland, another five stations were opened under the Galloway Water Power Act of 1935–6.

The promotion of all other hydro-electric schemes, whether for industrial or public purposes, proved abortive. Between 1936 and 1938, three Bills were promoted for the production of calcium carbide in the West Highlands and Glen Affric, but the House of Commons refused to give the Bills a second reading. In 1941 the Grampian Electricity Supply Company sought authority to develop the hydro-electric power potential of Glen Affric, and it applied for a Provisional Order under the terms of its original Act of 1922. The scheme was approved by a parliamentary commission, but later rejected by the House of Commons.

In the debate of 1941 the Scottish Secretary of State referred to 'the vehemence, and indeed violent controversy' which had surrounded the question of hydro-electric power. Political parties and Scottish opinion were divided. Meanwhile, the Highlands sank 'into deeper depression and the greater part of the very valuable water power resources are still running to waste'. No one disputed the need for some kind of development, and thereby additional employment, in the Highlands: everything revolved around what form that development should take.

During the consideration of the first Caledonian Power Bill of 1936 the Lord Advocate (deputizing for the Secretary of State) reminded the House of the need to broaden the range of economic activities in Scotland through the encouragement of new enterprises. The Bill provided 'the first concrete opportunity' since the Depression of 1929–33 to put various ideas into practice. In addition various ministries and defence services had emphasized the need for hydro-electric power in order to establish a carbide industry and thereby reduce dependence on overseas' supplies. For these reasons, the Lord Advocate advised the House to give the Bill a second reading so that it might then be referred to a parliamentary committee for 'a proper investigation'.[19]

Many members doubted whether the committee, by its constitution and procedures, could provide the kind of scrutiny required. Even the experts were divided as to the relative advantages of steam and water generating plant, and they disagreed as to the merits of different types of hydro-electric plant. The company had applied for extremely favourable rating concessions, especially at the outset of the project, in order to withstand competition from producers abroad. Members of parliament asked whether such help was necessary and, if so, whether it should not come from central government, rather than from the ratepayers of Inverness-shire. The Bill was rejected by 199 votes to 63.

When the second Caledonian Power Bill was introduced a year later, the rating provisions had been modified, and the desperate need for some kind of industry in the Highlands was stressed. According to Thomas Johnston, the Highlands were becoming a 'desert' in default of investment. Two parishes in the area affected by the proposed scheme had lost half their population in less than one hundred years. The Labour member for Inverness-shire and Ross and Cromarty described how the Highland people were 'very desperate for work', and many were emigrating. In view of this universal agreement on the need for more employment in the North of Scotland, the Secretary of State, Walter Elliot, suggested that parliament should concentrate on whether a carbide industry was needed and whether it was best located in the Highlands. These questions were so important that even if parliament rejected the Bill the government would be compelled to take up the question and make its own recommendations. With this implied promise of direct government intervention, the Bill was defeated by 188 votes to 140.[20]

A sub-committee of the Committee of Imperial Defence thereupon carried out 'an impartial examination' of the Bill and, during the debate on the third Caledonian Power Bill in 1938, the Minister for the Coordination of Defence,

Sir Thomas Inskip, reported that the Bill contained 'the most complete and satisfactory scheme for the production of calcium carbide'. Britain was the only important nation in Europe which did not manufacture the chemical, and the establishment of an industry would greatly ease 'our supply problems in time of war'. The entire hydro-electric and manufacturing complex could not be built in less than five years. If war broke out in the meantime, the output of calcium carbide could be started within twelve months by linking the plant to the national grid. An opponent of the Bill, Sir Geoffrey Ellis, argued that the scheme was useless. If there was to be a war, it would come soon and the factory would have to resort to the national grid. In that case, it would be much more efficient to locate the plant in an existing industrial area. He added that many depressed parts of the United Kingdom were in much greater need of new development than the Highlands. The Bill was defeated by 227 votes to 141.[21]

Hydro-electric schemes for the public supply fared no better. Under its Act of 1922 the Grampian Electricity Supply Company applied for parliament's consent to the erection of works in Glen Affric and Glen Cannich in 1941. Following normal practice, the application was heard by a committee of Scottish members of both Houses of Parliament. Although not unanimous, the Commission reported in favour, and the Secretary of State was thereupon obliged to ask parliament in September 1941 to pass a Confirmation Bill. No such Bill had ever been rejected, but a motion was put down on this occasion, opposing the Bill because of its contentious nature and on account of the fact that it could not be implemented straight away because of wartime shortages of labour and materials.

Proponents of the Bill stressed the time taken to carry out major civil engineering schemes and, therefore, the advantages of planning well ahead of needs. Adequate hydro-electric power was essential 'if any new industries are to be attracted to the North of Scotland, and, if the people of Scotland are to attain a standard of living comparable to that possessed by those in the South'. Opponents of the Bill fully endorsed the need for long-term planning, but insisted that this should be 'according to a definite plan set on foot by the Government of the day'. They accused the company of wanting to develop the most profitable areas for hydro-electric power, and of leaving the remainder to languish. As a leading consultant engineer told the House, it was essential for a government department to assume responsibility, so that 'a general, complete result will be attained', of benefit to the Highlands as a whole. In his speech, the Secretary of State, Thomas Johnston, conceded that preparations should be made for industrial development once the war had ended, but it would be wrong to 'mortgage the water forces of two glens and to do so for nothing'. The Grampian Electricity Supply scheme could not become operative during the war, whereas the government could work out plans for the comprehensive development of hydro-electric power and other natural resources, and for the location of industry. On Johnston's advice, the House rejected the Bill in order to take full advantage of a government initiative.[22]

North of Scotland Hydro-electric Development Act

The hint of an official inquiry into the entire question of hydro-electric power represented a major breakthrough after what one member of parliament described as twenty wasted years. As early as 1936 the Association for the Preservation of Rural Scotland had pressed for an inquiry into the benefits and impact of existing hydro-electric power schemes before granting consent for further projects. Whilst schemes might bring immediate benefits in the form of additional employment and large profits for the companies concerned, the real question was how far they permanently benefited the locality and 'how far the injury they inflict on the countryside is compensated by those benefits'.[23]

The role of individual Secretaries of State thereupon became significant. Although the incumbent Secretary of State regarded an inquiry as unnecessary, his successor, Walter Elliot, was more sympathetic. An office minute commented that he thought that 'there was a great danger of haphazard development, with the risk of unnecessary injury to amenity and other interests'. A letter from Sir John Stirling-Maxwell supported this view, noting that 'there seems to be a curious reluctance in this country to enquire into big questions of policy'. There had for instance been no attempt 'to thrash out the relative merits of road and railway transport for heavy goods'. Likewise, the scenery of the Highlands was being threatened before 'we know whether it is really better to use water power or coal'. Elliot was, however, soon replaced by another Secretary of State, who was advised that any chance of government support for hydro-electric development had been nullified by the ever-increasing crises abroad and the consequent need for financial stringency. The Secretary therefore concluded that the 'situation was already known'. Soon afterward, the relevant file in the Scottish Office was marked, 'the war has ended for the present at any rate the question of an Inquiry'.

The intervention of a further Secretary of State, Thomas Johnston, changed the situation dramatically. According to his memoirs, Johnston agreed to take office in February 1941 in order to 'inaugurate some large scale reforms', including the creation of a public corporation on a non-profit basis to harness Highland water-power for electricity. The progress and rejection of the Grampian Electricity Supply Confirmation Order added urgency to this aspect of his programme. Within a month of its defeat, a Committee was appointed under the Lord Justice Clerk, T. M. Cooper, to examine the feasibility and need for further hydro-electric generating plant in Scotland and to advise on the administration of such developments, taking the greater interests of the local population and amenity into consideration. Ten months later, in July 1942, the committee submitted a report in favour of further developments. According to Johnston, 'by common consent, [it was] a masterly production and a model of terse, constructive and courageous draftsmanship'.[24]

In December the report was published and the government introduced a Hydro-electric Development (Scotland) Bill, largely based on the recommendations of the Cooper Committee. The Bill was given a second reading in February 1943, and it envisaged the creation of a North of Scotland Hydro-electric Development Board to administer the generation and distribution of hydro-electric power on a non-profit-earning basis. The Board would give priority to providing 'ordinary customers outwith the areas of existing under-takers with electricity'. Surplus power could be sold to existing undertakers, large-scale industry and the Central Electricity Board for use in the national grid. 'Despite some Treasury hesitations', the Chancellor of the Exchequer agreed to the Board being given 'powers to borrow on the credit of the State up to £30 millions under a Treasury guarantee'. Any profits made from the sale of power were to be reinvested in 'reducing distribution costs and for developing new production and distribution schemes in the more remote areas'. The Bill passed without division: Johnston accorded much of the credit to the Cooper Committee which had provided a fresh appraisal of the Highlands, a feasible technical programme of development, and an end to 'the atmosphere of con-troversy'.[25]

The Committee's first task had been to decide whether large or small generating plant should be built. The opponents of the Confirmation Order of 1941 had advocated small hydro-electric power stations, 'perhaps one in every glen or strath in which you can expect a demand either for the needs of agriculture or of small industries'. They contended that this would not only be of direct value to the Highlands, but costs would be 'quite low, because you would not need any big reservoirs or conduits or transmissions, and, of course, such small plants would have the additional advantage of doing very little damage to the scenery'. The Cooper Committee took the opposite viewpoint. Local schemes would be far too expensive, even if agriculture and fishing were revitalized sufficiently to make greater use of the power. Even if medium-sized power-stations of 1,000 to 2,000 kw capacity were installed, it was doubtful whether they would attract the kind of light industry which generated employ-ment. The cost of power made up only a small proportion of operating costs and the cheapness of hydro-electric power would be offset by higher transport costs in the remote Highland glens. The absence of industry might lead to a large surplus of power, but not enough from each of the small generating stations to warrant the construction of transmission lines over long distances to other markets. The Committee therefore advocated the development of a number of large-scale schemes, which would, at least initially, export most of their output to the national grid south of the Border. Sales would not only help to bridge the gap between the construction of the generating plant and development of the distribution network and markets in the Highlands, but they might per-manently subsidize the use of electricity in the Highlands.

The Act incorporated the view of the Cooper Committee that the North of Scotland should be treated as a unit and that the most suitable sites should be developed for industry, based on large-scale hydro-electric schemes. Every effort would be made to attract (electro) chemical and metallurgical industries which depended on the availability of large quantities of relatively cheap power. There was a good chance that the prosperity, created in these areas of modern industry, would diffuse into the surrounding districts, including the crofting areas. There was no reason why these new centres should not be planned as model urban centres in a rural district.

There was considerable discussion over the degree of autonomy which should be given to the Development Board. The Cooper Committee and a group of members of parliament insisted on keeping the Board free from 'bureaucratic controls and needless references to Parliament', which could only lead to 'repeated delays in the performance of its task and unjustified postponement of the betterment of Scotland's condition'. Johnston conceded that the schemes could be implemented much more quickly if there were no checks, and he successfully opposed moves to make every proposed scheme subject to a public inquiry. Each scheme would however directly affect 'the location of industry, some branches of afforestation . . . agriculture and agricultural processing, the electrification of the railways and a tourist industry'. As Johnston asserted, the schemes would have such wide and considerable ramifications for industry and the countryside that it was wrong to invest them in a Board 'without preserving to Parliament the final rights of veto'. It was therefore agreed to make each constructional scheme subject to the consent of the Secretary of State, with recourse to a public inquiry where appropriate. Each scheme would be laid before parliament for forty days before being given statutory approval.[26]

AMENITY AND LIVING STANDARDS

Throughout the promotion of the hydro-electric schemes, much of the controversy focused on how much weight should be given to preserving amenity. As long ago as 1921 the Lochaber Water Power Act contained an 'amenity clause', whereby the company was obliged to preserve 'the beauty of the scenery' during the execution, maintenance, and working of the hydro-electric plant. Under the Grampian Electricity Supply Act of 1922 and subsequent Acts, the Secretary of State was empowered to appoint amenity committees to advise on how the obligations should be executed. The committees had to be given at least one month's notice of any project so that they could assess its impact on 'the beauty of the scenery'. If the companies ignored their views, the committees could appeal to the Secretary of State who, after hearing both parties, could make an Order.[27]

The advisory committees were prevented from making any recommendations which might 'imperil the financial success of the undertaking' and, according to some critics, this rendered the effects of the amenity clauses 'quite negligible'. This was hotly contested. The Galloway Water Power scheme had spent £20,000 on amenity provisions. Spoil heaps were made presentable, quick-growing trees and shrubs were planted as a screen to the pipeline at Glenloe, and over 30,000 daffodils and other bulbs were planted.

There were, however, limitations as to what even the most enlightened company could achieve. Under the Lanarkshire Hydro-electric Power Act of 1924, it was impossible to preserve the famous views from Stonebyres and Bonnington. The amenity committee for the Galloway scheme found it impossible to conceal or camouflage the surge towers on the reservoirs. It reported that 'we thought it best to refrain from attempting to make them look like castles, by adding battlements, as was suggested to us, or otherwise disguising them. They are, unfortunately, a necessary part of the equipment of a water power authority, and we think it best that they shall be frankly surge towers'.

Some loss of amenity was inevitable. In the debate on the Grampian Electricity Supply Confirmation Order of 1941, E. H. Keeling asserted that:

anybody who has seen Glen Affric and Glen Cannich, and has any capacity for appreciating beauty, must know that the wooded shores, heather-clad hillsides, rocky gorges, tumbling waterfalls of the glens form 25 miles of scenery not excelled in Great Britain. Under this Bill huge white concrete dams will be erected, the rivers and waterfalls downstream of the dams will virtually disappear, while in summer, when the glens are most visited, wide stretches of rotting vegetation and slimy mud will be exposed above the dams, with here and there the blackened skeletons of trees, submerged for half the year, projecting above the ooze

In the debate on the government Bill of 1943 the member for the Scottish Universities took up a more moderate stand. Although deploring the immediate impact of schemes, he described how the massive earthworks were soon 'mantled over with a covering of vegetation by Nature'. Whilst dams were erected and some streams ran dry, new lakes and vistas were also formed. In another debate Sir Archibald Sinclair cited how the hydro-electric power schemes of Austria and Switzerland had made a negligible impact on the scenery. It was a great mistake to suppose that developments would frighten away tourists. There had been an increase in traffic since reservoirs had been built. Most of the proposed sites for hydro-electric power development were situated 'in the loneliest and most inaccessible parts of the British Isles', and the Cooper Committee doubted whether they had been visited by 'one person in a thousand of the population of the United Kingdom'.

The question of water-power and amenity raised the entire question of the future of the Highlands. The Cooper Committee recommended that the region could be sterilized as a national park if it was desired 'to preserve the natural features of the Highlands unchanged for all time coming for the benefit of those holiday-makers who wish to contemplate them in their natural state during the comparatively short season imposed by the climatic conditions'. A few reservations could be left for 'the dwindling remnants of the native population'! The Committee hoped that the government would adopt an alternative course whereby the Highlanders would be given 'a future as well as a past' through water-power. A 'few localised interferences with natural beauties would be an insignificant price to pay for the solid benefits' which could come from hydro-electric power.

In the second reading of the Bill of 1943 Johnston declared his full support for preventing advertisements for 'somebody's beer or soap on the mountain-side of Sligachan', but he insisted that the term amenity included more than 'grouse-shooting, deer-stalking and salmon-fishing'. For him, the most important kind of amenity was 'social security, the right to work and the amenity which derives from remuneration for a useful service in the world'. At the present time, 'the amenities and comforts of civilisation have largely passed by the class from which Robert Burns sprang'. There were sufficient safeguards for scenic amenity. After all, the Secretary of State was also minister of planning in Scotland, and the Bill provided for the appointment of advisory committees to safeguard amenity and fisheries. Unlike earlier Acts, the new Bill made it possible for committees to make recommendations, irrespective of their effects on the financial soundness of the construction schemes under consideration.

In the debate on the Grampian Electricity Bill of 1941, Philip Noel-Baker described 'the provision of employment as the crux of the matter'. Throughout the inter-war period, members of parliament had shown that 'they would be ready to do anything, or almost anything, that would really solve the problem of poverty and unemployment'. Debates resolved themselves into how prosperity and employment might be best achieved, in the interests of the entire community. In discussions on the future of farming and the losses of agricultural land to building, policy-decisions tended to hinge on whether agriculture or some alternative industry might provide more employment and higher standards of living. In the Malvern Hills the contest between quarrying and the preservation of the Hills from disfigurement was largely decided on the basis of which could provide most employment. The losses of employment caused by the closure of the quarries were thought to be more than outweighed by the economic benefits otherwise conferred by preserving the amenity of the district. In the Highlands, economic prospects were so bleak that parliament eventually decided that the need for industrial development overrode all other considerations.

Whilst these debates were taking place, it was becoming increasingly difficult to define a rural community and its aspirations. As with other sectors of society, the experiences of the First World War had not only extended the horizons of many rural families, but had given them 'a greater self-confidence and feeling of personal worth in society'. In the words of Janet Roebuck, there was a greater 'determination to obtain their fair share of the good things of life', as measured perhaps in terms of labour-saving gadgets about the home, a greater variety of food and clothing, and access to the cinema. The widespread innovation of the rural bus service made it easier for country people to experience the amenities of urban life. In the view of some observers, the daily bus service pushed many villages still further 'to the edge of destruction by draining off the young people'.[28]

Whether such assessments were exaggerated or not, a paradoxical situation was developing whereby increasing numbers of townspeople sought a home in the countryside, whilst many rural families were leaving in search of a better life in the towns and cities. To stem these contradictory movements, the obvious solution was to provide an urban way of life in a rural setting. The ingredients for such a recipe were becoming available in the form of electricity, gas and mains-water, with all the improvements they brought to the home. The motor-coach and car made it easier to travel to work and shopping centres. There was the wireless and, a little further off, there was television. Slums were being cleared and new houses erected at an unprecedented rate. In time there seemed every prospect of an urban way of life being provided: the difficulty was in maintaining or creating a rural setting for that life. There was a risk of the greater uniformity in living standards being reflected in some kind of monoto-nous suburban landscape, neither urban nor rural.

There was considerable debate as to what form this suburban landscape would take. In his writings, Thomas Sharp described how the traditional antithesis between town and country would be replaced by areas of greyness and twilight, which were Neither-Town-nor-Country. Rural influences would neutralize the town, and urban influences would neutralize the country, so that 'in a few years all will be neutrality'. Another planner, S. D. Adshead, took a different view. He believed the physical effects of towns would always remain geographically limited because town and country were as reluctant to mix as oil with water. Towns would penetrate the countryside in streams and gather as pools, rather than cover the entire countryside in a film of development.[29]

Whatever view was taken of the urban–rural interface and its extent, one thing appeared to be certain to the inter-war generation. The countryside as an entity, occupying by far the greater part of the land surface of Britain, seemed to be threatened, and some of the more influential members of that generation felt a need to respond to this change. The main question for them was how, when and where to make that response.

CHAPTER IV

Preservation

Housing and industrial development, and the demands for outdoor recreation, became so ubiquitous that even the remoteness of the Highlands of Scotland was 'rapidly becoming a thing of the past'. The Principal Architect of the Scottish Board of Health told a meeting in 1928 that 'broad highways of glassy surface and teeming with traffic are replacing the rough, narrow and un-frequented roads of former times: huge industrial undertakings based on water power are projected, and in some instances already in operation'. Previously secluded areas were being invaded by 'thousands of city dwellers in search of rest and recreation'. The speaker warned that 'the time has passed when we can afford to leave these stretches of countryside to be ravaged by the accidents of commercial expediency and the vagaries of fortuitous development. Their beauty is easily destroyed and when destroyed is irreplaceable'.[1]

Nothing was sacrosanct: even the most precious and beautiful landscapes were threatened with the possibilities of change. As Clough Williams-Ellis wrote in 1928, the natural beauty of the countryside is so prodigal that it is taken for granted, 'like the air we breathe'. It was now time to take stock of the situation and look at the landscape and its abuse more critically. Had the English people fallen so far from grace that England would never again 'be an island of unsmirched country and ordered towns?' Williams-Ellis asserted, 'surely as human beings we ought to demand an ordered, reasonable human-istic setting for our lives and an end to this planless scramble'. Although we could not restore the charm of the past straightway, we owed it to our children and their descendents to at least begin the task of recovery. It was 'for that generation, perhaps remote, that we ourselves must hope and work'.[2]

Despite an overriding sense of shame at what men had done to the landscape, Clough Williams-Ellis saw grounds for hope.

Mercifully, and perhaps just in time, there is now a small minority fully, even passionately alive to our misdeeds both past and present, and determined that, so far as in them lies, England shall cease to grow less lovely year by year, but shall halt, then face about, and begin to regain order and beauty. Not necessarily, indeed not possibly, the beauty of the eighteenth or seventeenth or any other century, but a new beauty from a new and intelligent synthesis of needs and factors that are utterly different from any in the past.

At first, this small minority of concerned, awakened people concentrated attention on the preservation of particular aspects of the landscape. Some features and tracts of the countryside and coast were so outstanding and vulnerable that they had to be given special protection. Ways had to be found of insulating them from the harmful side-effects of building and industrial development. The Commons, Open Spaces and Footpaths Preservation Society was founded in the 1860s to help prevent the closure of commons. Under the inspiration of the printer and designer, William Morris, the Society for the Protection of Ancient Buildings was founded in 1877. The title of another pressure group, the Society for Checking the Abuses of Public Advertising (SCAPA) was just as self-explanatory. Formed in 1893, its members kept in touch with one another through the occasional journal, called *A beautiful world*.

Particular interest was taken in the historic and ancient features of the landscape: in 1894 the National Trust for Places of Historic Interest or Natural Beauty was founded, with the objects of promoting 'the permanent preservation, for the benefit of the Nation, of lands and tenements (including buildings) of beauty or historic interest; and as regards land, to preserve (so far as practicable) their natural aspect, features and animal and plant life'. By 1906 the National Trust owned 24 properties, and the need for some kind of additional protection for these sites became urgent. This was achieved in 1907, when a Private Act of Parliament enabled the National Trust to declare its land and buildings inalienable. They could not be sold or given away without the express consent of Parliament. Passed without opposition, the Act provided a valuable safeguard and stimulus to those who were considering giving further properties to the Trust for safe keeping in the national interest.[3]

The idea of 'removing' outstanding properties from the pressures of contemporary land use and management, and of according them a special status, was adopted in preserving archaeological sites. In response to mounting anxiety over the future of a number of famous archaeological sites, the First Commissioner of Works was given statutory powers in 1882 and 1913 to safeguard some of these 'ancient monuments'. The experiences gained in formulating and implementing these powers provided further insights into the utility and limitations of this kind of piecemeal, *ad hoc* protection.

Under the Ancient Monuments Act of 1882, parliament made it possible for the Office of Works to take into guardianship any of the sixty-eight ancient monuments specified in a schedule to the Act. They were prehistoric and famous sites, and included Avebury Circle, Maes Howe, Silbury Hill, and Stonehenge. These limited powers were widened by the Act of 1913, which introduced a system of scheduling, whereby landowners and occupiers were notified of the presence of any archaeological sites of national importance on their property. It was made illegal to damage a scheduled monument without first giving the Office of Works three months' notice.

In the period 1913–33 the number of sites placed in guardianship rose from 44 to 273. The number of scheduled sites increased from 344 in 1921 to 3,195 in 1932. If a developer persisted in his plans to destroy a scheduled monument, the Office of Works could issue a Preservation Order, which protected the monument for a further twenty-one months. To make the Order permanent, the Office of Works had to present a Confirming Order to parliament. The developer had the right to plead his case, and the final decision rested with parliament. As the First Commissioner of Works pointed out in 1938, such 'extreme measures were hardly ever necessary', and only one case reached the House of Commons. The Office of Works could not 'confiscate private property'. If a Preservation Order was made permanent, the Office of Works might have to buy the site or pay compensation for the restrictions imposed. This always made the Office extremely reluctant to use the full powers of the Act.

By the late 1920s there was growing concern as to the security of not only the sites but also the environs of many ancient monuments. In an editorial in a newly-founded journal, *Antiquity*, O. G. S. Crawford appealed to archaeologists to review their priorities. Instead of devoting so much energy to excavating sites which were in no danger of destruction, it would be much better to focus attention on those sites which were threatened by changes in land use and management. According to Crawford, 'conservation, not excavation, is the need of the day'. Any steps taken should include the 'conservation not only of purely archaeological features but [also] of the amenities which gave them half their charm'.[4]

Crawford stressed the urgency of the task. With 'the approaching electrification of Southern England', the impact of afforestation and the rising demands for aerodromes and military training grounds, 'the spread of bungaloid eruptions, and the threat of arterial roads and ribbon-development', it was 'unlikely that any open country or downland' would be left in southern England in a hundred years' time. A far-sighted policy was needed, which would begin by acquiring the more important archaeological sites before land prices rose.

This Chapter will describe both the wisdom and difficulties of responding to Crawford's call for 'a combined effort to preserve ancient sites *and their amenities*'. First, the Chapter will outline the difficulties of rehabilitating the downland around Stonehenge and of preventing the further destruction of lengths of Hadrian's Wall. Appeals for funds to save these ancient monuments were launched, and an Ancient Monuments Act was passed in 1931 specifically to help safeguard the environs of ancient monuments. Through case studies of Stonehenge, Hadrian's Wall, and Avebury Circle, the Chapter will assess the efficacy of the various strategies for protection, as indicated by the documentation of the Office of Works, the government department most closely involved.

STONEHENGE

Stonehenge is one of the most famous ancient monuments in the world, standing in 'weird solitude' on the otherwise featureless horizon of Salisbury Plain. In order to facilitate the protection and maintenance of the monument, it was included in the schedule of monuments to the Ancient Monuments Protection Act of 1882.

The Office of Works soon encountered two problems. First, the Act did not compel owners to hand their ancient monuments over to the Office of Works, and the owner of Stonehenge refused to do so. The Office of Works had to stand impotently by, even when the warnings of its Chief Inspector were ignored and 'one of the finest of the upright stones fell in a storm, breaking a smaller stone nearby and itself'. When the owner erected a fence round the monument and charged the public an entry fee, a High Court action was initiated. It failed, and a frustrated member of the Office of Works commented, 'one cannot but regret that in this country, unlike several Foreign States, there is no legal power to take possession of Stonehenge as a National Monument: paying the owner whatever may be the fair value of his interest in it'. The situation was not resolved until 1918, when Sir Cecil Chubb succeeded in buying Stonehenge as a private person, and thereupon transferred it to the Office of Works.[5]

By this time, a second threat had developed, namely the destruction of the 'weird solitude' of the monument. An aerodrome was built by the War Office within 600 yards of the Stone Circle, in order to take advantage of the nearby road. The hangars completely destroyed the 'sacred associations attached to this most venerable site,' and the War Office yielded to pressure from the Office of Works that a clause should be inserted into the requisition order for the site, stipulating that the structures would be removed at the end of the war.[6]

When the airfield was transferred to the Air Ministry at the end of the war, the Air Ministry gave an undertaking to derequisition the site as soon as possible, claiming that 'the temporary retention of the aerodrome is not conceived in any spirit of vandalism', but only out of military necessity. When the time for withdrawal came, the Office of Works and antiquarian societies were appalled to discover that the buildings would remain. The landowner had accepted them in lieu of compensation for reinstating the land. The Office of Works discovered that due to a muddle the Treasury Solicitor had never executed the original undertaking with the War Office.

The airfield became a pig-farm, and there the matter rested until 1927, when the secretary of the Wiltshire Archaeological and Natural History Society wrote to *The Times*, drawing attention to the fact that the pig-farm was about to be sold. He warned how it could 'fall into the hands of a speculative builder and be laid out as a bungalow town', and he appealed to the Office of Works, now the custodians of Stonehenge itself, to intervene and prevent 'the further disfigurement of the surroundings of the most important prehistoric monument in the British Isles'. The appeal was strongly reinforced by a former First Commissioner, the Earl of Crawford, who told his successor that 'a pig farm, and it is a big-farm too, is pretty distressing; but a row of "Stonehenge Villas" or "Druids Bungalows" would be more discreditable still'.

The Office of Works retorted that it had no powers to protect the amenity of monuments: it could only schedule the monuments themselves. In spite of the wartime blunder, the Permanent Secretary to the Office of Works, Sir Lionel Earle, was extremely doubtful whether the Treasury would sanction the purchase of land 'which they have never owned but merely occupied' during the war. In reply to a Parliamentary Question, a spokesman for the Office conceded that it would be 'a calamity if the surroundings of Stonehenge were disfigured', but the government had neither the powers nor the funds 'to purchase land surrounding monuments for the protection of their amenities'. He suggested that a public appeal should be raised for money to acquire the site and demolish the old hangars.

In a letter to the Office of Works, the Earl of Crawford warned that an appeal might 'encourage neighbouring people to erect pigsties, in order to be bought out by the archaeologists', but Earle had already recognized the danger and had, for several weeks, been instructing his Director of Lands and Accommodation to negotiate options secretly on the purchase of all property within one mile of Stonehenge. An internal minute confessed that 'we are incurring expenditure on these negotiations, but it will hardly be possible to criticise the use of public funds for such a purpose'. Once 'we have the necessary options', an appeal could be safely launched.

It was decided to organize the appeal in the name of the National Trust, with representatives of the Trust, Wiltshire Archaeological and Natural History Society, and learned societies forming an appeal committee, with J. C. Squire as secretary. In August 1927 the appeal was formally launched by a letter to *The Times*, signed by the Prime Minister (Stanley Baldwin), Ramsay MacDonald, the President of the Society of Antiquities (the Earl of Crawford), the Vice-President of the National Trust (Lord Grey of Fallodon), and the Lord-Lieutenant of Wiltshire (Lord Radnor). The letter described how Stonehenge would never be safe whilst the neighbouring land remained in private hands. Already 'an enterprising restaurateur had built a bungalow, the Stonehenge Cafe, within hailing distance of the stones, although happily just out of sight of them'. Unless urgent steps were taken, this would be the first of many developments and 'the monoliths will in time be surrounded by all the accessories of a popular holiday resort'. The aim of the appeal was to restore and maintain 'the solitude of Stonehenge' by raising £35,000 to remove existing buildings, prevent further development, and protect the valuable archaeological remains from ploughing.

Although the First Commissioner had no statutory powers to participate in the appeal, the Office of Works provided considerable indirect help. Before taking 'any decisive action' the National Trust was advised to consult those persons in the Office of Works who had secretly negotiated the options. The first meeting of the appeal committee was held in Lionel Earle's office, and he played a crucial role in publicizing the appeal and in obtaining contributions from leading figures in public life. In a letter of November 1927 he described how he was 'working like a beaver in the cause of Stonehenge', and, on another occasion, he wrote of how he was trying to persuade the Ambassador in Washington to assist in raising funds in that country.

The appeal started badly. 'Everyone was going for their holidays', and there were 'few large subscriptions from wealthy donors'. The £5,400 that had been raised in the first two months only just covered the costs incurred in taking up the option on the pig-farm. Another option was due to expire in late November

1927, and only £800 of the necessary £8,000 had been collected by the beginning of that month. The situation was only saved by an anonymous donation of £6,000.

Again, it was Earle who stimulated action by helping to organize the publication of an appeal leaflet, signed by Baldwin, Crawford, Grey, and Earle himself. The support of the *Daily Mail* was invoked, and O. G. S. Crawford and J. C. Squire wrote articles for the *Manchester Guardian* and *Evening News* respectively. By February 1928 half the funds had been raised, and the campaign received another boost from a luncheon given by the Lord Mayor of London. Further options were purchased, but a letter to *The Times* in December 1928 warned that £11,000 were still outstanding and that the last options were due to close in March. A revised appeal leaflet warned that 'unless partial success can become complete success the scheme will fail'. It was a close-run thing: the target was not reached until the very end of March 1929.

Although 'a very considerable sum of money was raised', and the National Trust took custody of the land acquired around Stonehenge, there was little ground for optimism. The success of public appeals could not be taken for granted, and the Office of Works still had no powers to offer direct, material assistance. There had been no attempt to lay down criteria on the amount of land which should be protected around ancient monuments, and the National Trust, for instance, was highly critical of the way in which the more distant views from Stonehenge were still unprotected.[7]

HADRIAN'S WALL

With the Stonehenge appeal accomplished, public attention shifted to Hadrian's Wall, where the neighbouring countryside was similarly threatened by change. As the Chief Inspector of the Office of Works, Sir Charles Peers, remarked, 'there can hardly be any monument in Britain which has more to lose by the alteration of its setting than the Wall. The remote and almost uninhabited places through which it runs give a marvellous impressiveness to its scanty and half obliterated remains. Where modern buildings and roads encroach on its surroundings, it shrinks into insignificance'. Already the setting of much of the Roman Wall had been destroyed, but twenty-nine miles out of the total length of seventy-three miles were still worthy of preservation, falling into three sections of twelve, fifteen, and two miles.

Beside the amenity value of the Wall's setting, a letter written by fourteen eminent archaeologists to the Prime Minister in May 1930 emphasized the archaeological significance of the Wall and its environs. The area had become the focus of a considerable and systematic archaeological inquiry, which would take many years to complete. It embraced not only the structure of the Wall itself but the belt of country immediately to the south, which contained the 'forts and camps and other remains whose testimony would in due time be called for, but whose secrets will perish beyond hope of recovering' if quarrying and other forms of devastation were permitted to take place. In their letter, the archaeologists appealed to the government to take powers whereby the Wall and Vallum, and the land between and on either side, could be placed in the guardianship of the Office of Works.[8]

Together with a good deal of agitation in the press, this letter caused Ramsay MacDonald to write to his First Commissioner of Works, George Lansbury, demanding an urgent investigation into 'the whole question of how to deal with our national amenities'. In a personal reply, Lansbury wrote, 'I think the time has now arrived when I ought to summarize the position as it appears to me and ask your advice on the proposals I have to make'. He then described how a quarryman had bought the mineral rights of an estate at Melkridge, on the route of the Roman Wall, for twenty-one years, with an optional extension for a similar period. The local whinstone rock was the finest available for road-making, and the quarryman had already invested £20,000 in the venture. Production would eventually reach 200,000 tons a year, and a receiving and crushing plant would be erected, sixty feet high, and covered with galvanized sheeting. Although the quarry and the buildings would not endanger the Wall and Vallum, they would eventually destroy the Military Road which ran between the two features, and 'it is this historic setting of Wall, Road and Vallum on this whinstone ridge that constitutes the visual charm and the historic appeal of the Monument'. The 'meaningless cliff' formed by the quarrying would be out of 'all relation to the natural features which dictated its line when the frontier of the Roman Empire was being marked out'.

Lansbury confessed that if 'the scheme for quarrying had not already reached such an advanced stage, and if the question of employment did not enter into it so directly, I should have liked to have been able to oppose it in its entirety'. Having visited the site, Lansbury was convinced that any attempt to ban quarrying would incur heavy claims for compensation. About 200 men would be employed eventually in the quarry.

In his letter to the Prime Minister, Lansbury emphasized that the quarryman had done nothing illegal or improper, and that if the government took powers to stop quarrying completely, 'the House of Commons would take strong exception to what would practically amount to retrospective legislation, restraining a man from carrying out his business, even though he was compensated'. Some kind of compromise was needed, and Lansbury suggested the imposition of restrictions on the quarryman and the introduction of fresh legislation. The Office of Works was optimistic that the quarryman would agree to his being restricted to quarrying only a small part of his concession, where least damage would be caused. The quarryman could not possibly exploit the total area of his leasehold within the period of the lease: he had only taken such a large area in order to secure a monopoly on the production of the finest whinstone.

During the ensuing months, an agreement was successfully negotiated, covering the extent and appearance of the quarry. The intended quarry was soon abandoned when the quarryman ran out of capital. Meanwhile, the new legislation came in the form of an Ancient Monuments Bill, which gave the Office of Works powers to preserve the surroundings of ancient monuments. Compensation would be awarded to those landowners and occupiers adversely affected by the controls that would be implemented under a Preservation Scheme. It was anticipated that the first beneficiary would be Hadrian's Wall.[9]

While the Bill was making its successful way through parliament, the Office of Works began drawing up a Preservation Scheme for the outstanding lengths of the Wall. Sir Lionel Earle advocated a modest scheme because, apart from the costs of compensation, 'we are totally without experience in the matter of preparing preservation schemes'. His Chief Inspector, Sir Charles Peers, wanted a more ambitious Scheme. Although there would be large claims for compensation and 'a mass of detailed work', any delays would lead to even larger claims in the future. Already, the village of Heddon was expanding rapidly. The debate was not resolved until members of the Office of Works visited the Wall and decided to embark on a single, comprehensive Preservation Scheme. As an Assistant Secretary, F. J. E. Raby, pointed out, the amount of compensation was likely to be modest compared with the length of Wall being protected. Besides satisfying archaeologists, the 'great stretch of country from Heddon to beyond Lanercost would be "for all time" kept for the recreation and enjoyment of the public'.[10]

It was proposed to include 'all those stretches of country where the historic setting of the Wall is least altered, leaving out so far as possible, villages and areas where railway lines and other modern works have destroyed the significance of the surroundings of the Wall'. The area would comprise 150,000 acres, up to half a mile on either side of the Wall, and would affect 120 ownerships and 200 occupations. Almost all the area would be preserved as farmland, and only agricultural buildings would be permitted. Even their design and appearance would have to conform to standards laid down by the Scheme. Petrol stations and advertisements would be banned.

By the time the Preservation Scheme was prepared and the cost of compensation had been assessed at £30,000, the country was in the throes of an economic crisis. There was not the slightest chance of the Treasury incurring the full costs, and a member of the Office of Works observed in May 1932 that it would be wrong to press for funds in view of the fact that the original 'villain of the piece (at Melkridge) is quiescent, and with the slackening of expenditure on roads there is not likely to be a sudden increased demand for whinstone'.

Sir Lionel Earle still wanted to press on with the Scheme. He argued that the level of compensation would rise once the economy began to recover. The Scheme had the personal support of the Prime Minister, and the First Commissioner would incur 'very severe criticism' if the powers granted under the Act of 1931 were left unused. On the advice of Earle, the First Commissioner applied to the Pilgrim Trust for a grant toward the cost of the Scheme. The Trust refused to enter into any commitment until some 'definite proposals were available', and the First Commissioner made this an excuse to ask the Treasury for some indication of 'the seriousness of the government's intentions'. He wrote, 'we want to be in a position to get as much money as possible out of the Trust', and this would only be possible if the Treasury agreed to meet a large part of the cost of preservation. In his reply, the Chancellor of the Exchequer, Neville Chamberlain, refused to give any assistance, on the premiss that no immediate action was required. In the event, the Pilgrim Trust offered a grant of only £5,000.

The Office of Works was despondent. The Treasury had refused financial support, and the Pilgrim Trust had offered a grant representing only a sixth of the likely cost of compensation. It was extremely doubtful whether a public appeal for funds would succeed, especially as the proceeds would be spent, not on acquiring the land, but in paying individual owners and quarrymen compensation. The only hope seemed to lie in persuading the landowners and occupiers to waive or minimize their legitimate claims for compensation. Almost in desperation, the First Commissioner made a series of personal approaches to landowners in 1932–3, and he was able to report later to the Treasury that 'we were very agreeably surprised by their favourable reception of the scheme and by their willingness to forego compensation'. In a revision of his earlier estimates, the Chief Valuer of the Inland Revenue assessed the likely costs of compensation for the length of the central Wall, which included Melkridge and the Wall Town Quarry, at only £5,000.

In view of this comparatively small figure and the risk of the landowners and occupiers changing their minds, the Office of Works decided in March 1937 to abandon the concept of an all-embracing Preservation Scheme and to publish and approve a Scheme for only the central part of the Wall. In a letter to the Treasury, the Office stressed that six years had now elapsed since the Act and it had been impossible to prevent the news of the preparation of a Scheme from becoming public knowledge. Unless some positive step was made, 'the Department's prestige in the North, where it has a great deal of influence, and indeed all over the country, would be very seriously diminished'. The central part of the Wall was 'the most important part, including the wild country where the Wall runs along the top of the whinstone cliffs overlooking the Northumbrian lakes'. The letter concluded that 'in return for a surprisingly moderate expenditure, the State will be able to show with justification a really substantial and spectacular contribution to amenity preservation'. The Treasury and Pilgrim Trust agreed to contribute £2,500 each, and the Notice for the first instalment of the Preservation Scheme for Hadrian's Wall was published in the *London Gazette* in December 1938.

The published Scheme went as far as practical politics allowed, but its defects were soon apparent. In order to minimize costs and avoid throwing men out of work, the Preservation Scheme allowed the existing quarries to continue in operation until their leases expired, on the assumption that the damage to the Wall in the intervening period would be small. Early in 1939, the Office of

Works was appalled to learn that demand for stone had increased sharply and that there was a risk of the last section of the Wall in the Wall Town Quarry being rapidly destroyed. Local archaeologists, the Royal Society of Antiquities, and members of parliament protested vigorously. The Office of Works could have responded by issuing a Preservation Order under the Acts of 1913 and 1931, which would have immediately stopped all quarrying, but this would have been met with fierce opposition in parliament. Men would lose their jobs, and the supply of stone for military defence-works would be disrupted. Instead, the Office persuaded the company to concentrate on an area where the Wall was already ruined. The quarry-owner was paid £1,000 and the company £15,000 in compensation for the dislocation and the extra expenses incurred by adopting the alternative site. A Preservation Order was placed on the remainder of the Wall, and the Treasury met the costs.

The defects of piecemeal compromises became even clearer in 1943, when a company tried to buy the quarry rights at Melkridge where earlier proposals for quarrying had stimulated the 1931 Act. When news of the attempt became known, there were again demands for the government to intervene and end quarrying once and for all. The press campaign was even more virulent than in 1930–1. The Office of Works, now the Ministry of Works, was prepared to intervene if 'the necessary funds' were forthcoming. The cost of buying out the quarry rights was estimated to be £10,000. The Treasury, after some hesitation, agreed in principle, provided that 'the floating value' did not 'settle somewhere else along the whinstone ridge' and prejudice future negotiations. The Minerals Valuer warned that this might well happen.

It was again clear that a comprehensive and effective Preservation Scheme had to be introduced with the minimum of delay. The Ministry decided that the Preservation Scheme which had been published in 1938, but shelved because of the war, should be confirmed. The mineral rights should also be purchased as soon as possible. A supplementary Preservation Scheme should be drafted to include the remaining lengths of Wall. The Treasury raised no objection.

AVEBURY

With work proceeding on the Preservation Scheme for Hadrian's Wall, the Office of Works began to look in the early 1930s at ways of protecting other scheduled monuments before any threat to their amenity occurred and land values rose. In doing so, the Office of Works highlighted still more clearly the considerable problems encountered when according *ad hoc* protection to features in the landscape.

Owing to the personal involvement of the First Commissioner, W. Ormsby-Gore, attention was focused on the prehistoric site of Avebury, a roughly circular enclosure surrounded by a large mound on which sarsen stones were placed at intervals. The feature had an over-all diameter of 1,500 feet, and was already divided into four parts by roads. Part of the site was occupied by the attractive village of Avebury. According to Ormsby-Gore, it was impossible to overestimate the special value of Avebury, which was 'perhaps the most important prehistoric site in Europe'. Although it was impractical and unnecessary to sweep away every building within the Circle, no effort should be spared in preserving the remaining stones, improving the amenity, and encouraging further excavations on 'the whole Avebury "complex"—even including the West Kennet longbarrow'.[11]

Accordingly the Office of Works drew up proposals for a Preservation Scheme in 1933, whereby no further building and extensions in the Circle would be allowed without consent, the development of open spaces and erection of advertisements would be banned, and steps would be taken to acquire and redevelop, where necessary, such unsightly buildings as the village garage. Although finance would be a major constraint, the Scheme would seek to retain as much of the surrounding land as possible in agricultural use. A distance of at least 100 yards from the scheduled monument was regarded as the absolute minimum.

Just as the Office of Works was about to consider the advantages of placing a Preservation Order on the area within the Circle, Ormsby-Gore learned that the archaeologist, Alexander Keiller, wanted to purchase as large an area as possible, with the specific intention of preserving the archaeological interest and amenity of the site. Part of the area was already in the 'safe' hands of a body called the Avebury Trustees. The Office of Works straightway decided to leave the 'initiative' for protecting the scheduled site to Keiller and to withhold any Order, 'hoping that the acquisition of actual property—the only really satisfactory solution—might be effected step by step'.

Not only did Keiller purchase the land, but his excavations soon began to reveal the tremendous archaeological significance of the West Kennet Avenue and of other sites in the neighbourhood. According to the Office of Works, 'the finding of buried stones, human burials, occupation areas, flint and other stone implements, makes it essential that no new buildings of any kind should be allowed anywhere in or near the line of the Avenue throughout its whole course'. From the point of view of archaeology and amenity, Windmill Hill and the environs of Silbury Hill should be rigorously protected. Paradoxically, the most immediate threat to the neighbourhood was the publicity given to Keiller's excavations: the Office of Works feared that news of his finds would 'result in an immense increase in the tourist traffic, and the demand for new garages, inns, roadhouses and other perils'.

During 1934 Keiller and the Office of Works began surveying the area 'which should receive the most stringent protection possible', and it was soon clear that the area would be so extensive as to be well beyond the scope of the kind of Preservation Scheme envisaged under the 1931 Act. The Office of Works was extremely concerned about the magnitude of the task and the eventual cost of meeting claims for compensation from those adversely affected by restrictions on land use. The Office therefore proposed an alternative strategy, namely the incorporation of Avebury and its environs in a particularly effective planning scheme, devised under the Town and Country Planning Act of 1932.

Under this new Act, the Minister of Health had already approved a resolution whereby the whole of Wiltshire would be subject to a planning scheme devised by a leading planning consultant, W. R. Davidge, on behalf of a joint planning committee of local authorities. The Office of Works approached Davidge and impressed upon him the need to adopt strict controls over building development in the Avebury area. The Office suggested that four types of planning zone might be distinguished, namely (i) where buildings should be banned, (ii) where building land should be subject to any regulations laid down by the planning authority, (iii) where building densities should not exceed one to five acres, and (iv) where building should be permitted if in harmony with its setting.

Although the proposals of the Office of Works were accepted in principle by Davidge and the joint town planning committee, the Ministry of Health warned that there was no chance of the local authorities contributing toward the cost of compensation. They would 'probably take the view that this was a national responsibility, which ought to be dealt with by the use of powers under the Ancient Monuments Act'. The Office of Works thereupon asked the Pilgrim Trust whether the £5,000 earmarked for the preservation of Hadrian's Wall could be temporarily diverted to Avebury. As a letter from the Office stated, 'the danger of development at Avebury is certainly more imminent than near the Roman Wall, and it is certain we shall be some time—perhaps some years—in bringing the latter claim to the point of compensation'.

Although it did not expect to exercise the same kind of veto as under the Ancient Monuments Acts, the Office of Works was anxious to exert as much influence as possible over the implementation of a planning scheme. The First Commissioner, therefore, asked the Pilgrim Trust to further help by stipulating that any donation should be adminstered by a special body and not placed 'in the hands of an unintelligent, if well meaning Rural District Council'. In the event, the Pilgrim Trust decided to offer a grant of £2,000 toward the scheme, to be adminstered by an *ad hoc* body approved by the Office of Works and Ministry of Health.

Although much of the land was already owned by Keiller and the Avebury Trust, and many landowners had waived any claims, the cost of compensation was expected to reach £5,000. Because the Wiltshire County Council and the Rural District Council refused to provide any financial assistance, a public appeal was required to supplement the grant of £2,000 from the Pilgrim Trust. There were, however, two practical difficulties. First, the timing of the public appeal had to be carefully synchronized with the progress of the planning scheme, otherwise news of the appeal's success might prejudice the willingness of landowners to waive their legitimate claims for compensation under the scheme. Secondly, the initiators of the scheme for protecting Avebury, the Office of Works, had to proceed unobtrusively. As the Office warned, if the man in the street learned that it was a government scheme, he would say 'if the Government feels all that about it, why don't they do it themselves'. It had to be made quite clear that this was 'a planning scheme and not a scheme in which a Government Department is appealing for money from the general public'.

With the help of the National Trust, an appeal raised over £1,300 within a month of its being launched in 1937. This sum, together with the grant from the Pilgrim Trust, was enough to meet the claims for compensation. The National Trust agreed to administer the fund, and to use it to make payments to the Wiltshire County Council, whenever claims for compensation arising from the planning scheme had to be met. The Minister of Health gave his statutory approval.

AD HOC *PRESERVATION*

The attempts to preserve Avebury once again demonstrated the difficulties of securing the administrative resources and funds for such piecemeal ventures. By the late 1930s the Office of Works had resorted to every device available for the protection of ancient monuments. All had their weaknesses. Stonehenge had shown that the preservation of the amenity of famous sites could not be left entirely to the efforts of voluntary bodies, and success was not even assured when the Office of Works gave assistance on an informal basis. The efforts to save the environs of Hadrian's Wall and Avebury soon exposed the limitations of *ad hoc* legislation in the form of an Ancient Monuments Act.

The story of the efforts to save the environs of Stonehenge, Hadrian's Wall, and Avebury provides a valuable case study in expediency. It graphically illustrates the kind of tortuous negotiations that could arise between landowners and developers on the one hand, and the preservationists on the other, and between the various kinds of preservationist, whether within the voluntary or official bodies. Even the most modest proposal could have major ramifications. The Office of Works found itself becoming embroiled in the wider issues of regional unemployment and the optimal use of land resources—issues that were well outside its terms of reference. Perhaps most significantly, some observers began to doubt whether the campaigns needed to save each ancient monument were worth the effort involved.

There was, similarly, growing disenchantment with the other examples of *ad hoc* preservation being practised during the 1920s and 1930s. In response to public pressure, legislation had been passed in 1907 and 1925 to regulate the erection of outdoor advertisements through bye-laws issued by local authorities. In 1928 an Act gave local authorities powers to prohibit the location of petrol stations in specified areas, and to regulate their appearance in others. In addition to the administrative confusion caused by these various piecemeal measures, their interpretation and implementation were largely left to individuals lacking both an expert and experienced insight into the wider issues involved. With respect to advertisements, the controls could only be imposed where the hoardings disfigured, for example, 'the natural beauty of a land-scape', and numerous actions were lost because magistrates decided that the scenery in question did not merit preservation. The legislation related to petrol stations did not begin to touch the most fundamental question of all, namely how many stations should be permitted and where they might be erected in the interests of the entire community.[12]

No matter how great the individual successes, the efforts of the voluntary bodies were proving inadequate. Of the 200 properties preserved by the National Trust in 1934, there were only forty-seven to the north of the latitude of Derby, and thirty-one of these were concentrated in the Lake District. Many properties had been saved at high cost, often as a result of the last-minute intervention of a generous and anonymous donor. And for what purpose? In the words of C. E. M. Joad, writing in 1934, a few hundred acres had been preserved. In themselves they were no more beautiful than the surrounding countryside. They were simply better-known as a high vantage-point, or for their oddly-shaped rock or some historical association. Meanwhile, the sur-rounding country was 'surrendered to the enemy'. Once the landscape was destroyed as an entity, the value of each part was greatly diminished. It was not so much that the beauty of the National Trust's property had been destroyed, but that it had been embalmed. It took on the mummified air of a museum exhibit: it had become a 'beauty spot'.[13]

Recognizing both the confusion and over-all ineffectiveness of these palli-atives, Ramsay MacDonald wrote to the First Commissioner of Works, George Lansbury, and the Minister of Health, Arthur Greenwood, in 1931, emphasiz-ing the need to consider 'the whole question of how to deal with our national amenities'. In an obvious reference to the earlier Stonehenge appeal, he asserted that 'we cannot go on dealing with this part and with that separately, raising funds for purchase and so on', otherwise 'the vandalism that is going on in our country will soon destroy some of our most precious historical monu-ments and our finest bits of natural scenery'. It was time the government devised 'some national policy regarding them'.[14]

In his reply Greenwood agreed on the need for 'general control' over changes taking place in both town and country. In early 1930 a Cabinet memorandum had been drafted, proposing the appointment of a departmental committee to review ways of preserving rural amenities, composed of a government official and representatives from the business world and preservationist bodies, under an independent chairman.[15] This course of action was soon abandoned, and Greenwood, in his letter, commended his Town and Country Planning Bill, which was being drafted to extend greatly the scope of statutory planning. As the example of Avebury Circle was to indicate, statutory planning was able to provide a framework within which account could be taken of such aspects as ancient monuments and, for that matter, advertisements and petrol stations. Although the Ancient Monuments Act remained on the statute-book until 1979, its powers to protect the amenity of ancient monuments were used only once. The Preservation Scheme for Hadrian's Wall was the first and last scheme of its type, and the following chapters in this book will look in closer detail at the alternative strategy adopted, namely that of comprehensive land-use planning.

CHAPTER V

Statutory Planning

In seeking to ensure that land was used to the optimum, one of two strategies could be adopted. One was to concentrate on protecting the most outstanding examples of each class of land and to leave the remainder to the vagaries of fortune. This approach was exemplified by the Ancient Monuments Acts. The other strategy was to introduce controls over all land, both in towns and the countryside. For practical reasons the controls would not be so stringent as under the first strategy, and might be inadequate for the protection of the most outstanding areas, but the controls would at least be comprehensive and provide minimal safeguards for the optimal use of land. Although both strategies were considered and, in some cases, implemented during the inter-war period, preference was given to the more comprehensive approach, called town and country planning.

Although the successes of the Office of Works and such voluntary bodies as the National Trust were encouraging, the piecemeal and limited nature of their achievements only heightened the sense of frustration felt by many who urged the preservation of rural England. As Patrick Abercrombie, the distinguished planner, wrote in 1926, 'we speak eloquently of the obligation that is on us to preserve and save from destruction the ancient monuments of this land, visible signs of our history . . . but we are apt to forget that the greatest historical monument that we possess, the most essential thing which *is* England, is the Countryside, the Market Town, the Village, the Hedgerow Trees, the Lanes, the Copses, the Streams and the Farmsteads'. No single organization had the resources to look after the countryside as a whole and, as early as 1898, the Society for Checking the Abuses of Public Advertising (SCAPA) convened a meeting of various bodies to explore ways of co-ordinating action 'in defence of the Picturesque and Romantic Elements of our National Life'.[1]

Although nothing came of this initiative, the need for a co-ordinating body became even more sharply felt in the 1920s. In a paper of 1926 Patrick Abercrombie advocated the setting up of a National League for the Preservation of Rural England, which might take the form of a strong joint committee, representing a wide range of propagandist, learned, and administrative voluntary bodies. The League could make a single, simple, and direct appeal to everyone concerned with the preservation of the countryside. The constituent societies, and more particularly their branches, could undertake any detailed executive action required.

The idea of forming such a comprehensive body found favour, and a Council for the Preservation of Rural England (CPRE) was created, made up of twenty-two constituent members and a larger number of affiliated bodies. The Association for the Preservation of Rural Scotland (APRS) and the Council for the Preservation of Rural Wales (CPRW) were founded on similar lines in 1927 and 1928 respectively. The APRS defined its objectives as being:

(i) to organise concerted action to secure the protection of rural scenery and of the amenities of country towns and villages from disfigurement or injury
(ii) to act either directly or through its members as a centre for furnishing or procuring advice and information upon matters affecting the protection of such amenities
(iii) to arouse and educate public opinion in order to ensure the promotion of these objects

The APRS emphasized in its literature that it was not 'merely a negative force'. Part of its policy was 'to promote suitable and harmonious development and to encourage the rational enjoyment of rural areas by urban dwellers'. The more positive aspects of protection were also emphasized by Abercrombie. The aim was to exploit the countryside without destroying its essential qualities. Through the use of contours, tree screens, grouping, harmonious colour, and suitable shapes, it should be possible to absorb the many human additions into the landscape.[2]

By seeking to control and regulate growth, Abercrombie asserted that 'we are merely continuing the work of the past. Planning in England is no new thing'. It was novel only in two ways: it was more consciously directed toward bringing together activities that had been previously compartmentalized, and, secondly, the planning agent had changed. It was no longer possible to hope that somehow a general harmony would result from 'individualistic satisfactions'. The private landowner could no longer be depended upon to strike a balance between preservation and development, whereby 'certain parts must be left preserved, intact and inviolate', and others, after experiencing change, would be transformed into a new kind of beauty. Instead, legal powers had to be adapted and fresh ones devised; the initiative was now transferred to the statutory authorities, voluntary bodies and the general public. To achieve results, 'education all round was wanted—in Landscape Design, in appreciation of the Country and in a detailed Survey of its features'.[3]

As Abercrombie indicated, the programme was not a light one; the support of government was an essential prerequisite. In 1932 this was given through a new Town and Country Planning Act, which strengthened and extended existing statutory planning legislation. The story of the remaining seven years of peace is one of how the comprehensive planning schemes envisaged by the Act were formulated and, in a few cases, introduced. Seven years was a short time for so profound a shift in public attitudes toward the use of land resources, and progress has been described as inadequate and ineffective.

There may be three reasons why this verdict on the inter-war period may be unduly harsh. First, there was a tendency to publicize the defects, rather than the attributes, of inter-war planning when the subsequent Town and Country Planning Bill of 1947 was being drafted and promoted. Secondly, the initial confidence in the 1947 Act encouraged many to think that if the 'right' kind of legislation could be devised, it would automatically bring beneficial results. Thirdly, historians have tended to analyse inter-war experience through the eyes of one sector of informed opinion, the planner and his journals, and they have given perhaps undue emphasis to the more technical aspects of planning.

In the event the 1947 Act was subjected to many of the strictures of its predecessors, suggesting that the problems faced in the 1920s and 1930s were more fundamental than many had supposed. The publication of volumes in the *Official history of environmental planning, 1939–69*, has helped to stress 'the essentially political nature of planning'. Based on official archives, the volumes described the severity of political constraints, even during the latter stages of the Second World War when there was unprecedented support for the concept of statutory planning.[4]

It is the purpose of this and the following Chapters to reappraise town and country planning in the inter-war period, largely on the basis of official records now preserved in the Public Record Office.

INTRODUCTION OF STATUTORY PLANNING

The introduction of statutory planning was not a leap in the dark, but the outcome of trends in urban life, and the perception and interpretation of those trends in the late nineteenth and early twentieth centuries. Cherry has described how many of the social and economic problems of the period were attributed to the overcrowded and insanitary living conditions that prevailed in parts of many towns and cities. Conditions were so appalling that they appeared to preclude any real hope of moral improvement and the elimination of drunkenness, vice, and crime, for which those areas were notorious. Physical health also suffered: many were shocked at the numbers of men rejected as physically unfit to serve in the army during the Boer War, and unfavourable comparisons were drawn between Britain and Germany in the levels of absenteeism and low productivity in industry caused by ill-health and poor living conditions. From these and many other instances, it was clear that the physical condition of towns, where the bulk of the population lived, was having a considerable and adverse effect on all sectors of national life and survival.[5]

This is not to deny that there had been some striking improvements in urban life as a result of public health and housing legislation in the nineteenth century. From the point of view of water supply, refuse disposal, street lighting and paving, conditions were often as good as those encountered in any country, if not better. The enactment of building bye-laws under a series of statutes had checked the worst excesses of overcrowding and had introduced minimal standards of air-space, lighting, ventilation, sanitation, and fire safety, but, for many observers, these piecemeal remedies were no longer enough—a more comprehensive approach was needed. It was, for example, inefficient to depend on slum clearance, street widening, and the provision of better utilities when a more comprehensive approach would have also ensured adequate housing standards, communications, and services right from the start. If good design and layout could be made the prerequisite of urban development, there would be a dramatic improvement not only in the health and prosperity of towns, but in their visual amenities.[6]

The chances of securing a more concerted attack on areas of deprivation were nevertheless bleak. High land values and low rates of return on investment, together with competition from more remunerative forms of investment, meant that the private builder was little interested in providing working-class housing. Private philanthropy could only do so much, and 'it was not yet timely for local authorities to build subsidized houses on any considerable scale'. The only possibility seemed to lie in encouraging suburban development which, even if it was too expensive for the working classes, might encourage others to move and thereby relieve the pressures on accommodation in the town and city centres. The most effective way of accelerating suburban development was to provide an attractive return on investment by keeping the cost of land purchase and development as low as possible. This could be best achieved through adopting a comprehensive approach, whereby land could be apportioned to its most appropriate use and an efficient network of roads and public services laid out. In the words of Cherry, the advocates of housing, social and land reform found a common cause in promoting suburban development and, in doing so, they played a major role in extending 'the century-long process of sanitarianism, bye-law control and public works into one of land-use control and comprehensive urban management'.

The shift of interest away from the centres of towns and cities coincided with, and was reinforced by, a feeling that towns had somehow failed modern society and that the time had come to once again graft some of the attributes of the countryside on to town life. Instead of the various activities of the town taking place cheek by jowl, they should be separated. The introduction of fast and relatively cheap forms of public transport made it possible for increasing numbers of workers to live at some distance from their employment, and thereby enjoy an urban way of life in a more rural, suburban setting. The time had come 'to empty the slums into the country', which, according to J. S. Nettlefold, writing in 1914, 'must be the real country, not a fresh slum'. Never again should bricks and mortar 'thrust out into the country in a solid phalanx'. The houses should be built at densities of no more than ten houses per gross acre, so as to leave adequate land for allotments, playgrounds, and playing fields. This would be possible if building costs were kept to the minimum and plenty of cheap land was available.[7]

It was against this background, and with the explicit intention of improving sanitary conditions, and of enhancing the amenities and conveniences of urban life, that planning powers were included in the Housing, Town Planning, &c. Act of 1909. For the first time, it became possible for borough, urban, and rural district councils to regulate nineteen activities if those councils wished to do so, and if the Local Government Board gave its consent. These activities included the regulation of street and house construction and the preservation of open spaces and 'objects of historical interest or natural beauty'. The planning powers could be applied to any 'land which is in course of development or appears likely to be used for building purposes'. After obtaining consent, a planning scheme would be drawn up, which defined the area affected and the way in which the planning powers would be implemented. Before statutory consent was given to the eventual scheme, advertisements were placed and public inquiries held. Once approved, the scheme had the force of the Act itself.[8]

Ashworth has stressed how the Act was only permissive: it did not compel or indeed stimulate any one to take action. Indeed, the Act was subject to 'a welter of administrative controls'. Parliament simply redirected 'activity rather vaguely in a new direction', away from piecemeal remedies toward a more fundamental approach to urban layout and design, based on suburban growth.[9]

The limitations of the Act were clear for all to see and yet, as Alwyn Lloyd said many years later, the very act of passing the Bill was a great achievement. It would have been a great mistake to have attempted too much in a 'first' Bill. The promoters of the early Ancient Monuments Bills of the 1870s had made that mistake, and the result was failure. It was only after they had put forward a much more modest measure that parliament passed the Ancient Monuments Bill of 1882. The advocates of town planning made no such mistake in 1908/9: they sought to enact a modest measure and met with success first time. And yet the advances made by the Act should not be underrated. The measure set a precedent for public involvement in the use and management of land, and included the word 'amenity' for the first time. Although owners' rights were safeguarded, the Act served as a warning that there were limits to which these rights could be exercised, and that it was in the long-term interests of private owners to collaborate with public authorities.[10]

The Act of 1909 has often been criticized for its vagueness. Although it used the words 'town planning', the term was not defined. The Act did little more than identify the nineteen issues which could be covered by planning schemes.[11] The absence of definitions in this and later legislation should not, however, be taken always as a sign of a lack of precision or purpose on the part of the government. On the contrary, the planning Acts were both practical and ingenious in the way in which they conferred legal respectability on the regulations imposed on land use, whilst allowing a large measure of flexibility in their interpretation and implementation. A tersely worded definition might have reduced a Minister's room for manoeuvre at a later date, or have led to endless wrangles in parliament as to what should be included in a definition. The risks were clearly displayed when a private member's Bill, the Rural Amenities Bill, was introduced in 1929. This rashly defined 'rural amenities' as:

the beauty of the landscape or rural scenery and the enjoyment of the countryside, including fields, trees, woods, hills, valleys, cliffs, foreshores, streams, commons, open spaces, village greens, ways, buildings or groups of buildings, spaces about buildings, gardens, and other features with picturesque characteristics, historical associations, archaeological interest or architectural merit.

Critics immediately complained of the omission of 'geological interest', and at least one government department, the Department of Health for Scotland, concluded that, whilst the definition was 'a good one', it would be much simpler 'to use the word "amenity" without definition'. When drafting the Town and Country Planning Bill of 1931, the Ministry of Health (which succeeded the Local Government Board in 1919) soon decided that a definition of 'amenity' was 'unnecessary'.[12]

George Pepler became the Chief Town Planning Inspector of the Ministry of Health in 1919: some years later, he emphasized how the Act of 1909 had been primarily intended to improve the layout of housing estates. The advocates of statutory planning were interested in planning mainly from the housing point of view, and they took the logical step of including the necessary provisions in Housing Bills. In the short term this was 'a good strategic line of approach' in winning support in parliament, but it soon led to 'a great confusion in administrative practice'. Under the Housing, Town Planning, &c. Act of 1919, a system of housing subsidies was introduced in order to help alleviate the desperate shortage of working-class housing, caused partly by the war. Although the subsidies were regarded as only a temporary measure, housing and planning were clearly embarking on different courses—there was no Exchequer aid in the form of subsidies to facilitate planning. During the drafting stages of the Housing of the Working Classes Bill of 1924 it was decided to draw up completely separate codes for housing and planning. The code for statutory planning was effected by the Town Planning Act of 1925.[13]

The Housing, Town Planning, &c. Act of 1919 made it possible for local authorities to combine together and co-ordinate their separate planning schemes through the appointment of joint planning committees. In this way more attention could be given to 'the assignment of districts for different industries, for residential purposes, for open spaces, and the like, according to their suitability'. The Ministry of Health did its utmost to encourage this kind of liaison. As an Assistant Secretary, I. G. Gibbon, wrote in 1921, 'if we can get neighbouring authorities with common economic interests to act together and to combine in securing a scheme of development of which the main outlines are good, a big step in advance will have been taken'.[14]

In 1929 parliament passed the Local Government Bill. It was one of Neville Chamberlain's greatest achievements during his long period as Minister of Health. At first, the Act caused considerable confusion and some ill-feeling between local authorities (p. 94) but, in the longer term, it facilitated regional planning. Under the Act, the Ministry of Health endeavoured to place each area under a form of local government appropriate to its needs and status; awkward, anomalous, and confusing boundaries were removed, and detached parts were absorbed into neighbouring districts. By 1937 the number of rural district councils in England and Wales had been reduced from 752 to 486, and urban district councils from 783 to 649. Whereas the 5,000,000 inhabitants of Scotland had previously been administered by as many as 1,300 local authorities, every major function, including statutory planning, was now transferred to the county councils and burghs of over 20,000 people. In England and Wales the county councils were given powers for the first time to participate in planning, either by becoming members of joint planning committees or by taking over responsibilities relinquished voluntarily by the district councils.[15]

The value of this more co-ordinated approach was severely limited, however, by the geographical inadequacy of statutory planning. Although schemes could be devised for any 'land which is in course of development or appears likely to be used for building purposes', this did not cover the redevelopment of built-up areas or the control of rural land. It was soon clear that city life could not be completely rejected or ignored, and city centres left to languish as best they could. As early as 1914 Nettlefold accused the Act of ignoring 'the first object of town planning, which is to deal with towns as a complete whole'. Experience in Oxford led to a clause being inserted in a Housing Act of 1923, which enabled areas of special architectural or artistic merit to be included in statutory planning schemes. Between 1926 and 1932 nineteen local authorities, mostly city corporations, obtained powers under Local Acts to draw up statutory schemes for their centres.[16]

Whereas cities and towns suffered in a negative sense, the countryside was harmed more directly as a result of low-density suburban development. The break-up of large estates and the resumed depression in farming caused land values to fall; building costs were comparatively low and, as a result, low-density housing of about twelve per acre became a 'sound business proposition', even without recourse to the Act of 1909. Soon a new kind of protest was heard, arising from the loss of extensive areas of countryside to suburban sprawl. In many cases, the sprawl and scattered development became even more obtrusive than the previous 'solid phalanx' of growth.

Suburbanization did not take place in a vacuum. An urban *and* rural perspective was required, and this could best be achieved by extending statutory planning to *all* rural areas. A Ministry of Health minute of 1931 warned that 'systematic development has reached a stage beyond the control of private individuals'. The magnitude of the building boom of the post-war years was now fully grasped. In the Home Counties and other relatively prosperous areas, building was now so ubiquitous that it was quite impossible to forecast where it might occur next. The assumptions of the 1909 Act and its successors were clearly outdated.

In view of the depressed state of the coal-mining industry, it was paradoxical that it was the exploitation of a new coalfield that provided one of the earliest examples of the need for a new approach to planning. A new coal industry was being developed in the Garden of England—Kent—and Patrick Abercrombie was commissioned to draw up an East Kent Regional Plan. He soon discovered that his main task was to prevent the despoliation of a rural area, rather than to rehabilitate an area already desecrated by industrial or urban growth. The need was for preventive medicine, rather than surgery. In his report of 1925 Abercrombie suggested the most appropriate ways of introducing new industries and settlement, with the minimum of disruption to the life and appearance of the countryside.[17]

This kind of planning, which was concerned with not only the form, but also the location, of building development, took statutory planning into a completely new dimension. On the prompting of the CPRE and other voluntary bodies, a Conservative back-bencher, Sir Edward Hilton-Young, introduced Rural Amenities Bills in the parliamentary sessions of 1929–30 and 1930–31. Their main purpose was to extend statutory planning to all rural areas, and both Bills were given a second reading without division. The Ministry of Health opposed them for tackling only part of the task; it advocated the promotion of a general measure for both town and country. Citing the support given to the Rural Amenities Bills, and the precedents set by the Surrey County Council Act of 1931 (see p. 15) and other Local Acts, the Ministry drafted a Town and Country Planning Bill in 1930–31. In a brief to Parliamentary Counsel, Gibbon described the difficulties that had arisen in administering the existing legislation. Public pressure had been so strong that the Ministry had had to 'construe' its powers in 'a most liberal spirit', but even when the 1925 Act was 'stretched almost to breaking point', it was not possible to deal with all the situations where some kind of statutory planning was clearly desirable.[18]

Under the proposed Bill, the entire country would come within 'the ambit of the Act'. It would be possible to follow the lead of the United States and Germany in regulating the redevelopment of town and city centres. It would be easier to achieve 'the right correlation of place of work and place of residence', and thereby secure 'the maximum of public good and inestimable benefits to industry'. A memorandum prepared within the Ministry of Health described how 'the Bill is a bold attempt to deal comprehensively with the urgent need for systematic planning', so as to ensure the best possible use of national resources and the preservation of amenities. It would 'give local authorities powers which are badly required for dealing with modern problems', and would enable them to render even greater service to the community.[19]

In April 1931 the Minister of Health, Arthur Greenwood, obtained a second reading for his Town and Country Planning Bill. It was lost owing to the demise of the Labour Government. Neville Chamberlain once again became Minister of Health but, following the general election, Ramsay MacDonald appointed a new Minister in the National Government, Sir Edward Hilton-Young, on Chamberlain's recommendation. As a back-bencher, Hilton-Young had been sponsor of the earlier Rural Amenities Bills, and he lost little time in reintroducing Labour's Town and Country Planning Bill. This was passed in a modified form, and remained the basis of statutory planning until the Town and Country Planning Act of 1947.[20]

THE TOWN AND COUNTRY PLANNING ACT

The town planning profession gave the Bill of 1931 a generally favourable reception. In a letter of March 1931 Raymond Unwin told Greenwood that the passing of the Bill 'would be highly appreciated by all those, who are interested in the improvement of towns or the preservation of the countryside, irrespective of whether they belong to our party or not'. Unwin also added his appreciation of 'the energy and zeal with which Mr Gibbon had worked at this Bill and his willingness to go to endless trouble to try and solve many difficulties'.[21]

Greenwood and Hilton-Young realized that all-party support for the Bill was essential. As Greenwood told Ramsay MacDonald in June 1931, 'the Bill is, I believe, a really useful measure, but it is complicated and affects so many interests that I am convinced it is essentially a Bill which must be carried into law by agreement'. Faced by a much more conservative parliament in 1932, Hilton-Young found it prudent to stress the consolidating nature of the Bill. At the second reading, he claimed that 'it is simply to perfect the existing powers, to make them efficient, to run more in the directions in which actual experience has shown that it would be useful to supplement them and to round them off'.[22]

The consolidation and extension of earlier legislation was by no means a foregone conclusion. The fact that there were no divisions during the second readings of the Rural Amenities Bills and the Town and Country Planning Bills was deceptive in giving the impression that there was little opposition. Until 1932, the debates were largely concerned with the general need for planning, on which there was 'practically unanimous approval'. In the debate of 1931 Greenwood devoted almost all his speech 'to neutral ground', namely to the desirability of improving both rural and town amenities. Chamberlain and other members complained of a lack of any explanation of the contents of the Bill which were of 'such complication and such intricacies'. When Hilton-Young reintroduced the Bill in 1932, members were much more fully briefed and consequently better able to criticize each section of the Bill. As a result, almost every aspect of statutory planning was challenged, in both debate and committee.[23]

This was not, of course, the first time that statutory planning had been criticized. In 1919 an article in the *Architectural Review* had attacked town planning as another expression of collectivism. It crushed individual liberty and sought to mould the masses into 'cast-iron conceptions and conventions' which petrified progress. In the writer's opinion, communities should be allowed to 'grow up and live and work in harmony without the shepherding of a grandmotherly Government'. In a civilized country like Britain, men should be free to work out their own lives. Whilst others might suffer from their mistakes, it was 'better for all that we should feel the moral responsibility ourselves; than that we should excuse ourselves by sheltering behind the rules and regulations of public bodies'. On that occasion, the professional planning consultant, Thomas Adams, took on the task of rebutting these criticisms. Adams asserted that it was the anarchy arising from the ownership and misuse of property that crushed individual liberty. Far from restricting freedom, he had been impressed by the extent to which town planning had extended liberty. An organized society had to impose some restrictions on the wrongdoer; co-operation was an essential prerequisite for individual development.[24]

In 1932 the root-and-branch critics had their first chance to mount an attack on the very concept of planning in parliament. The Marquess of Hartington asserted that the desecration of the countryside had increased almost exactly in proportion to the number of town-planning conferences. Leslie Hore-Belisha accused planners of showing 'a complete disregard for the necessities of civilis-ation, which is an expanding, a spontaneous civilisation. People are spreading out and doing things on the spur of the moment'. Not only was it wrong to impose further constraints, but critics castigated the decision to place these further statutory powers in the hands of local authorities. During the debate on the third reading of the Bill in 1932 the Ministry and local authorities were described as 'slaves to precedent'; unless checked, they would cover the entire countryside with 'dull, tame and uninspiring . . . piffling little garden suburbs'.[25]

These criticisms had some foundation in fact. Although the 1909 Act and subsequent legislation were expected to lead to a reduction in housing densities, no guidelines were offered as to how this might be achieved. Local authorities were simply asked to strike a balance between the too *intensive* development of the Victorian and Edwardian periods and the opposite tendency of too *extensive* building. Some degree of grouping or concentration was required. Not surpris-ingly, most local authorities lacked the finesse and experience needed for striking the optimal balance. Some simply treated the proposals made by the Tudor Walters committee of 1918 on housing densities of up to twelve per acre as a rule to be followed wherever possible. Others found it easier to follow the practice already adopted by local builders. Either way, town planning came to be identified with the principle of uniformly low-density housing develop-ment.[26]

With the change in government, and especially after the general election, the Bill was 'relegated to the political scrap-heap'. In advocating its reintroduction, leading figures from several voluntary and professional bodies reminded Ram-say MacDonald, in a letter, of how the Bill had eventually emerged from its Standing Committee as an agreed measure. Emphasizing its relevance to economy and the restoration of national prosperity, an editorial in the *Journal of the Town Planning Institute* described how planning was 'the surest, safest and cheapest method of insuring future economy in the development of the country'. Without the Bill, 'our beautiful countryside' would remain the prey of ignorant and foolish speculators, all gambling for a quick penny.[27]

Soon after he took office as Minister of Health in the National Government, Sir Edward Hilton-Young gave explicit instructions that a Town and Country Planning Bill should be drafted 'as much like the Late Government's Bill as possible', including the amendments made in the Committee Stage. There had, however, been a profound change in the mood of parliament, and considerable hostility was encountered in piloting the new Bill through the Committee Stage. In a personal letter to G. M. Trevelyan in March 1932 Hilton-Young wrote, 'I fear our Town Planning Bill is having a stormy passage, and I doubt but that "the waters wild" may yet go o'er our child. The truth is that it is little short of a miracle that it is still afloat'.[28]

In his presidential address to the Town Planning Institute in 1932 F. Longstreth Thompson accused the Ministry of making two tactical errors—first, by introducing the Bill so early in the life of a vigorous, but inexperienced, parliament, anxious to prove its zeal for economy, and secondly by codifying and clarifying existing powers in a Bill which was also designed to extend some of these powers. This meant that some of the longest-established principles came under hostile scrutiny. Gibbon retorted that a minister could rarely wait, and had to introduce legislation at the first opportunity afforded by the parliamentary timetable.[29]

Longstreth Thompson conceded that perhaps the most fundamental difficulty resided in the fact that town planning had still not justified all the claims that had been made on its behalf. A considerable body of opinion remained 'distinctly sceptical', especially of the techniques and administration of planning, as practised by the local authorities. In order to offset some of this scepticism and save the Bill, the Ministry had to make many concessions before the Select Committee of 1932. In doing so the Ministry forfeited much of the confidence placed in the original Bill by the professional and voluntary bodies.

Under considerable pressure to exclude from planning schemes all areas where there was no likelihood of development, Hilton-Young obtained a compromise, the form of which was designed to satisfy his critics on the Select Committee and the content of which was intended to leave the Minister and local authorities with the maximum of room for manoeuvre. Under the amendment, the Minister could not approve the planning of an area unless he was satisfied that:

in the case of land which is neither already built upon nor in course of development, nor likely to be developed, that the land is so situated in relation to land which is already built upon, or in course of development, or on which development is likely to take place, as to make its inclusion in a scheme expedient, or that it comprises objects or places of natural interest or beauty.

The areas excluded from planning schemes under the amendment were described by Hilton-Young as 'static areas'.

The professional and voluntary bodies put the worst interpretation on the amendment, and accused Hilton-Young of betraying the fundamental principle of the original Bill, whereby all types of land were to be included in schemes. John Dower represented many when he asserted that no area of town or country could be safely regarded as 'static'. According to Dower, 'motor transport alone by its ubiquity threatens the remotest valley with an unplanned mushroom growth of bungalows and petrol pumps, and by its intensity is daily making the centres of our towns more hopelessly chaotic and out-of-date'. The concept of static areas was simply one more example of parliament's lack of nerve for planning. As in the case of 'all progressive and stimulative legislation', risks had to be taken, and in this case they were fully justified by 'the imperative need for nation-wide planning for the economic and orderly use of the land (which a system of exceptions must grossly impair), and by the educative force of planning activity, which is our best chance of an improved local government'.[30]

For its part, the Ministry regarded such fears as exaggerated. An internal memorandum prepared by Pepler suggested that the amendment would mean little in practice. Since competition was the chief instigator of change, only the most pre-eminently suitable areas for a particular use might remain 'static', and therefore excluded from statutory planning. For example, there was little chance of the well-equipped industrial complex of Trafford Park, or the world-famous luxury shopping centre of Bond Street, being converted to other uses. Likewise, Wembley and Willesden would almost certainly remain residential suburbs. But change could take place subtly in other areas. Many of the larger houses in the resorts of Bournemouth and Eastbourne, and in the formerly fashionable parts of St Pancras and Islington in London, were being converted into flats. In practice, local authorities would always be able to find excuses for introducing planning schemes for most areas.[31]

Hilton-Young's attitude toward the concessions was revealed in a hand-written, personal letter to Ramsay MacDonald in June 1932. He assured the Prime Minister that all was well. It was 'true that we had to accept and invent a lot of amendments to wriggle through the committee, but no main or useful purpose of the Bill has been compromised'. The Bill still extended planning powers to built-up areas if they were likely to undergo redevelopment or included buildings or objects of architectural or historic interest. Rural areas could be included in planning schemes irrespective of whether they were likely to be developed if they contained places or objects of natural interest or beauty, or required to be included because a scheme for an adjoining area might be otherwise less effective. Hilton-Young wrote that 'we are confident that within these wide categories can be included all land that can be usefully planned. If a local authority allows itself to be taken by surprise by development, it will be its own fault, not the fault of the powers under the bill'. In the event, the Minister approved every resolution that was submitted for a planning scheme during the 1930s—the only exception being one for the Inns of Court submitted by the Corporation of the City of London![32]

Hilton-Young stressed that the concessions 'amounted in substance to much less than they did in form'. Of course, the government could not proclaim this, and 'most of the dissatisfaction amongst the Town-planners' arose from this impediment. Hilton-Young expected them to 'grouse' until they saw how the Act worked out in practice. In reply MacDonald agreed that some 'very critical letters' from 'ardent town planners' were only to be expected, but he made the general point that 'we must be very careful to keep in touch with the more liberal elements in the Government and supporting the Government, or we shall find ourselves very quickly regarded as a mere party Government with all these elements in opposition'. In a further letter, Hilton-Young agreed, but added, 'what our experience on the Planning Bill does is to illustrate the difficulties that will beset legislation of the sort that appeals most to that (liberal) element in this peculiar parliament—especially when it is out of the limelight, in Committee upstairs'.

This exchange of correspondence underlines the point that the greatest defect of the Act was the circumstances in which it had been passed. This was the first occasion on which serious opposition to the growth of statutory planning had been encountered, and the scale of the opposition made it difficult to judge its extent and nature. As Cullingworth has written, it was difficult to foresee how far the new powers would be welcomed or rejected in practice, and whether the Minister would be able to use his wide discretionary powers to exploit and extend the opportunities contained in the Act. Much of the impetus usually derived from the passing of a new Act was accordingly lost.[33]

As expected, the professional town planner gradually came to recognize the subtleties contained in the 1932 Act. Speaking in 1938, S. D. Adshead divided the years since 1909 into three periods. Both before and immediately after the first world war, there had been a tremendous exuberance and enthusiasm among planners. Then for about ten years, this had been replaced by dis-enchantment, as planners believed the old ideals had been lost in regulations and the 'perfect entanglement of confusion'. Planning had now entered a third and more encouraging phase. Guided by officials in the Ministry, a distinction was now being drawn between 'what was purely statutory and what was ideal'. The planning schemes were becoming 'more and more just legal documents, leaving opportunities within the statutory net for the realization of ideals'. In this way, Hilton-Young's prognostications were borne out. The trouble was that it took a highly professional and experienced planner to recognize this potential in the Act: the subtleties were lost on most other people.[34]

FINANCIAL ASPECTS OF PLANNING

Planning authorities were given almost unlimited powers to control develop-ment in the interests of 'amenity' and 'convenience'. To offset this, ways had to be found of making sure that nobody suffered or benefited unduly from the planning schemes. It was clear that planning would have an uneven impact on land values: those areas scheduled as agricultural reservations or open spaces would lose any potential building value, and the value of other properties would be enhanced, not only by the consequent reduction in the amount of land available for development but also by the general improvements made by the planning schemes to amenity, health, and the local economy.

In order to achieve equitability, the planning authorities were required in most cases to compensate any owner 'whose legal rights in his property were infringed by a planning restriction' and, as parliament and the government correctly forecast, this liability acted as a very effective check on unduly harsh planning controls. In fact, local planning authorities were very reluctant to impose any restriction which might incur claims for compensation.

There were three methods by which authorities could impose controls without incurring claims for compensation, and these accordingly became the basis for statutory planning. First, the authority could acquire the land and, for example, the Ministry of Health sanctioned loans of over £3,000,000 for this purpose in 1936–7. But this was only appropriate where beauty spots, parkland or cliffside areas required protection. It was quite impracticable to buy ordinary agricultural or rural districts in this manner.

The second method was to enter into agreements with landowners, either to preserve their properties in their existing state or to limit severely the number of new buildings to approved sites. As part of the agreement, the owners waived or drastically reduced their claims for compensation. The initiative for the earliest agreements of this type came from landowners who wanted to retain their estates as agricultural land, but who were afraid the land might be assessed on its building potential for the purposes of death and estate duties. They discovered that if they entered into an agreement binding on themselves and successors in title not to develop the land, this automatically deprived the land of building value. Starting as a method of evading death and estate duties, the Ministry of Health and preservationists capitalized on the attractiveness of the restrictive covenant in persuading the owners of tracts of outstanding countryside to enter into similar agreements. The statutory powers of the planning authority to enter into such agreements, and later enforce them, were codified under Section 34 of the 1932 Act. By 1937 sixteen schemes of this type had been negotiated in Buckinghamshire covering 19,000 acres. The largest affected 5,200 acres in Waddesdon and Eythrope, and the smallest covered only twenty acres.[35]

In spite of the importance of these two methods, the fundamental part of almost every planning scheme comprised those restrictions which parliament had allowed to be imposed without any liability for compensation. Under the 1909 Act these included restrictions reasonably imposed on the height, density, and character (later defined as size, design, elevation, fabric, and use) of buildings. Under the 1932 Act, 'immunity' was extended to prohibitions on development where the land was unsuitable or the proposed change in land use would be 'injurious to health or seriously detrimental to the neighbourhood'. This was designed to prevent a recurrence of the case where a Middlesex Rural District Council was threatened by a claim of £14,000 in compensation if it prevented a housing estate from being erected on land liable to flooding by the river Thames.[36]

These exemptions from liability for payments of compensation 'inevitably determined the shape of schemes'. Planning authorities tried to leave ample land for future building development immediately round existing village centres so that they could reasonably preserve the remainder of the area from excessive numbers of non-agricultural buildings. They could limit the density of buildings to one house per 5, 10, or 25 acres. In Hampshire over 35,000 acres of the Ringwood and Fordingbridge district, 18,000 acres of the Petersfield district, and 10,000 acres of the New Forest district, were controlled in this way without incurring a liability for compensation. Although 'fiercely criticised by the amenity groups' as not being strict enough, the Ministry of Health regarded the densities, except for the one-to-five ratio, as 'really low' and sufficient to maintain the agricultural and rural appearance of most areas.[37]

The planning authorities were given powers for the first time in 1932 to impose a temporary reservation or 'time zone' on land not yet ripe for development. During the 1920s, there had been many cases of development taking place without the adequate provision of access and public services, and in spite of any damage caused to amenity. Local authorities became increasingly worried lest this kind of loose, uncontrolled development might reach such a scale as to force them, in the wider interests of the community, to provide the necessary roads and utilities at great and otherwise unnecessary cost to existing ratepayers. The most notorious examples occurred where speculative companies acquired tracts of countryside or coast, and then subdivided the land into plots for individual development. The 'official' guide for Peacehaven in Sussex (see p. 10) boasted of the variety of scenery and lack of overcrowding in this new settlement on the clifftops of the Sussex coast. Many of the avenues were 'grass-covered, with footpaths on either side'. The participants in a land-use survey in the early 1930s interpreted the amenities of Peacehaven rather differently: they described how the plots were laid out in a 'colonial' fashion without any regard to relief or drainage—one proposed road intersected a large pond. There were no made-up roads and much space was wasted by the many vacant plots left between the scatter of houses of varied design and building materials. Many years later, early residents still recalled how the odd plot might be fenced or pegged out, but in the main most plots remained as lines on a map. It was often impossible to establish the ownership of plots, which had become covered with the rank grass, bramble and thorn of many years' growth.[38]

A number of authorities tried to prevent this kind of development by promoting a Local Bill: one for Poole in 1928 forbade any development unless the local authority was satisfied that access to the proposed development was adequate. The wider powers taken by the Surrey County Council have already been discussed in Chapter II. The Act of 1932 gave all authorities powers to temporarily prevent general development in specified areas, without incurring any liability for claims of compensation. The procedure was to designate sufficient land to cope with immediate building needs, and then to delimit this further zone where planning consent could be withheld if the operation would endanger public health through a lack of services, if the provision of these services was premature and costly, or if immediate development would injure amenity. There was a right of appeal to the Minister, and the local authority was obliged to review the case for issuing a General Development Order, removing restrictions, every three years. The Ministry nevertheless described the powers as far-reaching. They would help to secure more orderly development and curtail much of the spasmodic and ribbon development that had aroused so much opposition in the past.[39]

A fundamental weakness of the legislation was the explicit exclusion of agricultural considerations from statutory planning. According to Abercrombie, this arose out of apathy toward farming, rather than as a result of a 'Hands off Agriculture' campaign. It meant that farmers remained free of any constraints which might otherwise have been imposed on agricultural buildings and on the scale and disposal of farmland. On the other hand, the failure to include agricultural considerations in the system of statutory planning was a source of weakness for the agricultural industry as a whole. It meant that planners had no statutory responsibility to divert development to poorer land when this was in the interests of food production.[40]

It was clear that the restrictions which could be imposed free of claims for compensation did not provide 'a cast iron code for preservation'. Difficulties could arise under even the most enlightened and resolute administration. In 1937 the Tendring Rural District Council in Essex imposed a density of one house per five acres, having drawn attention to the large amount of land available for development around the villages in that district. None the less, a speculator who had previously bought seventeen acres for subdivision into one-acre building-plots appealed against the proposed density as being unreasonably low. Following a public inquiry, the inspector appointed by the Minister advised that the appeal should be upheld on the grounds that a density of one per acre would be more reasonable for land only half a mile from a village and railway station. A member of the Ministry agreed, claiming that housing densities would otherwise vary from four per acre to one per five acres within a very short distance of one another.[41]

Other members of the Ministry supported the Rural District Council, claiming that to allow the appeal would open the way to the kind of pepper-pot development that had been so widely criticized. Furthermore, there was nothing wrong in an abrupt and striking change in housing densities: one of the attractions of English villages was that the resident or visitor could walk from the village street directly into open country: 'a diminishing straggle of houses' was to be deprecated. The appellant was 'merely a land speculator who, having produced one blighted area, has bought another'. The fact that he knew of the zoning density when he bought the land made it easy for the Minister to reject the appeal and, therefore, any claim for compensation. The Minister was nevertheless warned that whilst 'you would have the weight of informed opinion in Parliament and elsewhere behind you in supporting' a policy aimed at maintaining a clear-cut distinction between town (or village) and country, zoning restrictions could lead to a serious depreciation in the value of properties. There would be occasions when the policy would lead either to heavy claims for compensation or considerable losses to the owners.[42]

Various proposals were made to offset the costs of compensation. Under the 1925 Act, local authorities could recover up to half the value of the benefits conferred by a scheme, and the proportion was raised to three-quarters in 1932. The original intention had been to allow a 100 per cent levy, but this had to be dropped due to opposition from the Conservative party and fears lest this should take away all inducement for landowners to support and participate in planning schemes. As the Ministry of Health expected, the betterment levy brought in little revenue. The difficulties of assessing liability were so great that there was bound to be a strong bias toward the property owner. The main value was to secure the mutual release of all claims for betterment and compensation in many cases.[43]

The failure to offset compensation by betterment levies was the greatest deterrent to effective statutory planning. Even the relatively advanced and much-praised planning scheme for the Hailsham Rural District in East Sussex was obliged to exclude several areas worthy of preservation because of the likely costs of compensation. Even the most prosperous authorities, including county councils, were deterred. In spite of exceptionally high rateable incomes, the Middlesex and Surrey County Councils could achieve little in view of the correspondingly higher land values. In order to protect the Guildford and Godalming bypass from ribbon development, the local authorities in Surrey would have incurred claims for compensation along twenty-two miles of frontage, in just one of the eighty-eight schemes proposed for the county.

The financial impediments considerably weakened the force of statutory planning. When Ramsay MacDonald demanded 'stronger meat' during the drafting stages of the Town and Country Planning Bill of 1931, Gibbon shared his sentiments but retorted that this could only be done if all liability for compensation was waived. This 'would clearly not have the remotest chance of becoming law'. He asserted that the Bill went as far as parliament 'seems likely to accept', and he accurately forecast that even this compromise would encounter considerable opposition at the committee stage.[44]

Throughout the 1930s cost continued to be the main 'bugbear' of planning, particularly in towns. Although local authorities had powers to acquire holdings which were 'too small or inconvenient to ensure good development', the cost of acquiring land precluded even the most prosperous urban authorities from taking 'effective action'. The only remedy was for the Treasury to provide assistance, acting on the precedents of the Housing Acts of 1930 onwards, which had greatly facilitated slum clearance. But the analogy with the Housing Acts served only to highlight the differences in the attitude of parliament, which was prepared to intervene directly on the housing question, but was content to leave planning as a purely local issue.[45]

CHAPTER VI

Local Planning

Far from being 'a centralising Bill' the 1932 Act was designed to stimulate and assist local, voluntary action. It sought to create the means by which a partnership of local authorities, voluntary bodies and individual persons could safeguard and enhance the countryside and town. Statutory planning was entirely local and permissive.

This was hardly surprising because much of the stimulus for the 1909 Act and subsequent planning legislation had come from the local authorities themselves. The support of the Association of Municipal Corporations, for example, had made legislation politically possible. Such authorities as Birmingham had already a long tradition of housing and sanitary reform, and the 1932 Act and its predecessors were firmly based on the practical experience of those authorities 'who would be responsible for the execution of town planning'.

As expected, there was a wide range of response to the legislation. The County Borough of Halifax applied for authority to plan two areas of 800 acres and 756 acres as early as 1912. The Local Government Board gave its approval, and a preliminary statement was adopted in 1922. The combined and extended schemes were the subject of a public inquiry in 1929. In a publication of that year, the Corporation looked to the future with optimism, and spoke of 'the beneficial effect of perhaps the most far reaching legislation of modern times', which promised at last to end 'the evil and enormous expense which had attended the congested development of the past'. The schemes designated zones for housing and industrial development, with adequate roads, shopping centres, and public utilities. The main aim was to secure the 'good grouping' of development and plenty of open space in the form of gardens, tennis-courts and playgrounds. These would be the lungs of each community, and help to keep the children off the streets. The Corporation stressed that the actual development of privately owned land would remain outside the control of local authorities and could not, therefore, be accurately forecast. Nevertheless, the schemes allowed plenty of flexibility so that details could be modified to accommodate any changes in industrial or social life.[1]

The Frimley and Camberley Urban District Council in Surrey may be cited as an authority which adopted a diametrically opposite point of view. The chairman claimed that development was already taking place on 'town-planning' lines and that a statutory scheme would create 'artificial monopolies', raise the 'already extravagantly high' land prices and rents, and 'press hard on the poorer classes'. A considerable sum would be required 'in the first stages of town planning to meet claims for compensation', the council was sceptical as to the practicability of long-term planning, and 'could not overlook the fact that town-planning made considerable inroads into private rights, and that advocates of town-planning found it difficult to show real benefits'.

Some commentators believed that the Local Government Board and its successor, the Ministry of Health, were equally prejudiced against statutory planning. Writing in 1914, Nettlefold accused the Board of being so steeped in 'old and out-of-date methods' that it completely failed to grasp the concept of planning and that, having been forced to introduce legislation in 1909, the Board had introduced so many regulations as to prevent anything useful coming out of the Act. It took, for example, three years for a scheme to become operational, during which time property-owners had at least seven opportunities to oppose the scheme. Without the strong force of public opinion, Nettlefold believed the needless complexities, delays, and costs would have entirely killed the Act.[2]

Nettlefold argued that there was little point in improving the 1909 Act until its sympathetic and effective administration were assured. To achieve this he advocated the replacement of the Local Government Board by a more dynamic department, which would explain 'to local authorities and the general public what town planning really means'. A more constructive attitude can be discerned, following the creation of the Ministry of Health in 1919. In that year, for example, the Housing, Town Planning Act simplified procedures for drawing up planning schemes and made the preparation of such schemes obligatory for boroughs and urban districts with over 20,000 inhabitants.

The Ministry of Health tended to adopt the policy of concentrating on 'the willing authorities' and of publicizing their achievements as an encouragement to the remainder. George Pepler played an important role in this 'missionary work'. Not only a great tactician and administrator, he was described as 'something of a lawyer'. Acting as 'expert consultant', he averted many local crises as, for example, when the Audenshaw Urban District Council threatened to leave the executive Manchester and District Joint Town Planning Committee because of fears that the district might be 'taken over' by the regional planning scheme.

Even where local authorities were sympathetic toward statutory planning, the lack of resources made long delays inevitable. Housing always took priority, and in the immediate post-war period the Ministry opposed anything which would divert the attention of local government officials from the main and all important purposes of getting on with new houses. Instead of emphasising 'town planning in general', the Ministry had to 'concentrate on areas (such as the South Wales and Doncaster coalfields) where there were likely to be big, early developments and where, therefore, town planning was the more urgent'.[3]

One such crisis arose in 1918, when the Penybont Rural District Council applied for consent to introduce a scheme for the parishes of Pencoed and Coychurch Higher, an area of 2,038 acres. Pepler was appointed inspector for the purpose of the public inquiry, and heard from witnesses of how four collieries had already been sunk in this otherwise agricultural area and of how further pits would be dug as soon as the war had ended in order to exploit the valuable Southern Outcrop of coal and provide employment for hundreds of men. At present most men had to walk many miles between the pits and their lodgings, and a spokesman for the miners claimed that the men would be prepared to pay higher rents for better living conditions. In his report recommending that a scheme should be prepared, Pepler described how the area was 'developing into a colliery centre. The surroundings are quite beautiful and it is most desirable that the development of the area should be on proper lines so that the amenities may be preserved and every convenience may be provided.'[4]

Throughout the inter-war period, town planning slowly evolved as a responsibility of local government and as a new profession. Although some authorities, such as Birmingham, were used to promoting and implementing statutory controls, many more lacked the necessary expertise and experience. Herbert Griffin, the secretary of the CPRE, complained to Pepler on several occasions of how local councillors, especially in rural districts, were absolutely ignorant of the powers which existed and were frequently muddle-headed. In many cases, they treated town planning as yet another chore to be delegated to the architect or highway engineer on the council's staff.

Of the existing professions, town planning impinged most directly on the architect, and it was an architect, Raymond Unwin, who wrote one of the first texts on the practical aspects of town planning, with the significant subtitle, 'An introduction to the art of designing cities and suburbs'. The readiness of the profession to exploit the opportunities of the concept soon had important repercussions on statutory planning. The bias and prejudices which the architect brought to planning were clearly illustrated as early as 1911, when the Town Planning Committee of the Royal Institute of British Architects (RIBA) published a series of 'Suggestions to promoters of town planning schemes'. Having reviewed the need for surveys, and for providing roads, centres of development, and reservations for open spaces, the Committee concluded by defining town planning as 'an architectural problem'. Although other professions might provide data, the architect would play the major role in actually drawing up the schemes. The Committee explained that:

the work consists in applying upon a wider field and with greater scope the same principles which govern the designing of individual buildings. The appreciation of the relation of masses and voids, the apprehension of the right points for emphasis, and the power to combine into one creation many differing parts by bringing them into harmonious proportion are equally required in the field of town planning, if there is to be produced that rhythm in the plan, and that spacious breadth of ordered elevation in the groups of buildings, which so largely constitute the beauty and grandeur of cities[5]

The fact that statutory planning was largely restricted to regulating suburban development until 1932 made it even easier for the architect to emphasize the visual aspects of building development. Nevertheless, this concern with the 'outward appearances' of development caused many to ignore one of the principal reasons for statutory planning, namely the alleviation of social deprivation in the cities. It failed to tackle the fundamental question of how much land in a locality or a region should be converted from one use to another.

In 1912 the Town Planning Institute was founded and, under its aegis, a professional code and standard evolved. The trained planner nevertheless faced a long struggle to win a place, let alone an influential role, in local government. As late as 1945 there were nearly twice as many local authorities with planning powers as had appointed qualified planners. The expert planner often faced the formidable task of having to educate his masters before he had won the right to an intelligent hearing. His post was often so lowly that even if the salary attracted a trained man of high calibre his views could only reach the ears of councillors through some uninterested senior official, trained in another profession.[6]

Some authorities embarked on statutory planning by appointing a privately practising consultant. Two of the leading consultants of the period were Thomas Adams (1871–1940) and Patrick Abercrombie (1879–1957). Having worked as a farmer and journalist, Adams set up what was probably the first planning consultancy in Britain in 1906. For a short period, he was hired by the Local Government Board as its town planning inspector. He was then invited by the Canadian Prime Minister to join the Canadian Commission of Conservation. In 1923 he returned to Britain and again set up a consultancy, this time with another planner, Longstreth Thompson, and the architect, E. Maxwell Fry. Over the next two decades Adams contributed to almost twenty commissioned reports, in addition to writing a number of books and many articles on specific and more general issues of the day. Abercrombie was Professor of Civic Design at Liverpool, before moving to University College, London, in 1935. In partnership with S. H. Kelly and others, Abercrombie helped to draw up sixteen regional schemes. He openly exploited the practical experience that he gained from this consultancy work. Dix has argued that the external contacts and experiences which arose from the various commissions made a substantial contribution to the development of planning theory and to the strength and reputation of planning as an academic discipline.[7]

Planning consultants of this calibre provided a vital link between the planning theorist and those with the executive powers. Abercrombie freely acknowledged his debt to Patrick Geddes (1854–1932), who had emphasized the close relationship between human settlement and the land, as expressed through the functioning of the local economy. This was summarized in the triad, place–work–folk. Geddes also recognized the essentially dynamic character of this relationship, and he accordingly insisted that before physical planning could take place, the past and the present had to be reviewed, analysed, synthesized, and projected. He gave planning its logical structure, as expressed in the sequence: a survey of the region and of its characteristics and trends, followed by an analysis of the survey, and then the preparation of an actual plan. It was the professional consultant, such as Abercrombie, who publicized these concepts and methods, and applied them to actual tracts of land and land-use issues. It was the task of the consultant to make planning intelligible and attractive to councillors and public gatherings, and to provide both guidance and encouragement to those drafting and submitting schemes to the Ministry of approval.[8]

One of the main criticisms of statutory planning centred on the long delays between the resolution to make a scheme and the implementation of that scheme. To some extent, this was inevitable. First, time was needed to prepare up-to-date maps of the area to be planned (see p. 143) and, secondly, there was the need to consult all the interested parties at each stage in drawing up the scheme. The Ministry attached special importance to the need. In 1921 Gibbon asserted that councils should positively invite the views of business ·men, landowners, parties concerned with transport and building (including the speculative builder), and the various 'social agencies'. The Ministry would contact central bodies and 'concert with them measures by which their local Branches shall take a real live part in any scheme under weigh in their respective districts'.[9]

Within the Ministry of Health, delays occurred as a result of a shortage of staff and the lack of balance in the nature of the work. The importance attached to statutory planning may be gauged by the fact that it was only one of six aspects covered by one of the seven divisions of the Ministry. As late as 1939 there were only an Assistant Secretary, four Principals, and up to twelve Inspectors engaged on planning. Because no one had experience of the new legal and administrative machinery, the Ministry had to scrutinize the earliest schemes 'with meticulous care'. Local authorities needed help not only in making full use of their powers, but also in remaining strictly within the limits of those powers. A great deal of time had to be spent redrafting individual clauses rather than in 'dealing with the substance of the schemes'. Writing in the 1960s, Evelyn Sharp recalled how 'much time was spent in the Ministry crawling over minor issues on enormous maps'.[10]

There were soon signs that some local authorities were treating the preparation of a planning scheme as a once-and-for-all affair. As a result, they were trying to take account of every possible eventuality in their schemes, with the result that there were even further delays and frustration. To obviate this, the Rural Amenities Bills proposed a system whereby schemes could be introduced by instalments, so that early protection could be given to the more vulnerable parts of the landscape. The Ministry opposed this on a point of principle, arguing that it was not only wrong to safeguard such features as open spaces and woods in isolation, but that the first instalment would be 'very largely restrictive in character and would not offer the advantages and facilities for development afforded by the full schemes'. The opposition which was aroused might prejudice the acceptance of the entire scheme.[11]

The Ministry advocated a quite different approach to planning. Gibbon observed that 'it would be a mistake to think that a plan is made once and for all'. There would always be a need for periodic revisions 'to keep abreast of prevailing conditions'. In London, for example, many areas which had been previously residential had become, in recent years, invaded by offices. The answer was to introduce a broad plan for the area as a whole and as quickly as possible, which would then provide a framework for more detailed (supplementary) plans whenever they were needed. The 1932 Act granted the necessary powers.

Until a planning scheme came into operation, a developer was not obliged to seek planning consent before building. Because of the delay in formulating and introducing schemes, this meant that the value of the eventual schemes could be seriously prejudiced by any development which took place in the interim period, especially as developers would be tempted to complete as much building as possible before any controls were imposed. To offset this danger, a device called the Interim Development Control was introduced. This did not legally bind a developer to obtain consent, but it contained a clear warning that unless the approval of the local planning authority was secured there was a risk of the venture being destroyed or altered without compensation if it failed to conform with the eventual planning scheme. Realizing that such uncertainty would make it difficult, if not impossible, to obtain a mortgage or sell a property, nearly all developers thought it prudent to apply for consent under the interim development procedure.

Interim development control, introduced as a stop-gap measure and with great reluctance on the part of the Ministry of Health, led to three unexpected results. First, planning authorities discovered that they could exert considerable influence over development through interim controls without having to go to the trouble and cost of completing and implementing the eventual planning scheme. Although the Ministry might cajole them, there was no practical limit to the time taken to prepare a scheme. Secondly, and as a result, the interim development controls became so widely used that the public grew used to an unwritten, adaptable planning policy. Many decisions were taken before the contents of a draft scheme had been finalized, let alone announced. Gillie has observed that if such an arbitrary or loose form of control had been proposed in the original Acts, in advance of practical experience, it would almost certainly have been rejected as investing the planning authorities with unacceptably arbitrary powers. Thirdly, and related to this point, interim development controls made it possible to formulate policy step by step, as experience and opinion evolved. Most of the policy discussions took place in the context of interim development. Where an authority refused to grant an interim development order, the developer could appeal to the Minister on the grounds that the order had been withheld unreasonably. The Ministry assessed these appeals in terms of notional future schemes, and this made it possible for planning policies to be tried and tested long before the schemes became a reality and were cut and dried.[12]

Sadly, the Ministry's files dealing with these various appeals have long since been destroyed by the weeding process and cannot be studied today. All that survives is a volume or index to the important precedents established during the 1930s. This includes, for example, reference to the case of a developer being refused permission to build one house per 2.5 acres in Hambledon Rural District in Surrey in 1933. Because the land was an impermeable Weald Clay, considerable public expense would have been incurred in providing sewers and piped water. In another case the Minister himself took the decision to dismiss an appeal against a decision by the Docking Rural District Council in Norfolk in respect of a proposal to build a bungalow, not because the building itself was likely to cause damage to amenity, but rather because its construction would open the way to further building which would, taken as a whole, destroy the amenities of the coastline. From this kind of casework a set of guidelines emerged, covering every aspect of planning policy.[13]

Although interim development control was surprisingly effective, and provided unexpected opportunities for experimenting with a wide range of formulae, it became clear that the planning schemes could not be postponed indefinitely. Interim controls could not act as a permanent substitute for a planning scheme. In practical terms, there was a large element of bluff behind the controls, and there were soon fears that this bluff would eventually be called by developers. Although the threat of demolition without compensation was usually enough to prevent undesirable development, great publicity was given to exceptional cases where a developer took the gamble. The most serious cases occurred where houses and shops were built without an interim development control order, and later sold to a succession of 'innocent people . . . whose only crime was their failure' to check the status of the properties before buying them. The Surrey County Council cited several instances of this, and warned that the task of evicting these people would be so unpleasant that many of the buildings would have to remain although they did not conform with the eventual planning scheme. If developers exploited this loophole on a large scale, irreparable damage would be done. The County Council tried to make unauthorized development within Surrey an indictable offence under a Local Bill of 1936, but the Ministry opposed this, arguing that legal prohibition would automatically lead to claims for compensation from the prospective developer and, if the claims were upheld, assessments would have to be made of liability before the statutory scheme had been finally determined and imposed. This would be 'quite out of accord with the theory of town planning'. The Ministry emphasized that the only effective way to exert planning control was to complete and implement a planning scheme with the minimum of delay.[14]

Clearly, such questions as the content of planning schemes, the merits of supplementary schemes, and the nature of interim development controls were highly complex issues, in both a theoretical and practical sense. A close working relationship was needed between the Ministry and local authorities before they could be resolved and the opportunities for statutory planning fully exploited. And yet, paradoxically, there were limits to which the Minister could act as an adviser and sounding-board for the local authorities. His role was both ambiguous and constrained. Although popularly expected to act as a guide and initiator, he was, in the eyes of the law, primarily a regulator and judge. He had to assess all the planning schemes to ensure that they complied with the Act. He held public inquiries to seek out and consider all points of view as to the merits or otherwise of schemes. The Minister considered appeals against the refusal of local authorities to grant interim development or general development orders. These were not empty duties: they were highly responsible and laborious tasks. By 1936–7, the Minister considered over a thousand appeals each year, mostly related to interim development.

Because of this ever-increasing quasi-judicial role, the Ministry found it particularly difficult to advise local authorities, even informally, on specific schemes or interim decisions which might later be challenged and referred to the Minister for adjudication. His impartiality would soon be called into question: he would be accused of acting as advocate and judge. Appreciating this difficult position, local authorities often refrained from seeking consultation when they clearly needed guidance. On occasions, the Ministry was forced, or used its quasi-judicial role as an excuse, to take a 'strictly neutral' stand, when its intervention might have greatly benefited the development of executive planning. The dilemma as to the optimal role of the Minister was another factor bedevilling planning throughout the inter-war period.[15]

In view of all these real and imagined difficulties, it was not surprising that many observers regarded statutory planning as 'lengthy, cumbersome and unsatisfactory'. The problems were not over when the schemes became operative. Planning authorities could not approve proposals which did not comply with the scheme. Neither could they refuse proposals which conformed with the scheme but which, in the fulness of time, proved to be ill-advised or harmful. Indeed, the developer did not have to apply for planning consent if his proposals complied with the scheme. Operative schemes could only be modified by preparing and submitting 'amending schemes', a process which was expected to be as formidable as that required for the original schemes.

Many argued that a more flexible system should be introduced, which recognized the need to adapt schemes to changing circumstances and requirements. They suggested that the existing schemes should be replaced by outline plans, drawn up for periods of, say, ten or fifteen years. The local authorities would not be obliged to stick rigidly to the plans and, in any case, developers would be required to seek planning consent for all new buildings and substantial changes to existing structures. The situation would be analogous to that of the interim development stage, except that there would be no final, once-for-all scheme. Not only would this alternative provide greater room for manoeuvre on the part of the planner and remove the kind of extravagantly wasteful contingency planning which occurred under the existing system, but it would introduce a much needed sense of reality in forecasting land-use trends.[16]

Others argued that this would cause the pendulum to swing too far in the direction of imprecise and arbitrary planning. The planning officer for the North Riding of Yorkshire recalled, in later years, how it was the clear and definite nature of the planning schemes, as introduced under the 1932 Act, which most appealed to developers and planners. Because the standards imposed by the schemes were binding on both parties, the developer could prepare proposals confident of their complying with planning requirements. The need to submit every proposal for fresh consideration in the context of periodically revised outline plans would lead to much greater uncertainty. Decisions might hinge on the membership and attitudes of a planning committee or office at any one point in time.[17]

PREVENTING WHAT IS BAD

In 1937 a Member of Parliament, Arthur Bossom, put down the following Motion:

this House deplores the destruction of beauty in town and country and the danger to houses of historic or architectural interest, declares that these are matters of national concern, and is of opinion that the Government should take active steps to ascertain whether its existing powers are adequate or whether they require substantial reinforcement

In moving the motion and asking the government to review its legislative powers, Bossom asserted that 'we have already had sufficient piecemeal legislation. The next time we touch it we want to make a thorough and final job of it'.[18]

In view of the overwhelming support of the House for the Motion, the Minister had no alternative but to accept the Motion and to refer the entire question to his Town and Country Planning Advisory Committee. This body had been set up in 1931 as a sop to Lloyd George and the Liberal Party, who had wanted Town Planning Commissioners to be created. The Ministry was never keen to have an advisory committee which, in fact, did very little until 1937. The Permanent Secretary, Sir Arthur Robinson, warned against creating a committee 'containing a strong "long-haired" element', and Gibbon took the precaution of appointing the Ministry's Solicitor and Legal Adviser (E. J. Maude) as chairman and another member of the Ministry (first E. S. Hill and later Miss Evelyn Sharp) as secretary. These appointments made it possible for the Ministry to exert considerable influence over the timing and content of meetings attended by the representatives of various voluntary and professional bodies.[19]

Bossom's Motion provided the Advisory Committee with its first opportunity to study a major issue and in 1938 it published a report called *The preservation of the countryside*. In the words of John Dower, the report was 'complacent, half-hearted, inconclusive and dilatory'. It looked as 'if some editorial blue pencil had been over the Report in final draft and struck out or qualified every suggestion of vigorous action by the Ministry of Health'. In the sense that the report represented the considered views of the Ministry rather than a distillation of a wide range of viewpoints from 'outside', Dower was right. On the other hand, the task of drafting the report helped to focus the minds of both the Ministry and members of the Advisory Committee on some of the more fundamental problems of rural planning within a local or regional context.[20]

In a preliminary sketch of the Committee's report, Miss Sharp emphasized the need to 'remember that the countryside is not the preserve of the wealthy and leisured classes. The country rightly prides itself on the fact that since the War there has been an unparalleled building development, a development which every Government has done its utmost to stimulate, and whose effect has been to create new and better social conditions for a very large number of persons'. Slums had been cleared and over 3,500,000 houses had been built in England and Wales by 1938. To achieve this the population had spread out from the towns and 'vast numbers of small houses for persons of very limited means' had been built. Any serious attempt to reverse this trend would 'undoubtedly run counter to the wishes of a large section of the community'.

Given these conditions, the secretary asserted that 'no planning could avert the absorption of large areas of green fields and woods within building estates, with an accompanying loss of beauty'. Controversy did not centre on whether to build, but on how and where to build. It was not easy to be dogmatic, but the published report of the Committee asserted that when all allowances were made, there had been a great deal of quite unnecessary destruction caused by misplaced development and buildings which were of poor design and character. By far the greater part of the damage had been inflicted before the 1932 Act came into operation in April 1933.

According to Miss Sharp, the two main questions raised by the motion in the House of Commons were whether the destruction of the countryside was proceeding at the rate suggested, and whether the powers conferred by the 1932 Act were now strong enough to stop further unnecessary destruction. In the absence of 'a detailed survey of the whole country it was impossible to attempt any qualitative answer'. Each member of the Advisory Committee could only speak from his personal, albeit wide, experience, and so it was decided to make on the spot inquiries in three sample areas, the Witney district of Oxfordshire, the Sevenoaks district of Kent, and the Cornish coast.

Two members of the Advisory Committee, together with Miss Sharp and G. L. Pepler, made a two-day visit to the Witney urban and rural districts. These were administered by a joint planning committee and covered 86,000 acres. There had been comparatively little development since the war, largely because most of the land remained in the hands of large landowners, including several Oxford colleges, and this had tended to exclude the small building speculator. The joint planning committee regarded its statutory powers as adequate; a preliminary statement on the planning of the area had been approved in 1933, and zoning of rural parts at a density of one per ten acres was thought to be sufficient to prevent inappropriate development.

A similar visit was made to the Sevenoaks Rural District, where development was at its most rapid. In this district, only thirty-five minutes from Charing Cross Station by electric train, nearly 3,500 houses had been built since the war, mainly in the Darenth valley. Planning powers appeared to be adequate. Although the pretty, but not outstanding, valley had been spoiled, Miss Sharp believed that it would have been impossible to have prevented development. Much more significantly, there had been no 'serious damage to the North Downs'.

The Advisory Committee expressed much more concern over the third study area, the Cornish coast, where there was need for a 'complete prohibition of any building except what is natural to an agricultural or rural area'. Many places would have been 'spoiled' by any kind of building development. In fact, there was a 'shocking example of ribbon development' above Marazion, and there was a new house at Perran, completely out of keeping with the steep valley running down to the sea. Meanwhile 'plans are coming in steadily for more and more building in the many little coves' along the east coast of Cornwall.

The West Cornwall joint planning committee wanted to designate a thin strip around the coast as a private open space, but none of the landowners on the north coast would agree to forgo compensation because of the high potential building value of this beautiful and comparatively accessible coastline. On the south coast, one major landowner had withdrawn his agreement, and another's decision to waive his claims for compensation depended on all others making a similar sacrifice. The planning authorities would be too poor to meet the inevitably large claims for compensation. Effective planning would fail unless financial aid was forthcoming from outside or some way could be found of reducing the liability to pay compensation on this coastal strip.

The Cornish coast clearly raised fundamental planning issues. Two of the members of the Advisory Committee, Raymond Unwin and E. C. King, demanded a 'radical revision' of the terms of compensation and betterment in the 1932 Act, but the chairman, Sir John Maude, insisted that the important thing for the Committee was to find ways of making immediate and practical improvements, without recourse to new legislation. Due to pressures on parliamentary time, there was practically no chance of the government agreeing to further legislation. Only five years had elapsed since the 1932 Act came into force, and rural planning authorities were only just beginning to appreciate how much control they could exercise. They were still working out their policies; 'many experiments for controlling development within the four corners of the Act' were being carried out under interim development control. Until a planning scheme for an extensive rural area had been submitted to the Minister for approval it was premature to think about further legislation.

Instead, the Advisory Committee confined itself to making extremely modest recommendations, which included the strengthening of controls over outdoor advertisements and the inclusion of agricultural buildings under the regulations controlling the external appearance of buildings. Whilst approving of these proposals, Dower and fellow critics totally refuted the argument that more drastic changes should await further experience—while the doctors are experimenting, the patient is dying fast.

The Advisory Committee believed that what was really needed was a great improvement in the quality of administration. On the evidence of the three sample studies, the priority seemed to lay in 'skilled and determined administration'. To achieve this, the local authorities were urged to appoint competent and skilled officers who had the time 'to spend on the details of plans, re-drawing them if necessary, and keeping in constant touch with developers'. The Ministry should encourage a greater interchange of ideas and experiences between planning authorities.

Experience in the Witney district had shown that controls over design were adequate if properly applied: the joint planning committee had induced developers to break up straight lines and plan houses in circles round small, open spaces. In many cases the committee had secured the use of local Cotswold stone with concrete roof tiles, and even where this was beyond the resources of the developer the committee's insistence on an 'absolute simplicity of design combined with harmonious colourings' produced very pleasing results. The Advisory Committee attributed much of this success to the planning officer, who 'really knows what is wanted' and carried out 'extensive negotiations with developers'. His perpetual vigilance had led to 'a general readiness among developers in the area to co-operate with the planning authority'. Some years previously he had produced a threepenny booklet, explaining what planning meant and what materials and designs would be most suitable in the Witney district: the Advisory Committee attributed 'the good appearance of the new buildings in the area' very largely to the clear lead given by this modest publication.

Things were very different in Cornwall, where Miss Sharp commented, 'they should have begun planning long ago'. The West Cornwall joint planning committee had only resolved to make a scheme in 1935, and a scheme for the entire area of the East Cornwall planning committee had only just been approved, and the committee 'were still very uncertain of what they should do'. Both Cornish committees badly needed expert advice. Even during the two-day visit, the Advisory Committee had been able to make a few suggestions for 'stricter control'. Miss Sharp concluded that 'if they could be more actively helped and advised, we believe that there should not be any ground for serious anxiety about the preservation of their area'.

Whilst conceding the need to improve administration, Dower argued that it was still unreasonable 'to ask local authorities to fight their best with needlessly defective weapons'. Whilst planning authorities could set 'fairly drastic low density zonings' and impose temporary bans on all building, there was no way of *permanently* prohibiting *all* development without incurring a liability for compensation. Experience in Cornwall and elsewhere indicated that many landowners were not prepared to waive their rights to compensation.

To meet this point, the Ministry drew up proposals for a new kind of planning zone, a Rural Zone, where it would be possible 'to safeguard the countryside as long as possible by allowing proper rural development without hindrance and by keeping development other than proper rural development down to a reasonably low figure'. Within this new zone, there would be free entry for buildings connected with agriculture and the 'smaller type of rural industry and the winning of minerals'. Other buildings required the consent of the local planning authority, which could impose stipulations as to the number of houses and rates of construction without incurring any liability for compensation. New country dwellings of over five acres, and rural industries 'of a more extensive kind' needed the consent of the authorities. No other new buildings could be erected without this consent *and* the right of aggrieved parties, including local amenity societies, to appeal against this consent being given.[21]

The concept of rural zones was considered by the Town and Country Planning Advisory Committee, and was recommended in its report. George Pepler stated that several authorities were prepared to designate rural zones by way of experiment, and an internal Ministry memorandum suggested trying a range of different planning controls, otherwise 'we might well be open to criticism in the eyes of our successors if we had not tried out a number of experiments'. Whatever the type of control adopted, the trials would provide the pretext for giving the local authorities much more information and assistance. As a Ministry memorandum emphasized, 'it is important to get a circular with concrete suggestions out as soon as possible, not only because there is a rising agitation on these matters but because every week planning authorities are involving themselves in agreements and negotiations on the wrong lines for want of guidance'.[22]

The outcome was Circular 1750, a letter addressed to local authorities in England and Wales, which set out the terms by which rural zones could be designated under the 1932 Act without risk of incurring liability for compensation. The Circular stressed that the zone should only be applied to 'genuinely rural' areas, and that there should be adequate provision for ordinary development in and around existing towns and villages outside the zone. The zone was intended not so much to prevent development but to foster grouped development in suitable places.

Circular 1750 also provided protection for the coast where 'the Minister felt there was need for an immediate check on the kind of ribbon development which had already 'ruined the charm of so many miles of beautiful coast'. Not only had the Minister's Advisory Committee expressed grave concern as to the future of the coast but in 1938 the CPRE, National Trust, and Commons, Open Spaces and Footpaths Preservation Society had formed a Coastal Preservation Committee specifically to stress the moral duty of each generation to preserve 'the precious heritage of the coast'.

The Coastal Preservation Committee had sent questionnaires to every maritime local authority; about sixty-five per cent replied, reporting an extremely slow rate of progress in drawing up planning schemes, negotiating voluntary agreements with landowners for preserving amenity, and in acquiring open spaces for outdoor recreation. Urban authorities were usually able to purchase public open spaces on their seafront and compensate landowners adversely affected by planning decisions. Brighton and Bournemouth, for example, had 'fulfilled all obligations' and, in any case, had little open coastline left to protect. In contrast, rural authorities frequently had such a low rateable income that they were deterred from any scheme which would incur claims for compensation. In many cases, the longer the coastline, the poorer the county, and Cornwall and Pembrokeshire had achieved comparatively little progress.[23]

An internal minute of the Ministry of Health admitted that the committee had 'put their finger on what is probably our most vulnerable spot', namely that planning controls were far less effective in coastal districts. The Coastal Preservation Committee described compensation as the 'real bug-bear' for 'the very popularity of the areas puts up the building value'. The Committee recommended that either all claims for compensation along the coast should be waived, or that the Treasury should make grants for offsetting the liability of the poorer authorities. The Ministry believed the problem could be largely resolved by adopting the new rural zone.[24]

Circular 1750 described how to protect substantial strips of land along high cliffs, with or without dry beaches below, and along flat coasts, coombes, or low cliffs with accessible beaches. The developers of permanent holiday camps would have to seek planning permission, and every opportunity was to be taken to gather holiday-huts into groups in the 'most inconspicuous places'. The Circular offered guidance on the siting of car parks in order to counter the 'growing tendency to bring motor cars down on to the sea shore or as far down the approach to the shore as possible'. As with so many initiatives taken during this period, war intervened before their efficacy could be assessed.

CHAPTER VII

Regional Planning

The main object of regional planning was 'to obtain unity of purpose for a comprehensive area in which for geographical, industrial, or other reasons, there is a special community of interest'. With these words, George Pepler exhorted the local authorities in Cumberland in 1928 to join together to form a joint regional town planning committee for the northern part of the Lake District. As the Chief Town Planning Inspector of the Ministry of Health, Pepler attended the inaugural meetings of every joint committee, providing encouragement and practical guidance. At the meeting at Carlisle in 1928 he described how each part of a region should be made 'truly productive'. Minerals should be exploited; the most effective sites found for industry; room should be set aside for healthy and convenient residential areas; recreation areas had to be provided. In the Lake District, 'the maintenance of harmony and landscape' had to be given special consideration.[1]

Following the conference at Carlisle, almost every local authority joined the joint committee, a technical sub-committee was set up, and Patrick Abercrombie was appointed as an expert consultant. With S. H. Kelly, he drew up a draft Regional Planning Scheme, which was published in 1932. It suggested subdividing the region into four planning areas, served by joint advisory committees made up of the relevant local authorities. Although the report was approved in principle, comparatively little happened.[2]

Paradoxically the Local Government Act of 1929 made it harder to initiate regional planning schemes in the early 1930s. The Act should have greatly facilitated regional planning by reducing and rationalizing the number of local authorities, but its immediate effect was to cause considerable hostility and resentment, particularly between the county councils and urban district councils, and between the urban and rural district councils. For a few years this made it very difficult to secure the level of goodwill and co-operation necessary for regional planning. Because the reorganization of the local authorities in Cumberland practically coincided with the publication of the Abercrombie and Kelly report, it was decided to suspend work on the Report until the reforms had been completed and the inevitable animosity had subsided.[3]

In spite of the missionary work of Pepler, there was widespread misunderstanding of the purposes and consequences of regional planning. On one occasion the Ministry of Health had to deny vigorously that there was any 'intention whatsoever of applying urban practice to rural districts' through regional planning schemes, and claimed that it was instead 'the essence of proper planning to fit measures to the particular circumstances. The aim will be to provide the minimum of control which is required to safeguard rural amenities and to secure that such building development that does take place is most in accord with rural surroundings'. There were also fears lest regional schemes might reduce the rateable income of some constituent authorities and unduly favour others. The Ministry admitted that there was often an overwhelming case for concentrating industry in one area, and for giving priority to 'agriculture and other forms of open development' in another. But the Ministry emphasized that any such allocation would have to be fully justified and all points of view considered.[4]

In spite of these assurances, it was very rare for all the local authorities in a region to participate in a regional planning scheme. When the Dorset County Council tried to form five regional planning committees to cover the county, Beaminster Rural District Council refused to join because 'they saw no good reason to undertake the planning' of their district. The Flintshire County Council met with similar setbacks. The Rhyl Urban District Council refused to join the proposed joint committee because it was cheaper to embark on a separate scheme than to contribute to one which covered the entire area of Flintshire: the district contributed a quarter of the county rateable income.[5]

In spite of the comparatively early head start of the South Devon Joint Town Planning Committee in 1929, its scheme was not even approved by the outbreak of war. The committee included three boroughs, eight urban and six rural district councils, together with the county council. The Regional Surveyor defined the objectives of the committee as 'the general safeguarding of the residents and by planning for the future to make adequate provision to ensure that the district may retain its attractiveness to people seeking desirable places to visit or in which to live'. Even when detailed work began on the scheme in 1931, a great deal of time had 'to be given to the necessary foundation work', which the Regional Surveyor defined as 'the education of the general public in the elementary principles' of planning.[6]

Perhaps the cohesion of regional planning committees was most at risk when the time came to implement the planning scheme. In a lecture of 1925 Patrick Abercrombie described how a group of local authorities, united for the first time after years of antagonism, might contribute to a fine scheme and perhaps the publication of a monumental report, but, he asked, did this guarantee that they had 'staying power to carry it out'? Was there not a danger of the joint approach to planning disintegrating at the point when individual sacrifice was called for? Was there not a risk of the authorities departing from the broad policies laid down by the regional scheme when it suited their individual interests?[7]

By the mid-1930s, a great deal of discussion centred on how the planning schemes might be administered. In a lecture to the Town Planning Institute in 1937 Abercrombie advocated the conversion of the joint committees that had prepared the schemes into joint boards for their administration. Although this proposal found a good deal of favour, some of his audience opposed the setting up of yet another body in local government. The chairman of the South Devon joint planning committee heard the lecture. He agreed with Abercrombie that the ideal course was for regions to be administered by joint committees, but he also believed that local autonomy should be the paramount consideraration in local government. He therefore proposed a compromise to his joint committee, whereby the joint committee acted as a meeting-place and clearing-house. Each local authority would be responsible for its particular district, and the county council for the administration of regional open spaces, and the control of advertisements and petrol stations. The formula was accepted.[8]

The many instances of delay and lack of effective planning have often been interpreted as evidence of impotence on the part of individual local authorities and of the antipathy which existed between them. Clearly these traits were present and significant, and the local approach to statutory planning magnified their effect, but they do not entirely explain the lack of strong executive action. Impotence and mutual antagonism were frequently only the symptoms of frustration, as the local authorities encountered for the first time some of the more fundamental problems of rural planning.

It is the purpose of this chapter to look at these various fundamental problems, first through a case study of the South Downs Preservation Bill, which was promoted by the East Sussex County Council in 1934. The papers preserved in the County Record Office make it possible to reconstruct the circumstances in which the Bill was conceived and introduced to parliament, and they help to explain why the measure was later rejected by a House of Lords committee. It is a story of the failure of regional planning. Failure is just as instructive as success for the purposes of the chapter.

THE SOUTH DOWNS

Perhaps the beginning of the saga of the preservation of the South Downs was in 1923 when Alderman Carden proposed that the County Borough of Brighton should prepare a town development plan. It was immediately realized that no scheme would be complete without the participation of the neighbouring Borough of Hove. Other councils soon became involved, and in 1926 a Brighton, Hove and District Joint Town Planning Committee was formed, made up of twelve constituent authorities. Meanwhile, a similar Joint Town Planning Advisory Committee was formed in 1925, covering the County Borough of Eastbourne, Seaford Urban District, and the Rural Districts of Eastbourne and Hailsham. A comparatively detailed planning scheme for the Eastbourne and District area was published in 1931, and a preliminary report for the Brighton, Hove and District area was produced in 1928, with a final report in 1932.[9]

The downs of East Sussex, therefore, fell into two planning schemes, proceeding along similar lines. By means of zoning, the Brighton, Hove and District scheme made provision for an aggregate population of 500,000 and the preservation of the South Downs above the 300-foot contour. The Committee's final report emphasized the vulnerability of the Downs. 'Relatively small in scale, they stand out so nobly because of the smooth unbroken lines of their summits and escarpments. Break one of these lines by an artificial erection and the scale is lost, the harmony destroyed'. In view of the need for more residents and holiday-makers in the Committee's area, the report defined 'the preservation of attractiveness, beauty and amenities' as the main objective of town planning. Not surprisingly, the sentiments were warmly endorsed by the Society of Sussex Downsmen, a voluntary body that was founded in 1923 to facilitate the preservation of the downs in their natural state and agricultural use.

The value of regional planning was stressed. It was widely assumed that the plans prepared by the joint town planning advisory committees would be implemented by joint committees, to which each council would devolve its statutory planning powers. The Corporation of Brighton was especially keen that this should happen, but some of the other authorities were reluctant, particularly those which had already embarked on their own separate planning schemes and were naturally unwilling 'to be held up or to forfeit the credit for what they had already achieved'. The East Sussex County Council was in a particularly difficult position. Representatives of the County Council simply attended meetings of the joint advisory committees as non-voting members, and yet the county council would be considerably affected by any future developments within the administrative county. As early as 1928 the Finance Sub-committee of the county council warned that a conflict of interests might develop. As self-appointed guardian of the rural districts, the East Sussex County Council urged the councils not to establish an executive joint planning committee, on which the coastal boroughs would have a major influence. Brighton had only just succeeded in extending its administrative boundaries, and might easily use a joint planning committee as a device for making further inroads into the administrative county.

The difficulties of planning the South Downs on a regional basis were greatly accentuated by the land-holding interests of some local authorities. By 1934 Brighton Corporation had spent £410,000 purchasing 10,000 acres of downland, a third of which was outside the borough boundaries (see figure 6). The prime object was to preserve the nearby downland from building and other kinds of development that might reduce the volume or purity of water derived from these valuable water-gathering grounds. The future status of Brighton and other fast-expanding resorts would be imperilled unless water-supplies could be sustained and extended. The Corporation also recognized the amenity value of the new estate. The best-known part was the Devil's Dyke, which Alderman Carden bought in 1926 in order to prevent its falling into 'the wrong hands'. With the encouragement of the Society of Sussex Downsmen, the sum of £9,000 was raised for the purchase of the site by the Corporation. At a ceremony marking its acquisition, the Duke of York observed that 'you have the cordial support of all who love our countryside. The Downs of Sussex are not merely a local but a national possession'. Brighton Corporation agreed with these sentiments, and looked forward to contributions toward the cost of such ven-

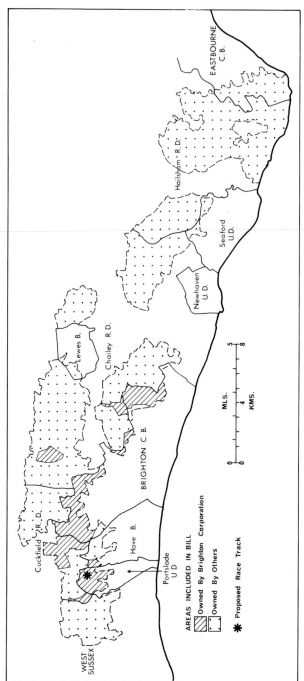

Fig. 6. The area of the South Downs affected by the South Downs Preservation Bill of 1934

no money for planned proposals

tures coming from the government, the county councils and other local
authorities in Sussex, neighbouring counties and their local bodies, especially
those of London, and from the public generally. None came.

Although a major disappointment, the lack of external assistance gave
Brighton Corporation a freer hand and, scarcely two months after the Duke of
York's speech, the Corporation agreed in principle to lease 1,100 acres of its
downland estate, west of Devil's Dyke, as a motor-racing track. The lease was
subject to the Racing Club being able to prove to the Corporation that it had the
financial capacity to meet the rigorous conditions laid down in the lease.
Members of the Corporation noted that a half-day Easter meeting at the famous
Brooklands race-track drew a crowd of 21,000, and that visitors to the Isle of
Man motor-cycle races spent £29,000 a year. A Brighton councillor observed
that 'looking at it from a business point of view, there must be money in it' for
Brighton.

Advocates emphasized how the track would conform with the natural contours among the wide open spaces of grassland. The terms of the lease specified
a six-foot high fence, painted in a neutral tint, around the track-area. The
grandstand would be collapsible, litter would be collected, and the timing of
meetings controlled. The Society of Sussex Downsmen vigorously protested.
The Times argued that the restrictions were not of 'the faintest importance'. The
proposal for a track cut 'right at the root of the whole town planning scheme for
the preservation of the Downs'. If Brighton could reconcile the construction of a
track with the preservation of the Downs, other landowners would demand
similar latitude, and the regional planning strategy for the South Downs would
be in ruins.

The site of the proposed track was in Portslade Urban District, and its
council protested that if 'this was a fair example of what Brighton was going to
mete out in the future, it was not to be wondered at that small local authorities
doubted the advantages of handing over their powers to (joint executive planning) Committees'. A local newspaper, the *Sussex News* was even more
emphatic, warning that there was no longer the slightest chance of a joint
executive planning committee being formed. Because of the action of Brighton,
most constituent authorities regarded even the advisory committee with deep
suspicion.

A breathing-space was now provided by the fact that the whole scheme was
dropped owing to a lack of funds on the part of the track-developers. In the
meantime, seven of the largest landowners in the South Downs pledged their
'active co-operation and support' to the local authorities in preserving the
South Downs. Whilst they would not surrender completely their rights to claim
compensation where building development was banned, a letter which they
wrote to *The Times* in 1929 contained a strong hint that they would hold claims
to the absolute minimum.

In view of this suggestion of support for statutory planning, there was an even
greater furore when proposals for a race-track were revived in 1933. As the

Sussex Express commented, 'it would be strange indeed if the sacrifice required of private landowners for the public good were not supported by equally dis-interested endeavours by the public authorities'. The leader continued, 'what is condemned as selfish in private owners becomes almost a virtue in the public body if it is accompanied by some doubtful or temporary monetary advantage. Surely it is for public authorities to show an example'.

Opposition from other local authorities, the Society of Sussex Downsmen, and national amenity organizations had the effect of making Brighton Corporation even more determined to lease the land. In a letter to *The Times*, Councillor Aldrich pointed out that Brighton had spent £410,000 in acquiring the downs. This was 'no pious pretence at preservation . . . it is a substantial sum, paid in hard cash by her ratepayers'. Having made such an investment, Brighton was hardly likely to throw it all away just for a race-track. Brighton deserved to be trusted to impose proper safeguards on the building and management of the track.

Carden accused the other members of the joint advisory committee of 'blind, unreasoning prejudice' and, in disgust, Brighton resigned from the committee in January 1934. He described how the committee had refused to turn itself into an executive joint planning committee. It had become 'a mere debating society and a luxury', which Brighton could no longer afford to support. Within a month the joint advisory committee had collapsed. Brighton had contributed three-fifths of the cost of running the committee, and the other authorities were not prepared to take over the burden.

Regional planning had come to an end, and Portslade Urban District Council received an application for an Interim Development Order from the track-developers. The developers stressed how the track would raise the rate-able income of the district substantially, and they warned that a refusal to grant planning consent would eventually lead to a claim for £10,000 in compensation. As the Clerk to the East Sussex County Council noted, the pretended guardians of the downs, or their lessees, threatened to 'fine' the people of Portslade £10,000 for preferring an open space to a race-track. Much to the relief of opponents of the track, the Urban District Council rejected the application. The developers thereupon appealed to the Minister of Health against the decision, and the councillors who had voted for the rejection of the application were defeated in the ensuing council elections.

THE SOUTH DOWNS PRESERVATION BILL

Meanwhile, the county councils were becoming involved in the track issue. The West Sussex County Council was comparatively well advanced in drawing up statutory planning schemes for the South Downs within its boundaries, using the powers devolved by the local authorities. Many agreements were being negotiated with landowners, whereby they waived all or part of their legitimate claims for compensation. The Clerk of the County Council, J. Edward Seager, was therefore alarmed lest the construction of the proposed track in East

Sussex, so near the county border, might disrupt these delicate but far-reaching negotiations.

In December 1933 Seager wrote to the Clerk of the East Sussex County Council, Hugh McIlveen, as a matter of urgency. At that time, the revival of the track issue was still only a rumour, and Seager was able to evince very little in the way of a response. Indeed, McIlveen was rather resentful at the inordinate interest being taken in an East Sussex problem. McIlveen's attitude soon changed, however, when the joint advisory committee collapsed and an application was received from the track-developers for an Interim Development Order. In a series of telephone calls, Seager proposed to McIlveen that the two county councils should jointly promote a South Downs Preservation Bill, which would prevent the Downs from being used for any purpose other than as a 'private open space'. It would, for example, have the effect of prohibiting the construction of a race-track. Although compensation would have to be awarded, the sum would be 'spread over the two counties' and would be modest in view of the 'considerable measure of agreement' already reached with the principal landowners.

Seager stressed that the participation of the East Sussex County Council was essential in any Bill because of 'the Brighton proposals' and the need to treat the entire length of the South Downs in a similar manner. By now, McIlveen was just as keen to participate. Instead of being a bystander, the Bill promised to make the county council the most powerful planning body in the Downs and would fill the vacuum left by the demise of the joint advisory committee. Within a month the necessary resolutions had been passed almost unanimously by the county councils, parliamentary agents were engaged, and the CPRE, National Trust, and Society of Sussex Downsmen gave their 'wholehearted support' to the Bill.

The official position of the Ministry of Health was inevitably one of neutrality because of its quasi-judicial role in adjudicating the appeal made by the track developers against the Portslade Urban District Council. Privately, the position of the Ministry was much more confused. There was relief that the issue had been referred to parliament in view of the major conflict of interests: the adjudication of the appeal was suspended. Unofficially, the Chief Planning Inspector, George Pepler, pledged 'all possible assistance' to the principle of the Bill, and the Permanent Secretary, Sir Arthur Robinson, told the Minister that 'my own desire is that this Bill should go through, because whatever claims may be made on behalf of Town Planning', there was no practical way of preventing the disfigurement and spoliation of the Downs under existing legislation.

In February 1934 the promoters of the South Downs Preservation Bill suffered their first major setback. Legal counsel pointed out that the 70,000 acres of downland covered by the Bill were extremely varied in character. It would be much simpler to promote two Bills, one for each part of Sussex. In view of the urgent need to protect the area of the proposed race-track, the East Sussex Bill should be the first to be introduced. The county councils were at first

two bills → varied landscape

extremely reluctant to follow this advice because of fears lest any separation should be interpreted as a divergence of policies and, thereby, weaken the individual cases. They therefore struck a compromise by choosing the river Adur, rather than the county border, as the dividing line between the two Bills (see figure 6). The river was the most natural subdivision of the Downs, and the arrangement would ensure that West Sussex had a direct, albeit minor, involvement even in a Bill for the East Sussex downs.

Legal counsel made a further significant recommendation by pointing out that the Bills were being promoted to protect a natural region and so it was logical to include the downs falling within not only the administrative counties but also the county boroughs. The county councils agreed very reluctantly to this. Although each council would be responsible for implementing the Bills in its own area, the concession gave such boroughs as Brighton a direct involvement in deciding the over-all content of the Bills.

Up to this time, McIlveen had only sent details of the proposed Bill to the Town Clerk of Brighton 'as a matter of courtesy'. Now he had to brief the Corporation more fully, and he expressed the hope that Brighton could agree to the terms of the Bill and leave the question of the race-track, on which their views were 'so diametrically opposed', to the decision of parliament. The Corporation replied by attacking the entire Bill as 'a dead set at Brighton over the Motor-Racing Track'. By excluding Brighton from the earlier discussions on the Bill, the County Council was clearly trying to unite all interests in taking common action against the County Borough. Brighton did not need further powers over the downs within the Borough because the Corporation owned most of them, and the Bill would considerably reduce the Corporation's freedom of action as a landowner in the administrative county.

McIlveen replied by stressing that the Bill was concerned with all downland areas, and not just the site of the race-track. The Sussex coast was already popularly known as Channel Street, and unless action was taken much more of the downland overlooking the sea would become covered by an unsightly and expensive sprawl of buildings. At Peacehaven 650 houses had already been erected over 650 acres of cliff-top. In Brighton's view, the force of these arguments was diminished when East Sussex County Council decided not to wait until the next parliamentary session and introduced the Bill as a 'Late Bill', giving as its reason the threat of the race-track. Brighton, together with the Borough of Hove and an hotel-owner, challenged the Bill as not complying with parliamentary standing orders. The Parliamentary Examiners agreed, but a committee of the House of Lords allowed the Bill to proceed on condition that any powers of compulsory purchase should be struck out because landowners had not been given sufficient notice of the Bill.

With this inauspicious start, the South Downs Preservation Bill was introduced by Lord Zetland, the chairman of the National Trust, given a second reading, and referred to a Select Committee for Opposed Bills, under the chairmanship of Lord Redesdale. After 22 days of hearings and a long adjournment, the Committee recommended that the Bill should not proceed to a third reading. When Lord Zetland initiated a debate in the House of Lords in March 1935 on the consequences of the Bill's failure, Lord Redesdale gave an unusually full account of the reasons why the Bill had been rejected by his Committee.

Was the Bill necessary?

In his speech during the debate of 1935 Lord Redesdale described how the Select Committee had faced three major questions: (1) was special legislation required? (2) what was meant by the word preservation? and (3) were the proposals in the Bill equitable?

The Bill tried to preserve the Downs in their natural condition by adopting most of the recommendations contained in the report of the Brighton, Hove and District Joint Town Planning Advisory Committee. No part of the Downs should be used for any purpose unless explicitly permitted under the Bill. Agriculture, the designation of public and private open spaces, mining and quarrying, and any uses in existence before 1934, were to be permitted. The Bill forbade any excavations or the erection of any structure or fence without the written confirmation of the relevant council that they conformed with a permitted use. The erection of posters and advertisements would be illegal, and no letters, emblems or drawings could be cut in the downland turf. The local authorities could place preservation orders on trees of over a specified size.

From the first meeting of the Select Committee, Lord Redesdale expressed a preference for proceeding under the Town and Country Planning Act of 1932, but the Counsel for the East Sussex County Council protested that it took too long to formulate and approve town planning schemes, and in the meantime considerable damage would occur. Acting as a witness for Brighton Corporation, Sir Herbert Carden described how 'you cannot build a brick on the Downs anywhere or make a road or do anything'. Because all the authorities could withhold Interim Development Orders, no one would risk unauthorized development in case it was later destroyed without compensation. Witnesses for the County Council denied the effectiveness of this kind of control. At Chanctonbury in West Sussex an Order had been refused for a kiln, but the company proceeded to build the kiln because they knew that the venture would yield sufficient profit before the town planning scheme was approved and any steps were taken to demolish the buildings. The quarry would remain as a permanent memorial to this form of 'catch-cropping'.

The promoters further contended that it was 'pretty hopeless to expect that there will be any joint action under the Town Planning Acts' to provide over-all protection for the Downs. Fifteen boroughs and districts were involved, some representing seaside resorts and others purely agricultural areas. The Bill was essentially 'a short cut' to bring into immediate effect a town planning scheme for the Downs without having to wait for all the different authorities to agree. On points of disagreement, parliament was being asked to arbitrate.

Counsel for Brighton claimed that if the Bill, an essentially anti-race-track measure, was dropped, the Corporation would help to reconvene the joint advisory committee as a preliminary to establishing the proposed joint executive planning committee. Counsel for the Promoters poured scorn on this suggestion, accusing Brighton of using the joint advisory committee as 'a sort of omnibus into and out of which people get as they please; it is a convenient vehicle while it goes their way, but when it goes the other way to that they want to go, then they get out'.

In the absence of a joint executive planning committee, the local authorities would have to draw up and implement schemes on an individual basis. In spite of the progress made by such authorities as the Hailsham Rural District Council, the Counsel for the promoters emphasized that local schemes were generally impractical owing to the inevitably large claims for compensation. If the local authorities could not meet these claims, they would have no alternative but to permit the proposed developments, and Counsel reminded the Select Committee that Portslade Urban District Council, for example, was threatened with a claim for £10,000 if consent for a race-track was refused. Under the South Downs Preservation Bill, the claims for compensation would be submitted in the same way as under the Town and Country Planning Act of 1932, but the cost of meeting these claims would be met by the precept of the County Council rather than by individual district councils. By spreading the burden more widely, preservation could become more effective.

The meaning of preservation very important.

A great deal of confusion surrounded the use of the word preservation. The County Councils called their measure the South Downs *Preservation* Bill, but their opponents attacked the measure for threatening the preservation of the Downs. It was the controversy over the race-track that most clearly demonstrated the acute differences in attitude and perception.

Proponents of the track assessed each part of the Downs on its intrinsic merits, whereas opponents saw each part in a wider context. Proponents described how the proposed site for the track was the only suitable area near Brighton, where it would occupy 'a small portion of the Downs which not one in ten thousand Brighton people had any interest in and which probably not one in 50,000 had ever visited'. There were no rights of way, most of the valley was cultivated (see figure 7), and amenity was already impaired by derelict farm buildings, a water-tower, and an isolation hospital. According to the opponents of the track, this did not justify the building of the track. One should protect not only the most picturesque parts of the Downs, but the entire region. A correspondent to *The Times* compared the Downs to a picture, and wrote, 'because one finds in a picture some shadows or dark patches one does not cut these out of the picture and leave only its prettier aspects. The picture has to be regarded as a whole'.

There was another fundamental difference of view. Proponents of the track

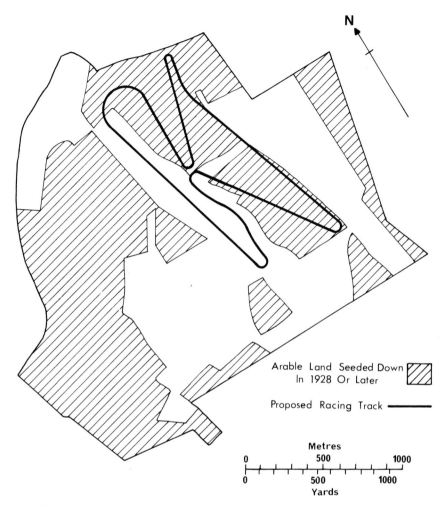

Fig. 7. The site of the proposed race-track

emphasized the way in which large numbers of people would visit the Downs because of the races. During the second reading of the Bill, Lord Buxton replied, 'I say frankly it is not so much the actual track itself to which I object. It is more the fact of there being that track, which will bring immense numbers of people there, over the Downs, to the destruction of the amenities. The pro- moters estimate that some half-a-million people will attend the meetings'. According to the *Brighton and Hove Herald,* this remark raised

a nice point of ethics. Which was the higher morality? Ought we to preserve the Downs for the privileged few, who enjoy the Downs only because they have them to themselves? Or ought we to make one very small and rather ill-favoured portion of Downland, on the outskirts of a growing town, accessible for the enjoyment of half-a-million? Is it good ethics for a few hundreds who have all the . . . Downs to choose from, to deny one poor square mile of bare Downland to half-a-million of their fellow men?

The newspaper pointed out to an inconsistency in Lord Buxton's attitude toward the Downs by applying Lord Buxton's argument to the long-established horse-races at Goodwood in the Downs of West Sussex:

The Goodwood Races mean the invasion of one of the loveliest of all the lovely areas of Downland by a hundred thousand people. The race followers who go to Goodwood invade, not a piece of farming ground, or the outskirts of a town already menaced by the builder. They invade one of the most opulently delightful pieces of scenery in Sussex. But who proposes, for that reason, to abolish Goodwood Races? Is not the reason put forward for the holding of them that they give pleasure to so many people?

The newspaper concluded with the words:

Therein is the sum and substance of the reasons for consenting to the motor-track. The loss to Downland beauty will be negligible, and will be genuinely felt by few. The pleasures that it will create will be appreciated by hundreds of thousands. Moreover, the human traffic will be canalized, compressed into the open space. And the lovers of Downland solitude will have all the rest of the Downs to themselves

During the debate of 1935 Lord Redesdale recalled the feelings of his Committee during the consideration of the Bill in 1934. He said 'it is no exaggeration to say that every member of your Lordship's Committee . . . had a feeling almost amounting to indignation at the very idea' of a race-track in the Downs, 'but, after hearing the arguments and evidence on both sides, and, above all, after inspecting the proposed site, the Committee were unanimously of the opinion that the track should be allowed,' because it would not interfere with the amenities of the Downs.

By granting victory to Brighton, the Committee deprived the County Council of the main reason for becoming deeply involved in downland preservation and for promoting the Late Bill. In view of parliament's decision, the Portslade Urban District Council had no alternative but to reverse its earlier decision and grant an Interim Development Order to the track developers. Perhaps the crowning irony was that the company was never able to take up the lease and build the track because of a lack of funds.

The County Council lost not only the battle but the war. In his speech of 1935, Redesdale identified two forms of preservation. A small minority wanted to absolutely sterilize the Downs for all time: a rather larger group wanted to turn the Downs into a noisy, crowded entertainment centre. It was the duty of the Select Committee to steer a middle course and preserve the amenities of the Downs for the 'average public'. The Committee was impressed by the moderation shown by Brighton Corporation: it had spent over £400,000 in acquiring areas of downland largely for preservation purposes and its advocacy of the track showed a genuine desire to make the downs more accessible to the public. Redesdale deprecated those who scorned Brighton and other resorts. They fulfilled a pressing public need by allowing the average holiday-maker to indulge in every kind of relaxation and amusement imaginable during his few days away from work each year.

Redesdale accused the County Council of taking up a more extreme position. The Bill wanted to maintain the *status quo*: it provided the general public with no extra rights of way. Visitors would continue to see the Downs only from existing rights of way or from afar, as a backdrop to Brighton and other coastal resorts. Redesdale commented, 'by all means exclude the public from the Downs, but then you must not say you are preserving the Downs for the public. At least be honest and say you are preserving the Downs for the Society of Sussex Downsmen and the actual inhabitants of the Downs'.

This remark highlighted a dilemma faced by local authorities in trying to implement effective preservation schemes. In order to minimize the claims for compensation, the authorities had to pay special attention to the wishes of the landowners, and this almost inevitably led to clashes with other sectors of the community. In promoting the Bill, the County Council had been successful in gaining the support of all but six of the 350 landowners in the South Downs, and there was a good chance of most landowners waiving all or part of their legitimate claims for compensation. But the landowners were only prepared to make this sacrifice if the restrictions were imposed uniformly on public and private owners. Whilst they accepted the need for building controls, they refused to allow any greater public access to their land without compensation, and the County Council had to give an undertaking that the Bill would not give the public any greater access to the Downs.

The Council's opposition to the race-track and its inability to promote casual rambling in the Downs made it easier for critics to lampoon the County Council as a collection of 'autocratic Country gentlemen, living at a considerable distance from Brighton'. Councillor Aldrich, a member of the Brighton Town Council, pointed out that five-sixths of Brighton had been built on former downland, and that it was 'absurd to say that at no time in the future should a blade of grass or a bramble on the downs be disturbed for some new development'. The County Council sounded like those persons who had earlier objected 'to trains, to motor-cars, and on principle to anything new'.

Was the Bill equitable?

The third major issue for the Select Committee was whether the Bill would cause undue hardship for individuals or communities. Although most of the petitions against the measure were concerned with technical points and were soon resolved, the opposition of Brighton and Hove Town Councils was more fundamental.

Lord Redesdale insisted that any scheme for the preservation of the Downs must have the co-operation of Brighton and Hove. In view of the universal agreement that the Downs should be preserved, he therefore adjourned the Select Committee on the eighteenth day and gave the parties three months to come to an agreement. He hoped that 'it might be possible by an additional provision or by agreement outside the Bill to effect what is required within the walls of the Bill itself'.

Many observers expected Redesdale to say, at this point, that 'if you fail to agree we will make a scheme for you'. The County Council had stressed right from the start that it wanted parliament to arbitrate on any outstanding disputes so that, even if the original proposals in the Bill were rejected, parliament would have provided some form of planning scheme to fill the void in the Downs. It was, therefore, a bitter blow to discover that the Select Committee could not act in this way. Redesdale emphasized that the Select Committee 'was not competent . . . within the four walls of the Bill before them, to make a satisfactory scheme, and in no circumstances could they go outside the four walls of the Bill'. For this reason, Redesdale had no alternative but to adjourn the hearings by saying that 'if you fail to agree, the Bill will not pass'. This meant giving victory to the Bill's opponents.

This insistence on unanimity and equitability made Brighton and Hove masters of the situation. The County Council agreed to the Brighton Corporation becoming the planning authority for property which was partly within and partly outside the borough's boundaries. It rejected a proposal that the Corporation should also become responsible for any further land acquired, which was adjacent to areas already under Brighton's control. This would have meant Brighton becoming the authority for an indeterminate area of virtually unlimited extent, and this might soon have led to demands for a further extension in Brighton's borough boundaries. As a compromise, the County Council offered to consider all applications from Brighton for an extension in authority if and whenever Brighton acquired further land.

The County Council also rejected a proposal for a special zone in and adjacent to Brighton where the downland could be used for 'various additional purposes'. The Council claimed that it would be difficult to define such a zone in the featureless downland, and it would reopen 'the whole question of negotiation with landowners and from what we know of the view of the landowners we do not think they would be at all agreeable'. The County Council concluded that 'we think it would be very complicated', but again it offered to make 'a very considerable sacrifice' and, in special circumstances, to allow 'any use of land or the erection of any structure, subject to the approval of the Minister in cases where objections are made to the proposal'. Brighton regarded these concessions as inadequate, and still opposed the Bill when the Select Committee was reconvened in October 1934. Redesdale did not regard the differences as serious and, according to an internal document of the Ministry of Health, he was prepared for the Committee 'to help resolve them'.

The dispute with Hove Town Council was much more fundamental. In its petition against the Bill, the Hove Town Council claimed it 'certainly [had] no desire to develop or encourage development on that part of the South Downs which lies within the borough', but circumstances might change and the Bill was inequitable in depriving Hove of any chance of expansion in the future.

There was another reason for opposition. Hove compared its status as a coastal resort with that of Brighton and argued that, because the resorts had an equal interest in the Downs, they should contribute similar amounts to their preservation. Brighton was, however, a County Borough and, under the Bill, was only liable for claims for compensation arising within the borough boundaries. Hove was in the administrative county of East Sussex and was expected to help meet the county's liability. Since Hove contributed a third of the county's rateable income, the Town Council realized that it would be asked to contribute a far higher sum to the preservation of the Downs than its rival resort, Brighton. Hove insisted that it should contribute only 20 per cent of the county's costs, which it considered exceedingly generous in view of the fact that only 3 per cent of the Downs covered by the Bill fell within the borough's boundaries.

The County Council noted that Brighton's low liability reflected not only its County Borough status but also the fact that the Town Council had spent large sums in buying the downland for water-gathering purposes, which had contributed to preservation and obviated the need to compensate private landowners for any future development restrictions. Hove agreed, but noted that the cost of these purchases had been met from Brighton's revenue as a water-undertaker, and Hove had contributed 36 per cent of this income for its share of Brighton's water. This meant that Hove had already spent over £100,000 buying Brighton's downs and now it was being called upon to pay a third of the county's costs in compensation, estimated at £600,000.

The County Council could not agree to a differential rating for Hove as this would be a departure from 'the normal principles of local government'. The preservation of the South Downs was 'a matter of common interest to all ratepayers in East Sussex', and accordingly they should contribute in proportion to their rateable value. Far from deserving privileged concessions, Hove was so near to the Downs that it stood to gain far more in benefits than such boroughs as Rye or East Grinstead, which were not even within sight or easy reach of the Downs. Hove Town Council agreed that it should pay its fair share toward comprehensive county services, but drew a distinction between financing a mental hospital, or a road scheme, and preserving the amenities of each part of the county. Inasmuch as Hove would benefit from the preservation of the downs outside the borough, so the remainder of the county 'benefits immensely from what Hove has done in preserving the amenities of its borough along the sea front and providing these facilities and amenities for the enjoyment of the place'.

The County Council regarded the entire argument as irrelevant. Under the Bill, the individual ratepayers in Hove would pay exactly the same amount in the pound toward the preservation of the Downs as ratepayers elsewhere in the administrative county. If Hove's demands were accepted, the ratepayers would contribute less, and the remainder of the administrative county would regard this, quite justifiably, as grossly inequitable.

Lord Redesdale decided that this impasse was 'insuperable', and he told the respective parties at the last meeting of the Select Committee that 'the Committee will report to the House that the Bill is not to proceed'. Brighton regarded the verdict as 'a remarkable vindication to the furthest possible extent of the attitude taken by Brighton throughout the whole prolonged and painful business'. The County Council was appalled to discover that the promotion of the failed Bill had cost £10,000. All parties agreed that an acceptable preservation scheme had to be found, which steered a middle course between the 'grave abuse and spoliation' of the Downs and what opponents believed to be 'the rigidity of the Bill'. The problem was in finding the middle course.

FINDING ANOTHER STRATEGY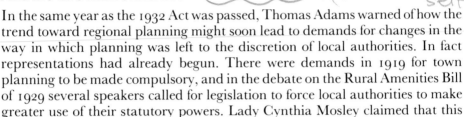

In the same year as the 1932 Act was passed, Thomas Adams warned of how the trend toward regional planning might soon lead to demands for changes in the way in which planning was left to the discretion of local authorities. In fact representations had already begun. There were demands in 1919 for town planning to be made compulsory, and in the debate on the Rural Amenities Bill of 1929 several speakers called for legislation to force local authorities to make greater use of their statutory powers. Lady Cynthia Mosley claimed that this was the only way 'reluctant and backward authorities, the timid and the unseeing local authorities' would ever act.[10]

The Ministry of Health regarded such proposals as futile. A memorandum of 1919 emphasized that the whole essence of a town planning scheme was that it should be 'carefully and thoughtfully devised', and this would never be achieved by simply compelling local authorities to participate. Many would comply with the letter of the law by merely submitting schemes that were entirely unsatisfactory and impractical. In his reply to the debate of 1929 the Minister, Arthur Greenwood, highlighted a further difficulty, when he pointed out that the costs of any statutory controls had to be met by the local authorities. As a result, he could hardly compel them 'to do things they do not want to do'. A few laggards had to be expected in any system which gave free rein to the enterprising and energetic.[11]

As a professional planner, Thomas Adams was equally sceptical about the value of compulsory powers. To be effective, the driving force for planning had to 'grow upward from public opinion and not downward from dictation of government bodies'. The only way to end haphazard and wasteful land use was through educating 'town planners, public authorities, and the general public, in the principles of town planning'.[12]

The Ministry constantly emphasized the need for voluntary bodies and local ratepayers to stimulate local authorities into action. Far from ignoring voluntary organizations, the 1932 Act had made them even more important. By granting the local authorities powers to make schemes wherever they thought necessary, it was essential that these powers should be fully understood and correctly applied. The Ministry's attitude was illustrated in 1937, when the

Parliamentary Secretary, R. S. Hudson, replied to criticisms of the lack of statutory protection for old buildings and the countryside. He asserted that 'the real solution lies not in coming to Whitehall and saying that the Central Government must act, and tell the local authorities to disallow this, that or the other'. Instead, the voluntary bodies should exert the necessary pressure on the local authorities, who already had extensive powers.[13]

In extolling the role of voluntary action, the Ministry may have been under an illusion or simply ahead of its time. It presupposed that the various societies already had strong, active, local branches throughout the country. Even the CPRE found this hard to achieve and, even where firmly established, it took a long time before a branch had any perceptible influence over the activities of the local authorities. Meanwhile, harmful changes in the use and management of the countryside continued, and the voluntary bodies had no alternative but to appeal to the government for further legislative aid.

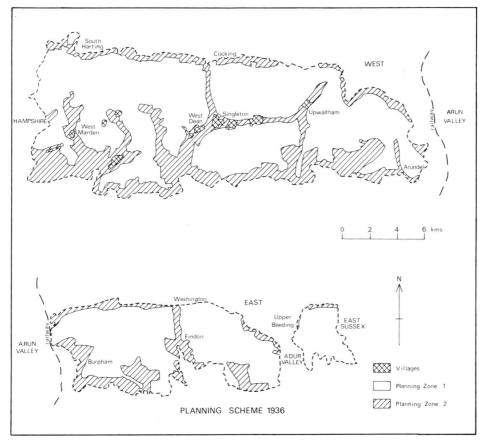

Fig. 8. The Planning Scheme for the west and east parts of the South Downs, as proposed by the West Sussex County Council

One of the most important testing-grounds for local and regional planning continued to be the South Downs. In West Sussex, the eight district councils with planning responsibilities for the South Downs delegated them to the County Council which, by 1936, had drawn up a planning scheme, covering 77,281 acres. The scheme was based on a conception of two planning zones: zone I comprised the higher parts of the Downs, and a smaller zone II occupied the area up to a quarter of a mile from the north scarp and those parts below about 200 feet on the dip slope (see figure 8). The only buildings that could be 'erected and used' without planning consent in zone I were those required in connection with existing uses of land, for the most part agriculture. In zone II, this concession was extended to include dwelling-houses. Unless special consent was given, the average density of building units was not to exceed one per hundred acres in zone I, and one per five acres in zone II. The height of buildings was limited to 35 feet, and disputes over the external appearance of

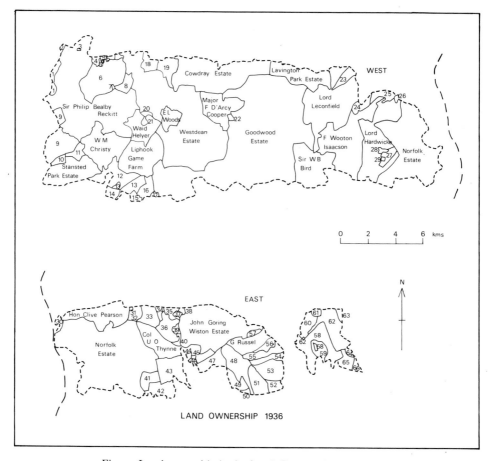

Fig. 9. Land ownership in the South Downs of West Sussex

buildings were to be settled by a tribunal of three persons, who would be Justices of the Peace or who would be drawn from the professional bodies concerned.[14]

The West Sussex County Council went to great pains to secure the support of landowners. Their task was made much easier by the fact that only 101 owners were involved (see figure 9). Most were large landowners, who found it comparatively easy to make compromises involving some economic sacrifice of potential development values. By the time that the Public Inquiry was held into the scheme, the Council had satisfied all but two of the original sixty-nine objectors. The Inspector drew attention to the remarkable unanimity of support, and recommended the scheme's implementation with the minimum of delay. The two outstanding objections related to properties of 400 and twelve acres, where the owners wanted scope to develop at higher densities than permitted by the scheme. The Inspector opposed this on the grounds that the owners were not 'likely to suffer any serious loss', and the larger owner had bought the property after the council had announced its proposal to include the area in the scheme.

In East Sussex, the search for a compromise was more tortuous. The eastern part of the South Downs was more open, and it was felt that even the low densities permitted in West Sussex were too high. Furthermore, the district councils were far less eager to delegate their planning powers and yet, as was emphasized before the Select Committee, these authorities could not afford to meet the cost of claims for compensation. To prevent the situation deteriorating still further, the East Sussex County Council decided to intervene under the 1932 Act and indemnify the district councils against any claims for compensation arising out of statutory planning, where the cost exceeded the capitalized value, spread over thirty years, of a farthing rate. Under this arrangement, the councils would allow the Downs to be used only for agriculture and as a private open space. Any buildings or other major changes would require the consent of the County Council.[15]

All the relevant authorities in the administrative county agreed in principle to the arrangement, but unfortunately the conditions laid down by the County Council were found to be *ultra vires*, inasmuch as they would have illegally fettered the individual councils in the discharge of their statutory duties under the 1932 Act. Accordingly, some 'legal gymnastics' were required, whereby the councils were asked to delegate their statutory responsibilities to the County Council, which would then delegate them back to the councils. Delegated powers could be fettered! This aroused the suspicions of some councils, jealous of their statutory powers, and three authorities took advantage of the difficulties to withdraw from the agreement. The remainder agreed to relinquish their position as statutory planning authorities and, indeed, three of them decided later not to seek any delegation of the powers back to themselves.

Once agreements with the local authorities had been reached, the County Council began to negotiate with as many landowners as possible under Section

34 of the 1932 Act (see p. 76). The aim was to secure as many voluntary agreements as possible by the time the County Council submitted to the Minister a planning scheme for the entire area. This would effectively minimize opposition to that scheme and help to ensure that the Downs were protected not only by a statutory scheme but also by agreements in perpetuity duly registered as land charges. Most land was thus protected without demands for compensation. By the outbreak of war, negotiations had been completed for about 24,700 acres of the 34,600 acres for which the Council had assumed responsibility, at a cost of £62,700. Of the remaining 10,000 acres of 'unprotected' land, about 2,000 acres were owned by the Crown Estate and by Brighton Corporation, 720 acres by the National Trust, and 3,000 acres fell within the Hailsham Rural District planning scheme, which came into operation in 1938.

By 1938 the County Council was anxious to complete negotiations with all the landowners in the Downs because funds were available and war appeared to be imminent. Nevertheless an internal minute advised caution: 'it is quite easy to spend £13,000 on compensation, the more difficult problem is to get value for money'. McIlveen warned that 'the less said about the payment of compensation the better', otherwise the County Council would be faced with greatly inflated claims. The Council tried to stop the Society of Sussex Downsmen and the National Trust from launching appeals for the purchase of key areas of downland, lest this might also deter landowners from making voluntary planning agreements.

This policy of stealth was very frustrating to the County Council, which wanted to publicize the great success of the scheme of assisted compensation. The secrecy surrounding the Council's preservation programme made it easy for voluntary bodies to misinterpret the Council's motives, and often it was wrongly accused of being apathetic and even hostile toward the preservation of the Downs. The fact that the running battle with Brighton continued seemed only to confirm that the local authorities were still playing politics and ignoring changes taking place in the 'real world'. In fact, there was even the prospect of improvement in this theatre of conflict: a compromise was being negotiated for the treatment of the Corporation's property when war broke out.

It was all too easy for the public to find examples of bad development and overlook the fruits of the essentially negative forms of planning possible under the 1932 Act. As the Minister of Health, Walter Elliot, wrote in 1938, 'particular pieces of unfortunate development get publicity, but no one hears of the unsatisfactory projects for development which are being day to day successfully prevented by planning authorities or transformed under their influence and made more attractive'. One consequence was that the voluntary bodies and their supporters gave short shrift to the efforts being made by the local authorities. They often had no idea what was being negotiated and accomplished behind the scenes, but even if they had been better informed it is doubtful whether such critics would have been impressed. Many had turned their backs on statutory local and regional planning, and were busy advocating a more radical, comprehensive, and positive concept of planning, within which national parks were a key component.[16]

NATIONAL PARKS

Clearly the strategy eventually adopted for the South Downs was not a perfect one, and it could do little to deter the search for more effective and straight-forward means of protecting areas of outstanding scenery and recreational value. A way had to be found of ensuring that protection became the paramount concern of these areas, and that positive steps could be taken to enhance amenity and recreational opportunities.

An increasing body of opinion believed that this could only be achieved by appointing an *ad hoc* group of commissioners, who would designate a series of national parks. In other words, planning in these park areas would be taken away from the local authorities and given to a national parks authority. The Ministry of Health was never keen on the idea because of the practical difficulties involved, but it joined with the voluntary movement in looking for ways of providing additional protection to areas of outstanding scenery within the existing pattern or framework of statutory planning. It is not the purpose of this Book to provide another detailed account of the concept and location of a series of proposed national parks, but, instead, this Section will look at some of the key issues raised and debated within the government departments.[17]

Lord Bledisloe, the Parliamentary Secretary to the Ministry of Agriculture, made a private visit to the national parks of Canada and the United States in 1925 and, amid considerable publicity, he described how 'they not only provided beautiful sanctuaries for wild animals and birds, as well as for the wild flowers and ferns of endless variety and beauty, but, in particular, they constituted a most perfect holiday resort for persons of all classes engaged normally in strenuous work'. Bledisloe was accordingly receptive to the ideas of Major-General Sir Frederick Robb, who not only suggested the creation of a series of national parks in Britain but actually calculated the costs of equipping a national park in the Forest of Dean with the requisite tourists' camps. As a local landowner in the Forest, Bledisloe decided in 1928 to write to the Prime Minister and First Commissioner of Works, recommending the conversion of the Forest of Dean into a national park, equipped with at least three holiday camps run on American lines. With a General Election in the offing, he described to Stanley Baldwin how 'thousands of votes' might be secured for 'relatively trifling Treasury expenditure', namely £30,000. The First Commissioner, Lord Londonderry, was sceptical: it was debatable whether the Forest was the best suited area for a national park and whether there would be sufficient public support to make the venture a success.[18]

Nothing came of the suggestion, but shortly after the General Election and the formation of the Labour Government in 1929, the CPRE submitted a memorandum to the new Prime Minister, Ramsay MacDonald, asking for an inquiry into the need for a series of national parks in Britain. MacDonald responded by appointing an inter-departmental committee in 1929 to investigate the need for one or more national parks for 'the preservation of the natural characteristics, including flora and fauna', and 'the improvement of recreational facilities for the people'. In its report of 1931 the committee recommended the creation of a national parks authority with a budget of £100,000 per annum for five years in order to create a series of parks. The Minister of Health, Arthur Greenwood, accepted the proposal, but decided to make no further moves until the enactment of his Town and Country Planning Bill, which would help prepare the way for the parks. By the time the 1932 Town and Country Planning Bill was passed, the country was in the throes of a severe financial crisis, and the new Minister of Health, Sir Edward Hilton-Young, decided that it was pointless to ask the Treasury to approve any expenditure on national parks.[19]

In order to sustain interest in the national parks issue, a Standing Committee on National Parks was formed under the auspices of the CPRE and CPRW in 1935, largely on the initiative of a local pressure group, the Friends of the Lake District. As soon as the economy showed signs of recovery, demands for national parks were renewed. The Ministry was now more hesitant in acceding to these demands. Although the 1932 Act had helped to prepare the way, it also provided an alternative means of preserving amenity. The Ministry pointed out that statutory planning schemes were being prepared for most of the proposed park-areas, and that any *ad hoc* statutory intervention was unnecessary and would be a damaging blow to the morale of the local planning authorities.[20]

The advocates of national parks responded by claiming that the statutory schemes were too weak to preserve amenity because the planning authorities were generally too poor to meet the inevitable costs of compensation. They cited the instance of Pembrokeshire, where a penny rate raised only £1,000. The Ministry agreed that some local authorities had 'meagre resources', but insisted that they could achieve much more than they had without incurring heavy claims for compensation. The preparation of planning schemes appeared to be well in hand wherever there was need for controls. There was no evidence that 'the preservation of important areas was failing through the inability of the local authorities to find money'.[21]

When the Standing Committee on National Parks asked the Minister to meet a deputation, the Ministry warned that 'the deputation must prove that key areas are being ruined through lack of adequate finances before an Exchequer grant can be secured'. The deputation met the challenge by submitting a detailed memorandum to the Parliamentary Secretary in 1937. Although the Ministry believed it failed to prove the general inadequacy of statutory schemes, internal memoranda conceded that it had highlighted those parts of the country where considerable improvements were urgently needed. As a member of the Ministry, Miss Evelyn Sharp, remarked, 'the examples they give do show the difficulties of getting satisfactory preservation in remote and undeveloped parts of the country if one relies completely on local resources and

I think none of us disputes that a great deal more could be done if outside assistance were more available'. The successes in Surrey, where rateable income was high, and in Sussex, where landowners had voluntarily waived their claims to compensation, should not 'obscure the fact that while the preservation of the countryside is an object of national policy, the National Exchequer makes no financial contribution towards the attainment of this policy'. Until it did so, Miss Sharp concluded that statutory schemes would be unable to provide certain protection, particularly in those areas where 'the local authorities have slender resources, preservation is required more for national than local interest, the proportion of land needing control or reservation is unusually high, and the attractiveness of the districts makes the early possibility of sporadic development a particularly real danger'.

The exceptional difficulties in protecting the potential park-areas were graphically illustrated by Kenneth Spence. He wrote of the Lake District that:

our main difficulties very often arise from the fact that unlike other districts where you can say to the builder or the garage owner or the electricity undertaker: 'You can't do this here, but it will be quite all right just there, round the corner', with us there is no 'round the corner'; the whole area is or should be kept beautiful

One of the areas facing this kind of dilemma was the Ulverston Rural District in the Lake District, an area of 127,000 acres and only 4,700 inhabitants. Interim Development Orders had been granted by the council for development on the banks of Lake Windermere at a density of four houses per acre, and another for buildings at a density of one per acre at the head of Ullswater. The Standing Committee on National Parks protested that, whilst this kind of density 'might be suitable for ordinary rural areas', it made 'a mockery of planning' in the Lake District. The Ministry agreed, and an internal minute conceded that undoubtedly 'the fear of compensation lies at the bottom of such zoning'.[22]

Miss Sharp concluded that:

the Government will be exposed to serious criticism and discredit if a purely negative reply continues to be given to the large body of opinion in favour of definite action for the preservation of the countryside. The National Parks appear to provide the best opportunity of making a gesture to indicate the reality of the Government's interest in the problem of preservation, applied to that portion of the problem in which the national interest is greatest and the opportunity of finding an alternative solution the most remote

The real crux of the question was whether the Exchequer would provide financial assistance. Without this, Miss Sharp regarded a national body, set up to select and supervise national parks, and 'to guide, support, co-ordinate and supervise local authorities . . . [as] a pale and rather useless shadow'.

The Deputy Secretary, Sir John Maude, commended Miss Sharp's memorandum to the Minister in July 1937. As usual, the main difficulties revolved around finance. He was surprised that no one in parliament or elsewhere had drawn attention to the fact that Planning had remained the Cinderella of 'all the social and local government services started in the early years of the century. Planning had never received a penny of Exchequer grant'.[23]

Events took a dramatic turn in May 1937, when the Amenity Group of members of the House of Commons met the Chancellor of the Exchequer, Neville Chamberlain, primarily to discuss ways in which landowners might make gifts of land and buildings to such bodies as the National Trust in return for an exemption from death duties. The Group also referred to the value of the Treasury providing funds for the preservation of outstanding buildings and scenery, and Chamberlain, speaking as 'a friend rather than as Chancellor', suggested that the voluntary bodies should submit a formal request for a grant toward a specific project.[24]

Chamberlain's remark caused embarrassment in both the Treasury and the Ministry of Health. The Treasury emphasized that the Chancellor was in no way committed to looking favourably at any request for aid, but an internal memorandum conceded that from now on 'the Government are virtually committed to financial assistance in some form or other to the National Parks project'. It was significant that even Herbert Gatliff, a member of the Treasury and leading figure of the Ramblers Association, thought the Chancellor's comment was premature. In a private capacity Gatliff had tried to persuade the voluntary bodies to establish a national parks fund, and then approach the Pilgrim Trust or another charitable body for substantial grants. Once this had been done, Gatliff believed the voluntary bodies would have a decent case to put before the government. In various memoranda Gatliff reminded the Treasury that none of these steps had been taken.[25]

Chamberlain had also embarrassed the Ministry of Health. There were fears that if the Ministry pressed the Exchequer for funds to set up national parks, this might prejudice the chances of securing assistance for other, more important, projects which the Ministry had in mind. Although a strong case had been made for planning grants, Sir John Maude believed that 'Housing, Milk for Mothers and a cancer scheme' should be given higher priority. In the event, the Minister, Sir Kingsley Wood, decided to include in his 'Bill' to the Treasury an 'item in respect of the National Parks Organisation for which the CPRE and so many other idealists are pressing'.[26]

Now began the difficult task of deciding how much money should be requested from the Treasury, and how it should be allocated to the parks. The Ministry rejected the concept of a national parks authority, and suggested an alternative scheme to the Treasury, whereby the amenity organizations should set up a new *ad hoc* body, or nominate an existing organization, to select and administer up to six national parks in accordance with criteria laid down by the Minister. The Exchequer grant would not exceed the amount raised from other sources, and would in any case be limited to £150,000 per annum for three years. Local authorities would be allowed to contribute funds. The grant would be spent on administering the parks and compensating landowners for voluntarily accepting restrictive covenants on the development of the park areas. The

Minister's approval would be required for such payments.[27]

The Treasury warned that by taking the initiative in setting up a new body, defining its functions and procedure, and imposing Ministerial control over its expenditure, the government would in effect be making itself responsible for the success of the scheme. Landowners might become less generous, and local authorities less careful in incurring claims for compensation. Once initiated, it would be difficult to confine the scheme to 'a few obviously attractive areas', and soon claims would be lodged 'wherever any beauty spot—even a small one—is threatened'. The Minister would soon be under considerable pressure to exceed the limit of £150,000 per annum.[28]

The Treasury believed these difficulties could be avoided if aid for national parks was given in the form of an ordinary grant-in-aid, involving no administrative control over expenditure. In this way the Ministry's level of support would not be related to the costs of the parks: it would merely be awarded 'on the usual recognition basis as a Government encouragement to private effort'. A fixed contribution of £20,000 per annum over an initial period of five years was suggested. The obvious candidate for this grant was the National Trust, which had the public confidence and was the best equipped to carry out a national parks scheme. By 1937 the Trust had acquired 58,000 acres of land and had negotiated restrictive covenants over the use of a further 14,000 acres, including Buttermere, Loweswater, and Crummock Water in the Lake District.[29]

In a review of the Treasury's proposals on national parks, an Assistant Secretary, Eric Twentyman, was under no illusions as to how the formula would be received by the advocates of national parks. He wrote: 'if the conservation of particular areas as Natural Reserves or National Parks be accepted as an object of policy, the case for a National *ad hoc* authority is I think unanswerable'. He recognized, however, that it was imprudent to enter into relatively large financial commitments in view of present and prospective demands on the Exchequer, and he reluctantly agreed to the proposed fixed grant-in-aid to the National Trust. But he emphasized that 'it can only be defended on grounds of financial stringency'.

Meanwhile the Ministry of Health had asked its Chief Planning Inspector, George Pepler, to nominate a number of national parks eligible for grant-aid. Pepler soon pointed out the difficulties of choosing the areas. The Lake District, Snowdonia, Peak District, and Dartmoor were the most popular suggestions, but Pepler contended that coastal areas were in far greater need of protection. Whereas most tracts of coastline formed comparatively minor components of planning schemes, nearly every park area fell within schemes which had the preservation of natural beauty as a primary objective. Some of these schemes were far advanced, and all but one would be ready for the Minister's approval by 1939. In many cases, landowners had waived their legitimate claims for compensation, and Pepler warned that any announcement of Exchequer aid would throw them back into the melting pot. The whole atmosphere would change, and 'a quite substantial amount of Exchequer money might find its way into the pockets of landowners without any appreciable result in securing further protection'.

At a meeting in February 1938 Sir John Maude and an Under-secretary in the Treasury, Sir Alan Barlow, examined the 'risk of the market hardening'. Barlow suggested a new formula, whereby the Ministry would approach the amenity bodies 'in the strictest confidence and intimate that if and when after negotiations with the planning authorities they could satisfy us that they were in a position to secure valuable concessions from the landowners . . . the Exchequer would make suitable contributions towards the expense involved'. The Ministry disliked the formula for three reasons. First, the need for secrecy would prevent the government from displaying its real and growing concern for the countryside. Secondly, news of the offer to voluntary bodies would eventually leak out, probably in a misleading and ill-digested form. The third and most fundamental objection was that this formula did not ensure good planning. In a letter to Barlow, Maude took the example of the Lake District, where there was every possibility of the park area being divided between three and possibly four planning schemes, and it was 'doubtful whether the Exchequer ought to contribute, however indirectly, to planning organised on these lines'. The only chance of persuading the local authorities to join in one scheme might be to offer financial assistance, but this would have to be done in 'a direct and open manner'. Secret help to the voluntary bodies would not suffice.

It was decided that Pepler should again visit the Lake District 'as part of his normal duties' in order to assess the situation more closely. In a more hopeful report, Pepler insisted that any Exchequer help should be given to the local authorities, but warned that even if this were done 'the delay involved in scrapping the existing schemes in their various stages and starting *de novo*' would be scarcely worthwhile. The overriding need was to implement the planning schemes. As a Ministry memorandum remarked:

as long as schemes are in the resolution stage we do not know what local authorities are doing with them: we can say that local authorities have the planning controls, but we cannot say how they are exercising them or how strong is *their* desire to preserve what others think worthy of preservation. They do not know and we cannot say how far the Minister would support them if they did take a strict line

This uncertainty could only be resolved when a number of schemes was approved, and that meant avoiding the kind of disruption and delay which would inevitably follow any announcement of Exchequer assistance.

Pepler also reported a considerable improvement in the preparation of the planning schemes in the Lake District. One was submitted to the Minister for approval, and others were nearly ready. As Maude told Barlow, 'none of these schemes is perfect, but we think that, given tolerable administration, they will effect most of what reasonable persons require. They will certainly not satisfy the Friends of the Lake District and other extremists, who, in effect, wish to put the whole district under a glass case'. Because of the need to expedite the schemes as quickly as possible, the Ministry decided to leave the question of Exchequer assistance in abeyance.

It happened that a fortnight later, the Chancellor of the Exchequer received a copy of a pamphlet, *The case for National Parks in Great Britain*, which the Standing Committee on National Parks intended to publish and send to all members of parliament. The pamphlet restated the case for a national parks authority, and described how the existing local authorities lacked both the legal powers and financial resources to safeguard the park areas. There was no means of identifying those areas worthy of 'national park treatment' or any statutory recognition of the positive aspects of park management. The pamphlet emphasized how it was important 'not only to secure and increase access, and to provide hostels, campsites and other facilities, but also to preserve wildlife and to maintain landscape beauty and effective farming use. For such activities the local authorities have, in general, no mandate and no resources'. Recourse should be had to a specially appointed national parks commission.[30]

On reading the pamphlet, Eric Twentyman confessed that 'our recent discussions with the Ministry of Health have been inspired by the hope that we might stave off the demand for a full blooded National Parks policy by action under the powers given by existing legislation'. The pamphlet had put forward convincing evidence of their inadequacy, and Twentyman concluded that 'some announcement of Government policy should be made fairly soon if the technical position is not to be worsened'.

The threat and then the outbreak of war prevented the announcement being made. There was a lull until the national parks question was once more taken up in discussions as to the shape and purpose of the government's post-war reconstruction programme. Pressure from the Standing Committee on National Parks encouraged the government to appoint John Dower as a research officer to investigate national parks, and his findings were eventually published as a Command Paper in 1945. Dower proposed the formation of a national parks commission, with executive planning powers, in order to select, establish, and maintain a series of national parks. Meanwhile the government was preparing a new Town and Country Planning Bill, which finally reached the statute book in 1947 and awarded the local planning authorities unprecedented powers. By doing so, it became politically impossible to transfer the recently-awarded planning powers to a new, non-elected national parks commission. The result was a compromise in the form of the National Parks and Access to the Countryside Act of 1949, which split responsibility for national parks between a National Parks Commission and the local authorities. Although statutory provision was made for a series of parks, the Commission was granted only advisory planning powers.[31]

In essence the search for compromise and expediency in 1949 was very similar to that of ten years previously. The fundamental dilemma remained unresolved, namely whether it was worth risking the disruption of the entire framework of town and country planning for the sake of the most outstanding parts of rural England. The arguments put forward for national parks and a more comprehensive statutory planning system during the war and immediate post-war period merely sharpened the dilemma, and the compromise presented in the 1949 Act satisfied no one completely. Far from providing a fresh start, the war simply interrupted the long search for ways of creating a more effective and responsive pattern of regional planning.

CHAPTER VIII

National Planning

The debates as to the optimum size and functions of local and regional planning authorities, and the need for greater intervention on the part of central government, closely reflected parallel discussions as to the wider objectives of managing the land resources of Britain. Many felt that there was an undue emphasis on the more negative aspects of planning, and that this had inhibited the promotion of new and more positive developments in town and country planning. As Patrick Abercrombie said in 1937, statutory planning was almost entirely concerned with preventing 'what is bad', rather than with 'creating what is good'.[1]

In advocating a more positive role for statutory planning, increasing reference was made to the wider economic and social benefits conferred by the concept of planning. In 1935 twelve leading planners combined to present a paper on 'Positive planning in Great Britain' to an International Congress. They described how statutory planning had played an important part in reducing the amount of misuse, waste, and ugliness, but concluded that its objectives were too narrow and negative. A positive counterpart was urgently needed, which would stimulate the creative and progressive forces in national life.[2]

In their opinion, the time was ripe for a shift in emphasis from negative to positive forms of planning. First, the economy was more stable and large supplies of capital at low interest rates were available for bold, imaginative schemes which would alleviate unemployment and help to modernize Britain. Secondly, the decision to end slums and urban overcrowding through systematic rehousing schemes opened the way for an attack on all depressed areas and the redistribution of industrial growth. Thirdly, the introduction of centralized schemes for marketing farm produce, the creation of a national electricity grid, and the greater co-ordination of transport services, implied a greater willingness to adopt larger measures of economic planning. Fourth, the rise in the amount of personal leisure time meant greater demands for recreational facilities, and, fifthly, the value of statutory planning had now been proved: the overriding need was to strengthen and extend it.

The Ministry of Health responded to this kind of advocacy by pointing to the successes of the essentially negative statutory powers and to its readiness to adopt more positive measures, if they appeared practicable. Negative powers had prevented the construction of further slums, factories in the middle of residential areas, and development across the route of future highways. In the countryside, the greatest need was for negative powers to fill the vacuum left by the disappearance of so many large landowners. The Ministry claimed it had 'direct knowledge of many cases where ribbon development had been stopped, sporadic building had been induced to group round existing villages, and pseudo-Tudor or Gothic has been replaced by something in harmony with the tradition of the countryside'.[3]

A report to the Minister in 1936 described how a wide range of initiatives was being taken under the 1932 Act. Statutory schemes for such outstanding areas as the Lake District, Norfolk Broads, the Peak District, and Dovedale were making good progress. The Carnarvonshire County Council had commissioned Patrick Abercrombie to prepare a scheme for Snowdonia and, with the material support of landowners, the Sussex County Councils were saving the South Downs from sporadic development. On their own initiative, several 'public-spirited landowners' had entered into voluntary agreements with the planning authorities for the preservation of parts of the Thames Valley.

The Ministry recognized its responsibilities in helping to maintain and create the conditions whereby local and private initiatives could flourish. Confusion arose when the Ministry missed opportunities to promote more positive planning, not because it did not believe in 'creating what is good', but rather because it was difficult to discern where the priorities for positive forms of assistance should lie. For administrative reasons, it was always harder to be positive than negative. This may be illustrated by reference to two examples, namely attempts to assist the National Trust and support given to the garden cities movement.

National Trust

In 1930, the National Trust wrote urgently to Ramsay MacDonald, asking for an exemption from estate duties. It described how the Trust was obliged to contribute £2,300 in the year 1928/9, and that there was now a liability of £1,800 on Bodiam Castle, bequeathed by Lord Curzon. The National Trust could not sell or mortgage any of its properties, and depended entirely on donations and subscriptions for income. At Bodiam Castle, it would take eight years to raise the necessary sum and, in the meantime, urgent repair work had to be postponed. MacDonald asked the Board of Inland Revenue 'to look sympathetically' on the request for exemption from estate duties. The Board replied that there was no objection if the concession could be confined to the National Trust, but clearly other societies would demand similar treatment. Using a draft prepared by the Treasury, MacDonald told the National Trust that the scope of any concession would have to be carefully considered and that there was no time to do this before the next Budget. A year later, in 1931, the Finance Act exempted from death duties any land and buildings which had been given to the National Trust and were declared inalienable.[4]

Earlier in 1929 the Treasury had considered ways of making an annual grant to the National Trust. Its immediate response was to reject the idea as being fatal to the National Trust inasmuch as it would discourage persons and local authorities from giving support at a time when they were beginning to bestir themselves. After a little more reflection, the Treasury conceded that 'theoretically, a small State grant of e.g. £1,000 a year might encourage the National Trust without destroying individual initiative, but the grant would surely grow, and how could it be given without whetting the appetites of innumerable other societies'. In his reply to a Parliamentary Question, the Financial Secretary to the Treasury stressed the impossibility of singling out 'one particular society for exceptional treatment by giving it a grant from public funds'.[5]

It was a disappointing outcome for the National Trust that no positive government assistance was forthcoming. But at least the government was sympathetic, and the refusal to help reflected not only administrative difficulties but also the Treasury's interpretation of the needs of the preservation movement. The government believed it was acting in the best interests of government *and* the National Trust by refusing to give a direct grant. The position was very different with respect to Garden Cities, another movement which might have expected generous government aid. In that case, the government became less and less sympathetic toward the concept of new towns and garden cities.

Garden Cities

In spite of the difficulties in launching Letchworth Garden City, Ebenezer Howard and his supporters continued to promote the concept of the garden city, and work began in 1920 on a second Garden City at Welwyn in Hertfordshire. Although the plan prepared by Louis de Soissons was a striking improvement on the 'rash of unplanned speculative building and ribbon development' otherwise taking place around London, the project nearly ended in financial disaster. It was saved only by a loan from the government, the writing off of £420,000 of share capital, and removal of limitations on share capital dividends. By the 1930s fortunes had revived, and 18,500 people lived in Welwyn Garden City by 1940.[6]

The Town Planning Act of 1925 incorporated earlier powers, whereby the Public Works Loan Board could advance loans for Garden Cities, subject to Treasury approval. The Act also made it possible for land to be compulsorily acquired for laying out garden cities. When the Town and Country Planning Bill was being drafted in 1931, these powers were automatically included for re-enactment. The first difficulty arose when the parliamentary draftsman proposed leaving them out because they were not 'directly part of town planning'.

When this was successfully resisted, much stronger opposition was encountered from the Treasury, which had assumed that the powers 'would die a natural death and that the Welwyn case would be the first and the last to be actually dealt with'. A total of £322,677 was still outstanding from an advance of £407,102 made by the Public Works Loan Board. Neither the Board nor the

Treasury were 'keen to extend or repeat the experiment', and, by re-enacting the powers under the new Town and Country Planning Bill, the Ministry would be bringing them back to life. If the powers could not be repealed, the Ministry should leave them as outstanding from the 1925 Act.

The Ministry of Health replied that it was quite impossible to leave a single section of the 1925 Act on the statute-book. The Ministry reminded the Treasury of how, during the debate on the Bill in 1931, the spokesman for the Conservative Party, Neville Chamberlain, had criticized the Bill for providing so little encouragement for the garden city movement. In addition to re-enacting the old powers, he had called upon the government to set up 'some sort of machinery for the multiplication of garden cities in the future'. As the Ministry pointed out, Chamberlain was now the Chancellor of the Exchequer in the new National Government! The powers did not automatically involve the country in great expense and there would be plenty of opportunities to ensure that there was no waste or misuse of public funds. The Treasury reluctantly withdrew its opposition.

Having successfully fought off this challenge, there was increasing reluctance within the Ministry to provide positive encouragement and material assistance to garden cities. This sprang from doubts as to the wisdom of the concept itself, and in 1931 the Ministry readily agreed to Liberal demands for a departmental committee to review the entire question. During the debate on the Bill of 1931 even E. D. Simon admitted that 'we do not quite know whether it is the right thing to take bare patches of land and build there, or whether it is better to take small towns which are well planned and in good centres and encourage them to grow'.[7]

The Ministry's attitude was conveyed in an internal document, written by the Permanent Secretary, Sir Arthur Robinson. He wrote:

beginning as a supporter of garden cities, properly so called, I have in process of time changed my views on them—they are fine theory but in practice they do not seem to work. What is properly called a satellite town is a much better method of approach. In such a case as Dagenham industries gradually follow it and it is that part of the garden city idea which is in practice so vulnerable. But the satellite town is just what several of the large housing schemes of local authorities are producing and the line of progress is to encourage it

Housing schemes would make further statutory help unnecessary. When trade revived, the greater part of the new work should be 'diverted to some of the existing boroughs of small size but with good rail and road connections, and a nucleus of population and services on which to build'.[8]

The National Trust and the garden city movement met with considerable success during the inter-war years. Other writers have described how the Trust acquired some of its outstanding properties during this period, and how the concept of the garden city became a living reality. In both cases a considerable fund of experience and expertise was built up, which was put to good effect after the Second World War. But these achievements received little government assistance. The reasons for the lack of support were many, but perhaps the most important was the difficulty of giving help in a positive or material form. The ramifications of any positive response on the part of government were felt over such a wide field that it was even more important to ensure that the concepts being promoted were sound and relevant to national needs.

A NATIONAL PLAN

Whereas previously the emphasis of statutory planning had been placed on health and amenity, it became more prudent in the late 1920s to emphasize the economic advantages. The economic aspect had never been entirely forgotten: Nettlefold had stressed the business aspects of planning in his book *Practical town planning*, published in 1914, and Gwilym Gibbon of the Ministry of Health had asserted on numerous occasions that planning was a 'firm business proposition'. In the promotion of the 1932 Act, it was stressed how town planning had brought 'wonderful increases in value', where it had been attempted in the United States. The improvement of Michigan Avenue in Chicago had cost 16,000,000 dollars, but had raised property values by over 100,000,000 dollars. In notes prepared for a Ministerial Broadcast in 1932, Gibbon described how 'the old laissez-faire of the past, the old haphazard methods will no longer suffice. We have to organise to a larger extent and to exercise more forethought, in other words, to plan. This new outlook is as essential for economy and for prosperity in the development and redevelopment of our towns and in directing changes in our countryside as it is in other spheres'.[9]

It was the Slump of 1929 and the emergence and persistence of localities marked by a chronic level of high unemployment that caused an increasing number of commentators to ask whether statutory planning could bring more immediate benefits to areas of great economic and social stress. There was even a possibility of planning becoming a party political issue. Amid considerable publicity, Lloyd George and a section of the Liberal party began to extol the value of planning schemes as 'a rapid means' of 'initiating schemes for the relief of unemployment', and they threatened to oppose the Town and Country Planning Bill of 1931 unless 'positive proposals' were incorporated for bringing work to the depressed areas. The Ministry of Health was extremely sceptical of the value of planning for this purpose but, in order to safeguard the government's position, Ramsay MacDonald appointed a committee under Lord Chelmsford to consider the thirty-six regional planning surveys already published in order to assess how far they identified projects which would help to offset unemployment. Lloyd George was consulted as to the committee's terms of reference and membership. As the Ministry predicted, the committee reported six months later that there was 'no greater volume of additional work to be found immediately available within the Regional schemes'. Planning could not offer any immediate palliative to unemployment.[10]

Thereafter, the government drew a clear distinction between the longer-term objectives of statutory regional planning and the short-term stimulation of employment. As Gibbon commented:

anyone who knows anything of the subject at all realises that the object of town planning is to lay out what the development of a suitable area ought to be over a period of years . . . when this is once done—and it means studying development years and years in advance—then as the area develops the local authority knows where to put its roads and parks and working class houses, and industry knows where its factories and so forth must be[11]

Nothing more was heard of the Chelmsford committee, but the effects of Lloyd George's intervention may have persisted for the rest of the decade. Gibbon was right to emphasize the long-term nature of planning, and it was understandable that he should have resented seeing his draft Bill of 1931 threatened and delayed by what he regarded as the political manoeuvrings of Lloyd George. Nevertheless Gibbon and his colleagues in the Ministry may have exaggerated the need to draw a distinction so sharply between statutory planning under the 1932 Act and other devices to improve economic and social well-being.

Given time, the Ministry of Health believed the 1932 Act would provide all that could be reasonably expected from statutory planning. The prevailing attitude was summarized in a report to the Minister in 1936, in which the Permanent Secretary wrote:

it is in the nature of planning that results are in the future, but already a great deal has been achieved and nobody who goes about the country today can fail to observe that the tide of sporadic, unregulated development that threatened to engulf the south after the war, is being stemmed, and that planning is beginning to leave a visible mark on the English countryside

Although there had been many amendments to the original Bill of 1931 for the safeguarding of private interests, and the procedure for making a planning scheme was still complicated, statutory planning was not only effective but the private person was assured of fair play and knowledge that his views would be heard. The Permanent Secretary concluded that 'the co-operation which land-owners, both large and small, have willingly extended to the planning authorities, has been one of the most striking features of the administration of the past three years, and has shown that there is genuine support for planning in all classes of the community'. The Ministry's Annual Report, published for 1936/7, spoke of the remarkable increase of interest being taken by the public at large in planning, and a member of the Ministry at that time, F. B. Gillie, later recalled how the years 1937 to 1939 were a stimulating time for 'the staff of the Town and Country Planning Division, all felt they were making valuable progress'.[12]

Compared with what had gone before, progress was impressive. Whereas only 7,000,000 acres of England and Wales were subject to Interim Development Orders in 1931, half the country, or 19,500,000 acres, were covered five years later. This area included the half where building development was taking place on a large scale or where 'some particularly fine stretch was threatened with spoliation'. The parts which were slow to start were 'those where little is stirring—Cornwall, Wales, Shropshire, the remoter parts of Yorkshire, Northumberland, and the Lincolnshire, Ely and Norfolk fens'.

The Ministry confidently predicted that 'the next few years should see the completion of a task of great magnitude commenced in some cases many years ago and carried on in circumstances of exceptional difficulty'. One of the great strengths of statutory planning was the flexibility of a system which involved district, borough and county councils in the planning of individual regions which could, if required, correspond with such natural features as a river basin or range of hills. In 1931 Gibbon dismissed suggestions that the planning powers of the rural district councils should be transferred to the county councils as 'not a practical proposition at the present time'. The district councils were in closest touch with land users and they were themselves responsible for many major housing, sewerage and water supply schemes. Their staffs knew 'every inch of the country for miles around', whereas many of the more elaborate surveys prepared by regional joint planning committees tended to be remote and academic.[13]

The Ministry asserted that the local authorities, through their ability and increasing willingness to combine 'for the purpose of executing regional schemes on a larger scale' would soon bring about 'a real measure of national planning'. By 1936 about 120 executive joint planning committees had been formed by local authorities, covering three-fifths of the total area being planned (see figure 10). This had 'enormously increased the effectiveness of planning control, particularly in relation to rural preservation; by enabling a wide view to be taken, by providing better qualified staff, by strengthening administration, and not least by spreading the financial burden'. The counties of Herefordshire, Huntingdonshire, Pembrokeshire, and Wiltshire were being planned as single units, and the report to the Minister in 1936 commended the initiatives being taken by the county councils, who were giving 'cohesion to regional planning'. Many were 'spending heavily, not merely on planning administration, but on the preservation of open spaces'. Whereas the Ministry had sanctioned loans of £793,667 for the preservation of public open spaces in 1932/3, the level had risen to £2,467,245 in 1935/6.

There were, however, serious drawbacks to this kind of national planning. As the Chelmsford committee noted in 1931, it was impossible to make any kind of national appraisal until all the regional planning reports had been completed to the same level of detail. Even when they were available, the national plan could be little more than a patchwork of schemes of varying criteria, sizes, and merits. Their subject matter was hardly likely to capture the public imagination and therefore patronage at a time when the depression and unemployment were uppermost in the public mind. The plans failed to provide the basis for the perception and management of the nation's land resources as an entity.

The weaknesses of the existing approach to statutory planning were highlighted by the treatment of industrial development. The Ministry of Health freely admitted that the approach gave no comprehensive picture of the distribution of industry, still less of its causes. A draft memorandum explained how the distribution pattern reflected commercial, economic, and psychological factors, and the Ministry and planning authorities were concerned only with

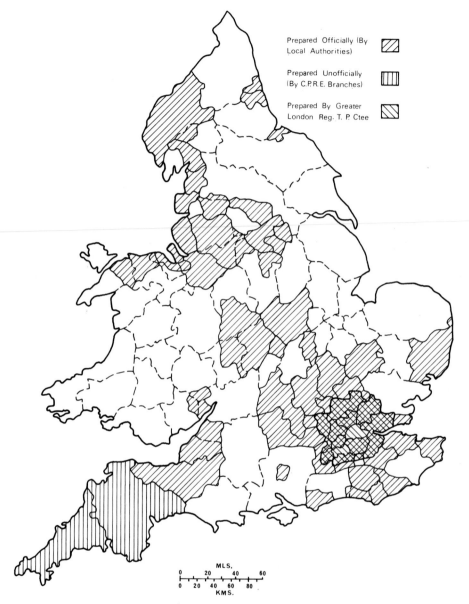

Fig. 10. Areas for which advisory regional planning reports had been prepared by 1939, as compiled by John Dower

public health and local government. If some kind of national plan was envisaged, either through such inducements as trading estates and satellite towns, or directly through a central licensing authority, the plan would have to be drawn up quite separately from the existing system of statutory planning. Not only did the local authorities have no experience of such a complex issue, but there would often be conflict between national and regional/local interests. The planning schemes so far drawn up by these authorities had taken the industrial and commercial setting as given, and had made little attempt to modify it explicitly. The most any plan or scheme sought was to designate a zone for industry if and when the need arose. The Ministry summed up the situation in 1937 by stressing that:

it is important to appreciate that planning, as at present understood, consists mainly in a series of restrictions on private enterprise. Thus local authorities do not lay out trading estates, or private housing estates, or build fine shopping arcades as part of their plan. They do not even say that in certain parts of the area development by private enterprise is to take a certain form. They only say that certain forms of development will be permitted freely and other forms not be permitted, or permitted only under conditions, in the various parts of their area[14]

There was no statutory way of introducing new industry to new areas or of resuscitating those areas that had become obsolescent.

A different approach to national planning was advocated by a symposium of planners in 1930, which envisaged a system whereby all forms of land use, the distribution of population and industry, and the development of transport, public utilities and services, would be made to conform to a national plan. Instead of the national plan being allowed to evolve, it would be imposed 'from the top' on the basis of a national survey of national resources, food supplies, transport, urban development, industrial growth, and the scope for further expansion.[15]

Far from being a revolutionary concept, the advocates of this form of positive planning argued that the ideas of planning development had been in the minds and writings of planners for more than half a century and had found visible, if limited, expression in such pioneer planning efforts as Port Sunlight, Bournville, Letchworth, Welwyn, and Wythenshawe. In order to convert these ideals into practice it was essential for statutory planning to be given effective control and guidance over all kinds of major development, so as to ensure harmonious and orderly development. In the paper presented to the International Congress in 1935 the authors concluded that:

it is clear that new towns cannot be healthy and efficient organisms unless their sites are well chosen for industrial development and their industries and populations grow in pace with each other. Equally, old towns cannot be made healthy and efficient unless steps are taken to prevent an excess or deficiency of industry and, in many cases, unless slum clearance is applied not only to worn-out dwellings but also to worn-out workshops and factories. To achieve these purposes some degree of control over the location and density of industries is obviously essential, while a wider control over the national distribution of industries will be required, if the 'depressed areas' problem is to be adequately tackled[16]

The Ministry regarded such proposals as being another device to replace local planning authorities with a new central executive 'with unlimited Treasury money at its disposal for wild cat schemes'. In a book written after his retirement from the Ministry in 1935 Sir Gwilym Gibbon remarked that such a 'notion of comprehensive planning arises partly from a mechanistic mentality, from thinking of the life of society in simple terms without realizing the un-measured complication of means and motive, as in the individual life of man'.[17]

Gibbon illustrated the impracticability of a centrally imposed plan by noting how 'the crux of national planning lies in the location of industries, using the term in its broadest sense'. There was so little information on this vital issue that any plan would 'be largely a leap in the dark'. Very comprehensive and detailed information would be required, which related not only to 'the present relative advantages of different localities (for industry), but also future developments'. The imposition of a national plan would be 'a stupendous task requiring prolonged research, and only research by the very competent could justify any faith at all in the findings and even then with dubiety'.

Some members of the planning profession shared this scepticism as to the practicality and efficacy of national planning. Thomas Adams argued that if national plans were sought, they should be limited 'to a skeleton system of the main lines of communication and perhaps power transmission. It was not practicable to prepare a comprehensive national plan to cover the same ground as a regional plan. No planner could intelligently comprehend the physical problems of a country as a coherent whole'. There was every need for caution and circumspection. Planning was not a perfect instrument, and as much injury could result from poorly conceived planning controls as from following 'the road of drift'. Adams emphasized that town planning should be conceived of as a form of guidance, whereby the planner helped towns 'to evolve in a state of freedom'.[18]

By the mid-1930s, the term 'planning' had become something of a cliché. In his study of 'Economic planning and international order', the economist Lionel Robbins described Planning as 'the grand panacea of our age'. In popular discussion it stood for almost any policy that was thought to be desirable, and, in Robbins's view, ambiguity went a long way towards explaining the attractiveness of planning. Although there were obvious links between them, there was an increasing tendency to blur the distinction between planning in a physical sense and planning in the form of a managed economy.[19]

A CENTRAL PLANNING AUTHORITY

By the outbreak of war, the value of complementing negative controls over land use with more positive measures had become generally recognized, especially with regard to the economic aspects of planning. The problem was to find ways of providing the necessary guidance or leadership without incurring charges of being dictatorial at a time when one democracy after another was succumbing to Fascism or Communism. Worse still, it was easy to accuse the aspiring 'national planners' of seeking to impose their will, in spite of their minimal knowledge and experience of planning on such a large scale.

There was a lingering belief that planning would somehow erode freedom, whether of a government department or of the individual person. The Next Five

Years Group, in their five-year programme for action, published in 1935 (see p. 5), emphasized that the real alternative to planning was not freedom but improvisation. The programme, endorsed by 150 distinguished signatories drawn from all professions and political persuasions, described how 'at present an elaborate and extensive system of State control is being built up haphazardly, successive measures being determined by emergencies or by the successful pressure of some sectional interest, and neither related to any general conception or scheme nor co-ordinated between themselves'. Far from being an academic issue, the promotion of national surveys and planning was designed to end the waste and inefficiency borne out of improvisation.[20]

Restriction of ribbon development

The penalties of there being no central survey/planning agency in the government service and local government were highlighted in regard to traffic management and land use, particularly during the debates on the Restriction of Ribbon Development Bill of 1935. For many years there had been mounting concern as to the damage caused to rural amenity and road safety by the construction of buildings and access roads along main roads. Patrick Abercrombie likened it to cancer—'as a growth of apparently healthy cells but proceeding without check or relation to the whole body'. A deputation of members of parliament reminded the Prime Minister, Ramsay MacDonald, in 1934 of how extensive lengths of the Great North Road and Kingston bypass were already aligned by ribbon development, and of how land abutting the new Maghull road in Lancashire was being sold for £800 per acre, clearly for further ribbon development. The Ministers of both Transport and Health conceded the imperative need to halt this form of 'uncontrolled development', and MacDonald told them that 'I want complete powers of control . . . The delay in tackling the problem has been criminal.' Already immense damage had occurred.[21]

Ribbon development was one of many land-use issues that fell within the purview of both Ministers. As early as 1930, Thomas Adams had emphasized the close interrelationship between the road system and building development. An administrative schism had nevertheless developed between traffic management and land-use planning. The construction and maintenance of roads were regarded as primarily civil engineering matters. It was the Ministry of Transport that decided how the Exchequer grants, made available through the Road Fund, should be spent, and accordingly it was that Ministry which controlled in practice where roads should be built or widened, corners removed, and bridges erected. The exact timing and location of the work were often influenced by their value in alleviating local unemployment. In spite of the obvious bearing of roads on the use and management of neighbouring land, the responsibilities of the Ministry of Transport did not extend to land-use planning or the preservation of amenity—these fell under the purview of the Ministry of Health.[22]

The restriction of ribbon development was, however, only one of the many planning issues within the Minister of Health's wider responsibilities for health and local government. Although the 1932 Act was intended to help control ribbon development, Sir Edward Hilton-Young conceded that 'the town planning powers are too slow and necessarily too slow to overtake such an elusive thing as ribbon development'. In many parts, planning had not commenced, or the schemes were still being formulated and interim development control could do no more than 'threaten' retribution at some uncertain point in the future (see p. 85). Even where schemes were operational it was often difficult to ensure the uniform treatment of a road passing through the areas of a number of schemes. Whereas the Ministry of Transport could both stimulate and directly influence initiatives by its ability to make grants from the Road Fund, the Ministry of Health had no such carrot to offer the local authorities. There were no Exchequer funds to finance the protection of amenity or facilitate land-use planning.

In this situation, there was general agreement within the government, and some professional and voluntary bodies, that any major new powers would have to be granted to the Minister of Transport, Leslie Hore-Belisha. Ribbon development was taking place on such a large scale that it threatened both the efficacy and safety of the nation's newest, most important and expensive roads. Any controls would necessarily impinge on the common-law right of access to the highway—a question of obvious importance to the Minister.

In preliminary discussions two different kinds of approach were advocated. Ramsay MacDonald and the Minister of Health believed that the problem was so serious that the highway authorities, namely the county councils, should be given powers to control road frontages, without incurring any liability for compensation. Hore-Belisha warned that this would incur bitter hostility from a section of the government's supporters and that there would either be a long parliamentary battle or the powers would have to be dropped or hedged in 'with so many safeguards and restrictions as to make them of little more value than the numerous existing provisions which appear upon the Statute Book and have in practice proved ineffectual'. Hore-Belisha favoured a less radical approach, namely that the precedent set by the Surrey County Council Act of 1931 (see p. 15) should be extended to all county councils. They would be given powers to acquire or sterilize land to a substantial depth along scheduled roads, subject to a liability to compensate those adversely affected. In order to help offset the council's liability for claims of compensation, the Ministry would take over responsibility for trunk roads as soon as possible. This latter concession was fiercely contested by the Treasury.

The result of protracted discussions within the government was the Restriction of Ribbon Development Bill of 1935. In spite of its name the Bill was mainly intended to help highway authorities plan the construction or improvement of roads well ahead of actual need. They were given powers to prevent the erection of buildings within specified distances of projected or actual roads. This ensured that sufficient room would be left for roads and verges, and possibly for service roads running parallel to the main road. The power did not, in itself, prevent ribbon development; it merely pushed any development further back from the road and therefore made it more expensive for the building speculator on account of the extra cost involved in providing sewers, lighting, and other services. It was hoped this would act as a deterrent to building in many cases. The highway authorities were obliged to compensate those landowners adversely affected, but the Bill made it possible to offset costs with grants from the Road Fund. In order to safeguard amenity and further prevent ribbon development, another clause in the Bill gave the highway authorities powers to ban the construction of access roads or the erection of buildings within 200 feet of a classified road. This could be extended to other roads, subject to the approval of the Minister. The costs of compensation incurred under this clause could not be offset by the Road Fund, which the government insisted could not be used to safeguard amenity.[23]

In the debate on the second reading of the Bill, the spokesman for the Opposition, Arthur Greenwood, attacked the government for failing to use the Road Fund or some other national fund to offset the costs of prohibiting ribbon development. The measure was a 'colossal bluff'. Whilst pretending to lead the battle against ribbon development, the government had placed the entire cost of imposing controls on the backs of local authorities. The Act would soon become a dead letter, especially in the poorer areas where the highway authorities would be unable to meet the very high costs of compensation. The Parliamentary Secretary to the Ministry retorted that the burden of compensation would be no greater in a poorer area with a low rateable income because land values would be correspondingly lower than in a richer area with a larger rateable income.[24]

Greenwood also criticized the government for attacking ribbon development from the wrong angle. Ribbon development was a sociological and aesthetic problem, and could already be tackled under the 1932 Act if the government and local authorities showed greater resolve in using their existing statutory powers. And yet the Minister of Health maintained silence throughout the debate and allowed another Minister, Hore-Belisha, to introduce the Restriction of Ribbon Development Bill, thereby leading to further impotence and confusion.

In spite of these criticisms the very act of passing the Bill demonstrated that parliament was opposed to ribbon development as a form of suburbanization. It became possible, for the first time, to apply automatic and uniform controls over all classified roads. The controls could be enforced immediately by resort to the courts, and a series of pragmatic devices minimized any administrative confusion between the powers of the two Ministries. The 1935 Act was gradually subsumed by statutory planning, especially after the inception of the Rural Zone in 1938 (see p. 92). It was discovered that whereas the prohibition of building development under the 1935 Act usually incurred claims for compensation, the same development could often be opposed under the 1932 Act

without any such liability. By the outbreak of war the stop-gap measure had
served its essentially political purpose: planning under the 1932 Act was now
sufficiently widespread and effective to ensure a large measure of protection for
the interests served by both Ministers.

The furore had, however, highlighted the defects of a compartmentalized
approach to land use and management. It was clear that the regulation of
ribbon development was most effective, and caused least confusion, in those
areas where the highway and planning authorities were the same body, namely
the county or county borough councils. The control of ribbon development
demonstrated in a striking manner the advantages which would accrue from
creating some kind of organization at the local, regional, and national levels to
monitor every form of land use and activity taking place on the land.

Grant-aid to the Highlands and Islands

Whilst there was scope for co-ordinating and rationalizing the responsibilities
of the individual government departments, the streamlining of government
would not, in itself, guarantee the quick and certain resolution of problems
affecting land use. This was made abundantly clear from experience in Scotland
where, for historical reasons, a single government minister, the Secretary of
State, had uniquely wide responsibilities, including those for health, education,
and transport. Even this did not guarantee a response on a scale large enough to
tackle the problems of Scotland, whether on Clydebank or in the Highlands and
Islands. Every initiative had to take account of wider administrative and
financial considerations, as perceived by the Treasury, and it was the duty of all
government ministers to operate within the guidelines set by the Treasury. In
practice this proved to be a major constraint.

The kind of difficulties that could arise may be illustrated by an initiative
taken in 1936, when an *ad hoc* group, the Scottish Economic Committee, set up
an inquiry in close consultation with the Secretary of State. The inquiry, under
Major E. L. Hilleary, was appointed to review the economic plight of the
Highlands and Islands, and to make proposals for economic and social improvement. In its report of late 1938 it recommended the appointment of a
Highland Development Commissioner, who would organize further surveys
and take steps to accelerate the renewal of the region. Both the general and
detailed proposals aroused considerable support and, as the months passed,
there was mounting pressure on the Scottish Office for their implementation, in
spite of the rapidly deteriorating international situation.[25]

The Secretary of State, John Colville, responded by rejecting the appointment of a Commissioner because this would require an act of parliament, a
considerable support staff, and might overlap with the existing responsibilities
of government departments and local authorities. Likewise, he rejected such
detailed suggestions as the creation of a central marketing agency. He thought
that the work should be undertaken by the existing Agricultural Organisation
Society. In a debate of August 1939 Colville told members of parliament that it

would be far more 'expedient to concentrate on projects which do not require the creation of special machinery', and he thereupon announced extra government aid toward the control of bracken, promotion of lobster-fishing, organization of training schemes, and the construction of roads and piers. Even this modest programme had incurred considerable opposition from the Treasury. Colville had originally asked for £114,000 per annum to be available for grant-aid. The Chancellor of the Exchequer replied that approval could only be given for £50,000, and that subject to a time-limit. Colville protested that 'frankly, I find it difficult to face the House of Commons with a programme' based on a sum of £50,000, when members knew that much greater sums of money were being spent on helping refugees from overseas countries.

In the end, Colville was able to announce a programme of £65,000 per annum, extending over five years. In doing so, he reminded parliament that this was in addition to the £2,000,000 that had already been given to the region in the form of State grants. The seven crofting counties received far more aid per capita than any other part of Scotland. In an Adjournment Debate, members agreed that the international situation was grave and that the Highlands and Islands were not the only region of the British Isles in need of government aid, but Sir Murdoch MacDonald described the measures as nevertheless a very small and halting step. It was another example of administrative and financial expediency. MacDonald believed it would have been far better to have introduced a thorough and drastic scheme immediately, rather than to have continued 'dribbling money into an almost bottomless pit and not get a proper return on it'. A month later, war broke out.

Location of industry

The most famous debate as to the need for a coherent national strategy was centred on the practicality of a central planning agency to control the location of industry and its work-force. It was an issue that not only affected many government departments, but also challenged many of the preconceived assumptions of the Treasury. By the mid-1930s, it was clear that the massive dislocation of heavy industry was no temporary aberration of the British and world economies. The richest and poorest nations of the world were all unable to find employment for a significant proportion of their populations. Not only the working classes, but also the middle and professional classes, suffered from a sense of insecurity. For them the concept of a planned economy had a powerful appeal, and great interest was taken in the Roosevelt New Deal and the Soviet Five Year Plans.

In 1934 the government was persuaded to appoint Commissioners under the *ad hoc* Special Areas Act to help revive the especially depressed areas of Scotland, South Wales, West Cumberland, and Tyneside. The report of one of these Commissioners, Sir Malcolm Stewart, urged the introduction of curbs on the growth of Greater London as a means of securing a 'more evenly distributed' pattern of regional prosperity. For its part, the government conceded that the continued expansion of the capital and other cities created problems for public health, communications and made the country more vulnerable in time of war. As the situation in Europe deteriorated, and fears of aerial bombing grew, increased importance was attached to the strategic aspects of industrial location.[26]

It was at first proposed to appoint a Royal Commission on the growth of Greater London and other large cities, but at the instigation of the Chancellor of the Exchequer, Neville Chamberlain, the terms of reference were widened, and in July 1937 it was announced that a Royal Commission under Sir Montague Barlow had been appointed 'to inquire into the causes which have influenced the present geographical distribution of the industrial population of Great Britain'. Chamberlain was keen to include a representative planner on the Commission, but Sir John Maude of the Ministry of Health opposed his nomination of Sir Raymond Unwin and Sir Theodore Chambers on the grounds that neither would approach the question with 'an open mind'. As an alternative, Maude successfully nominated Patrick Abercrombie. In their deliberations, the Commissioners soon confirmed that a large-scale drift of industrial population was taking place from the depressed regions of England, Scotland, and Wales, into a central coffin-shaped area between south Lancashire and the Home Counties. Changes in the fortunes of industry and the consequent movement of peoples were clearly of national concern.[27]

The Commission emphasized how the location of industry affected agriculture, land, water transport, roads, amenities, and many other aspects of national life. The solution to problems of location had therefore to be sought along lines of national inquiry and guidance. Although the Ministry of Health had responsibilities for housing the industrial population and for approving statutory planning schemes which might include areas of existing or potential industrial growth, other major aspects of industrial location fell within the purview of other ministries. Markets were the responsibility of the Board of Trade, labour and transport fell under their respective Ministries, electric power under the Grid authorities, and the Ministry of Agriculture was concerned with protecting agricultural land.

The Royal Commission believed that the only way to secure the necessary national response to the problems of industrial location was to destroy administrative confusion by creating a new central authority, which would help secure the redevelopment of congested urban areas and the decentralization or dispersal of industries and industrial population from those areas. In these ways, a better regional balance of industrial development would occur. The advice given and action taken by the central authority would be based on 'the collection and co-ordination of information' obtained from government departments and elsewhere. The authority should have the right to inspect town-planning schemes and 'to consider, where necessary, in co-operation with the Government Departments concerned the modifications or correlation of existing or future plans in the national interest'.

Dissension occurred when the Royal Commission turned to defining the executive powers and status of the new central authority. In March 1938 Sir John Maude reported to the Treasury that 'the Commission is making very little headway and there is every likelihood of its Report being a fiasco'. Maude suggested that the relevant government departments got together to see whether there was any line of action that they could recommend, however unofficially, to the Commission. The result was a proposed 'half-way house between compelling industry to go where it is wanted and *inducing* it by bribes of various kinds'.[28]

In the event, the Royal Commission produced a Majority and Minority Report. The majority of members believed the new central authority should take the form of a National Industrial Board, made up of a chairman and three members appointed by the Board of Trade in consultation with other ministers. In addition to research, advisory and publicity functions, the Board would have executive powers to regulate additional industrial building in London and the Home Counties. Three members of the Commission believed these negative powers should not only be used over the whole country, but that positive inducements should also be offered to those industries established outside the London area. In a Minority Report, a further three members, who included Patrick Abercrombie, described the need for executive action on a national scale as being so urgent that the new central authority should take the form of a ministry exercising full executive powers. In order to fit the ministry into 'the scheme of central and local government' it should absorb, for example, the planning and possibly housing functions of the Ministry of Health, and some of the responsibilities of the Ministry of Transport. Finally, Abercrombie submitted a 'dissentient memorandum', which summarized the development of statutory planning powers and further emphasized their weaknesses, particularly in regard to such questions as the regulation of industrial development.

The reports of the Royal Commission were completed in August 1939, but not published until January 1940. The timing was significant. The findings predated the outbreak of war and, as a result, analogies can be drawn between the proposals later made for post-war reconstruction in the 1940s and those made in the closing stages of the First World War in so far as they drew their inspiration from the pre-war period, rather than from the war itself. Writing of the experiences of the First World War in a social context, Arthur Marwick has stressed that war did not 'create a body of knowledge and theory which was not there before, but it brought a violent awareness of the need to apply it'. The same may be said of the relationship of the Second World War to planning.[29]

The role of the war may be assessed in the context of a lecture given by Sir Ernest Simon in 1937, in which he drew unfavourable comparisons between the planning experiences of Moscow and those of Britain. He believed British planning had been so weak and ineffective because of a failure to remove the burden of compensation, the lack of political stimulus and leadership, but above all from a lack of enthusiasm and imagination on the part of the public. Planning would never be effective by itself: fine planning could 'only come as part of a new spirit', engendered by 'a reunified democracy determined to build a new civilization'. It is in this respect that the contribution of the war to planning was so important. As the war situation began to improve, and plans for reconstruction became more relevant, the nation's mood began to change, so that by 1944 there was an almost universal desire for radical change and an enthusiasm for planned and orderly post-war reconstruction. The earlier investigations and preparation of reports made it possible to exploit this brief and adventurous interlude in public outlook.[30]

The implications of this change in outlook may be illustrated by the fortunes of the Barlow report. At the time of its publication in 1940 the Treasury conceded that the Commission had 'collected a good deal of useful information on planning', but had 'thrown back at the Government' the very problem the Commission had been appointed to investigate, namely how it was possible 'to reconcile the obvious disadvantages of interfering with the freedom of industry to choose its own location with the social advantages, which inevitably follow a redistribution, geographically, of national prosperity'. Sir John Maude agreed with the Treasury that there was 'very little of value' in the report. In a debate on the report in 1940 his Minister, Walter Elliot, warned that 'it is no use pretending that, merely by the device of setting up a new Minister, we shall get away from the difficulties of deciding where industries should be located and continued'. There would still be the difficulty of reconciling the economic reality with social well-being.[31]

In the debate, the Minister argued that the more practical recommendations of the Commission's report were already being implemented. The government was encouraging war industries to be located in the previously depressed regions. Far from there being too little control over location, there were complaints of 'too meticulous examination, of having to consult Department after Department, and that it is very difficult to get a decision and to get the job carried through'. His remarks excited little sympathy in the House. One member, Kingsley Griffith, spoke of the Minister's 'profoundly negative attitude', so that 'wherever an idea found its way out of the pages of the report of the Commission, he set himself to chase it back in'. During the debate, there was no opposition to the concept of planned industrial location, and no rift emerged between those members representing the depressed areas and the Home Counties. Herbert Morrison and Lewis Silkin, representing London constituencies, described how 'the continued drift of the industrial population to London and the home counties' constituted a grave social, economic, and strategic problem, demanding fundamental changes in policy and administration.

The debate was therefore symptomatic of the new spirit which was developing. In Simon's words, the war had 'reunified democracy' and had created a determination to build a new civilization, where expediency gave way to resolute action. As the war situation improved and resources could be spared for planning post-war reconstruction, the Commission's report was to form the basis for further inquiries and discussions, leading first to the creation of a Ministry of Works and Planning, and then to a Ministry of Town and Country Planning in 1943, charged with the task of securing 'consistency and continuity in the framing and execution of a national policy with respect to the use and development of land'.

The impact of the new spirit may be illustrated by a memorandum prepared within the Ministry in December 1943, which concluded that 'land-use planning must inevitably involve a large measure of economic and social planning', which was for the most part the responsibility of other government departments. Because planning was indivisible, this meant that the new Ministry would have to provide a common meeting-ground for these various departmental interests. A single integrated and comprehensive land-use policy could evolve in no other way. In the words of the memorandum, 'the waging of peace and the production of the munitions of peace demanded a single strategy no less than do the requirements of war'.[32]

Brian Hackett, writing in the late 1940s, described how Britain led the world in the extent and range of its planning powers. Other war-damaged European countries had tended to institute emergency reconstruction programmes, with little reference to the national or regional implications. In taking the broader, longer-term view, Britain was perhaps drawing on the hard-won lessons of the inter-war period.[33]

CHAPTER IX

Survey and Research

Although Patrick Geddes was the first person to draw attention to the value of an extensive, yet detailed, survey of individual localities and regions, it was Patrick Abercrombie who did more than anyone else to popularize the survey and make it an essential prerequisite for statutory planning. Speaking from first-hand experience, Abercrombie described how 'the plain practical man' thought he knew his town from pillar to post. He carried his knowledge around in his head and scorned such cumbrous things as a map. But Abercrombie warned, this man knew no more about his town 'than his tongue does about the state of his teeth'.[1]

There were two particular advantages in having a fully documented, well-illustrated survey. First, it would help to relate planning theory and pre-conceived ideas to local requirements, and thereby take account of the immense variety of conditions encountered. Secondly, a survey would help to highlight the relationships between the various activities in a region. There was a tendency for individuals to see things from a particular point of view, perhaps with respect to factories, housing, traffic, or ancient monuments. A survey would help to prevent undue bias toward any one particular viewpoint. A more comprehensive, balanced perspective, based on what Abercrombie called 'a scientific study', could play an important role in substituting controlled planning for the kind of blind evolution that had all too commonly arisen from the activities of the speculative builder and the self-centred instincts of the manufacturer in the past.

LAND-USE SURVEYS

By the First World War the Ordnance Survey had published large-scale maps of almost every part of Britain. They were of unsurpassed accuracy and detail, but economies imposed on the Ordnance Survey from 1918 onwards soon made it impossible to maintain the high standards. It was decided that maps at the scales of 1:2500 and 1:10560 should be revised at forty-, as opposed to twenty-year intervals in those areas where the population was under 100 per square mile. As part of the economies imposed on the Civil Service in 1922, the establishment of the Ordnance Survey was halved. The publication of 1:2500 maps fell from 2,500 per annum to just over 500 in 1933. Meanwhile, there developed an unprecedented demand for up-to-date maps, largely as a result of the implementation of various Housing Acts, the town planning Acts of 1925 and 1932, the Land Registration Act of 1925, the Land Drainage Act of 1926, and the Local Government Act of 1929. In many cases local authorities could neither buy the maps nor find surveyors to bring the existing maps up-to-date.[2]

The failure to revise the published maps at frequent intervals led to special difficulties for town and country planning. Under the 1932 Act, a scheme had to be adopted no more than two years after the planning authority had resolved to make a scheme. The time-limit was usually exceeded manyfold, often because the local authority discovered that the relevant Ordnance Survey maps were so out-of-date. In 1934 the Dagenham Urban District Council asked for an extension of three years in order to provide time for the council's staff to revise the maps. Over 20,000 houses had been built since the last revision of 1920, and the Ordnance Survey could not hold out any prospect of further revision for several years.

The Minister of Agriculture was the government minister responsible for the Ordnance Survey and, in 1934, the Ministry of Health complained to him of the way in which the progress of statutory planning was being jeopardised by the lack of up-to-date maps. In addition to an official letter setting out the consequent difficulties, the Minister sent a personal letter to the Minister of Agriculture, Walter Elliot, in which he made two points. First, the local authorities expected the National Government, which had passed the 1932 Act, to be responsible for supplying them with the means of complying with the Act. Secondly, there was a grave risk that if planning became difficult and expensive, the public would not only lose confidence in town and country planning but also in the wider concept of economic planning, a subject which was of considerable personal interest to Elliot.

In reply the Minister agreed that the earlier economies in the Ordnance Survey had been a mistake, made before 'the importance of good maps for almost every kind of social activity' had been recognized and before 'the immense growth in building' had been foreseen. The Minister warned, however, that even if the Treasury approved an increase in staff, it would take up to ten years to appoint and train the additional field-staff required.

Meanwhile there were complaints from many quarters, including a Parliamentary Question that drew attention to 'the expense and delay to local authorities with statutory housing and town planning obligations consequent upon the backward state of the Ordnance Survey'. The new Director-General of the Ordnance Survey concluded that the only way of keeping pace with the ever-increasing rate of building development was to replace the concept of cyclic revision with one of continuous survey. This would be more costly and take up to ten years to introduce, and he warned an inter-departmental conference in February 1935 that the Treasury would have to be convinced that continuous revision 'was necessary and, in the long run, economical'.

In order to help promote the concept of 'continuous revision', and to examine a wide range of other issues, including the needs of town planning, an interdepartmental committee of inquiry was appointed, under an 'outside' chairman. As a first priority the Committee, under Lord Davidson, reviewed the provision of maps for town planning purposes. An interim report of 1936 described how questionnaires had been sent to each local authority that had resolved to make a planning scheme. These revealed that a revision was urgently needed of 1,400 maps at a scale of 1:2500. The Ordnance Survey warned that it would take two years to revise even 200 of the maps, and that even if extra staff could be recruited several years would be needed to train them. To save time the Committee recommended that an interim edition of the 1:2500 maps should be produced for planning purposes, which would be restricted to recording significant and visually striking changes, such as new buildings, roads, and field boundaries. Together with an increase of staff to the 'maximum practicable', this would allow 800 maps to be produced in two years, and a further 600 in three years.[3]

The government approved these proposals, and a final report in 1938 recommended the retention of the existing series of published maps and the introduction of a new series at the scale of 1:25000. A National Grid would be used on all maps, and there would be further experiments in the use of aerial photography as an aid to ground survey. Although these recommendations laid the foundations for the remarkable achievements of the Ordnance Survey in the post-war years, two decades of valuable time had already been squandered in the inter-war period.

Even where modern maps were available they did not reveal the detailed use and character of each parcel of land. An earlier series of economies had taken its toll. At one time, it had been the practice of field surveyors to make a land-use survey, whereby the incidence of arable, pasture, and other forms of land use was systematically noted. Although the practice continued as late as 1918, none of the information was published after 1882 and, as a result, there remained an almost total dearth of information as to the distribution and character of land use at the national, regional, and local scales.[4]

The anomalous situation was highlighted by what might otherwise have been a modest initiative, taken by the teachers of Northamptonshire in the 1920s. During a series of courses run for teachers on the 'Teaching of geography in elementary schools', it was discovered that most schoolchildren had a woeful lack of knowledge of their home localities. With the direct encouragement of the County Secretary for Education, and the financial support of the Elementary Education subcommittee, a geographical survey was made of each parish by schoolchildren, under the supervision of their teachers. Almost every school took part. The incidence of arable, pasture, woodland, and waste was recorded on Ordnance Survey 6-inch maps, and the information was later reduced and printed by the Ordnance Survey in the form of three sheets covering the county, at a scale of 1-inch to the mile.[5]

The land-use maps of Northamptonshire drew attention to the way in which the valley bottoms were occupied by pasture, with arable largely confined to the drier slopes and mixed soils of the valley sides. Most of the cultivated land was adjacent to roads and lanes, whereas the more remote fields were under grass. The organizer of the Survey was a teacher in the Northampton Town and

Country School and, in a paper later published in the journal *Geography*, he described how the value of the work did not lie solely in the maps. Rather, 'the work of preparation and the collection of the data provided a piece of definite geographical work calling for the cooperation of teachers and children. It gave a definite aim for outdoor lessons and expeditions. A new interest was aroused in the local area'.[6]

The experience gained from this and more limited surveys encouraged Dudley Stamp in deciding to organize a Land Utilisation Survey of the entire surface of the United Kingdom, whereby schools and other educational institutions would similarly record land-use information on Ordnance Survey 6-inch maps. By early 1931 surveys were under way in eighteen counties. In addition to the educational benefits conferred on those taking part in the Survey, Stamp stressed how the maps would show 'a snap-shot of Britain in the years 1931–35, which can serve as a standard of comparison with the past and a basis of planning for the future'. The Survey had no political or ulterior motive: it simply attempted to determine the existing use of every acre of land, record the information, and then make it readily available in the form of published maps and a series of county monographs.[7]

By 1938 the task of survey was almost completed and the protracted publication of maps and county monographs was under way. Already, there were lessons to be drawn from the maps and, in a paper, the Organising Secretary, E. C. Willatts, demonstrated the penalties of treating the countryside as 'a blank sheet of paper' for the laying out of 'fanciful schemes for future development'. In south-west Essex, the Land Utilisation Survey recorded a remarkable concentration of cultivation on the loam terraces. The importance of this cultivated land had been completely overlooked by a recently-published South Essex Regional Planning Report. In spite of the emphasis given by the Report to the need 'to arrive at an understanding of the character of the Region', the authors had been concerned with the potential of the land only for urban use. There was a total lack of appreciation of the losses which would follow any further loss or fragmentation of the valuable market-gardens. Far from being 'virgin country', the Land Utilisation Survey indicated how the subtle differences in past and present land use helped to indicate the optimum use of land in the future.[8]

Meanwhile a leading physical geographer, S. W. Wooldridge, emphasized the need for greater precision and thoroughness when taking account of the physical environment in planning. A perfunctory reference to geology was no longer enough: more attention had to be given to structure, morphology, and the superficial deposits covering landforms. Only rarely could this information be obtained in a readily digested form: data had to be collected and interpreted in terms relevant to planning.[9]

Geographers were particularly vocal in calling for greater rigour when carrying out surveys and, in a presidential lecture to the Geographical Association in 1938, Patrick Abercrombie emphasized three ways in which geographers could help the planner, namely: by describing natural conditions, including geological factors, soil and water, and the natural vegetation; by studying the historical growth of town and country; by conducting surveys of the present-day environment. The Land Utilisation Survey was already under way, and should be supplemented by the surveys of traffic, population, occupations, public services, land values, and all other aspects of the geography of a district, region, and nation. In providing the essential data for a scientifically formulated planning policy, geographers, in concert with other disciplines and interests, had an important role to play.[10]

LANDSCAPE SURVEYS

Because statutory planning was at first an essentially suburban affair, attention was naturally focused on the appearance and character of the suburb. As soon as it became clear that the government intended to extend statutory planning to all parts of the country, it became even more important to study and understand the landscapes over the entire land surface. In the words of Patrick Abercrombie, 'if we are going to have powers to control the development of the country and the interior of our towns', it was important to consider some of the fundamental principles that should govern design. Planning schemes required an aesthetic basis.[11]

The first need was to distinguish town from country. Whilst no one could say precisely where a town began and the countryside ended, their poles of influence could be easily identified. According to Abercrombie, the one was characterized by all that was conscious, artificial, and regular, whereas the other was instinctive, natural, and picturesque. Difficulties arose because these attributes were rarely encountered in a pure form; Nature intruded on the pure formalism of the town and the countryside had become equally sophisticated through human handiwork. The challenge was to ensure that urbanism prevailed in the Town and that the Country remained distinctively rural.

During the 1930s several attempts were made to adapt statutory planning to the needs of landscape preservation, both in the countryside and on the coast. The concept of the Rural Zone 'stretched' the Act of 1932 as far as was possible (see p. 92). In a lecture on 'The landscape and planning' in 1944, John Dower suggested an alternative approach, whereby the planner should first study the landscape and then consider what kind of planning policy should be applied. This method would help to concentrate the planner's mind on strategy rather than tactics—on the end rather than the means of landscape preservation.[12]

To illustrate this Dower began his lecture by defining the landscape as 'what we see about us when we are out of doors in the countryside'. It was primarily a vision, reinforced by the senses of hearing, smell, and touch, and involved 'a continuous relation or partnership between objective and subjective, between the countryside and ourselves'. Each person had a capacity to blend his selective perception of the countryside with personal memories and fantasies, and it was this instinctive ability to obtain a generalized impression of each stretch of countryside 'as seen from a variety of view-points, under varying skies and at varying sessions', which formed 'the indispensable foundation for all effective appreciation of landscape values and for all sound work in landscape treatment and design'.

The scope for landscape appreciation was tremendous: no other country possessed such a wealth of landscape beauty. Other nations might have higher mountains, greater forests, and longer rivers, but the British Isles surpassed them all in terms of quality, as expressed 'in diversity of landscape types, in delicacy of detail, in harmonious wealth of colour, in concentration of human interest, in ease of enjoyment'. Human activities enriched this intrinsically unique assemblage of landscapes. Even in the relatively simple case of a heather-moor, the effects of draining and controlled burning, sheep-grazing and grouse-shooting, led to further differences in the vegetation and, therefore, the appearance of the landscape.

There was nothing virgin about this scenic heritage: everywhere, beauty was the 'joint product of nature and man's handiwork'. The nature reserve of Wicken Fen in Cambridgeshire was often quoted as a primeval patch of country, but its sedges were annually harvested and the dykes cleaned out. Even the balance of vegetation and animal life on the most exposed rocky summits or cliffed coastline might be subtly different without the influence of human activities elsewhere in the vicinity. Everywhere the landscape had been affected by man 'more or less continuously spread over countless generations, of every degree of intensity, and of infinitely various and ever-changing purposes and effects'.

The process had begun, according to Abercrombie, when the early inhabitants had started to clear the forests and had erected their mighty earth-works which, in some parts, remained the most outstanding examples of the human modelling of the landscape. The Roman system of roads, towns, and camps represented an early example of country planning, much of it done in a modern mechanistic way. The Saxons had established the English village system, where the essential feature was grouping and compactness without overcrowding. The biggest visible contribution of the Normans was architectural: they endowed the English countryside with its human climax—the cathedral and church. Until recently human activity had usually enriched the beauty of the landscape. In this respect Thomas Adams drew analogies between the landscapes created by earlier generations and a collection of great works of art. In both cases the creator may have acted out of self-interest, but the results were for all to see and enjoy.[13]

The fact that this landscape was a *used* landscape added greatly to the complications of assessing its beauty. Not only was Britain composed of many thousands of separate land-holdings of all sizes, but each was devoted to a greater or lesser degree to cultivation, grazing, forestry, quarrying, and other purposes. If the beauty of this natural/man-made landscape was to be retained and enhanced, it was not enough to guard it from 'urban intrusions and other specific injuries'. The forms of land use and management which had led to the creation of beauty and interest had to be sustained and perhaps extended.

Because almost every part had been 'tamed' by Man, the fragments of relatively wild country had 'a specially enhanced scarcity value'. They should be managed according to 'a specially rigorous conservation policy'. The wilder tracts of countryside were the most suitable for rambling and other outdoor holiday pursuits. Extensive areas should be set aside as nature reserves, so as to provide ecologists with opportunities to compare the plant and animal communities present with those of more intensively used parts of the country.[14]

These wilder areas were not only important in themselves, but also formed part of a larger, composite picture. In the Lake District it was not only a delight to reach the top of a peak or crag, but to see 'the combination and interweaving of the same wild mountainsides with adjoining land which has been tamed—harmoniously tamed—for some more intensive human use. It is a landscape in which the cultivated valleys and lakesides have as much beauty as the uncultivated fells: the richest beauty is when they are seen all together against the moving background of sky and cloud'.

In his book *Town and countryside* Thomas Sharp complained of a widespread tendency to follow Ruskin's lead and to concentrate, almost to the exclusion of all else, on wilderness areas. All the energies of the preservation movement were marshalled 'on behalf of the spectacular, the abnormal, the beauty spot'. Public appeals for money and support were always directed toward preserving 'special areas, such as the Lake District, the North and South Downs, the Devonshire moors, the Seven Sisters, Stonehenge, Friday Street, and so on. The National Trust, admirable body though it is, is similarly concerned with the abnormal'. The national parks movement followed the same pattern, with 'hardly a passing reference to the one unique national possession, the *ordinary* countryside'.[15]

Sharp reiterated these sentiments during the discussion following Dower's lecture to the Town Planning Institute in 1944. Dower agreed that landscape assessment should not mean 'putting all our money on beauty-spots and none elsewhere'; the entire countryside mattered, whether in remote upland areas or around the fringes of towns. The essential point was that 'different kinds of country wanted different treatments', and priorities had to be carefully worked out on the need for special protection and management measures and the effectiveness of any treatment given. Some 'sort of grading or testing of landscape types and uses was essential' for effective national and regional planning. The fact that an area was excluded from a beauty spot or national park did not mean that it should be ignored or abused. It was still an important component of the countryside.[16]

Even when the history and present-day status of the landscape had been studied, and the various qualities in the landscape discerned, there was still the need to draw up an agreed basis for assessing and grading the landscape for the purpose of positive, creative planning. It might be argued that 'every man to his taste' and that 'one man's taste is as good as another's'. Such solutions as 'refer it to a committee' and 'put it to the vote' often worked, but Dower insisted that in matters of landscape beauty it was only too clear that these remedies did not *work well*. Was there an alternative way of obtaining a consensus of opinion which would, 'with the appropriate legislation and administrative sanction, increase rather than diminish the sum of our country's beauty and its public enjoyment'?

There were two relatively straightforward methods of landscape assessment. One was to measure the popularity of particular areas for recreation and holidays in order to see what gave visitors the greatest pleasure. In doing so, a distinction had to be drawn between what visitors knew to be available and what they would prefer. Just because 30,000 people took a railway to the top of Snowdon this did not mean that it was all the public wanted. The concentration of numbers was largely a reflection of the fact that most visitors were un-adventurous, keeping close to the familiar and reluctant to go where there were no signposts to lead them.

The other method of landscape assessment was to seek the advice of various learned professions and academic disciplines: geologists and geographers could describe and delimit landforms; ecologists and naturalists could identify sites of high wildlife importance; archaeologists could help discover and safeguard ancient monuments. Sometimes the experts could fulfil two roles, writing guides for the many visitors venturing into the countryside, and simultaneously providing a factual basis for landscape assessment and for any 'special conservation' measures. One of the most outstanding examples of the period was A. E. Trueman's *The scenery of England and Wales*, written and illustrated largely from the geological point of view.[17]

Of these disciplines it was perhaps the geographer who showed the earliest interest in landscape assessment. In a presidential address to the Royal Geographical Society in 1920 the explorer and great authority on Central Asia, Sir Francis Younghusband, appealed to geographers to take 'a less material and a more spiritual view of the Earth'. Not only was an appreciation of beauty relevant to 'geographical science', but also it was the duty of geographers to provide expert guidance in comparing the beauty of one region with that of another. As Younghusband told his audience, 'we are considered as a Society for the purpose of diffusing geographical knowledge, and I trust that in future we shall regard knowledge of the beauty of the Earth as the most important form of geographical knowledge that we can diffuse'.[18]

One of those to respond to his call was Vaughan Cornish, a productive and versatile geographer, who had made his reputation by research on aeolian and coastal landforms. During the last thirty years of his life Cornish devoted most of his attention to 'the analytical study of beauty in scenery'. He set out to discover the principles. He devised the following technique:

... abandoning sketch-book, notebook, and all other appliances, I wandered free, open to impression; being careful to remain long enough in the field to let busy thought quiet down. The outstanding impressions were afterwards noted, and the physical conditions under which they occurred were investigated later by the ordinary methods of the observational sciences ... nothing is described at second hand, for, as mental impression had to be analysed, I considered it essential to rely entirely upon personal experience. It remained, however, to test the normality of my impressions, and this I did by delivering to an educated audience a course of lectures, each of which was followed by a half-hour class for discussion, and it was found that my impressions were shared in every essential particular by the audience[19]

By this method Cornish formulated what he described as 'a general aesthetic of Geography which could be applied *ad infinitum* in the description of localities'. He defined aesthetics as a concern for the beauty which enthralled the observer. It was a beauty which depended upon a grouping, where one part enhanced the other, and created a harmony. It was because of this dependence upon grouping that the beauty of scenery varied both as to place and season. In 1937 Cornish published a book on *The scenery of England: a study of harmonious grouping in town and country*, and in 1943 a manual, *The beauties of scenery: a geographical survey*, with chapters dealing in turn with the sky, land and water, natural vegetation and wild life, and the scenery of civilization. Through his writings Cornish provided a remarkably comprehensive, detailed, and uniform treatment of the scenery of England and Wales, but his observations were naturally intensely personal and anecdotal. For effect, they depended completely on the reader's having sympathy with his perception and interpretation of scenery.[20]

In this context an earlier initiative taken by the CPRE and the Geographical Association was significant. A subcommittee was set up to prepare 'a geographical manual on scenic amenity, with Cornish as one of its members. When a synthesis of all the attitudes represented on the committee proved impossible, O. J. R. Howarth was entrusted with writing a book, *The scenic heritage of England and Wales*. In parts, the book tended to become an inventory and, therefore, flat and dull. It began by relating the heritage of scenery to the formation of rocks and landforms, development of vegetation, and history of man, and then looked at the individual experiences and character of each of the regions into which the country was divided (figure 11 and table 1). The book was intended as an educational and stock-taking exercise. As Howarth explained, most people were capable of admiring scenery and, the more they understood what they saw, the more this would strengthen their 'instinct' for preserving what they admired.[21]

Table 1. *The regions of England and Wales, as identified by Howarth in his study of their scenic heritage*

1	London	8	Western Marches and Severn Plain
2	Weald	9	South-west
3	Chalk Belt	10	Wales
4	East Anglia and Essex	11	Pennines
5	Hampshire Basin	12	Durham and Northumberland
6	Limestone Belt	13	Lake District
7	Midlands		

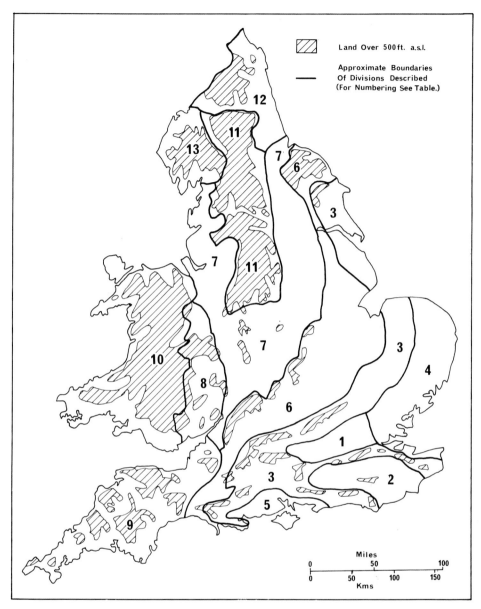

Fig. 11. The regions of England and Wales, as identified by O. J. R. Howarth in his study of their scenic heritage

Dower believed the key to success was to involve as many people as possible, and especially those with some kind of authority or professional expertise, in making surveys and assessments. In recruiting them, the most important attribute was 'a love and experience of the countryside, of country ways, of the trees, grasses and flowers, rocks and streams that compose the landscape and that are the living materials of the country planner's work'. There had to be a willingness to learn from earlier guides and interpreters of the countryside, of which Dower acclaimed Wordsworth to be the most outstanding. For Dower, the *Guide through the district of the Lakes* had been 'of unfailing inspiration ever since my delight in landscape beauty, in cross-country walking, and in other rural pursuits began, in the late 1920s, to express itself in work for rural preservation and planning'. Wordsworth's *Guide* was 'unique in its fusion of poetic appreciation and masterly generalization with detailed description and critical and practical advice on true and false taste in the treatment of landscape and disposition and design of buildings'. By giving heart and mind to the cause, and with this kind of inspiration, Dower thought it would not be long before 'we are sufficiently sure and united to assume a leadership which the rest of our fellow-countrymen are sufficiently ready to follow'.[22]

Experience had shown that there was a surprising number of people who could provide the necessary aesthetic judgements by their 'disinterested love and long study of the landscape'. The main problem was that many of these 'simple folk' had been given few opportunities to express themselves, and most were 'more or less lacking in *comparative* experience', which meant that their observations tended to be inarticulate and unreliable outside their immediate locality. There were very few who, like Vaughan Cornish and Anthony Collett, had visited, studied, and appreciated almost every part of England and Wales. Dower rated Collett's book, *The changing face of England*, second only to Wordsworth's *Guide*.[23]

If a team of experienced landscape-lovers could be found, and their judgements collated, Dower believed it would be possible to draw up and apply 'a scale of landscape values' on a national or local scale. Priorities could be set—a national park here and a nature reserve there, with perhaps a public open space or green belt in another part. All this might be achieved through a discriminatory use of statutory planning powers. Through informal negotiations and the formal conditions attached to planning consents, it should be possible to complement the more negative controls of planning with positive programmes for the maintenance and enrichment of the rural landscape.[24]

BRISTOL AND BATH REGIONAL PLAN

How relevant were the concepts and techniques of land use and landscape surveys to the drawing up of a planning scheme? What part could they play in persuading those with the executive powers that a proposed scheme was both desirable and practicable? Abercrombie was under no illusions as to the magnitude of the task. Whereas landowners had often had long and close family connections with their respective estate, parish, or county, and were 'saturated' with the atmosphere of the place, a planning authority lacked this kind of intimacy. Study would have to take the place of deep-seated instinct. As a first step, every aspect of the countryside would have to be annotated, catalogued,

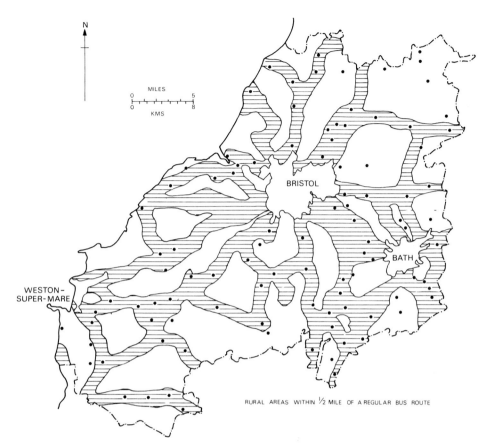

N

MILES
0   5
0   8
KMS

BRISTOL

BATH

WESTON-
SUPER-MARE

RURAL AREAS WITHIN ½ MILE OF A REGULAR BUS ROUTE

Fig. 12. Accessibility to regular bus services in rural areas, based on a diagram in the Bristol and Bath regional planning scheme

and mapped. A synthesis of the component parts could then be attempted in order to provide a basis for what Abercrombie described as the 'difficult and personal task' of appraisal.[25]

The scope of a regional survey may be illustrated by an unusually comprehensive, and yet detailed, survey completed of the Bristol and Bath region in 1929 by Patrick Abercrombie and B. F. Brueton, the Town Planning Officer of the Corporation of Bristol. The Corporation was the first to contemplate statutory planning in the area, and recognized, as early as 1923, that there was little point in drawing up a scheme for the undeveloped parts of the City without the closest liaison with the neighbouring rural and urban district councils. The outcome was a conference in Bristol, attended by representatives of fifteen local authorities, including the Cities of Bristol and Bath, and the Gloucestershire and Somerset County Councils. The Chief Town Planning Inspector of the Ministry of Health, George Pepler, took the chair. A motion for the setting up of

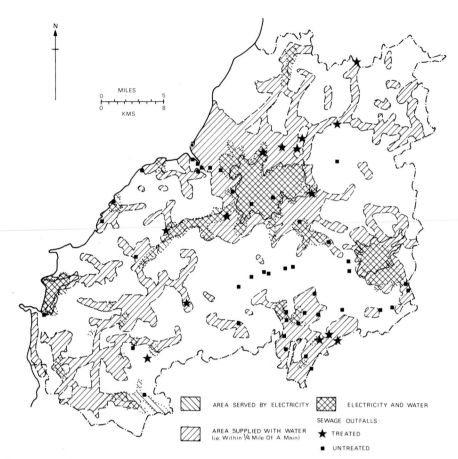

Fig. 13. Availability of piped water and electricity, as indicated by diagrams in the Regional planning scheme

a Bristol and Bath Regional Joint Town Planning Committee was passed and, a few weeks later, a meeting of surveyors from each of the constituent authorities decided that an expert planner should be appointed to prepare an outline plan.[26]

Patrick Abercrombie was offered the post and, together with Brueton, he submitted a printed draft of a survey and plan to the Joint Committee in 1927. It consisted of four parts, namely (1) a survey of the region, with sections on physical features, history and archaeology, communications, administration, population, landscape disfigurements, and public services; (2) a regional plan, comprising sections on zoning, communications, open spaces, and public services; (3) the effects of a regional plan; and (4) the realization of the plan.[27]

The authors observed that the Report was not the place for laying down the principles of rural planning and landscape development, but this did not preclude Abercrombie from introducing large sections of a paper, 'Planning of

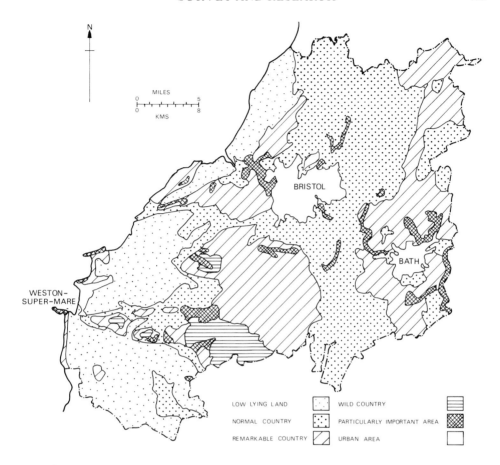

N

MILES
0   5
KMS
0   8

BRISTOL

BATH

WESTON-
SUPER-MARE

LOW LYING LAND   WILD COUNTRY

NORMAL COUNTRY   PARTICULARLY IMPORTANT AREA

REMARKABLE COUNTRY   URBAN AREA

Fig. 14. A landscape survey, based on a diagram published in the planning scheme

town and country', which he published in the *Town Planning Review* in 1930. The Report provided, after all, a unique opportunity for the expert planner to 'educate' the minds of the decision-makers, namely the members of local councils and their officers. The approach adopted in the Report may be illustrated by the section on roads, which began by defining the three objects of a modern road system, and described the development and defects of the existing pattern of roads in the region. A map was included, showing the relative accessibility of each part of the region to bus and rail services (figure 12). Almost every village and hamlet had a bus service. A series of proposals was put forward for improving the road system.

The section of the Report on public services included maps indicating the areas provided with piped water and electricity (figure 13). It drew attention to the fact that of the forty-eight communities which depended on inland water for their drainage thirty-four discharged untreated sewage directly into the water-

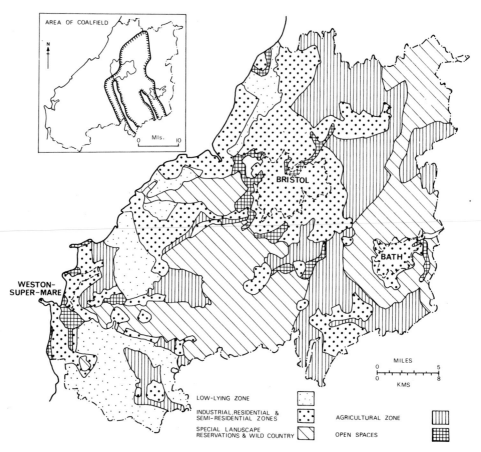

Fig. 15. The character zones proposed by P. Abercrombie and B. F. Brueton, based on a diagram
published in the planning scheme

courses. There was a complete lack of co-ordination between local authorities,
and between neighbouring villages. Among other detailed recommendations,
the authors insisted on a co-ordinated drainage scheme for the Chew Valley,
and that urgent attention should be given to schemes for the fast-growing
settlements.

The Report stressed that so far the region had not suffered as severely as
many other parts of England from disfigurement. A map was compiled, which
distinguished six landscape divisions (figure 14). A distinction was drawn
between 'normal' agricultural land or country, and seven tracts of 'remarkable
country' which were scattered about the region. The Mendips were the most
outstanding example of another category of landscape, called 'wild country'.
The Cheddar Gorge was one of sixteen sites identified for their particular
beauty or landscape value.

The landscape survey, together with data on geology, topography, and climate, was used to form the basis for a series of 'character zones' (figure 15). The authors identified industrial and residential zones, and a semi-residential zone which would act as a buffer between the residential zones and the normal agricultural zones. In another zone, called the 'special landscape reservation', the emphasis would be on 'conserving the existing landscape character and on preventing straggling development'. Water-gathering grounds and tracts of 'wild country' fell into another class of rural reservation, and finally the proposed system identified two further zones, namely low-lying areas and open spaces.

The system of zoning had to be modified in the coalfield, where the authors recommended that mining should be allowed in the normal agricultural zone, if existing amenities were not harmed. In the residential zone and special landscape reservation, any associated works around the pitheads should be kept to the absolute minimum.

Sections of the Report were devoted to Bristol and Bath, and to the urban and rural centres in the region. Rather than create new satellite communities, the authors believed the growth of some of the region's 150 villages should be stimulated. The Report drew attention to the value of making a detailed survey of each settlement, perhaps under the aegis of the CPRE. This would record such aspects as physical and historical features, buildings, traffic, public services, open spaces, land use, natural history, and disfigurements.

The authors emphasized that their plan was merely 'a forecast, an attempt to visualise the future'. It was not intended to compel people to lead different lives, but rather 'to stimulate their natural tendencies in the right direction'. By explicitly identifying the optimum use of an area of land, it would be easier to encourage all parties, including landowners, developers, and public utilities, to co-ordinate their individual efforts by having common objectives throughout the region. Logically, a plan might lay down very detailed guidelines, perhaps in the form of precise routes for electricity lines, sewers, or new bus services, but the authors warned that 'this would be pushing the planner's zeal too far'. The planner's task was to provide 'accurate plans' of the present situation and to hope that each activity in the region would be 'scientifically and co-operatively extended in accordance with the Zoning Map'. With this kind of Persuasive Planning, the Plan became 'a real power, not of compulsion, but of constructive growth'.

After the publication of the Survey and Plan in 1930, the Joint Planning Committee met at very infrequent intervals, but to little practical effect. The impetus passed to the two County Councils, which appointed town planning officers and were in a better position to act as overseers of planning. By 1937, when the Joint Committee was formally dissolved, individual schemes were being prepared for all parts of the region except central Bristol. Abercrombie attended the 'funeral service' for the Joint Committee. The fact that nothing very tangible had come directly from his work did not entirely detract from its long-term value. What was needed in the 1920s and 1930s was a model—

something to strive for. Although there was no hope of the perfection of the model being attained, the fact that councillors and officials became aware of the model represented at least the beginnings of a new and important approach to practical planning on a local and regional scale.

NORTHAMPTONSHIRE IRON-FIELD

The need to formulate a planning scheme was predictable, and preparations could be laid over many months. But what happened when the community was suddenly faced with a crisis? What resources could be deployed in identifying and helping to resolve a problem in land use and management through survey and research? As an illustration, this section will trace the investigations made into the effects of the iron industry of Corby on the neighbouring Northamptonshire countryside.

The existence of iron ore had been known since Roman times, but little had been excavated for some 200 years before the construction of the Midland Railway around 1850, when large quantities of high-grade ore were found in the numerous cuttings and tunnels. A new industry developed, centred on the outcrops where any overburden could be removed by hand and the land later restored to agricultural use. Elsewhere the overburden was too thick, and underground mining was both costly and difficult. It was not until the 1930s that the industry began to have a devastating effect on the countryside. A Scottish steel-making firm, Messrs Stewarts and Lloyds, obtained a government loan to set up a modern, integrated steel-works at Corby in order to exploit the iron-ore deposits more intensively. The introduction of large electrical shovels and walking draglines made it possible for one machine to lift 600 tons per hour from depths of up to 100 feet.[28]

By the autumn of 1936 the local authorities had become extremely anxious about the extent and nature of the excavations. Although it would have been against the 'national interests to sterilize the rich resources of iron-ore', and the industry provided much needed employment, the authorities drew attention to the ever-increasing area that was being converted into a 'ridgy-desert', known locally as hill-and-dale. The Chief Town Planning Inspector of the Ministry of Health, George Pepler, shared this concern, and, at his instigation, a meeting of representatives from the Ministries of Agriculture and Health, the Board of Trade, and the Geological Museum, was arranged. At the meeting, the Clerk of the Northamptonshire County Council posed three questions: what should be done with the land already excavated; could the ore be excavated in such a way as to facilitate restoration, say, by preserving the top soil for later use; who should be responsible for carrying out the restoration work?

The local authorities insisted that central government should take a positive lead by appointing an informal, expert committee of inquiry. They maintained not only that the future of the devastated land was a national issue, but also that the government was better placed to conduct the relevant inquiries. The operators were, for example, very reluctant to reveal their plans for further exploitation and restoration to the local authorities in case the information might become public knowledge and be used by landowners when negotiating with the companies for further leases and royalties. The operators were more likely to be forthcoming before a government committee, taking evidence in closed session.

For its part, the Ministry of Health agreed that it had an important role to play, and a number of *ad hoc* inquiries were initiated. Pepler wrote to German colleagues, asking how areas affected by lignite mining were restored. The most important need was for a technical appraisal of the scale of devastation and feasibility of reinstatement. One of the engineering inspectors of the Ministry of Health, G. M. McNaughton, visited the area in December 1936, in the company of the consulting engineer and assistant manager of Stewarts and Lloyds. He learned that 1,600 acres of land had already been transformed into hill-and-dale around Corby. The current rate of conversion of 160 acres per annum was expected to rise when a new furnace came into operation. McNaughton estimated that an area of twelve square miles would be affected within twenty years. Taking into account the activities of the eleven other companies operating in the iron-field, which occupied at least as much land as Stewarts and Lloyds, he warned that as much as twenty-five square miles of the county were threatened with dereliction.

The scope for restoration appeared to be bleak. McNaughton learned that the latest machines created ridges of up to twenty feet in height, and up to sixty feet from crest to crest. His report contained a number of case studies of individual pits. He estimated that it would cost £320 per acre to reinstate the farmland, which was originally worth up to £15 per acre. Not surprisingly, the operators which had leased the land for up to £360 per acre were content to pay a 'fine' of £30 per acre, rather than attempt to restore the land at the end of their lease, and the landowners seemed content to leave the land in its derelict state. McNaughton confirmed that the only economic use for the hill-and-dale was afforestation, which might cost £60 per acre, plus £3 per acre per annum for subsequent management. There had been some tree-planting, and Stewarts and Lloyds promised more, but McNaughton was unimpressed by what had been achieved to date, and he expressed serious doubts as to whether afforestation should be left in local hands.

McNaughton's report was considered by a further inter-departmental conference in May 1937. There was no denying the seriousness of the situation. Landowners and operators were making large profits, and a visitor from Mars might well think it was reasonable that they should be compelled to contribute toward the cost of reinstatement of the land after excavation. There was every prospect of the problem getting worse. The demand for ore was rising rapidly, and the scale of the individual pits was likely to increase because of the greater costs of dismantling and moving the huge excavating machines to new sites. It was noted how the inquiries had so far concentrated on Stewarts and Lloyds, which had located their furnaces and associated housing in the middle of the iron-field, whereas most other operators excavated the ore and simply exported it by rail to South Wales and other parts of Britain—they would take even less interest in the well-being of the Northamptonshire countryside.[29]

Representatives of the various government departments agreed that, whilst the exploitation of the iron-field had to continue, it was impossible 'to contemplate so large an area being left permanently ruined and derelict'. Surprise was expressed that there had been no outcry from the 'amenity interests', as represented by the CPRE and other bodies. The greater scale of operations would soon lead to such an outburst of indignation.

The inter-departmental conference agreed that 'no constructive action could be taken without a good deal more detailed examination of the situation and without decisions on several important points of policy'. It was important, for example, to discover more about all the companies operating not only in Northamptonshire but also in the iron-fields of neighbouring counties. In view of its general responsibilities for local government and planning, the conference decided that the Ministry of Health should take steps to appoint an official committee of inquiry, which would investigate and, in the longer term, draw public attention to 'the magnitude of the questions'.

The Ministry of Health proceeded with the utmost caution. Because of the contentious issues raised, the question of a committee of inquiry would have to be fully aired in the Cabinet, and it was essential for the Minister to know beforehand that he would have the full support of colleagues in the relevant departments. In a letter drafted by the Deputy Secretary, Sir John Maude, the Minister warned the President of the Board of Trade and Minister of Agriculture of the implications of setting up such an inquiry. He wrote:

I think we must face the fact that if the inquiry is to give the Government a useful lead it must not be confined to the technical aspects of the matter, but must deal with the broad question whether it is right that those in control of land should be at liberty to reduce it to this devastated condition without taking any steps to restore it to a useable state, and, if not, whether the landowners or operating companies, or both, ought not to contribute in some form towards its restoration.

Although this was a large and controversial question, the Minister believed it could not 'be burked if any adequate examination of the problem' was to be made.

Any misgivings which the President of the Board of Trade may have had on behalf of the iron and steel industry were allayed by the fact that his own Import Duties Advisory Committee had recently drawn attention to the disruption caused by the iron-workings, as part of a wider study of trends in the industry and the consequences of the transfer of plant and labour to such new centres as Corby.[30] The Cabinet approved the appointment of a committee of inquiry in October 1937. The fact that the Minister of Health was so well supported by departmental colleagues probably helped to overcome the misgivings of the Chancellor of the Exchequer as to the financial implications of any measures that might be recommended by the committee.[31]

Meanwhile there were discussions on who should be chairman and members of the committee. Eventually, the Treasury's nomination of a former Minister of Health, Lord Kennet (formerly Sir Edward Hilton-Young), as chairman, prevailed. Some proposed members declined to serve because of other commitments, and one was found to have a direct interest in the iron-field. The final list of five members comprised the chairman of the First Garden City, an ex-President of the Land Agents' Society, a business man, the Lord Mayor of Sheffield, and the Clerk of the Cheshire County Council. When the Clerk of the Northamptonshire County Council protested that 'somebody living in or with intimate knowledge of Northamptonshire' should have been included, he was told that every opportunity would be given for such persons to offer evidence to the Committee.

The Kennet Committee was appointed in January 1938, met twelve times, and visited the affected areas. Evidence was received from a wide variety of sources, and the Committee's report was published in March 1939. According to Sir John Maude, the Committee had met the original objectives of the Minister by providing 'outside' support for the views held by the Department, namely that the land had 'to be restored to some serviceable condition' and that the main cost should fall on the landowners. The Committee proposed that an *ad hoc* Ironstone Areas Restoration Board should be appointed, made up of representatives of the local authorities, operators, landowners, and Forestry Commission, with an independent chairman appointed by the Minister of Agriculture. The Board should secure the reinstatement of land, wherever possible, and make use of compulsory purchase if necessary. The costs would be defrayed by a levy of £40 for every acre taken over, derived from the landowners, companies, and local authorities in the proportion of 3 : 2 : 1, respectively.[32]

Whatever the merits of the Committee in tackling the major policy issues, considerable difficulties were encountered in gathering and interpreting the technical data on which its recommendations for future policy had to be based. The larger operators convened an *ad hoc* committee to present evidence, which the Committee found both confusing and guarded. The operators denied that they were trying to be secretive or obstructive, and attributed any inconsistencies in the evidence to the wide range of geological and commercial considerations affecting the various pits. They argued that such questions as royalty payments were 'a private matter for the individual firms'. The operators emphasized that these difficulties could only be overcome by appointing someone to collect and collate the information for the confidential use of the Kennet Committee, and they suggested that McNaughton should undertake the task. This was agreed and acted upon.[33]

After its Report had been published, the secretary of the Kennet Committee recorded his conviction that 'a big mistake' had been made in not appointing an engineer as a member. The lack of such expertise on the Committee made it easier for critics to cast doubts on the validity of its conclusions and recommendations. He wrote that 'it would not have occurred to the authorities to set up a committee on abortion without a doctor or a committee on the construction of hospitals without an architect'. Right from the start, it was clear that everything depended on the highly technical question of how much it would cost to move a given volume of waste material under given conditions, and it was hardly surprising that a committee of laymen 'sometimes floundered'. There were often difficulties 'even in establishing the most elementary engineering facts and calculations owing to the play which trade witnesses were able to make of drawbacks, reservations, etc. due to their superior knowledge of the subject'. Although the Committee managed to extricate itself largely owing to the assistance given by McNaughton, as an outsider he could only appear as a formal witness and could not be used to cross-examine the technical witnesses of the ore-producers.[34]

War broke out before a Cabinet Paper could be prepared, recommending the drafting of a Bill for the implementation of the recommendations of the Kennet Committee. By then, three years had elapsed since the problems of the iron-fields had been identified as a national issue requiring urgent attention. Much of the time had been spent merely in setting up the machinery for an inquiry. In view of this delay, it was reasonable to suggest that some kind of standing committee, capable of carrying out adequate surveys and research, would have been much more efficient and effective. However, the inquiry into the iron-fields also illustrated the difficulties of distinguishing technical issues from questions of public policy. Even the most technical query could quickly lead to contentious questions affecting, for example, the rights of property and the propriety of public expenditure. This raised the question of the status of the survey and research bodies and their relationship with government departments, the Treasury and, ultimately, the Cabinet.

NATIONAL SURVEY COMMISSION

Patrick Abercrombie was one of the earliest advocates of some kind of permanent body to carry out surveys at a regional or national scale. He warned in 1919 that there was little to be gained from replacing the self-interested business acumen of the developer with obtuse, official bungling. If such a fate was to be averted, there had to be a scientific basis for the post-war reconstruction plans that were being devised at that time. Drawing on Canadian experience, Abercrombie proposed the creation of a permanent Reconstruction Board, which would carry out a systematic survey, region by region, of national resources. By surveying past and present trends, there would be a basis for forecasting the future. The compilation of a national soils map, for example, would have a direct bearing on programmes for agriculture and forestry; accurate and detailed population maps would help decide where industry might be located, and diagrams of traffic flow would help in identifying the need for new roads. With this unique and comprehensive body of information, the Reconstruction Board could provide guidance to the government.[35]

Nothing happened, and the experience of the 1930s was far from encouraging. In spite of the extraordinary organizing abilities of Dudley Stamp and the

participation of over a quarter of the nation's schoolchildren, the Land Utilisation Survey very nearly collapsed through a lack of funds. When grants from the
Rockefeller Foundation and Pilgrim Trust came to an end in 1936, Stamp was
forced to take complete financial responsibility for the Survey, which he then
financed largely out of the profits made from writing textbooks. Throughout the
inter-war period, the amount of material aid given by official sources was
negligible.

This inability and unwillingness of the government to collect and publish
data of relevance to the physical environment was severely criticized by Sir
Gwilym Gibbon, in his book *The problems of town and country planning*. Having
just retired from the Ministry of Health, Gibbon drew on his recent experiences
in demonstrating how government departments could play a large part in
interpreting past and present trends, and in predicting future changes. As he
asserted, 'an enormous amount of information comes to the Central Departments in the course of their daily work. It would be useful to the Departments
themselves and not less to local authorities and private organisations and
persons, concerned with planning, if this information were more systematically
scrutinised and that part of it likely to be of general value published.' Government departments could easily provide this kind of assistance if definite
arrangements were made.[36]

The tasks of collating and disseminating the information would help to
identify gaps in knowledge—the areas where further investigations and research were required. Very little research had been carried out, and statutory
planning would benefit in two ways. First, the planner would be able to make a
quicker response to problems and, secondly, the relevant research might help to
reduce the obsessive search for utopias. In Gibbon's view, there was a tendency
'to look upon development as something mechanical, as something of which the
parts can be moved about at will as though society were made up of a number of
bricks'. Gibbon strenuously denied this, claiming that 'society is organic,
location of industries and residences and other needs are determined largely by
forces operative within the body social, and these forces must be understood if
planning is to be effected to the best purpose'. It was time that all planners took
a closer look at 'actual conditions, with their advantages and shortcomings,
their possibilities and their harassments'.

A demand for a National Survey Office, attached perhaps to the Cabinet
Secretariat, came from another quarter, namely Max Nicholson, the General-
Secretary of the Political and Economic Planning (PEP), Research Group. In a
paper of 1936 he described how town and country planning dealt with definite
and limited geographical areas and all their needs. It had a territorial, rather
than a functional, basis and, so often, this role was prejudiced by some government department or other agency that was quite oblivious of the territorial
consequences of its actions. Such *ad hoc* devices as the payment of subsidies or
creation of marketing boards might have a considerable, and yet varied,
regional ramification. Nicholson called for the creation of 'a properly equipped

agency to watch, measure and report' upon the effect of such activities, 'just as the Treasury was kept informed of each item of revenue and expenditure, or as the directors of a business are kept informed of production of each product and each plant, and of sales in each market'. Nicholson believed that if such a National Survey Office could put the facts before them, politicians and administrators might take very different decisions, which might assist, rather than hinder, the work of the planning authorities in each locality and region.[37]

The demand for more surveys and research became more strident in the late 1930s. The report of the Town and Country Planning Advisory Committee in 1938 complained of the impossibility of making a quantitative assessment of the destruction of the countryside and efficacy of planning controls in the absence of 'a detailed survey of the whole country'. Speakers in the debates on the hydro-electric power Bills complained of a similar lack of basic data on which policy decisions were required for the Highlands.

In this context, it may be instructive to look more closely at a proposal to set up a National Survey Commission for the purpose of making a National Survey of Rural Resources. The proposal was made in 1937 by an *ad hoc* committee convened by Patrick Abercrombie. The members were 'all concerned in some manner with rural affairs', and included John Dower, C. S. Elton, Geoffrey Jellicoe, C. S. Orwin, L. Dudley Stamp, R. G. Stapledon, and A. G. Tansley. They submitted a memorandum containing the proposal for a National Survey Commission to the Prime Minister in March 1937.[38]

In a letter accompanying the memorandum, Abercrombie drew attention to the way in which building development was often allowed to destroy first-class agricultural or forestry land, or occupy areas which were ideally suited for playing fields. Often these harmful developments occurred because of a lack of information as to the quality of the land or likely trend in urban and rural social needs. Even where remedial action was taken, assistance was often on a piecemeal basis. The government had sought to improve rural prosperity by providing assistance in marketing farm produce and by extending water, gas, and electricity supplies, but those responsible for these initiatives rarely had a chance to carry out 'a comprehensive scrutiny of the facts'. As a result, 'decisions of great consequence are daily being made without adequate knowledge of the inter-related facts and the wider implications of the steps taken'.

Abercrombie believed that a National Survey Commission could provide 'an independent comparative survey on a national basis'. It would 'co-ordinate existing material, arrange for further surveys where necessary, and present the whole of the results on a comprehensive and uniform basis'. It was estimated that the cost for the first five years would be £500,000 per annum. The necessary work could be undertaken by a 'comparatively small group of specialist surveyors working under an able administrator', and supported by existing Government surveys, universities, and research bodies. The work would have to be done under government auspices.

The memorandum outlined four types of survey, namely: air surveys, regional surveys, land-use surveys, and a miscellaneous category. Some of the proposals had long been advocated: others were comparatively novel. The role of air photography was stressed, particularly if the photographs were taken stereoscopically and at a large scale. The memorandum commended their use in compiling geological and soil maps, delimiting water catchment areas and plant communities, and in producing plans for land reclamation, afforestation, and new roads.

The role of the National Survey Commission as an initiator and co-ordinator was clearly set out. The Commission should be empowered to make grants toward the collection and publication of soil data. It should cooperate with universities, the British Ecological Society, Welsh Plant-breeding Station, and Forestry Commission, in making a vegetation survey of the United Kingdom. It was suggested that the Commission should (1) make a survey of wood-working industries and craftsmen, (2) classify woodlands according to type, condition and form of management, together with an estimate of their content and yield, (3) identify areas suitable for afforestation, and (4) help to determine the species most suited to different regions.

In a review of the increasing use of the countryside for outdoor recreation, and the scope for conflict with other land users, the memorandum proposed a survey of potential and actual recreational areas, both public and private. The National Survey Commission would give special attention to footpaths and the provision of refreshments and other facilities for the visitor from the town and city.

Having noted the influence of landownership and tenure on the pattern of land use and management, the memorandum proposed surveys of farm size, types of tenancy, those estates managed primarily for amenity, and farm and forest land substantially affected by game preservation. The availability of this kind of information, recorded on maps, would help to make the variations in land use and management much more intelligible.

Abercrombie's letter and the memorandum were referred by the Prime Minister's office to the Treasury. The proposals affected the interests of the Ministries of Agriculture and Health most closely. Rather than letting the Ministry of Health 'loose', the Treasury referred the proposals to the Ministry of Agriculture, with a request 'to consult other Departments as they think fit'. A wide range of departments was consulted, and both the underlying assumptions and detailed proposals for a National Survey Commission were challenged. There were serious doubts as to whether it was desirable to place such a heterogeneous collection of inquiries under one body. The memorandum laid great stress on presenting all the results in cartographic form, but the Director-General of the Ordnance Survey warned that this would lead to the inevitable suppression of a great deal of information. In many cases, statistical tables were the only means of presenting survey data.

The Department of Agriculture for Scotland challenged, in particular, the basic premiss of the memorandum that no policy for the better use of rural resources could be framed without the wide range of proposed surveys being undertaken. The Department claimed that no new facts were needed to prove that farmland was being wasted by ill-informed town-planning. The basic need was to rouse the public conscience, and this might be 'more easily achieved by an *ad hoc* public inquiry' than by the proposed Commission. Nor was a National Survey Commission needed to identify gaps in knowledge. Where gaps arose, they were usually caused by a lack of resources rather than of insight. If increased funds became available, it was 'a pertinent question whether they could not be more effectively used in extending the scope of local enquiry rather than on embarking on such grandiose schemes as a National Survey'.

There were doubts as to the utility of some of the proposed surveys. For example, the Forestry Commission claimed that a general survey of potential forest land would be of little practical value unless the government allowed the Commission powers to compulsorily acquire land and enforce good management. There were fears that parts of the Survey would be out of date before they were completed, and that some of the regional surveys would be too superficial for departmental needs.

In spite of these criticisms, the Ministry of Agriculture opposed the 'outright rejection' of the memorandum. In its submission to the Treasury, it stressed how the proposals were another manifestation of a widespread feeling that the State should have access to 'a much wider range of information than has been necessary in the past' because of its intervention 'to an increasing extent in what used to be private or semi-private affairs'. In the Ministry's view, 'this point of view would seem to be fundamentally reasonable whatever may be the objections to the detailed proposals'. Secondly, there was a *prima-facie* case for improving the flow of 'useful and interesting' information between government departments. At present there was no machinery available for an interchange of data, except by semi-official consultation. Thirdly, the memorandum had served a useful purpose in reminding departments that it was not enough to have sufficient information to administer existing policies: they would increasingly have to obtain 'sufficiently reliable data' to form the basis for future development policies.

The Ministry drafted a letter for the use of the Prime Minister. It began:

you will agree that the programme outlined in your memorandum is an ambitious one. While not questioning the utility of many of the items in it, I must confess to grave doubts whether the results would be commensurate in value with the cost; nor am I satisfied that the cost would be covered by the sum mentioned in your memorandum. In drawing up a programme of enquiry of this sort it is very important, in my opinion, to avoid prejudicing the results by undertaking too much. With regard to the number of enquiries you propose, I am advised that useful results could only be achieved by a considerably more detailed and consequently more costly type of investigation than the memorandum appears to contemplate. In other cases, it seems desirable to await the outcome of existing research investigations

On receiving the draft letter and the reactions of the various departments, the Treasury decided to reject out of hand the proposal for a National Survey

Commission. There were many more 'deserving objects'. The estimated costs would soon be exceeded, and the Survey would have to become permanent because 'the information collected would clearly be continuously obsolescent'. Far from stimulating government action, the imposition of advisory commissions tended to cause delay and confusion. The Cabinet would always attach far more weight to 'the accumulated knowledge and experience' of Ministers and their departments than to any recommendations made by an external body.

In forwarding the Ministry's draft to the Prime Minister, the Treasury amended the final paragraph of the letter, so that it read as follows:

I have no doubt that the work of Government Departments in collecting information on rural conditions will continue to expand in the future, as it has done in the past; and I fully appreciate the need for proper co-ordination of this work. I am not persuaded that existing arrangements are inadequate, either in respect of co-ordination or in respect of the character of the work undertaken, but I am taking steps to ensure that your views receive the continued attention of the Departments concerned

In January 1938 the amended draft of the letter was submitted to the Prime Minister for signing, and Neville Chamberlain did so without any further amendment being made to the text.

In view of the rejection of the Abercrombie memorandum the Treasury was annoyed to discover that the Ministry of Agriculture had independently convened a meeting with a view to setting up an inter-departmental committee to review ways of collating and disseminating information between government departments. The Treasury deprecated the move on the grounds that the committee would become permanent and was ill-equipped to tackle the task. As a stalling device, the Treasury proposed that a questionnaire should be sent to each department. By the time that the completed questionnaires were returned, the thoughts of each department had turned to the more immediate prospects of an outbreak of War.

With the imminence of War, each department was urgently looking for more rapid ways of improving the flow of information. In conversation with the Minister of Agriculture, the Prime Minister suggested that the Ministry should organize a land-capability survey as a means of helping to stem the loss of good agricultural land to widespread, indiscriminate building. Officials of the Ministry rejected the proposal as impracticable. It would take too long and require large numbers of skilled surveyors. Furthermore the quality of the land was not the only reason for the neglect and loss of land, and any survey which ignored the historical, economic and social factors would be very misleading.[39]

Having rejected the proposal, the Ministry was still left with the task of forming a wartime policy without adequate information. The Permanent Secretary described how the advice of individual landowners, farmers and land agents was necessarily based on their own, limited experiences and was coloured by their particular needs and prejudices. On the other hand, a sophisticated and objective survey of all the factors pertaining to food production was out of the question. The Secretary believed the solution was to make greater use of the Land Commissioners, who were appointed by the Minister, and who, 'while sympathetic to agricultural needs', were able to take a completely disinterested and impartial view of conditions in their particular districts. Their views would be collated by the Economics Intelligence Division. At the same time the Division would organize a statistical survey of land-use changes in each parish as recorded in the Ministry's Annual Returns of 1918, 1923, 1930, and 1935. This would help to identify those parishes where significant amounts of arable land had reverted to grass, and where any wartime ploughing-up campaign should be concentrated. Treasury approval was obtained, and the survey was completed in November 1938 in readiness for war.[40]

With the outbreak of war it was soon clear that these expedients were not enough. They did not locate the actual fields which had reverted to grass, nor identify those holdings and soils where conversion to arable would be most rapid and effective. Within only a few months the officers responsible for directing the food production campaign began to borrow the field sheets of the Land Utilization Survey—maps which the Ministry, as late as 1939, had dismissed as being too detailed for 'ordinary departmental purposes'. By the time over 5,000 sheets had been borrowed for consultation, the Ministry conceded that a payment should be made to the Survey, especially as a shortage of funds once again threatened to halt progress. The Treasury authorized an annual grant of £1,500 per annum, rising to £2,500 when the Department of Agriculture for Scotland began to make use of the Survey's field sheets. The grants continued until 1945.[41]

Meanwhile the Ministry was forced to embark on the kind of comprehensive survey which it had always dismissed as too impractical. After a trial survey of 1940 the decision was taken to mount a National Farm Survey in order to gather both quantitative and qualitative data. The former covered information on the size and layout of holdings, the state and number of buildings, the level of rent and nature of tenure, length of occupancy, and availability of piped water and electricity. This information was provided by the farmer himself. The staff of the War Agricultural Executive Committees in each county collected the qualitative data relating to the type and fertility of the land, the competence of the farmer and such aspects as the state of drainage. The major problem was the shortage of qualified and experienced recorders with the knowledge of national agricultural conditions to answer these parts of the Survey. In peacetime, special training courses could have been laid on, but this was impossible in wartime. Such were the penalties of leaving such surveys until the moment of actual need.[42]

During the 1930s, an increasing number of observers came to regard the implementation of a wide range of surveys and research programmes as an essential prerequisite to the rational use of town and countryside. Only by having the relevant information at his fingertips could the planner become competent. The Land Utilization Survey and other, more modest, ventures, provided hints of what was needed and of what could be achieved. The general attitude of central government, and of the Treasury in particular, was therefore extremely frustrating. It was easy for them to be critical of such proposals as that for a National Survey Commission, but until surveys and research programmes were carried out on an adequate scale, and this required government patronage, the art and science of data-gathering and synthesis would remain underdeveloped.

CHAPTER X

The Multiple Use of Land

By the late 1930s the need for some kind of national land-use policy was beginning to be recognized. As John Dower wrote, an agreed policy for the use and development of land resources was especially necessary in a country where 80 per cent of the people lived and worked on only 10 per cent of the land. Despite 'the great constructive efforts of the inter-war period, there was a vast heritage of misdevelopment, not only in the slums, overcrowding, confusion, and ugliness of our industrial towns, but also in the widespread misuse, waste, and disfigurement of rural and suburban areas'.[1]

Land resources were both misused and underused, and nowhere was this more evident than in the hill-lands. For the first time in history, upland areas could now be placed on a commercial footing, thanks to the great strides being made in raising productivity through cultivation and new seed mixtures of grass and clover. Many thousands of acres could now be worked by tractor. Meanwhile, the same internal combustion engine had greatly reduced rural isolation and had brought the hill-lands within reach of the holiday-maker. With proper planning, R. G. Stapledon believed that the uplands could be exploited on 'an entirely new scale of productivity' and, at the same time, be made a great playground for the urban population. At present their enormous potential was being wasted.[2]

This heritage of misdevelopment and waste had a bearing on many aspects of economic and social life, and it was therefore the responsibility of the entire community to find and implement a remedy. The use and management of land could no longer be left to the whims of individual landowners and occupiers: the land was far too precious. The use and management of each property should conform with guidelines which arose out of a consensus of public opinion. According to Dower the aim of these guidelines should be to allocate, use, and develop all parts of the country 'in an orderly, healthy and seemly manner' for the purpose to which, on balance, they are best suited—whether for farming or forestry, quarrying, or industrial development, commerce or residential use, transport, utility or social services, or for recreation. The aim should be to 'satisfy as fully and fairly as possible the legitimate needs and aspirations of every kind of user, from the individual to the nation as a whole'.

Dower wrote of the need for a National Declaration of Purpose, which would lay down guidelines as to the amount of land which should be allocated to each use. About 4,500,000 acres of England and Wales were already urbanized, and Dower suggested the conversion of 500,000 acres for further residential and industrial development, 500,000 acres for roads, railways and airfields, and a further 500,000 acres for golf courses, playing-fields, parks, reservoirs, and sewage schemes. So as to provide the maximum flexibility for planning, another 1,000,000 acres might be allocated for development, leaving the remaining 30,000,000 acres as rural land, which should be strictly preserved against 'any kind of urbanizing development'.

Stapledon believed the only way to achieve this kind of goal was to appoint 'the right sort of experts with the right sort of knowledge'. Voting people into authority was not enough. A properly equipped authority was needed, containing 'social biologists, psychologists, agriculturalists, foresters, architects, engineers, land agents, chartered surveyors, and such like people. Experts all'. Only then would 'scientific planning become a reality instead of a catch phrase, and the research worker and the scientist be in a position to serve the nation'. An expert body could tackle each region on its own merits and in relation to its topography, vegetation, and circumstances, and in sympathy with the particular national needs which the region could serve.

The need for this kind of approach became more widely recognized during the Second World War, as each major user of land began to draw up proposals for post-war recovery. In 1943, for example, the Forestry Commission published a White Paper on *Post-war forestry*, which envisaged the large-scale afforestation of up to a quarter of the hill-sheep lands of England and Wales. Dower was not unduly worried as to the effects of this loss on hill-farming because he believed the carrying capacity of the remaining hill-land could be doubled if the improvements in management proposed by Stapledon and other agricultural botanists were implemented. Rather, he castigated the Forestry Commission for considering the future of forestry in isolation. As Dower stressed, 'woods and fields must be thought of together'. When drawing up proposals for one type of land use, account had to be taken of the interests and requirements of other land users. For too long farming had 'been the Cinderella of British industries'; land devoted to agriculture had been regarded as 'merely undeveloped and fair game for any sort of change which will earn a capital appreciation for speculators'.[3]

There were two stages in devising an integrated policy for land use. The first was to select the optimum use for each tract of land, and the second was to allow as many secondary uses of the land as possible. For example, Dower believed that outdoor recreation would be perfectly compatible with upland farming. Despite the risk of vandalism and fires, 'a wise policy can provide generous facilities for the holiday and week-end enjoyment of the countryside . . . with very little temporary and no lasting harm to landscape beauty or farming'. Far from damaging 'the unique and delicate beauty' of the Lake District, fell-walking had increased the demand for 'farmhouse accommodation', and had helped to provide additional revenue, thereby helping to sustain the traditional hill-farms in lean years.

The concept of multiple land use was perhaps most fiercely contested by the owners of grouse-moors and water-catchment areas, who proved the most implacable opponents of the rambler during the debates and negotiations over the Access to Mountains Bill (see p. 195). Dower regarded the scope for conflict as grossly exaggerated: compromise would require only small concessions from each party. Ilkley Moor was 'open to all and thousands walk over it, but only a small proportion in fact go far off the recognized tracks, and the moor remains wild and lovely and still provides first class grouse shooting'. Where necessary, ramblers should be asked to stay away from the moors on shooting-days, and compensation ought to be awarded in the few cases where 'very heavy rambling' had clearly diminished sporting values. As for the infinitesimal risk of pollution caused by ramblers to water-catchment areas, the answer was to instal the necessary filtering equipment to safeguard the surface-gathered water. If water from the heavily polluted Thames could be made safe and clean for drinking purposes, the catchment-owners could surely instal much more modest equipment in the remote, upland areas, if they were a little less parsimonious.

Each type of land use and management would have to be reappraised if an integrated and multiple land-use policy was to evolve. Dower demonstrated the need for a more balanced view of land use during discussions, in 1944, as to the future role of forestry. He agreed that if afforestation was to be carried on as a strictly commercial undertaking, the amenities of the countryside could not be taken into account, but Dower challenged the very premiss that State and private forestry should operate on strictly commercial lines. Because of the long-term nature of afforestation, subsidies would always be needed to encourage planting schemes, and the best way of justifying subsidies was to take account of amenity and sporting, as well as commercial, considerations. Dower recalled how the finest landowners in the past had always adopted an '*all-round* responsibility for the well-being' of the land, and this meant a concern for amenity as well as profitability. Although there would be shifts in emphasis over time, the principles of good land husbandry should always be upheld. In this respect, the Forestry Commission was just another landowner—let the 'analytical economists keep separate "commercial" and "amenity" accounts if they wish, but don't let them split up the job and the responsibility' of being a landowner!

AFFORESTATION

The practical difficulties in securing an integrated, multi-purpose use of land were highlighted by the experiences of the Forestry Commissioners in trying to plant new forests during the inter-war period. One of the most striking land-use changes which took place in inter-war Britain was the large-scale afforestation of previously open countryside and the replacement of deciduous species with conifers in many of the traditionally wooded areas. There was considerable opposition to these changes in the content and appearance of the landscape. There were fierce clashes between the advocates of commercial afforestation and those who wanted to preserve amenity and promote outdoor recreation.

The conflict provides an important case study of the consequences of pursuing a single-minded land-use policy.

Using the contemporary files of the Forestry Commission and the Treasury, it is the purpose of this chapter to trace the changes in attitude toward afforestation in the inter-war period, and to note in particular how the Forestry Commissioners modified their planting policies, entered into closer liaison with other land users, and subsequently developed a series of National Forest Parks where outdoor recreation was of major importance.

Alarmed at Britain's dependence on imported timber, and its consequent vulnerability in times of war, the Forestry Commission was established by the Forestry Act of 1919 with the urgent tasks of promoting forestry, undertaking afforestation, and generally improving the production and supply of timber throughout the United Kingdom. Parliament established a Forestry Fund of £3,500,000 for the use of the eight Forestry Commissioners during the first decade. In spite of many setbacks, an area of 369,000 acres was afforested by 1939, of which two-thirds were planted with conifers.[4]

The proponents of outdoor recreation and landscape preservation soon declared their hostility to the physical enclosure and planting of the previously open grass heaths and moorland, and the replacement of oak and beech woods by conifers. The greatest opposition occurred in the Lake District, where the Forestry Commission bought 7,243 acres between the Esk and Duddon in 1934. The owner sold the estate on very advantageous terms on the explicit understanding that the land would be used for tree-planting.[5]

The Commission soon discovered that 5,140 acres of the open fell were unsuitable for planting, and so a more modest programme was announced, whereby planting would begin in Dunnerdale and finish with the afforestation of 740 acres in upper Eskdale. By this time, a society called the Friends of the Lake District had been formed under the chairmanship of Lord Howard of Penrith, which vigorously opposed afforestation in the Lake District and in Eskdale in particular. The Friends proposed alternative sites and even offered to buy Eskdale from the Commission at the purchase price.

The Commissioners refused the offer, claiming that it would break faith with the original vendor. But they offered to leave a further 440 acres of upper Eskdale unplanted if the voluntary bodies compensated the Commission at the rate of £2 per acre, namely the difference between the revenue from forest and open land. The Commissioners offered to plant the remainder of the area as 'a model forest', with a variety of trees planted along the contours and not in straight lines down the dale sides. Rides and paths would be provided through the plantations to allow pedestrian access to the higher, open ground.

The Friends of the Lake District rejected the compromise by claiming that even if the Forestry Commission could plant a model forest, the real issue was the preservation of open fell. The estate was 'in the very heart of the Lake District and the plantable portions formed the foreground to one of its finest mountain amphitheatres—Crinkle Crags, Bow Fell, Esk Pike and Scafell'. The

Friends launched a petition, asking the Forestry Commissioners 'to reconsider their desire to proceed with the afforestation of Eskdale and Dunnerdale' and stressing that any further afforestation in the Lake District would 'do most serious damage to a landscape unique in England'.

The petition was extraordinarily successful, in so far as over 12,000 signatures were obtained. These included the Lord Lieutenants of Cumberland, Westmorland, and Lancashire, the Archbishop of York and ten bishops, thirteen members of parliament (one of whom was Arthur Greenwood, the former Minister of Health), the vice-chancellors of six universities, 21 professors, 20 headmasters of public schools, and such leading 'economic experts' as Sir William Beveridge, Henry Clay, and Sir H. Llewellyn-Smith, the former Chief Economic Adviser to the government.

Criticisms were voiced in parliament. Lord Howard introduced a motion in April 1936, drawing attention to the petition and proposing a Select Committee to investigate the activities of the Forestry Commission. The government chose Lord Zetland, a government minister and president of the National Trust, to reply to the motion. Zetland agreed with the need to reconcile the inevitable clash between the Forestry Commission and the lovers of the Lake District, but he rejected the call for a Select Committee on the grounds that any inquiry would have to be peripatetic and deal with highly technical aspects. He stressed that it would be much better if the advocates of afforestation and the preservation of the countryside could reach a compromise by means of direct and informal discussions.[6]

During his speech, Lord Zetland made considerable use of a brief prepared by the Commissioners, which attacked the petition for giving the impression that the entire estate of 7,243 acres between the Esk and Duddon would be afforested, whereas only two-sevenths were intended for planting. The Commissioners described many of the signatories as persons who only looked upon 'the valleys as ideal places to spend any brief holiday', and who disregarded the fact that afforestation would help to alleviate the serious unemployment and poverty of an area otherwise dependent on farming.[7]

In their brief the Commissioners stressed the relevance of the Lake District to national forestry needs. The Forestry Commission had been established to create a reserve of 'standing timber to meet requirements for three years in a time of national emergency . . . provide reserves of timber against the time when the exhaustion of the virgin forests of the world begins to be felt . . . and to secure employment and increased production resulting from the conversion of uncultivated land into forest'. The Commission had been set a target of 1,750,000 acres of bare ground for afforestation in the thirty years up to 1949. So far, only 280,000 acres had been planted, which meant that the Commission was 100,000 acres behind its target, and was falling further behind by 1,400 acres a year.

The Commissioners warned that the target would never be reached 'if planting is banned in large districts such as the Lake District'. The areas of land intrinsically suitable for afforestation were far fewer than was commonly reported. In a confidential memorandum to the government in January 1935 the Commissioners had drawn attention to the serious effects of the economies imposed since the economic crisis of 1931, when the Forestry Fund was set at £450,000 per annum for five years. In order to make up the backlog of planting, it was essential for the Fund to be increased by £100,000 in order to acquire more land, and a further £80,000 were needed to expand the rate of annual planting from 21,000 acres to 30,000 acres over four years.[8]

The overtures were largely successful because the Treasury realized that an accelerated afforestation programme would also help to alleviate regional unemployment. Under the Special Areas Act of 1934, wide powers were granted for 'the initiation, organisation, prosecution and assistance of measures designed to facilitate the economic development and social improvement' of areas with exceptionally high unemployment. Forestry provided a high ratio of permanent work to total capital expenditure. In response to a request from the Treasury, the Commissioners described how it would be possible to acquire and plant 200,000 acres, and to lay out a thousand smallholdings, within and up to fifteen miles from the Special Areas designated under the Act. The proposals were accepted, and the Forestry Fund for 1936 was raised by 50 per cent in order to achieve a planting programme of 30,000 acres per annum.

Almost all the Lake District was within or up to fifteen miles from the West Cumberland Special Area, and the Forestry Commissioners chose to regard this as an instruction to give the maximum priority to afforestation in the Lake District. In their brief to Lord Zetland, they asserted that it was 'grotesque' to suggest that areas of 'landscape beauty and suitability for public recreation' should be excluded from planting programmes. This kind of exclusion could be applied to practically the whole country, except for the industrial areas. Some people would object to the establishment of plantations anywhere, regardless of the nation's needs.

THE JOINT INFORMAL COMMITTEE

In his speech Lord Zetland hoped that his pleas for compromise would not fall on deaf ears. Lord Howard's motion was withdrawn, in the hope that the Forestry Commissioners would heed the strength of feeling in parliament and the country at large.

Although the Commissioners were convinced that their course of action in the Lake District was reasonable and correct, they were already acutely aware of the need to improve their public image. In 1935 their chairman, Sir Roy Robinson, suggested that a small joint informal committee should be formed with the Council for the Preservation of Rural England (CPRE) to review complaints made against the Commission and to examine ways of 'making plantations more acceptable from the point of view of amenity'. The CPRE accepted the invitation, and thereafter representatives met periodically two Commissioners and an Assistant Commissioner, with Robinson in the chair.[9]

The Commission referred every criticism to the Joint Informal Committee, which was described in a report of 1943 as a vital channel of communication and 'the ultimate Court of Appeal on questions of amenity'. The Committee provided a valuable opportunity for identifying the various strands of opinion in the voluntary movement. When the Commissioners were considering their response to the petition of the Friends of the Lake District in 1935, they were encouraged to find that the CPRE representatives on the Committee considered that the Forestry Commission 'had had a raw deal', and that there had 'been some plain speaking between the CPRE and the Friends'. Clearly, the Commission's critics were not as united as they had appeared.

The Friends of the Lake District were the principal pressure group, whose uncompromising opposition to afforestation and aggressive publicity were the major factor in causing the future treatment of the Lake District to become a national, as opposed to a local, issue. Sheer tenacity in the face of obstruction from more powerful bodies brought its rewards—the arguments of the Friends eventually prevailed—but it is doubtful whether this could have happened without the interposition of the CPRE. The Forestry Commissioners would have regarded any concessions made directly to so 'radical' a group as the Friends as an unacceptable loss of face. The participation of members of the CPRE on the Joint Committee made it possible to present concessions as honourable settlements.

For its part, the CPRE regarded the Joint Informal Committee as a useful way of discovering the Commissioners' plans and of influencing the location and layout of future plantations. This was especially important in view of the Commission's inability to appoint a landscape adviser to its staff. On the other hand, the representatives of the CPRE found it difficult to act as a spokesman for all the constituent and affiliated bodies: they had the near-impossible task of reconciling the idealism of many of these bodies with the economic, technical, and managerial constraints of the Commission.

By 1937 there was need for greater liaison at both the general and detailed levels. The Forestry Commission was becoming increasingly irritated by those who condemned all tree-planting. Even from an aesthetic point of view, the Commission insisted that there was nothing wrong in preferring a wooded to an open country. When replying on behalf of the Commissioners to a debate in 1937, Sir George Courthope asserted that 'I love the Lake District as much as anyone does. To my mind, the one thing it lacks is more trees. While I respect the sincerity' of those who believe that 'the addition of large numbers of trees might destroy the beauty of the Lake District, I am equally sincere in my belief that it would enormously enhance it'. There was a genuine difference of opinion.[10]

Courthope may have been a biased observer, but his point of view won support from the Bishop of Gloucester in the columns of *The Times*, who wrote, 'the scenery of the (Lake) district would be very much improved by planting'. In his view one of the most beautiful valleys was the Vale of Keswick, where landowners had planted conifers in the early nineteenth century. They had provided both beauty to the landscape and valuable timber in the event of war. Trees would not grow at above 1,500 to 2,000 feet, and so the upper slopes of the mountains would always remain bare, adding further variety and beauty to an otherwise well-wooded landscape.[11]

The Commissioners were also resentful of the way in which critics were obsessed with the Commission's earlier plantations, such as those on the Whinlatter Pass and in Ennerdale, and failed to give credit for the more recent plantings, with their improved layout and appearance. In a letter to the *Spectator* in 1937, Sir Francis Acland described some of the difficulties faced by the early Commissioners. He wrote:

for some years after 1919, when we started from nothing, we had to concentrate wholly on planting. There was no tradition of real amenity planting anywhere in the Empire. Certainly the only men who could get planting work really well done lacked it. I was interim Chairman at the time and I take full responsibility for all those early appointments. But steadily more and more in recent years we and our officers have been learning to plant as beautifully as circumstances allow[12]

The Commissioners were accordingly very pleased when members of the Joint Informal Committee came to their support. When a correspondent to *The Times* accused the Forestry Commission of planting only conifers, G. M. Trevelyan pointed out that the officer in charge of Dunnerdale was under instructions to plant hardwoods wherever possible. He described how the Commissioners had decided to leave the meadows near Esthwaite Water unplanted. According to Trevelyan, 'they will neither be planted nor built upon, but will remain as the schoolboy Wordsworth knew them'. He concluded his letter to *The Times* by asserting that 'when the Forestry Commission really does a good thing for the amenity of the country it should be given the credit'.[13]

Robinson was keen that the Joint Informal Committee should examine specific areas, and in March 1935 the Committee started to examine the optimum extent of afforestation in the Lake District. When Lord Zetland rejected the call for a Select Committee on the Forestry Commission, he was able to stress that the Committee was reviewing 'the whole question of future planting in the Lake District so as to ensure that no land is acquired in parts where afforestation may be undesirable'. On behalf of the CPRE, John Dower prepared a map which indicated the area where the CPRE wanted to ban planting (figure 16). It included Eskdale and Dunnerdale. The Forestry Commission responded by proposing a much smaller area of 220 square miles. After prolonged debate, both parties eventually agreed to exclude afforestation from a central zone of 300 square miles. A further area, including Eskdale and Dunnerdale, was designated as a 'special area', where the Commission would seek alternative sites and consult the CPRE before carrying out any planting.[14]

The agreement reached by the Joint Informal Committee was published in July 1936. The Commission stressed its voluntary nature, noting that 'it is necessary to make the position clear because it has been suggested that some-

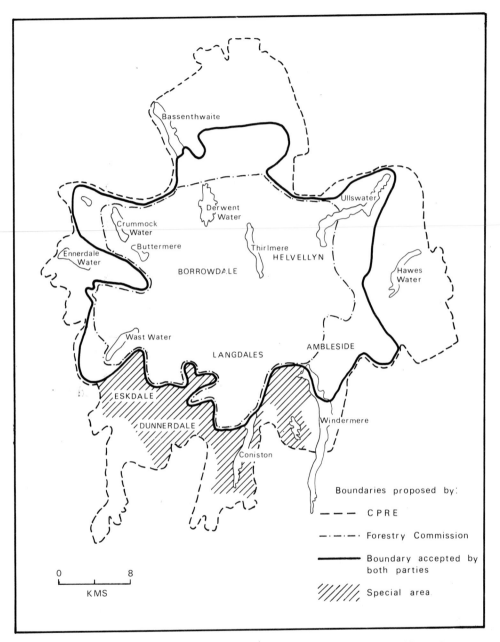

Bassenthwaite

Ullswater

Derwent
Water

Crummock
Water

Buttermere

Thirlmere
HELVELLYN

Ennerdale
Water

BORROWDALE

Hawes
Water

Wast Water

LANGDALES

AMBLESIDE

ESKDALE

DUNNERDALE

Windermere

Coniston

Boundaries proposed by:

- - - - C P R E

- · - · - · Forestry Commission

———— Boundary accepted by
both parties

////// Special area

0   8

K MS

Fig. 16. The restriction of afforestation in the Lake District, as agreed in 1936

thing analogous to *country planning* has been accomplished'. The CPRE representatives made it clear that they still opposed the exclusion of the 'special area' from the central 'protected' zone.[15]

It was soon evident that the compromise reached by the Committee had failed to satisfy critics. In December 1937 the House of Commons accepted a motion drawing attention to 'the anxiety that exists with respect to the activities of the Forestry Commission in the Lake District and other areas of great natural beauty'. The motion was introduced by Godfrey Nicholson, who emphasized that this was not a 'vote of censure': he recognized that the Forestry Commissioners had been conciliatory within 'their limitations'. They had created the Joint Informal Committee which had drawn up the agreement, but the Commissioners were unable to make substantial concessions within their terms of reference. Although 300 square miles had been excluded from afforestation, a further 400 square miles, including Eskdale, Dunnerdale, and the lakeside banks of Bassenthwaite, Haweswater, Coniston, and Windermere, remained unprotected.[16]

Another member of parliament, Henry Strauss, demanded the replacement of the Joint Informal Committee by 'stronger machinery' with the statutory powers to decide whether it was 'in the national interest that a conifer forest should be placed in Eskdale'. The new body would identify 'those areas of natural or historic landscape beauty which must not be disturbed, and areas suitable for afforestation'. If this survey was then made the basis for a carefully formulated and well-publicized planting programme, much of the anxiety and uncertainty surrounding the Commission's work would disappear.

Correspondents to *The Times* supported the views expressed in parliament. A letter from Sir William Beveridge, A. M. Carr-Saunders, Henry Clay, Reginald Lenard, and H. Llewellyn-Smith asserted that there were 'no sufficient grounds of economic, social, or national policy' to justify the afforestation of Eskdale. In another letter, seven bishops wrote that 'we cannot believe that the interests of timber-production, which the Forestry Commission exists to promote, are best served by its working in this atmosphere of perpetual controversy and persisting in enterprises which arouse this widespread opposition'. Although the Commission conceded in principle the importance of protecting amenity, the controversy was bound to continue until the principle was put into practice in a district 'so precious to lovers of mountain scenery'. The bishops concluded, 'the Lake District is a very small area and to ask the Government to protect it is not asking too much'.[17]

Up to this time, the Treasury had insisted that it was not directly involved in the Eskdale controversy, but the Forestry Commissioners increasingly defended their position by stressing how the government had placed them under explicit instructions to promote afforestation in Special Areas for the relief of unemployment. In this way, much of the criticism of the Commission's activities in the Lake District was deflected onto the Treasury. The Treasury responded by informing the Commissioners that the designation of West

Cumberland as a Special Area could not in itself constitute a sufficient reason for afforesting the Lake District. Large-scale planting programmes had not been envisaged for the Lake District when the Special Areas Act was passed and the Forestry Fund increased. As a member of the Treasury observed, 'I do not think that the Treasury could object to a halt being called in the Lake District provided that the unique qualities and associations of that part of the country are recognised to have made it an exceptional case'.[18]

Meanwhile the Treasury had become involved in another way. In December 1937 the Attorney-General, Sir Donald Somervell, wrote to the Financial Secretary of the Treasury, John Colville, describing his life-long interest in the Lake District and his 'very strong view that the Forestry Commission should not afforest Eskdale and the Duddon Valley. He stressed that 'owing largely to its geological formation, there is a greater variety of valley, lake and mountain scenery in the Lake District than there is in the same area probably anywhere in the world'. The Attorney-General doubted whether the opportunities for employment provided by afforestation would greatly exceed those lost through the dislocation of farming and, 'in any case, I myself feel that the preservation of the Lake District should be a matter of national policy, and even if the possibility of employment in that area was considerably greater than it is I think that preservation should be the governing consideration'. Somervell concluded by saying that 'there is a fairly strong feeling, with which I sympathise, that Governments have not sufficiently considered amenities in the past.' By stopping the further afforestation of the Lake District, the government would demonstrate its genuine concern for an area in which 'a very large number of people are interested'.

A few days later, the Financial Secretary received a letter from another government minister, Lord Balniel, who laid even greater stress on finding a solution. Balniel described how the Forestry Commission was continuing to acquire and seek out more land for afforestation in the Lake District. He wrote, 'one has no idea where it is going to stop . . . the Lake District is something unique in England. It is an ironical position that, with our various schemes for country planning, etc., to protect the countryside, a government commission should be allowed to destroy what is agreed by all to be the finest part of England'. Balniel ended his letter by asking, 'Can't you stop it? or rather, *won't* you stop it?'

At a briefing Colville agreed with the Treasury view 'that there was a very strong consensus of responsible opinion against the Forestry Commission as regards Lakeland'. The Commissioners should adopt 'as accommodating a spirit as possible'. In taking this view the Financial Secretary emphasized that the Treasury should avoid putting itself in a position where it '*told* the Forestry Commission to reverse its course'. As an Assistant Secretary pointed out, 'we have no direct control over or influence with the Forestry Commissioners who are an independent body'. Although the Treasury was 'on excellent terms with the Chairman', Sir Roy Robinson, there would be resignations if the Commission felt it was 'being coerced or its independence unduly interfered with'.

The prospects for a voluntary change of course were not good. Robinson insisted that the Commissioners were not prepared to compromise unless they were assured that, by so doing, the controversy would finally come to an end. No one could give an assurance of that kind, and so the dispute dragged on until the Treasury managed to convince the Commissioners that the clash over Eskdale was jeopardizing their success in promoting another venture, namely the promotion of outdoor recreation and a system of National Forest Parks. The next section in this Chapter will explain the significance of this new venture and its bearing on the Commission's future role.

THE RECREATIONAL USE OF WOODLAND

Afforestation was not the only change taking place in the countryside: the number of hikers and campers rose dramatically, and the possession of a motor car made it possible to reach the remoter parts. The New Forest was among the first areas to be affected: the Secretary of the Forestry Commission observed in 1925 that 'with the development of motoring the influx of picnic-parties has increased very greatly in recent years and, apart from the danger and nuisance of fires, parts of the forest are rendered unsightly through the scattering of waste paper and similar litter'.[19]

The Forestry Commission's first positive response to this trend in outdoor recreation came in a memorandum written by Sir John Stirling-Maxwell to his fellow-Commissioners in 1928. He warned that the question of amenity and access to forests was likely to become acute on several properties in northern England, and that the Commissioners should provide their staff with a clear policy, otherwise the officers would 'naturally take the line of safety and exclude all intruders who have no legal right of entrance'. Stirling-Maxwell described how, on fine Sundays, thousands of ramblers and cyclists 'traverse in thousands the road from Sheffield to Glossop through Hope Forest, and make much use of various rights of way. They are a rough looking lot. The farmers do not like them. They bring all they want in their riksacks and buy nothing. But they are out for exercise and the right kind of holiday'.[20]

The views of the Commission's staff were sought, and David Young, the Deputy Surveyor for the Forest of Dean, replied that 'it would be a mistake to attempt to exclude the public from the Commission's Forest areas'. The opening of the forests would 'go a long way to popularising the national programme' of afforestation, and there would be more immediate benefit. The Commission was increasingly worried about the cost of damage caused by people venturing into the newly-established nurseries and plantations, where they lit fires and dropped lighted matches and cigarettes. There were 409 fires during the long dry-spell of 1929, which cost £46,000. Nearly half were started by a careless act on the part of the public. It was impracticable to ban the public from the forests: instead, ways had to be found of guiding the visitors so that their 'contact and respect for the countryside developed together'. As Young pointed out, it was psychologically better to show the public where they *could* go, and he commended the German concept of marked forest trails.

In his memorandum, Stirling-Maxwell stressed the need to take amenity into account, especially in popular, tourist areas, where hardwoods and scrub were being replaced by conifers. At Gwydyr, the river banks should 'be treated for amenity rather than timber, and areas along road sides which tourists have been accustomed to use should be reserved unfenced for this purpose'. Traditional picnic spots should be left unplanted, and small camping grounds should be set aside, with water supplies and latrines.

After considering the memorandum and reactions from staff, the Commissioners issued instructions that 'the lay out of all Commission areas should take into consideration the question of amenities and endeavours should be made to meet all reasonable demands . . . Where any of the Commission's land carried ornamental scrub woods alongside public roads the fence should be erected a chain or so from the road'. The Forest Act of 1927 already granted powers for the Forestry Commission to issue bye-laws regulating recreation and, by careful management, the Commissioners hoped to produce commercial timber and permit public access wherever required and practicable.

In many ways the New Forest, 'with its extensive open heaths and recreational facilities', already fulfilled the functions of a forest park, and investigations were made as to the possibility of turning unplantable land on other properties into parks. At this point, the CPRE persuaded the Prime Minister, Ramsay MacDonald, to appoint an inter-departmental committee to review the need for national parks (see p. 115). Sir John Stirling-Maxwell represented the Commission on the Committee. The Forestry Commission suspended its own inquiry and told the Committee in 1929 that parts of Glenmore might form a national park if sufficient steps were taken to safeguard the plantations. A sum of £5,000 would be needed for capital expenditure and £250 toward road construction. Fees for camping and other facilities would help to make the parks self-supporting.[21]

As soon as it became clear that the government proposed to take no action on the report of the National Park Committee, the Commissioners resuscitated their own investigations and, following a tour of North Wales in 1933, they submitted a memorandum to Ramsay MacDonald which proposed alternative means of providing facilities for outdoor recreation. Instead of 'a limited number of national parks, specifically acquired for the purpose', the Commission should be given up to £20,000 to develop camping sites and hiking trails on their own properties and those of private persons who were prepared to provide certain minimum facilities. Huts and buildings might be provided at otherwise uneconomic rates, and some additional funds might be spent in acquiring 'interesting, unplantable land'. In this way, a systematic beginning could be made 'for what must inevitably come'.[22]

Ramsay MacDonald referred the memorandum to the Treasury with the comment that the outdoor 'movement described in the memorandum [was] an excellent one, but that everything depended on the bye-laws and the way in which these were enforced'. For its part, the Treasury argued that the financial reasons which prevented the implementation of the report of the National Park Committee applied equally to the Forestry Commission. Furthermore the Treasury-Solicitor advised that the Commission had no statutory powers to assume responsibilities for outdoor recreation, and an internal minute, written by the Permanent Secretary, Sir Warren Fisher, vigorously opposed any suggestion of legislation 'converting the Commission appointed to re-afforest Great Britain into an agency for promoting "hiking"'. If public money was required for the stimulation of outdoor recreation, this should be the responsibility of the Ministry of Health, but the Treasury concluded that hiking should be left entirely to such associations as 'the excellent Youth Hostels Association, who are fairly active at the present time'.

The Treasury therefore decided to reject the memorandum, but first the Prime Minister had to be informed. Much to its surprise, Ramsay MacDonald responded with a long minute which called for a reconsideration of the whole question. He believed that the Commission's proposals 'would be tremendously popular and would perhaps be the best way of regulating a habit which, hitherto, has grown up in a very disorganized way and unless carefully controlled may be a danger to public health and a serious blot on some of the most beautiful parts of the countryside'. During the summer, he had come across a 'very small piece of common land in Lanark near Tinto almost every inch of which was taken up by tents and caravans, and so was giving rise not only to serious inconvenience but dangers'. He saw many notices offering accommodation, and learned that some farmers were charging as much as 7/6d. per night for the right to pitch a tent. The Prime Minister concluded that 'sooner or later, especially when the flood spreads over desirable country like, for instance, the Cairngorms, something must be done, otherwise by fires and less disastrous incidents the countryside will be devastated except in very remote parts'. The longer action was postponed, the harder it would be to impose the necessary controls.

The Commission's proposals would be popular and inexpensive. Camping fees should cover the costs of administration and might even show a modest surplus. Whereas local authorities would find it difficult to regulate recreational activities in remote areas, the Commission might deploy its own staff for this purpose. It was often difficult to find employment of 'a strict forest nature' in summer, and the appointment of these woodsmen as wardens and custodians for the summer period would help to reduce seasonal unemployment.

In reply, the Chancellor of the Exchequer, Neville Chamberlain, emphasized that the Forestry Commission lacked the statutory powers to buy unplantable land for recreational purposes and to provide facilities on private land. Not only might these functions conflict with the Commissioners 'proper work', but the powers were largely unnecessary. There was already nothing to stop the Commission from providing reasonable access and modest facilities on their existing properties. The woodlands of Snowdonia, the Pennines, Lake District and Delamere Forest were accessible from Manchester, Leeds, and Liverpool; Cannock Chase was close to Birmingham; the Quantocks and Exmoor were not too far from Bristol. If the voluntary bodies were made responsible for supervising the holiday-makers and for providing the huts and tents, the small expenditure incurred by the Commission would be regarded by the Treasury 'as no more than incidental to the Commissioners' ownership of the land'.

The Prime Minister agreed with this compromise, and the Treasury informed the Forestry Commissioners that reasonable access should be offered to the public on existing properties; camping sites could be provided under proper control; direction posts might be erected on existing trails 'with suitable warning notices'. In April 1934 Ramsay MacDonald asked for a progress report, and Robinson informed the Treasury that the New Forest was the most popular camping area. Over 800 camping permits had been granted in the year up to September 1933, and a further eighty-nine free permits were issued to such organizations as the Scouts. Forty-five season tickets and over 2,400 day permits were granted for picking daffodils in the Dymock Woods of Gloucestershire. Several thousand people had used the footpath constructed in Puck's Glen, beneath Benmore, and the National Ramblers' Federation had assisted in marking routes in Gwydyr Forest. Buildings had been leased as youth hostels, and the bothy at Ennerdale had proved 'a mecca for all true YHA members'. An especially close liaison had evolved with the Scottish Youth Hostels Association, which had 'undertaken to do its utmost to inculcate a sense of responsibility in its members to assist in the extinguishing of fires and to ensure good behaviour'.

In their progress report, the Commissioners took the opportunity to reiterate their original proposals, and cited examples of how land could be acquired cheaply for recreational purposes. In view of the growing public interest, the Commissioners were still of the opinion that 'a separate subhead should be opened in their accounts for financing work of this kind and that money should be provided specifically for the purpose'. The Treasury still regarded these sentiments as 'rather dangerous', and decided to delete them from the copy of the progress report that was forwarded to the Prime Minister.

In spite of this censorship, the Treasury gradually became more sympathetic toward the Commission's involvement in outdoor recreation. This was partly because of the information obtained from one of its Principals, Herbert Gatliff, who attended meetings with the Commissioners on behalf of one of the voluntary bodies. Gatliff explained, 'I went as a hiker and youth hosteller, not as a member of the Treasury, but I had in mind the Treasury point of view', namely that the Commission should act as 'good landlords rather than amusement purveyors'. Through Gatliff the Treasury realized that the Forestry Commission would not only improve its public image by providing facilities for outdoor recreation but that these facilities might make it easier to safeguard the vulnerable plantations from fire. Gatliff described how a public footpath passed through the middle of a new plantation on the South Downs. It would cost many thousands of pounds to erect fencing and 'even then you can't be sure that people won't get through the fences or throw cigarette ends through them'. A more effective safeguard might be to leave the path unfenced and spend a modest sum on recreational facilities, thereby hoping to win the goodwill, and therefore the co-operation, of the visiting public. When the Treasury was informed that a hundred pounds were needed to provide toilets for an estimated 4,000 visitors from Glasgow in the forests of west Scotland on summer weekends, it replied that such modest expenditure should be treated as an integral component of commercial forestry. The creation of a subhead in the Commission's accounts, to cover such outgoings, would attract undue attention and 'raise questions of legal propriety'.

THE FORESTS AS PARKS

It soon became clear that the voluntary bodies could not provide all the recreational facilities required. Numerous practical difficulties arose: the Camping Club of Great Britain found that all the otherwise suitable sites in the Delamere Forest, and in Kent and north Wales, were either planted up or lacked water. The Youth Hostels Association (YHA) could not find any suitable buildings in the Delamere and Wyre Forests for conversion to hostels. The Forestry Commission would have to become more directly involved.

In their memorandum to the Treasury in 1935, setting out the need for an increase in the Forestry Fund (see p. 175), the Commissioners once again emphasized the value of exploiting the recreational potential of the new forests. On the basis of their experience in the New Forest and the 'experiments . . . in granting facilities to such bodies as the YHA', the Commissioners were certain that adequate facilities could be provided at modest expense. The memorandum admitted that the request for a special grant of £20,000 in 1933 had been too ambitious, but the Commissioners asserted that a grant of £5,000 per annum over five years would be sufficient to set up a series of National *Forest* Parks, where the plantable areas would be afforested and the remainder could be used on the lines suggested in the report of the National Park Committee in 1931 (see p. 116). Eskdale and part of Argyllshire were proposed as potential National Forest Parks.

This time the Treasury agreed, and a sum of £5,000 was allocated for 'fitting out' a National Forest Park of 35,000 acres in Argyllshire, comprising the unplantable areas of the Forests of Ardgarten, Glenfinart, Benmore, and Glenbranter. At the same time, the Glasgow Corporation decided to convert 19,000 acres of its adjacent estate of Ardgoil into an area for outdoor recreation. The first visitors to the National Forest Park arrived in 1936. Ardgarten House was opened as a park centre, and five hostels and four camps were in use by the outbreak of war in 1939. A park guide was published in 1938 which contained scholarly contributions on the geology, vegetation, and animals of the National Forest Park.[23]

The Argyllshire National Forest Park was the first extensive park of any kind in Britain, and the Commissioners were understandably hesitant about setting up further parks straight away. They wanted to gain more experience. A committee convened to advise on the management of the Park warned, 'it is difficult to estimate how many people could make use of the area for recreation without destroying the sense of remoteness and solitude which is its chief attraction'. The committee therefore recommended that the Commission should proceed cautiously and 'refrain from drawing undue public attention to what they are doing'.

However, time was not on the side of the Commission. As soon as the economy began to show signs of recovery, demands for a series of national parks became more strident (see p. 116). In 1934 Peter Thomsen read a paper to the conference of the British Association setting out the need for a national parks authority. One of the Commissioners, Sir George Courthope, warned Robinson that 'wild schemes of this kind must be nipped in the bud'. He added, 'it would be a good thing to push forward your proposals for recreational facilities in connexion with our forests', and soon all acquisitions and planting programmes were being reviewed with an eye to their future as national forest parks. When Plynlimon was acquired in 1937, Robinson directed that 'unusual care should be taken in the layout and amenity treatment' of the plantations.

By 1937 the Treasury was also becoming seriously concerned over the national parks movement (see p. 118), especially when it was learned that the Minister of Health was considering an application to the Exchequer for funds to set up a series of national parks. In a letter to the Chancellor of the Exchequer, the chairman of the Standing Committee on National Parks observed, 'if the Government appointed a National Parks Commission to direct and control National Parks it would not only be a great National boon but would give the Government very great popularity'. Treasury officials warned of the dangerous precedents which this would set, and the Principal Private Secretary, J. A. N. Barlow, concluded 'if we are to spend money on National Parks, it is probable that much better value could be obtained by extending certain recent activities of the Forestry Commission than by setting up a grandiose National Parks Authority'.[24]

The threat of a national parks authority led to a profound change in the Treasury's attitude toward the Commission's involvement in outdoor recreation and National Forest Parks. This was clearly seen in a letter which Barlow wrote to Sir Roy Robinson in November 1937. He wrote: 'I do not know whether it often happens that when you are acquiring land for planting there is land adjoining which would be no use for your purposes and has little except perhaps hill grazing value, but would be suitable for the kind of National Park which you have made in Scotland, and could as part of the deal be bought cheap.' Barlow was quick to point out that his suggestion did not mean that the Treasury would automatically grant funds for new National Forest Parks because 'a great deal would depend on the circumstances of the moment'. 'But', he continued, 'I imagine that cases such as I have indicated do from time to time arise and you might be able to convince us that a little extra money would in our own interest be well spent in warding off much less attractive pro-proposals.'[25]

As Barlow expected, Robinson assured him that 'we could pick up quite cheaply in the ordinary way of business considerable areas of the type of land which you have in mind'. Earlier in the year, the Commission 'could have bought a couple of thousand acres of the Cairngorms at 10 to 20 shillings per acre in connection with the purchase of our new Inshriach forest, but had refrained because most of it was unplantable'.

In Robinson's view, there was little steam behind the national parks movement. The idea was 'superficially attractive, makes good press copy, and the advocates are noisy', but 'an *ad hoc* National Parks Authority would un-doubtedly have to pay much more than we do for land, and incidentally might queer our market'. The Forestry Commission was able to make considerable savings by acquiring land 'gradually and at the individually favourable mo-ments' as an incidental part of its forestry activities. Robinson wrote:

I am quite sure in my own mind that the way we are going about the business is the logical and economical way . . . there is enormous and increasing pressure behind the desires of the urban dwellers to get into the country and to wander about the hills and woodlands. All the develop-ments of modern transport make it easier for them to do so. That is the real problem—how to give them generous facilities without spoiling the productivity (and amenity) of the countryside—half a dozen large National Parks will not solve it

Barlow followed up this initiative by writing to Sir John Maude, the Deputy Secretary of the Ministry of Health, advising him that:

When you are next pressed on the subject (of national parks) you might find it worth while to refer to us as to whether anything useful can be said about the activities of the Forestry Commission. They have a good deal of land not suitable for planting and of little agricultural or sporting value which they are compelled to acquire as part of larger purchases

The main difficulty in promoting the Commission's interest in outdoor recreation was the antagonism aroused by the battle over Eskdale and Dunner-dale, and in January 1938 a meeting was held in the Treasury to review the Commission's range of activities. Robinson began by refuting 'the exag-gerations and mis-statements of the recent campaign' waged by critics in the Lake District. Barlow responded by agreeing that 'the views expressed in the press' had been one-sided, but he emphasized that 'the writers were people of position and it might not be wise to ignore their influence in high quarters'. The Attorney-General had intervened, and debates in parliament had shown con-siderable disquiet over the activities of the Commission, especially in the Lake District.

Robinson retorted that 'we have been solid in our refusal to move out of Eskdale and Duddon because of the character of the agitation and also because we felt that similar arguments could be applied to almost all parts of the country. By taking a firm stand in the Lake District we had undoubtedly eased our position in Breckland and Snowdonia.' Barlow suggested that the Commissioners might be more successful in the long run in enhancing their prestige and paving the way for more National Forest Parks if they modified their attitude and entered into a *quid pro quo* arrangement with the amenity bodies. By doing so the government would find it easier to resist the strong pressures being exerted for a national parks authority and separate system of national parks.

The meeting concluded by agreeing to the wisdom of the Commission's withdrawal from Eskdale and Dunnerdale, and these views were conveyed by Robinson to the Commissioners at a meeting in January 1938. The Commissioners decided not to 'withdraw', but to issue 'a considered statement' and discuss the Eskdale plantings with representatives of the groups that had written to *The Times*. Soon afterwards a meeting was held with the Bishop of Blackburn, Sir William Beveridge, and W. W. Wakefield, representing the bishops, and academic and outdoor interests, respectively, with G. M. Trevelyan and Sir Lawrence Chubb also present. Robinson emphasized the Commission's statutory responsibilities, and Sir George Courthope stressed that 'the Forestry Commission did not go into the Lake District by choice: they had to go wherever land was available at a reasonable price'. Robinson later reported to the Treasury that 'we made some progress, first in getting our case appreciated and, second, in exploring a possible compromise'.[26]

At a meeting with the Attorney-General, Robinson discussed a possible compromise more fully, and he described plans for new National Forest Parks in the Forest of Dean and Snowdonia. While expressing considerable interest in the parks, Sir Donald Somervell emphasized that little could be achieved until the Commissioners 'retired gracefully' from Eskdale and Dunnerdale. An Assistant Secretary in the Treasury, Eric Twentyman, took the same view. He wrote:

I appreciate Sir Roy Robinson's desire to avoid the appearance of giving way to what he regards as 'crank' agitation; but the fact remains that it is preposterous that he should go on planting straight edged masses of conifer in the Cumberland valleys. Unless some genuine concession is made by the Forestry Commission to reasonable opinion in respect of the Lake District, the hope, if there is any, of endowing them with 'National Park' responsibilities will be nil and the credit we can derive from the National Forest Park activities will be discounted.

There was still considerable reluctance to compromise when the Commissioners met again in February 1938. Robinson merely stated 'that some concession might satisfy the more reasonable of their critics', but he then went on to emphasize that the Commission was 'at a critical point in its career; National Forest Park schemes were making an impression; National Park proposals were being revived', and there was a possibility that the Commission might be made the 'controlling body' of any new venture. In his view, the Commissioners should 'not merely be reasonable but must demonstrate the fact'. The Commissioners should 'not retreat from the Lake District', but should round off the plantings in Dunnerdale as an economic unit and leave Eskdale unplanted (figure 17). The amenity bodies would pay £2 per acre to the Commission in

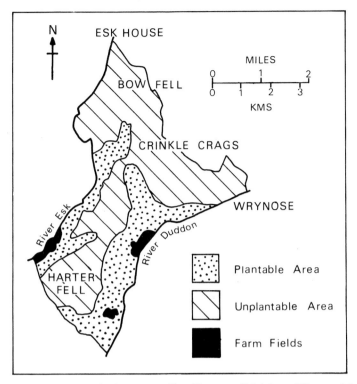

Fig. 17. The agreement as to the future use of land between Eskdale and Dunnerdale in the Lake District

respect of the 740 acres of plantable land in Eskdale which would not be afforested.

The Forestry Commission required the consent of the Treasury before entering into a formal agreement. Twentyman advised Barlow that the land was not being sold. The Commissioners would 'retain the farms, grazing rents, etc. What they are doing is to accept compensation for a restrictive covenant on the user of the land. Provided the compensation is adequate, this seems to me to be the right course to take in the public interest and to provide a satisfactory solution to the Eskdale difficulty'.

Consent was given, and the National Trust, CPRE, and the Commons, Open Spaces and Footpaths Preservation Society launched an appeal for the £1,480 required 'to preserve more than 5,000 acres' of Eskdale. The appeal was successful and, in 1943, the Forestry Commission issued a press notice, which described how 'all outstanding differences with regard to afforestation in Eskdale have now been settled and a Covenant between the Forestry Commission and National Trust has been agreed. By this arrangement, 827 acres in Eskdale will remain free from afforestation and public access will be assured to some 5,000 acres of unplantable fells.'[27]

ONE NEW PARK EVERY YEAR

The National Forest Park in Argyllshire was an immediate success. The number of people staying overnight (bed-nights) rose to 20,419 in 1937 and 30,870 in 1938. A National Forest Park of 23,000 acres was opened in the Forest of Dean in 1939, and another of 20,500 acres in Snowdonia in 1940. The main difficulty was that most of the plantations were still very young and extremely vulnerable to fire. In a letter to the chairman of the advisory committee for the Forest of Dean, Sir Roy Robinson emphasized that 'we have to bear in mind that timber production is still to proceed everywhere and that some of the young areas, such as Trellock, are still in a very inflammable state'. A proposal for a National Forest Park of 80,000 acres in the Kielder Forest was shelved in 1938 until the plantations were better established.[28]

In spite of these practical difficulties, the Forestry Commission became the most important statutory body for the provision of facilities for outdoor recreation, and during the war an assessment was made of a further twelve areas, including the Allerton and Langdale Forests of Yorkshire, and the Clunes, Inchnacardoch, Glengarry, Guisachan, and Glenhurich Forests of the Highlands. The Commissioners' report, *Post-war forestry policy*, published in 1943, claimed that 'one new Park might be established every year for the next ten years, at a capital outlay not exceeding £50,000. If on the other hand, it is desired to make a special feature of National Forest Parks, the provision of a further £100,000—making £150,000 in all—should enable the establishment of twenty Parks in all by the end of the first post-war decade.'[29]

The achievements and proposals did not, however, silence the advocates of national parks. The Standing Committee on National Parks stressed how recreation would always be subsidiary to the commercial interests of the Commission, and that National Forest Parks would necessarily be confined to the properties of the Commission. In their view National Forest Parks were a supplement, rather than an alternative, to national parks created primarily for their outstanding scenery and facilities for recreation. In 1939 John Dower drafted a National Parks Bill on behalf of the Standing Committee, which envisaged a national parks commission vested with statutory powers to achieve these ends.[30]

The Treasury also began to doubt whether the creation of National Forest Parks would provide 'a sufficient ground for refusal of Government assistance for National Parks of a more general character'. The cost of establishing a National Forest Park was only £4–5,000, and annual expenditure was as low as £1–2,000. There would clearly be funds left over for national parks, if the government believed them to be necessary.[31]

At this point, Herbert Gatliff wrote an internal memorandum in the Treasury which drew a distinction between north and south of the Scottish border. In Scotland the term 'national park really does mean wild mountains and the Forestry Commission happen to own some key spots'. The Argyllshire National Forest Park was already established and if the Commission could 'open up part of Cairngorm and allow some one to provide mountain huts there . . . that may prove a really dramatic move of considerable importance'. The position was very different in England and Wales, where the term national park covered a much wider range of landscape. In Gatliff's view, the Commission could not 'achieve anything very startling' because it did not own the 'key spots'. Even in the Lake District, a National Forest Park in Eskdale would not contribute very much because of the comparatively small area and the fact that 'there are so many other places where people can go freely in the Lake District'.

With the imminence of war, the national parks issue was soon dropped, but it was taken up again as part of the government's post-war reconstruction programme. In March 1943 a Ministry of Town and Country Planning was created with the responsibility for securing 'consistency and continuity in the framing and execution of a national policy with respect to the use and development of land throughout England and Wales'. The first steps to relate forestry to this responsibility were taken in June 1943 when the Minister met Robinson and emphasized the need for the Commissioners to consult the Ministry 'from the beginning on the selection of areas for post-war planting and in the use of land either for commercial plantings or for National Forest Parks'.[32]

Meanwhile, John Dower was appointed as a temporary civil servant to carry out an investigation of first 'the practical needs in certain potential areas' for parks and, later, the whole question of national parks. His report, completed in November 1943, repeated many of the proposals made by the Standing Committee in the 1930s, namely for a series of national parks and a national parks commission. On receiving a copy of his report, the Forestry Commissioners attacked Dower for being biased against forestry and for recommending a relatively expensive system of national parks, administered by a completely new body, when National Forest Parks would be much more practicable and an expert body was already in existence to administer them.[33]

At this point, the debate was abruptly terminated by the political considerations of the Ministry of Town and Country Planning and the Secretary of State for Scotland. In October 1943 the Forestry Commissioners decided to establish a National Forest Park of 40,000 acres at Glentrool. The Scottish Secretary was unaware of this until he received a letter inviting him to nominate a representative to the Park's advisory committee. As planning minister for Scotland, the Secretary took strong exception to the fact that he had not been consulted by the Commissioners when the idea of a new National Forest Park was first mooted.[34]

His complaint to the Lord Privy Seal, Clement Attlee, was upheld, and soon afterward the Secretary, Thomas Johnston, and the Minister of Town and Country Planning met to discuss ways of presenting 'a common front against any proposals by the Forestry Commission to pursue an independent policy with regard to national parks'. They affirmed that the primary responsibilities for national parks lay with the two planning ministers, and the Treasury was apprised of the situation 'so that they would know not to commit themselves to approving any expenditure on the establishment of a National Park in the Glentrool area' without first consulting the two ministers.

Although a National Parks Commission was established in 1949, and ten national parks were subsequently designated in England and Wales, the misgivings of the Forestry Commission over the Dower report were justified. It proved impracticable to appoint a National Parks Commission for Scotland, and no Parks were created in Scotland. Even in England and Wales, the management of the national parks was hampered by lack of funds and a lack of executive planning powers on the part of the National Parks Commission. Meanwhile the Forestry Commission not only maintained but extended its involvement in the outdoor recreational field. National Forest Parks were established in Glenmore (1948), the Queen Elizabeth Forest (1953), and Border Forest (1955). In aggregate, the eight Parks covered 430,200 acres, and recreational facilities were provided on a more modest scale in many other forests.[35]

CHAPTER XI

The Management of People

The countryside had long been regarded 'as a vast park or pleasure ground for the townsman', and, as the urban population grew in the nineteenth century, this role became proportionately greater. Even the poorer people tried to escape for a few hours, mainly to the urban commons where, traditionally, the commoners' livestock were grazed and fuel collected. As these common rights fell into disuse, the lords of the manors tried and often succeeded in enclosing part or all the commons for cultivation or building development. Either way, public access was severely curtailed, and the commoners were encouraged to challenge the legality of enclosure in a series of famous legal battles. Attention was drawn to 'the supreme necessity of preserving all that still remained open, for the health and recreation of the people'.[1]

The campaign to save Epping Forest succeeded and an Act of 1878 declared that the remnant of 2,300 acres would remain for ever open to public recreation and enjoyment, under the aegis of the Corporation of the City of London. The rapidly expanding population of late Victorian London and improving communications ensured the popularity of Epping Forest for visits at weekends and especially Bank Holidays. Individuals, families and organized parties came: an aggregate of between 100,000 and 200,000 people on a Bank Holiday in the 1890s. They were attracted by the rural environment and conscious provision of facilities for outdoor recreation: few actually strayed far into the woodlands. Refreshments and refuge from the weather were provided by the modest cottage tea-gardens, the existing hostelries, and the purpose-built 'retreats'. The latter were simply furnished wooden structures, positioned near beauty spots, where hundreds of people could enjoy inexpensive meals at one sitting. Some retreats had extra amenities in the form of coco-nut shies, roundabouts, helter-skelters and donkey or pony rides.[2]

This desire to escape into the countryside was not confined to the metropolis. J. B. Priestley recalled how Bradford had 'the good fortune to be on the edge of some of the most enchanting country in England. A sharp walk of less than an hour from more than one tram terminus will bring you to the moors, wild virgin highland, and every mill and warehouse will be out of sight and the whole city forgotten.' Men thought nothing of tramping up to forty miles every Sunday, and farmhouses supplied teas for sevenpence a head. The consequences of these rural tramps were enormous. Priestley recalled:

you caught the fever when you were quite young, and it never left you. However small and dark your office or warehouse was, somewhere inside your head the high moors were glowing, the curlews were crying, and there blew a wind as salt as if it came straight from the middle of the

Atlantic. That is why we did not care very much if our city had no charm, for it was simply a place to go and work in, until it was time to set out for Wharfedale or Wensleydale again.[3]

The popularity of the countryside showed no signs of abating in the inter-war period—quite the contrary. There were so many visitors to the Malvern Hills in the 1920s that the Conservators had to take steps to regulate the management of the Hills on their behalf. Under a further Malvern Hills Bill of 1930, they obtained powers to drain and renovate areas of turf, provide toilets and parking places, set aside land for organized games, exhibitions and displays, and formulate byelaws 'for the better regulation and protection of the Hills'. As the Chairman of the Conservators told a public meeting, 'it is essential in these days of thousands of cars congregating to have regulations, if only for the safety of the public'.[4]

On a return to Bradford in 1935, J. B. Priestley discovered that the local enthusiasm had not vanished. It had merely changed in character. Whereas men had once set out in twos and threes in their working-clothes, now there were 'gangs of either hikers or bikers, twenty or thirty of them together and all dressed for their respective parts'. They had an organized, semi-military, semi-athletic style. Another social commentator, C. E. M. Joad, was more concerned with the impact of these large numbers on the appearance and atmosphere of the countryside. He described a walk one fine Sunday morning in April from Hayfield along a path over the Derbyshire moors. 'It was a gorgeous path commanding wide views over miles of moorland country and finally descending steeply by Jacob's Ladder to Edale'. The path was unfenced: empty moorland stretched for miles on either side, and yet there were hundreds of walkers, both in front and behind Joad on that morning. He wrote, 'so close were we packed that we looked for all the world like a girls' school taking the air in "crocodile" on a Sunday afternoon'. The feeling of solitude and the wildness of the scenery was ruined.[5]

Joad blamed this congestion on the way in which visitors to the countryside were 'penned, cribbed, cabined, and confined' to the comparatively few rights-of-way left by landowners and tenants. In lowland England, attempts were frequently made to extinguish or physically destroy public rights-of-way, and the Commons, Open Spaces, and Footpaths Preservation Society, founded in the 1860s primarily to help preserve the commons around London, had to concentrate increasingly on safeguarding footpaths. Successes there were—the Essex County Council decided in 1933 on a general signposting of all public rights-of-way in the county, and the parish councils were asked to help in identifying such paths—but the general position was much less encouraging.[6]

The lack of public access was most serious on the upland grouse moors. On the uncultivated moorland between Manchester and Sheffield, an area of 230 square miles, there were only twelve footpaths over two miles in length. The bare plateau of the Peak itself was not crossed by a single path. The reason was that these heather-clad moorlands were preserved for grouse, and unrestricted public access would have made it more difficult to breed so many birds and to kill them so expeditiously. Joad argued that it was a question of values: whether it was better for a few people to enjoy their sport undisturbed, or for the close-penned populations of great industrial towns to have access to the natural beauty of the moors. It was against this background that the Access to Mountains Bills were introduced and debated, and one eventually passed in 1939.

Ever since the late nineteenth century, a long series of private members' Bills had sought to grant the public an automatic right of access to all mountains and moorlands for the purposes of recreation, subject to no damage being caused to property. The landowners had opposed the measures primarily because of the difficulties of defining such land and the inadequate safeguards granted to landowners. By 1938, however, the prospects for compromise were brighter, and the Access to Mountains Bill of that year received a second reading in parliament. Eventually the ramblers and land-owning factions reached a compromise whereby the areas of public access were to be defined and regulated much more rigorously than in the earlier Bills. The voluntary bodies, local authorities, and landowners were given the right to apply to the Ministry of Agriculture for an order to bring any area under the jurisdiction of the Act. As with so many compromises, it was a solution that pleased no one.[7]

Even if the Act of 1939 had met all the aspirations of the rambler, it would have been no solution to the more fundamental problems affecting outdoor recreation. In a lecture to the Royal Institute of British Architects in 1943, John Dower drew attention to the way in which recreation was becoming an extremely important form of land use. The increase in personal leisure time, the growing popularity of visits to the countryside and coast, and the rise in car ownership, had made the regulation of holiday-making an extremely urgent issue. It was not simply a question of discouraging the more obvious and disruptive types of outdoor recreation. The main problem was that so many people wanted to go on holiday. An increasing proportion of the working-population was eligible for holidays-with-pay. In 1938 a Holidays-with-Pay Bill was passed, which required statutory bodies enforcing minimum wages to provide at least a week's paid holiday each year. As Dower warned, there would be inevitable and complete chaos in the major resorts and recognized 'amenity' areas if the whole nation took a holiday at the same time. Irreparable damage would be caused to the very amenities sought by visitors in such areas as the Lake District, Snowdonia and Dartmoor.[8]

One way to alleviate the problem was to adopt a comprehensive planning strategy. Most holiday-makers wanted the noise, crowds, and amusements of a popular resort, holiday camp, or bungalow village, and Dower asserted that it would be 'ostrich-like folly' to ignore the great demand. One of the greatest challenges was to accommodate the need through 'good planning and gay-harmonious design'. To be successful, the new resorts would have to be on attractive, rather than dull or spoilt, lengths of coast. This might mean sacrificing a number of previously undisturbed coastlines, but this was surely preferable to the sporadic holiday development of all the coastline. By the conscious and adequate provision of what the 'crowds' wanted, the pressure would be taken off the more outstanding and vulnerable tracts of coast and countryside.

It is the intention of this Chapter to illustrate one way in which local authorities and government departments first recognized some of the harmful changes which outdoor recreation could bring to the environment. It describes how powers were taken to regulate pleasure-camping under the Public Health Act of 1936 which, together with more recent planning legislation, still forms the basis for controlling the holiday use of tents, caravans, and shacks. The Act represented an early attempt to accord the maximum amount of freedom to the holiday-makers and yet preserve the health and amenity of the country and coast.

HEALTH, GOOD BEHAVIOUR, AND AMENITY

Outdoor recreation could take several forms. Some liked to have a roof over their heads after a day's hike, and for them the Youth Hostels Association was founded in 1930. This provided cheap country 'inns' where young people on walking and cycling holidays could stay for a shilling a night, with breakfast for another shilling. By 1933 the YHA had 28,000 members, and over 270 hostels by 1935. Others preferred to erect their own shelter and, as an official committee observed in 1934, 'there can be no doubt whatever that there has since the Great War been a great development in camping. The value of an open air life as a means of improving health and developing physical strength and hardiness was being more and more realised.' Camping was 'an inexpensive form of recreation', ideal for those on 'restricted means'.[9]

Some campers joined a club, and the membership of the largest, the Camping Club of Great Britain and Ireland, rose from 1,400 in 1920 to 3,000 in 1927, and exceeded 6,000 by 1933. However, many more campers 'did not want to be under any regulations, and they pitched their tents here, there and everywhere'. Complaints were soon voiced: whilst conceding the benefits of camping, the Scarborough Town Council denied that every landowner and occupier should be allowed to let their land for camping purposes. The Wirral Rural District Council in Cheshire described in 1934 how hundreds of people invaded the district on fine week-ends, pitching 'tents in fields where there is neither water supply, sanitary conveniences, or receptacles for refuse, the result being that by Monday morning the tents have all disappeared, and the refuse therefrom is left lying about the ground, and ditches are polluted by sewage'.[10]

Confident of a continued rise in the number of pleasure-campers, a close scrutiny was made of existing statutory powers. The Public Health Act of 1875 enabled a local authority to intervene where public health was at risk. Under the Housing of the Working Classes Act of 1885 and Public Health (Scotland) Act of 1897, byelaws could be adopted to promote cleanliness in camps, subject to the consent of the Minister. The Ministry of Health reported 'many cases of success, but conceded that they were 'at a great price in time, energy and money, and without finality'. Very often, the powers adopted for the control of 'a few scattered gypsies and homeless people living in tents and dilapidated huts' proved inappropriate for the regulation of holiday-makers.[11]

Local authorities could only take proceedings when the structures were in position and occupied. The consequent litigation was so complicated, costly, and unpleasant that many local authorities advocated the introduction of a new system whereby all camping would be forbidden, except where the consent of the appropriate local authority was obtained. There would be provision for appeals to the courts against any unreasonable decision on the part of a council. The Home Office, however, opposed this, claiming that anyone who wanted to live in a caravan, tent, or shack should not have to go 'cap in hand' to the council. Instead, 'he ought to be allowed to live in this way without this necessity, subject to his not abusing the opportunity' and committing no nuisances.[12]

The Ministry of Health claimed that the licensing principle had already been adopted under the Public Health Acts Amendment Act of 1907 which required any person 'who erects or sets up a temporary building' first to obtain the consent of the local authority in order to ensure that adequate services and facilities were available. Because of the difficulties of applying a general definition of temporary building, local magistrates were left to decide 'on the merits of each case'. This caused so much uncertainty that local authorities had to apply to the High Courts for a declaration on the status of structures before deciding whether and how to take proceedings.[13]

Local authorities were further deterred by the difficulties of successfully prosecuting those persons actually committing nuisances. As the Clerk to the Epsom Rural District Council in Surrey remarked in 1931, 'you are continually getting fresh people. If you serve a notice on A, he goes, and B comes, and you have to serve a notice on B, and so you continue'. If an offender wanted to stay on a site, he could often evade a court order by reconstructing the offending structure a little differently or by moving it *in toto* to another site a few yards away.[14]

In these circumstances many authorities advocated prosecuting the site owner rather than individual campers, especially as the owner often made considerable profits from the camp and was 'more responsible and capable of understanding the law'. Using this method, the Leicester Corporation successfully applied to the courts under the Public Health Act of 1875 for the clearance of shacks and the prohibition of further structures for two years. But this case was exceptional: the Act stated that notice had to be served on the offender 'or, if such a person cannot be found, on the owner or occupier of the premises'. Usually, this was interpreted to mean that an action could only be brought against the owner if the local authority could prove the actual offender could not be traced, and this was rarely possible in practice.[15]

By 1936 seventy-six authorities in England and Wales, and three in Scotland, had tried to remove these limitations and ambiguities by taking extra powers under Local Acts of Parliament. A common-form clause evolved, whereby a licence was required before a tent, van, or shack could be occupied. It became illegal to let or permit any land to be used for these purposes until the local authority was satisfied that adequate services and facilities were provided. The Bills exempted all tents, vans, and shacks of less than three months' standing, and allowed appeals to the courts against any decisions of the local authority. Nevertheless the Home Office opposed the common-form clauses on the grounds that some authorities might use them to eliminate all campers, and especially gipsies. The promoters of the Bills denied this, asserting that they wished to regulate, and not eliminate, camping.[16]

Initially attention was focused on safeguarding public health, but by the late 1920s a number of local authorities had become equally concerned at the incidence of bad behaviour and damage to amenity arising from uncontrolled camping. As an illustration the local council at Formby in Lancashire described the considerable noise which arose from thousands of campers on the dunes and foreshore at summer weekends. Near the famous Surrey beauty spot of Box Hill, old underground and railway carriages, tramcars, buses, pantechnicons, and 'every sort of vehicle that is capable of being converted into a dwelling house' were parked. Although 'generally unpainted and dilapidated', and extremely detrimental to the amenities of the area, they did not constitute a risk to public health and so the local authority was powerless to intervene.[17]

From 1922 onwards the Rural District Councils Association tried to promote Bills to forbid all camping sites unless the local authority was satisfied that there was no threat from disorderly behaviour or damage to amenity or public health. This was opposed by the various camping interests which claimed that councils would make this an excuse for clearing entire districts of camping. The Home Office persistently blocked the Bills, lest some courts might accept 'aesthetic prejudices' as sufficient 'evidence of danger to amenity'.[18]

The threat to amenity was first recognized in Surrey, which was popular for camping due to its proximity to London and the beauty spots of the downs and heaths. Many campers were 'quite decent people, taking their holidays on the cheap', but the County Council contended that 'it is not right, if the amenities of this County are to be protected, that it should be open to these people or to anyone else to pitch their dwellings where they like without any regard at all to the effect that these unsightly dwellings are going to have on the neighbourhood generally'. In view of the exceptional circumstances of the county, the Surrey County Council obtained a new code for regulating camps under its Local Act of 1931 (see p. 15). Instead of the campers and site owners being required to obtain a licence (as under the common-form clauses of Local Acts), all the local authorities in Surrey were given the right to apply for a court order to close any camp where disruptive behaviour occurred or amenity was harmed. Appeals could be made to a higher court.[19]

Whilst the Local Acts' common-form clause and the Surrey clause helped their respective areas, they had two unfortunate effects: first, there was a great deal of confusion as to the powers held by each local authority and, secondly, the strengthening of powers in one district often had the effect of merely transferring the camping problem to the next. When the Mablethorpe and Skegness Urban District Councils took extra powers, the displaced caravan-dwellers simply moved to the adjoining rural district.[20]

Further complications arose when the Essex County Council tried to follow the precedent of Surrey. Unlike Surrey, Essex also wanted to strengthen its powers over public health, and both the Select Committees scrutinizing the Local Bill, and government departments, opposed the granting of the common-form clause and Surrey clause to the same districts. Accordingly, the Bill was amended so that the common-form clause was adopted in urban districts of over 20,000 inhabitants, where concern for public health was uppermost, and the Surrey clause elsewhere in Essex.[21]

Fresh difficulties arose when Plympton St. Mary Rural District Council in Devon promoted a Bill which included the Surrey clause, largely to control the activities of naturists. Although an Unopposed Bill, the Select Committee responsible for scrutinizing it refused to grant such powers to individual rural district councils. Instead, the council was allowed to adopt byelaws which safeguarded not only public health but also public behaviour and amenity. Recognizing that this added a further complication to the regulation of camping, the chairman of the Select Committee called for an urgent review of all general statutes and Local Acts as they affected camping.[22]

THE STATUS OF THE PLEASURE-CAMPER

By this time, even the government departments accepted the need for a fresh appraisal of camping legislation. On the personal initiative of the Secretary of State, a report was issued by the Scottish Council on Local Health, Administration and General Health Questions, which recommended fresh powers to control camping in Scotland. The common-form clauses should be 'blended' with the Surrey clause. Campers or alternatively site owners should be required to obtain a licence before erecting tents, vans, or shacks, and the licence would be granted only if the local authority was satisfied with respect to health, amenity, and orderly behaviour. The Department of Health for Scotland accepted the recommendations and 'entered camping on the list of subjects for government legislation'. The Scottish Secretary gave consent for a draft Camping Grounds (Scotland) Bill to be prepared.[23]

In England and Wales matters came to a head when the West Riding County Council started to promote a Bill for adopting the common-form clause throughout the county. It provided the occasion for a meeting in February 1933 at which representatives of the local government associations urged the Ministry of Health to introduce a Public Health Amendment Bill to codify and extend general legislation on camping. A member of the Ministry warned that parliament might not automatically generalize all the powers that had been granted to local authorities under earlier Local Acts. The local government associations would considerably strengthen their case by carrying out a survey of all councils to 'supply definite instances where experience has shown the existing law to be ineffective'.[24]

A survey was accordingly carried out and confirmed the 'extensive scale up and down the country, especially in recent years, of insanitary conditions arising from the erection of shacks and moveable dwellings of various kinds, and in a lesser degree from the use of tents'. However, the Ministry could not hold out much hope of early legislation, and advised the local government associations to promote a private member's Bill. The Minister would probably grant the Bill facilities if it was an 'agreed measure'. If hotly contested, 'it would probably have to go down in order to save the time of the House'.[25]

The main point of controversy was the extent to which holiday-makers, camping for a few days, should be regulated. The earlier controls were primarily directed against gipsies, tinkers, and vagrants, and had exempted those camping for periods of up to three months. But increasingly the counties most affected by pleasure-camping sought to remove this time-exemption. The East Lothian County Council claimed that short-term campers often caused far more trouble than longer-term campers who had a greater interest in the site and its environs. The Dunbartonshire County Council argued that local authorities should have a right to control holiday campers who required such services as scavenging and yet contributed nothing in rates. In Renfrewshire, Ayrshire, and Dunbartonshire, byelaws were allowed by the minister which regulated all campers who stayed for more than one, two, and three nights respectively. Shorter periods of exemption were also obtained under Local Acts: for example, the Bridlington Corporation Act of 1933 granted only a month's exemption.[26]

This soon led to warnings that 'it will be almost impossible for lovers of the open air to indulge in camp life'. Members of the Camping Club of Great Britain had recourse to about 2,000 sites in England, Wales, and Scotland by 1935, where the owners often derived little or no income. The Club feared that the owners would regard any regulations 'as official interference and to avoid this would refuse to allow the use of their land', leading to a serious shortage of sites.[27] Even a leader in the *Surveyor and Municipal and County Engineer* warned that the imposition of restrictions by over-zealous local officials would destroy the essential challenge of camping for 'the younger folk of the nation'. It stressed how 'the construction of latrines and incinerators, and the conveyance in buckets from the nearest pond or stream of the temporary water supply, were all part of the game'.[28]

Recognizing these differences of opinion, the Council for the Preservation of Rural England (CPRE) set up a committee in 1934 'to find a basis of settlement as between all the interests concerned which might form the subject of a Private Member's Bill'. The committee agreed unanimously on the need for regulation, and its chairman, Sir Lawrence Chubb, proposed a formula whereby no owner or occupier could let a site for camping without a licence granted by the local authority. The various camping organizations agreed, subject to campers staying for less than three months being exempted. The local government associations refused to make this concession, and deadlock ensued.[29]

The local government associations believed a private member's Bill with the three-month exemption would be useless: the Ministry of Health disagreed, pointing out that the survey of local authorities had identified only five rural and five urban cases where problems had arisen entirely through pleasure-camping. The Ministry was especially sceptical of the motives of those councils representing seaside resorts. In considering the Blackpool Corporation Bill of 1935 a member of the Ministry commented, 'one cannot help the suspicion about these representations from places like Blackpool that it is not only health interests which prompt them. Probably the interests of the apartment house-keepers (a very large proportion of the ratepayers) have a good deal to do with it'.[30]

For its part, the Rhyl Urban District Council claimed that the prosperity of its ratepayers was a legitimate reason for controlling campers. In a Local Bill of 1935, the council followed the Plympton St. Mary precedent in seeking powers to impose byelaws on campers for the protection of public order and amenity. A census of August 1934 had indicated that there were 2,340 tents and caravans crowded into the district. Hoteliers and boarding-house keepers not only resented the cheapness and informality of camping, but also the frequent bad behaviour of many campers which would 'drive away the better-class visitors'. In the local elections of that year, candidates warned that Rhyl had no industry and that any diminution in the number of hotels and other traditional holiday-making facilities would lead to serious local unemployment and fall in rateable income. Despite the benefits of camping, one class of holiday-maker should not be allowed to interfere with the comfort of residents and other visitors. The Select Committee scrutinizing the Rhyl Bill accepted this view: in spite of opposition from the Home Office and Ministry of Health, the Committee regarded the impact of pleasure-camping as so serious that no landowner should be allowed to let his land for camping without a licence granted by the urban district council. There would be no time-exemptions.[31]

A Central Committee on Camping Legislation was formed as early as 1928, mainly at the instigation of the Camping Club of Great Britain. This accepted the need to regulate unorganized camping and 'the increasing use of unsightly shacks and caravans', but the Committee insisted that the 'good campers should not be penalised because of the bad'. Many of the difficulties arose out of ignorance rather than malicious intent on the part of the campers. The Central Committee argued that it would be far more equitable and effective to encourage the efforts of bodies such as the Camping Club of Great Britain in their 'educational work'. Through their rules and the example of their members, novices would soon learn the rudiments of good camping.[32]

Local Act common-form clauses drew a distinction between military, religious (Salvation Army), and juvenile (Scouts and Guides) camps, and the remainder of campers. Not only did the Surrey, Plympton St. Mary and Rhyl

Acts follow this precedent, but the exemption from regulation was extended to cover the members and sites belonging to recognized camping associations, such as the Camping Club of Great Britain. Provisions were made for appeal to the Minister of Health in the event of any dispute over the status of an organization. The Home Office, however, condemned such concessions as discriminating against 'ordinary members of the public who prefer to be independent'. The concessions were objectionable inasmuch as the privileged societies would advertise the exemptions as a means of augmenting their membership. Far from being reasonable, the exemptions indicated 'the difficulties of formulating any proposals which are compatible with the freedom of roaming to which all persons are entitled'.

The Public Health Act of 1936

This account of the regulation of camping in the countryside has been complicated by the need to make reference to the various pressure groups, government departments, earlier legislation, and different kinds of byelaw. These details have been introduced because they provide the essential framework within which such questions as the personal freedom of the camper and the need to protect the common good were debated. Sometimes the framework can take on even greater significance, when, for example, the existence of a committee or piece of proposed legislation provides the stimulus for further discussion which, in turn, leads to new policies and concepts.

This was the case with respect to camping in the mid-1930s. As early as 1929 a departmental committee had been set up to recommend ways of securing greater clarity, uniformity, and precision in legislation affecting local government and public health. In 1936 the committee submitted a draft Public Health Bill which included the consolidation of all the general statutes related to camping. The new Bill made it clear that legal proceedings could be taken against either the camper or the owner of a site.[33]

The departmental committee believed that further powers should be taken to control semi-permanent camps used by 'gypsies and people of that kind' and the camps used by a succession of holiday-makers, where conditions soon became insanitary and unsightly. Further discussions were encouraged between the local government associations and camping bodies, and eventually a compromise was reached which was incorporated in the Bill. This introduced a general licensing system, whereby consent would be granted to campers or site-owners if the local authorities were satisfied about the number and class of dwellings, density, water supply, and sanitation. Exemptions were granted to those structures and sites (defined as areas of at least 100 yards in radius) used for less than forty-two consecutive days or less than sixty days in the twelve consecutive months.[34]

Exemptions were also available to those organizations which satisfied the Minister of Health that their grounds and structures were maintained to a very high standard. In the event, not only the guides, scouts, and Salvation Army received certificates of exemption, but also the Camping Club of Great Britain, in spite of some opposition from local authorities. The Camping Club regarded exemption as 'official recognition': membership of the Club would provide campers with 'a magic passport to camping freedom and independence'.[35]

This exemption was particularly important in view of an amendment made to the Bill when it was scrutinized by a Joint Committee of both Houses. The Ministry of Health had intended the extended powers to be automatically applied to only the borough and urban district councils: rural district councils would have to apply for an Order from the Minister before exercising such powers. This reflected the continued mistrust of rural councils and fears lest they would use any extra powers to clear, rather than regulate, camping. A member of the Parliamentary Counsel Office added, 'the big camps of semi-permanent caravans' were 'found almost entirely in the seaside resorts and places where there are attractions like cinemas and bands and music'. The parliamentary Joint Committee vigorously challenged this, citing examples where semi-permanent camps were located just inside rural districts, adjacent to a seaside resort. They insisted that the rural and urban authorities should be treated in a similar manner.[36]

Thereafter, any regulations imposed by a town planning scheme were based on those included in the Public Health Act. In 1947 the Town and Country Planning Act of 1932 was replaced by another of the same name, which required the owners of new camp sites in any part of the country to obtain the consent of the local planning authority. Reference would be made to the development plan of the area, conditions could be imposed, and appeals could be made to the Minister. In order to safeguard holiday-makers, a General Development Order was made under the Act, which exempted from regulation the use of land or placing of moveable structures for up to twenty-eight days in each calendar year.[37]

The provisions of the Public Health Act did not apply to Scotland, and the earlier report of the Consultative Council and contents of the draft Camping Grounds (Scotland) Bill remained confidential. The Department of Health waited to see how the new controls fared in England and Wales. Although the question of an *ad hoc* measure or a Public Health Bill for Scotland was occasionally considered, the outbreak of war blocked further progress.[38]

PERSONAL FREEDOM AND THE COMMON GOOD

The regulation of camping provided an early example of the difficulties of reconciling forms of outdoor recreation with the preservation of the environment. The efforts made to promote camping clauses in the various Local Bills and in the Public Health Act of 1936 indicate the extent to which outdoor recreation had begun to have an effect on the countryside and coast. In the words of the Department of Health for Scotland, the controls had the merit 'of following close on the emergence of the problem'.

It was not, however, enough to perceive an actual or potential threat to the environment. There had to be positive proof of serious damage before parliament could be persuaded to take remedial action. It was the object of the local government associations to provide this proof. The lack of basic data on camping was a serious handicap for all interested parties in reaching agreement as to the optimal level of control. It provided a further example of the general dearth of information on land use in Britain. Once the damage had been proven, there were two methods of making a response. One was to do everything possible to eliminate outdoor recreation. The second was to foresee and make provision for the invasion of visitors and, in the words of C. E. M. Joad, 'to educate the invaders and to canalize their inflow until they are educated'.[39]

In adopting the second course, a fine balance had to be struck between sustaining the personal freedom of the camper and the general need to preserve health and amenity. In his lecture on the holiday-use of land in 1943, John Dower described how most people tolerated a great deal of control over their daily lives, and applauded in principle the safeguarding of the countryside and coast, but they expected to be left alone 'to choose their holidays freely and to move about individually as they feel inclined'. Technically, a total ban on unlicensed camping was required, but politically this was impossible, and so the clauses in the Public Health Act of 1936 had to be a compromise.

CHAPTER XII

The Management of Amenity

Throughout the inter-war period, emphasis was laid on securing the protection of amenity and public access to the countryside. Comparatively little thought was given to how amenity and the public would be managed, once protection and access had been attained. Many assumed that Nature would look after herself and that the natural custodians of the countryside, namely the farmer and woodsman, would continue to keep the landscape looking tidy as a by-product of their everyday work. This assumption was no longer justified, and it gradually became clear in many parts of the countryside that amenity would only be protected and enhanced if management programmes were devised and implemented specifically for that purpose. Experience with the roadside planting of trees and grass verges soon indicated the practical difficulties which would arise from such new ventures in landscape management.

CUSTODIANS OF THE COUNTRYSIDE

According to the Scott report, published in 1942 (see p. 24), farming provided more than food and a source of income for rural communities—farmers acted as the natural custodians of the amenity of the countryside. Even if there were no economic, social, or strategic reasons for maintaining agriculture, the Majority report regarded amenity as so important as to justify sustaining and increasing the area of agricultural land. Farming was the cheapest, and indeed the only practical way, of preserving the countryside in anything like its traditional aspect.[1]

In the words of the Majority Report, 'the landscape of England and Wales is a striking example of the interdependence between the satisfaction of man's material wants and the creation of beauty'. The appearance of the landscape was neither natural nor static. It had been created or induced by man and his livestock, and would change in aspect and composition whenever changes occurred in the use and management of the land. The beauty and pattern of the countryside were the direct result of the cultivation of the soil and, the Majority Report emphasized, 'there is no antagonism between use and beauty'.

The events of the inter-war period illustrated how beauty suffered when the land was abandoned or neglected. As a result of the depression in farming,

less arable land was to be seen in the landscape; the number of derelict fields, rank with coarse matted grass, thistles, weeds and brambles, multiplied; ditches became choked and no longer served as effective drains; hedges became overgrown and straggled over the edges of the fields; gates and fences fell into disrepair; farm roads were left unmade. Signs of decay were to be seen also in many buildings. Barns and sheds were not put in order; farmhouses were allowed to deteriorate; agricultural cottages went from bad to worse. Whilst, when seen from afar, it retained the beauty of the old broad pattern, the landscape of 1938 had, in many districts, assumed a neglected and unkempt appearance.

Clearly, the protection of amenity did not mean allowing the countryside to go back to Nature. The countryside had to be farmed in order to retain 'those features which gave it distinctive charm and character'. The Majority Report described farmers as 'unconsciously the nation's landscape gardeners', and to help them secure their task of maintaining and enhancing the beauty of the rural landscape every effort had to be made to preserve farmland from industrial and other, alien forms of development. This aesthetic reason for preserving agricultural land was just as important as the need for more home-grown food and a contented rural population.

In his Minority Report, Dennison accused the remainder of the Committee and the voluntary bodies of exaggerating the damage inflicted on amenity by building and industrial development on farmland. Only a very small proportion of farmland would be affected. Between 1927 and 1939, only an average of 0.15 per cent of agricultural land was converted to other uses in each year. Dennison contended that even if this rate was doubled, the losses to amenity would be small, and statutory planning should be able to prevent development taking place in the most beautiful areas. It was not so much a stark choice between amenity and no amenity, as between more or less. Most of the countryside would remain as farmland. The real dilemma was how much of this farmland could be preserved for its beauty, bearing in mind the alternative uses and cost to the nation.

Dennison also attacked the premise that amenity depended on the pursuit of traditional forms of land husbandry. Beauty could take many forms: a predominantly pastoral or arable landscape could be just as attractive as a mixture of land use. Improved grassland could be as beautiful as wild moorland or a fellside. In the same way as man had created an attractive landscape in the past by farming, so he could create new landscapes and enhance the old by adopting new farming methods.

In support of his views, Dennison cited a section from a book by a leading agriculturalist, Sir Daniel Hall, published in 1941. In his book, *Reconstruction and the land*, Hall criticized those parts of the countryside which looked, from a distance, like woodland, where the numerous little patches of woodland and lines of hedgerow 'intruded on to good farming land'. Their value as timber and as shelter for livestock was far outstripped by their cost in providing havens for weeds, rabbits, and other vermin. Not only were the copses and small fields obstacles to farm machinery, but aesthetically they destroyed 'the noble contours of the ground . . . too much of our land looks overcrowded and fidgety'. Even if the creation of larger fields destroyed 'something of its snug, "comfortable" aspect', the countryside would benefit from being 'rendered simpler and of a wider sweep'.[2]

Amenity and the Ministry of Agriculture

Wildlife was an important ingredient of the amenity of the countryside. Naturalists and biologists were gradually building up a comprehensive, and often detailed, picture of the distribution and character of wild plants and animals in Britain, and it was in order to preserve both the amenity and scientific value of these wildlife communities that the first overtures were made for the Ministry of Agriculture to become involved more widely in the countryside.[3]

By the First World War, the National Trust owned thirteen sites of special interest to the naturalist, and in 1912 the Society for the Promotion of Nature Reserves (SPNR) was created, primarily to assist the National Trust and local societies in protecting further areas of wildlife interest. To this end, the SPNR organized a survey of areas 'worthy of protection', and notified landowners and occupiers of the importance of their properties. During 1915 a list of 273 areas 'worthy of protection' in England, Wales, Scotland and Ireland was submitted to the Board of Agriculture. On the basis of experience in Germany and elsewhere, the SPNR stressed that little could be achieved in protecting these areas without 'the approval and assistance of the Board'.

The Board of Agriculture supported the Society's successful application for a Royal Charter, and two members of the Board were nominated to serve on the Society's executive committee. In 1916 the Board seriously considered making a grant to the SPNR, but it was decided that the time was inopportune and that little could be achieved until after the war.

Later in 1916 the SPNR was alarmed to learn of plans for large-scale land improvement schemes in Cornwall and elsewhere, and the Society called upon the Board of Agriculture to help preserve the more important areas for wildlife as nature reserves. A member of the Board wrote:

from the entomological point of view there is a point in favour of these Nature Reserves which is perhaps just worth mentioning. Agriculture so interferes with the balance of nature that certain pests previously scarce are enabled to increase and do great harm. Artificial remedies—spraying, insecticides and the like are expensive and not always efficient, and it would be better from all points of view if we could discover the natural checks which formerly prevented the insects from becoming numerous. To do this however we must study the insects in their natural surroundings, i.e. in nature reserves, which therefore have a definite economic value

Despite this support for nature reserves, the Board decided to take no action. The President, R. E. Prothero, described the Society's fears as groundless: there was so much land that could be reclaimed for cultivation that there was not the slightest chance of all the 'natural beauty spots' being eliminated. In any case the Society's proposal to recommend the creation of nature reserves would be 'a considerable extension of the Board's active interest in the matter. It is one thing for them to be represented on the Council of the Society and quite another thing for them to communicate direct with local authorities or the public as to the value of Nature Reserves'. There the matter rested.

Between the wars, the Ministry of Agriculture adopted a somewhat ambivalent attitude toward statutory planning. The Ministry supported planning controls where they helped reduce the amount of farmland converted to other uses, but it vigorously opposed any attempt to regulate the construction or design of farm buildings. When the East Sussex County Council proposed, in the South Downs Preservation Bill of 1934 (see p. 100), to prohibit small-holdings and market-gardens because of the way in which the associated buildings would spoil the amenity of the South Downs, the Ministry threatened to block the Bill. This was in spite of the fact that the Bill was primarily designed to preserve the rural environment of the downland.

Throughout the inter-war period, the Ministry did its utmost to remain aloof from questions related to the protection of amenity and the promotion of outdoor recreation. It was only too happy to concur with the decision of Ramsay MacDonald that the issue of national parks should be left to the Ministry of Health. It was only by default that the Ministry of Agriculture became re-sponsible for regulating rambling under the Access to Mountains Act of 1939 (see p. 195). The Ministry was appalled at such an obligation, especially in view of the impossibility of forecasting how much work the issuing of orders would involve. The arrangement was, however, an essential part of the hard-won compromise, and the landowners rejected any idea of the Ministry of Health issuing the orders instead. Much to the relief of the Ministry of Agriculture, the outbreak of war soon provided an opportunity to suspend this part of the Act before any orders were made.

In 1942 the publication of the Scott Report inspired B. C. Engholm of the Ministry to write a memorandum calling for a more positive approach on the part of the Ministry of Agriculture to questions related to amenity and outdoor recreation. There had been a considerable increase in public interest in plan-ning, and the government had given a pledge to set up a central planning authority. The various voluntary bodies were pressing the government to include the protection of natural beauty among its responsibilities, and the Ministry of Works and Planning was already devoting a great deal of attention to such questions as national parks, access to the countryside, and footpaths. Engholm believed that the Ministry of Agriculture would be much better placed than any other Ministry to look after the interests of the amenity organizations.[4]

Engholm described how the Scott Committee had stressed the close inter-dependence of agriculture and the preservation of the countryside. Amenity depended on the land being well farmed, and farmers had to be protected from damage to their crops and fences. If the Ministry could help to persuade the voluntary bodies of 'the community of interests between agriculture and amenity', this would greatly help to strengthen the Ministry's hand. A large body of urban opinion would soon support 'a strong and progressive agri-cultural policy'. By taking the initiative, the Ministry would be in a much more powerful position to prevent any clash between farming and amenity.

There was a further reason why Engholm believed that the Ministry, rather than a central planning authority, should look after the interests of amenity. There was a strong feeling that the Ministry should concern itself with all rural matters and not confine itself to purely technical agricultural problems. 'Rural life, and everything appertaining to rural interests, is of the utmost importance from the agricultural standpoint', and Engholm contended that amenity was an essential part of that rural life. He cited the case of national parks, which would necessarily include a considerable number of farms and land suitable for afforestation. The Ministry would have to take a very close interest in the creation of national parks, and its task 'would probably be greatly simplified if it were to take an active interest in the amenity point of view as well'.

Not everyone agreed with Engholm's advocacy of a wider role for the Ministry, and a pencilled note on his memorandum indicates that the Deputy Secretary disagreed with the views expressed. The Ministry was overstretched in meeting its primary task of producing food to sustain a country at war, and its overriding priority after the war would be to establish 'a sound and progressive policy'. Whatever the merits of exploiting the goodwill of the amenity bodies, nothing should be done to deflect the Ministry from this central task. Accordingly, the initiatve for representing the amenity organizations remained with the new Ministry of Town and Country Planning, created in 1943.

AMENITY AND PROGRESSIVE FARMING

Like so many others, John Dower took a sanguine view of the impact of agricultural improvements on amenity, but he qualified his optimism by adding that 'he was not afraid of the sort of change that came properly and rightly from well-considered agricultural change'. By this he meant emulating the landowners of the eighteenth and nineteenth centuries, who had regarded the landscaping of farmland as something over and above the economics of farming. According to Dower, 'it should be the duty and pleasure of the land-owner to add to—or rather combine with—the sheer economics of farming the maintenance and creation of landscape beauties, by the "amenity" planting of trees and hedges and in other ways'.[5]

This presupposed that landowners and farmers were free agents in discharging their duties toward the landscape, but there was already evidence of their having to take account of wider issues to the detriment of amenity. As early as 1937 A. G. Street described the considerable pressures being exerted on some farmers greatly to extend their arable acreage. In order to compete with overseas' suppliers, this would inevitably mean the destruction of hedgerows and trees in order to make the fields larger for mechanical cultivation and harvesting.[6]

The Scott committee took a rather complacent view of the potential impact of farm mechanization. Although recognizing how tractors had increased productivity and had helped to extend the area of cultivation, the committee believed the over-all effect would be simply to revive the 'former well-kept appearance' of the landscape. There would be 'no striking change in the pattern of the countryside'.

Table 2. *Possible trends in land use in Great Britain, as indicated by L. D. Stamp in 1937*

Present Use	per cent	Use after Reconditioning	per cent	Total per cent
Arable—intensive (market gardening, etc)	2	→Arable—intensive (market gardening)	2	5
Arable—farm crops	20	→Arable—intensive	3	
		→Arable—farm crops	16	26
		→Orchards and fruit	1	
Permanent grassland First class	10	→Arable—farm crops	10	
		→Grassland—first class	16	16
Other	21	→Grassland—other	5	
Rough grazing in enclosed fields (derelict or idle permanent grass)	9	→Permanent grassland	9	22
Heathland, moorland and other rough grazing, mostly unenclosed	26	→Permanent grass	8	
		→Recreational, sporting, national parks	9	9
		→Forest and woodland, for timber	8	
Forest and woodland For timber	2.5	→For timber	3.5	11·5
Other economic	1.0	→Other economic uses	2.5	2.5
Scrubland and uneconomic	3.0	→Uneconomic	0.5	0.5
Orchards and fruit	0.5	→Orchard and fruit	0.5	1.5
Residual (housing, industrial, roads, etc.)	5	Residual (allowance for →improvement of housing, etc.)	6	6

In his book, *Reconstruction and town and country planning*, published in 1942, Sir Gwilym Gibbon took the opposite view. He wrote, 'the fact surely is that agriculture is passing through a revolution no less than industry, though in slower motion, and it is almost any man's guess how far the changes will go . . . that marvel, the modern tractor, is altering much and will alter more, and it has other fellow-machines which follow its trail'. Far from the Scott committee writing a new chapter for the countryside, the Majority Report was based on the assumptions of the Age of the Horse. Gibbon believed that the future of farming lay with the motor.[7]

In fairness, even the leading advocates of progressive farming were unclear as to the eventual impact of their revolution on land use. R. G. Stapledon described the scope for the upgrading of British agriculture as enormous. The extensive areas of pasture, previously used for rearing cattle and running sheep, could be improved by cultivation, new crop rotations, drainage, and fertilizers. In order to sustain the displaced livestock, there would have to be a programme to upgrade the 'now un-reclaimed and singularly unproductive regions of rough and hill grazing'. The implications of such a policy were further explored by Dudley Stamp, using the land-use statistics that were becoming available from his Land Utilisation Survey. Stamp's estimates of the potential for changes in land use are indicated in Table 2. Whereas previously, such large-scale changes would have been uneconomic, the 'nationalistic policies of self-sufficiency being pursued by each nation' were beginning to make such a programme feasible.[8]

Stapledon tried to allay fears of any threat to the appearance of upland scenery by stressing how it would be impossible to transform the entire area of rough grazings into a 'clean and well grazed fescue pasture'. Perhaps only a third of the land would be suitable for improvement, and the intermingling of improved and unimproved pasture would heighten the light and shade effects, and greatly enhance the contrasts of scenery in the uplands. In the words of Stapledon, the grassland-improver was an artist on a huge canvas; he enhances the beauty of the landscape.

In his book, *Reconstruction and the land*, Sir Daniel Hall also took a complacent view of the implications of mechanization, drainage, fertilizers, and other large-scale changes for the amenity of the countryside. In recommending the clearance of hedgerows and coppice, Hall assured his readers that 'one need not fear that England will be deprived of its trees; there is no lack of steep slopes and bad land that is better planted' with trees, where no machine would venture and no farmer would risk his capital. And yet, elsewhere in his book, Hall envisaged the reclamation of some of the most marginal and remote areas for intensive agricultural use. He described the reclamation of some 5,000 acres of Borth Bog, on the Mawddach estuary in mid-Wales, and of the inland moors on Hatfield Chase, near the mouth of the river Trent. Such peat mosses as Tregaron Bog in mid-Wales, the Fenn's Moss in Staffordshire, and the Lochar Moss in Dumfriesshire were 'susceptible of drainage and then of conversion into farmland by treatment with a certain amount of earth, lime and chemical fertilisers'.

These areas cited by Sir Daniel Hall were in many cases the last and most outstanding examples of that kind of 'wild nature', of considerable amenity and scientific value. In a survey of potential National Habitat Reserves in 1943, the British Ecological Society described Tregaron Bog, for example, as 'the best actively growing bog in England and Wales, the only perfect example remaining of a once common type of vegetation'. Clearly farmers now had an unprecedented capacity to transform the environment. Their ability and desire to act as guardians of amenity could no longer be taken for granted.[9]

Many preservationists were slow and reluctant to recognize this changing relationship with farming. This was well demonstrated during a two-day inquiry into the future of the Stanford Battle Training Area of Norfolk in 1948.

During the war the War Office had requisitioned 16,500 acres of this area of light, sandy soils in the Breckland of East Anglia for military training. Only 8,614 acres were farmland, and the remainder was heathland. Once the war was over, there was considerable agitation for the return of the area to agricultural use, and this was supported by the CPRE and other voluntary bodies. In evidence to the public inquiry they stressed how the Breckland region was famous for its scenery, archaeological sites and as an area well suited to outdoor recreation. The Norfolk Naturalists' Trust had recently created two nature reserves, and the Breckland Research Committee, composed of members of the University of Cambridge, stressed the scientific interest of the area.[10]

Far from opposing the reintroduction of farming, this Committee described how 'the tillage of land does not diminish the scientific importance'. There were 'many rare insects and plants which flourish best under the intermittent cultivation practised'. When the Inspector at the Planning Inquiry pointed out that restoration of the area to agricultural use would lead to cultivation on a far more extensive and intensive scale than ever before, the witness, representing the CPRE, denied that there would be any clash of interests. Modern farming would simply 'create a new sort of beauty'.

The Planning Inspector conceded, in his report, that the Breckland had 'a peculiar beauty' of its own, and that if a practicable means could be found for preserving this 'essentially primitive area . . . there would be no doubt a strong objection to using the heart of it as a battle training area'. However, change was inevitable, and the modern methods of farming were likely to have an even more damaging effect than military use. During the Inquiry, witnesses for various landowners, farmers, and the National Farmers' Union had described how 'modern machinery, fertilisers, and up-to-date methods of farming, including irrigation, had completely revolutionised the farming and output capabilities of these light lands'. The area under cultivation before the war could be reclaimed in two years, and eventually the entire range-area could be brought into food production. The Planning Inspector concluded that amenity and wildlife would be better served by leaving the grass heathlands under military control.

THE ROADS IMPROVEMENT ACT

The most effective way of preserving amenity was to manage the countryside explicitly for that purpose. Management usually took the form of planting areas of wood and grassland. Practical difficulties were soon encountered. It was not enough to plant trees, sow grass, and announce that the area was protected in the interests of amenity. Left to herself, Nature did not always provide or maintain beauty. Vigilance and skilled management were required to prevent saplings from dying, and the grassland from being invaded by scrub. Above all, conscious design and heavy investment of resources were required to create, maintain, and enhance the amenity of the countryside.

One of the first sectors of activity to demonstrate the practical implications of

landscape management was roadside planting. Files of the Ministry of Transport help in identifying the attitude of the Ministry and highway authorities
towards roadside verges during the inter-war period, following the Roads
Improvement Act of 1925. They provide one of the earliest examples of how
public concern for the rural landscape was translated into action. The files help
in explaining how, why and when a national policy toward the planting and
maintenance of those verges first evolved.[11]

As soon as the First World War had ended, work resumed on the construction of arterial roads and the widening of many existing trunk roads. Over 200
miles of roadway were built around London by 1924. This was generally
welcomed in view of the dramatic increase in the number of cars, lorries, and
omnibuses. The construction work often helped to relieve local unemployment.
But there was considerable concern over the impact of the roads on amenity.
Unlike the Roman roads, they had no history and had not been 'softened' by
age. The Parliamentary Secretary to the Ministry of Transport, Col. W. Ashley,
admitted that a road of up to 100 feet in width, bounded by concrete posts and
iron wire, was 'not a very graceful addition to the landscape'.

With the encouragement of such bodies as the Metropolitan Public Gardens
Association, Ashley went 'rather fully' into the matter, and agreed that a
well-organized tree-planting programme would reduce the 'rawness' of the new
roads and provide some compensation for the loss of trees during construction.
It might also help to reduce the incidence of land-slipping on the new cuttings
and embankments. There was a precedent, for a Local Act of 1914 had given
the Middlesex County Council powers to incur expenditure in planting trees
along the new Great West Road.[12]

In drawing up estimates for 1924–5, Ashley accordingly included up to
£12,000 for roadside planting, sought expert advice from the Forestry Commission and the Royal Botanic Garden, and actually 'mapped out what sections
of the roads and what particular trees should be planted'. In his words, 'all went
well until a vigilant officer in my Department discovered that I had no power to
do anything of that sort . . . The Minister could construct the road, drain the
road, maintain the road from the Road Fund, but the one thing he could not do
was to beautify the road in any way at all.' The situation was made even more
anomalous by the fact that urban authorities could plant wayside trees and
shrubs, under powers derived from the Public Health Acts Amendment Act of
1890. It is also relevant to note that Ashley had discovered a further anomaly in
his Ministry's powers: although £42,000,000 was spent on maintaining roads
and bridges, the Road Fund could not be used to finance experiments into
finding ways of improving their construction.[13]

Before a Bill could be promoted to remove these anomalies, a general election
led to the formation of the first Labour Government. But the new Minister of
Transport, Sir Harry Gosling, 'agreed departmentally with his political ad-
versary' and in May 1924 he asked the Cabinet for leave to introduce 'a short
useful Bill' to allow the Road Fund to be used for tree-planting, experimental

work, the erection of warning signs and direction posts, and the abolition of tolls. In a memorandum, he indicated how 'a great opportunity presents itself of adding to the amenity of new highways by the planting of suitable trees'. Although the Cabinet was 'in sympathy with the objects of the proposed Bill', Gosling was asked to make further inquiries as to whether the aims of the Bill could not be met without recourse to further legislation.

Gosling retorted that if the Cabinet wanted to beautify the roads and carry out research on road construction, the planting and experimental programmes had to be undertaken in a well-coordinated, carefully formulated manner, and for this a Bill was essential. There would be little opposition and 'the pressure on the Minister of Transport to take definite action' would increase as further arterial roads were built. The Cabinet later approved the Bill, but insufficient parliamentary time was left for a second reading. In November 1924 Ashley became Minister of Transport in a new Conservative government, and approval was given for the introduction of a new Roads Improvement Bill, almost identical with that drafted for Gosling. The Minister was anxious for this 'small, non-contentious measure' to be passed in time for the planting-season in the autumn of 1925.

Although the Bill was passed without division, it was challenged at all stages. A member complained that it should have been called the Beautification of Roads Bill: far from improving roads, trees would obscure vision, their roots would break up the road surface, and their leaves would block drains and make the roads more slippery. In the Commons, members representing rural constituencies regarded the tree-planting clause as further evidence of the government helping the towns at the expense of rural areas. Most of the trees would adorn arterial roads and urban bypasses, at a time when rural roads were urgently in need of attention.

Lord Banbury moved an amendment in the Lords to omit the tree-planting powers altogether, arguing that it was wrong to spend money on amenities when the country faced grave economic difficulties. He continued that, 'after all, we have now been in existence for some hundreds of years without planting trees along the roads' and it could easily be postponed. On behalf of the government, Viscount Peel responded that 'in view of the enormous advantages of turning these bare roads into shady highways, this is very small expenditure', amounting perhaps to only £30,000 per annum. Lord Banbury commented that small savings added up to large economies.

In view of these criticisms, Ashley was very anxious to demonstrate the practical value of his Bill for all sections of the community, and he accordingly agreed to incorporate the substance of a private member's Bill, designed to help eliminate blind corners on roads.[14] The new clause, added at Committee Stage, made Ashley's Bill 'twice as bulky' and gave rise to 'some caustic comments on the part of the Chief Whip'. Some members thereupon pressed for a further clause prescribing building lines along major roads. Ashley vigorously resisted this, but the Lords pressed so strongly for the amendment that Viscount Peel was obliged to agree to its insertion at Report Stage. The Bill finally obtained the Royal Assent in August 1925.

Reference must also be made to an earlier amendment which had very important long-term implications. The Ministry of Health noted that Gosling's Bill permitted only tree and shrub planting, whereas one of the model clauses inserted into most town-planning schemes enabled local authorities also to establish lawns and gardens alongside roads. The Ministry therefore suggested that Gosling's Bill should be expanded so as to make this clause unnecessary. The Ministry of Transport was sympathetic, but could only agree to add 'the establishment of grass verges' to Ashley's Bill. As a letter from the Ministry commented, 'we cannot go any further (and include gardens). Some members of parliament are already expressing alarm at the use of the Road Fund moneys for the purpose of providing local amenities.'

Implementation of the Act

A brief to the Minister described the Act as the first 'recognition of roadside amenities as a subject worthy of attention and expenditure by Local Administrators and the Government. It should not be allowed to become "a dead letter".' The Divisional Road Engineers (DREs) were asked to publicize the powers granted by the Act among highway authorities, and a memorandum on road layout and construction, issued in 1930, noted that 'the Minister specially desired that every care shall be taken not merely to safeguard existing amenities but to add to them'. Verges and the slopes of cuttings and embankments should be covered with soil, and then seeded, turved or planted with shrubs.[15]

At first, the Ministry had to proceed cautiously because it did not know how the Treasury would interpret the Act with regard to grants from the Road Fund. The Middlesex County Council soon put this to the test by applying to the Ministry for a grant toward the cost of planting twenty-six miles of roadway with 4,202 trees. In the event, the Treasury approved all that the Ministry requested. The implementation of the Act was further complicated by the fact that, whilst the Ministry had taken the initiative in obtaining tree-planting powers, only the local authorities could use them. Road-building and such ancillary activities as tree-planting were the responsibility of the local authorities, and the powers of the Ministry were limited to using the Road Fund to sanction, and thereby provide, grants of up to 50 per cent for the work on Class I roads and 25 per cent on Class II roads. It was soon clear that the Ministry's enthusiasm for tree-planting was not reflected by the local authorities—not even the more prosperous authorities around London.

Every authority complained of a shortage of resources and expertise. An horticulturalist, Wilfrid Fox, described how many county surveyors had a 'quite unjustifiable . . . belief in a beneficent Almighty'. Having once planted the trees, they left it to Him to look after them. The trees planted on the Kingston bypass had been hoed only once in three years, and as many died of neglect as of vandalism. In Buckinghamshire, bad pruning was blamed for the loss of many saplings. All the Ministry could do was to emphasize the need to 'educate' surveyors. The Chief Engineer, Charles Bressey remarked that 'it is only by quietly and persistently pegging away at the County Surveyors that we shall ultimately succeed in impressing them with the importance of careful maintenance'.

Setbacks to Planting

The failure to establish trees or grass swards soon led to fears lest the Act should fall into public disrepute. In 1931 Bressey tried to draft a memorandum, setting out ways of creating and managing grass verges, and its compilation provided an early case study of the limitations of legislation designed to set standards for amenity purposes. Although local authorities were used to imposing regulations 'for the public good', large-scale planting was an entirely new field of activity. Whereas research was being undertaken on ways of improving tree and grass growth, this was entirely oriented toward commercial forestry and agricultural objectives respectively. Although none doubted the need for a memorandum, almost every recommendation in Bressey's draft was challenged. The lack of data made its compilation premature.[16]

Bressey's memorandum described adequate 'ground preparation' as of the 'greatest importance'. Breeze or lime should be added to improve conditions, and the subsoil should be dug over, or cultivated by tractor, to a depth of at least four inches. This recommendation was, however, challenged by the firm of

Table 3. *Mixtures for the sowing of roadside verges, as proposed in an unpublished memorandum, 1931*

Suggested mixture for heavy soils (also suitable on chalk or limestone sub-soils)

By weight

10 per cent *Festuca duriuscula* (Hard Fescue)
10 per cent *Agrostis alba* (American Red Top)
10 per cent *Cynosurus cristatus* (Crested Dog's-tail)
70 per cent Dwarf Short seeded *Lolium perenne*—Ayrshire
          (Not the large agricultural variety)

Suggested mixture for light sandy soil (heathlands, etc.)

By weight

40 per cent *Festuca duriuscula* (Hard Fescue)
20 per cent *Cynosurus cristatus* (Crested Dog's-tail)
10 per cent *Agrostis alba* (American Red Top)
30 per cent Dward Short seeded *Lolium perenne*—Ayrshire
          (Not the large agricultural variety)

Alternative mixtures

By weight

87½ per cent Dwarf Short seeded *Lolium perenne*— Ayrshire
          (Not the large agricultural variety)   Variations in the percentage of this
12½ per cent Kentish Wild White Clover   mixture may be tried
          (or once-grown Kentish Wild White Clover)

James Carter (Carters), which argued that the 'texture of a clay soil for instance is constant and the structure is only temporarily modified by cultivation, as it will settle down to a natural consistency'. The draft memorandum suggested that 'selected vegetable soil' should be spread over the subsoil to a depth of three inches, but Carters regarded this as impracticable and 'appallingly expensive'. The DRE (North) warned how this would greatly increase the cost of such major road schemes as the Liverpool–East Lancashire road.

Carters were also critical of the amounts recommended for sowing, namely one pound of seed for areas of up to 40 square yards. Instead, the firm of seed-merchants recommended one pound per 16 square yards, and certainly not more than 24 square yards. An early version of the draft suggested sowing from mid-March until mid-April, or from mid-September until mid-October. The DRE (East) proposed that all autumn sowing should take place in September, otherwise there would be little time for the establishment of seedlings before winter. August was the optimum month if the mixture contained clover.

The draft recommended two seeds mixtures (Table 3). The mixture for heavy soils would cost £4. 17s. per acre, and that for lighter soils would be £6. 5s. per acre. This compared with £4. 5s. per acre for the mixture frequently used on road verges, comprising equal amounts of white clover and ryegrass. It was hoped that the faster-growing species in the mixture would quickly establish a turf and overwhelm any weeds: the finer grasses would 'fill up the bottom'. But the DRE (East) warned that even the small-seeded Ryegrass *Lolium perenne*—Ayrshire, grew so quickly that it would nullify any benefits to be derived from the comparatively expensive finer grasses. The seed-merchants, Sutton and Sons Ltd. (Suttons), warned that the inclusion of ryegrass would necessitate more frequent mowing.

Bearing in mind the cost of the seed mixtures, nature of the seed-bed, and the kind of turf required, Suttons recommended a mixture of Perennial Ryegrass and Wild White Clover. Quite independently, the DRE (East) suggested a similar mixture, in the proportion of 87 to 13, which would be up to 40 per cent cheaper than the other mixtures in the draft memorandum. The proposal was incorporated in the draft (Table 3), although the other seed-merchants, Carters, regarded it as a most 'wasteful composition of mixtures', with the 'white clover being altogether out of proportion to the ryegrass.

In August 1931 Bressey reluctantly concluded that an agreed set of recommendations could not be produced. It would be premature to issue a memorandum and, consequently, he called upon county councils to set up trials. Accordingly, trial sections were laid out on the Bath Road and along the London–Portsmouth road, which were reported to be 'making good growth' a year later. But Bressey had to admit a few years later that no trial had produced any 'definite results'. Plans for plots along the Llangurig–Rhayader road in the Wye Valley of Radnorshire were dashed when the county surveyor was persuaded by local farmers to use the seed from the local hay lofts instead of the mixture prescribed in the draft memorandum.

The need for expertise

The near-universal support for roadside planting and yet the equally wide-spread lack of resources and expertise emphasized the potential value of con-tributions from individuals and voluntary bodies. In 1928 Wilfrid Fox, the horticulturalist, suggested to Ashley that a voluntary body should be formed to provide the highway authorities with expert and material help in planting ornamental trees. The Ministry welcomed the idea, and, with considerable help from Bressey, the Roads Beautifying Association was soon formed, with membership open to all, Ashley as President, and Fox as the indefatigable secretary.[17]

In order to make an immediate public impact, it was decided to concentrate on planting a 'model' verge, namely part of the Kingston bypass, with up to forty-three different species arranged singly and in clusters, with smaller shrubs on the sides of the banks and cuttings, and a poplar tree at the four corners of each cross-roads. Ashley helped to select the species for planting and he canvassed the support of the Surrey County Council, noting that 'the road is worthy of something more than mere common-place lines of trees set up at uniform intervals. Landscape gardening should play an important part in the consideration of any scheme for the adornment of this highway.' The Highways Committee of the County Council gave its consent for planting to take place.

The technical subcommittee of the Roads Beautifying Association prepared a guide for county surveyors and others engaged in planting amenity trees. Called *Roadside planting*, it was published in 1930 and had a foreword written by Bressey. In the year 1931/2, the Association claimed that advice had been given for the planting of 2,000 trees on 50 miles of roadway. On receiving a request for advice, a panel of three to four persons was usually selected to visit the site. Its recommendations were considered by the Association's technical sub-committee, and a submission was made to the highway authority. Bressey observed that 'I have been impressed by the greater care which is now being devoted to the maintenance and after-care of wayside trees and shrubs—largely due to the propaganda conducted by the Roads Beautifying Association', and, in a brief to the Minister, he wrote, 'the Society is particularly helpful because its criticisms are constructive and not destructive'. Both Ashley and Bressey continued to be closely associated with the Association after they had left the Ministry, and a succession of Ministers of Transport served as vice-presidents of the Association.[18]

The most active member of the technical sub-committee was W. J. Bean, the Curator of the Royal Botanic Garden. When he retired in 1929, the Association suggested that the Ministry and Association should pay him an honorarium in order to retain his services. Bressey wholeheartedly agreed, and he wrote that 'Mr Bean would do much to prevent neglect and slackness on the part of the local authorities, to check questionable practices such as the hideous lopping which so often takes the place of judicious pruning, and generally to ensure the proper use of Road Fund monies allocated for roadside planting.' The Treasury approved the payment of a fee of 100 guineas a year for a period of not more than three years, subject to 'the actual amount of work involved being considerable'. A year later, Bressey asserted that 'I am constantly relying on Mr Bean's advice . . . so many complaints reach me in the manner in which wayside trees are planted and maintained that I much appreciate the advantage of being able to consult an unchallenged expert like Mr Bean.'[19]

Bean's report on the planting of the Liverpool–East Lancashire road, where the subsoil was composed of ashes and colliery waste for long stretches, may be cited as an example of his consultancy work. He gave advice as to the preparation of the verges, the age and species of the saplings, and suggested that the nurseryman who provided the trees should be responsible for looking after them for a period of up to three years. Bean also inspected the stocks of individual nurserymen in order to advise local authorities on where to obtain the best supplies for their particular needs.

There were, however, misgivings as to whether the savings on the Road Fund outweighed the cost of Bean's work. He made only twenty-five inspections in the first year and sixteen in the second, and the Ministry ended his appointment during the financial crisis of 1931, following Treasury demands for cuts in departmental spending. Attempts to revive the consultancy in 1935 failed. It was noted that the appointment had been an interim measure until the Ministry could obtain the requisite help from another official body, for example the Royal Botanic Garden. For its part, the Royal Botanic Garden insisted on its being given a new post in order to fulfil this advisory role.

Meanwhile the Ministry was accused of 'sponging' on the Roads Beautifying Association, which continued to pay an honorarium to Bean. Matters came to a head in 1938 when the Ministry took over responsibility for trunk roads: eventually, the Treasury agreed to an annual payment of £200 for three years in order to offset the expenses of the Association, when acting as official consultants.

Although no planting took place during the war, the Ministry envisaged 'a large scheme of planting' as soon as hostilities ended. The Minister of Transport in the post-war Labour government, Alfred Barnes, took a personal interest, and plans were laid in 1946 for the planting of 3,000 miles of trunk road over a period of ten years. The main question was how the planting work should be supervised and carried out. The Forestry Commission was unable to provide specialist advice or nursery facilities. The Royal Botanic Garden asserted that it was 'primarily a scientific institution' and could not accept essentially practical assignments without prejudicing its other functions. The Ministry, for its part, decided not to renew the pre-war arrangement with the Roads Beautifying Association. A memorandum described how the Association had been criticized both within and outside the Ministry for its tendency 'to overplant with exotics, without sufficient regard to the country through which the particular road passes'.[20]

The Ministry believed the time had come for the appointment of someone in its engineering section who would prepare, supervise and co-ordinate planting schemes on trunk roads and examine applications submitted by local highway authorities for grants toward tree-planting from the Road Fund. The Curator of the Royal Botanic Garden, E. J. Salisbury, advised the Ministry to appoint an horticulturist 'of some education and imagination, with a feeling for the country, who will be able to devise schemes of planting to harmonise with the surroundings, and to visualise what the road as planted, will look like in, say, 10 or 20 years time'.

Although a horticulturist and an assistant were eventually appointed, there were serious misgivings over the appointments, and the horticulturist was not replaced when he resigned a year later. There was even greater opposition from outside the Ministry. In February 1949 the President of the Roads Beautifying Association, the Duke of Devonshire, initiated a debate in the House of Lords, which not only called upon the Ministry to accelerate road-planting but protested at the way in which the Ministry had abandoned the Association, with its 'experience and accumulated wisdom'. The local government associations also protested at the expense of appointing an official to perform duties previously carried out by a voluntary body. A Member of Parliament, Peter Thorneycroft, described it as a 'monstrous thing that poor people should have to pay Purchase Tax in order to pay the salaries of gentlemen who then go out and plant our Highways'.[21]

Replying to the debate in the House of Lords, a government spokesman described how it often happened that voluntary bodies carried out pioneer work on a part-time basis. As the work expanded, perhaps as a result of legislation, the government had to employ a whole-time 'State paid expert'. The Treasury was unconvinced, and refused to make the posts of horticulturist and assistant established. Although they might be needed for a few years, a member of the Treasury wrote, 'I find it difficult to believe that, once the trees have been planted, you will need specialists full-time on the job.' In the event of an economy drive against the Civil Service, the posts would be the first to be abolished.

The Treasury's concern appeared to be justified by events, when the original plans for road construction were drastically reduced as a result of economies imposed by the Cabinet. A brief to the Minister in 1949 described how it was impractical to embark on tree-planting schemes 'when ordinary road maintenance has had to be reduced well below the normal pre-war level'. In the event, a compromise was reached with the Treasury over the employment of an horticulturalist. It was agreed that officers of the National Agricultural Advisory Service should be seconded to the Ministry to provide the expert help required for tree-planting schemes.

In spite of early plans to appoint a Landscape Advisory Committee, nothing happened until 1959, when twenty members were appointed. They included nominees from the appropriate amenity and professional bodies. Soon afterwards, the established posts of Landscape and Horticultural Advisers were created within the Ministry. The Landscape Advisory Committee not only inspected the routes of proposed motorways and major roads, but gave advice on wider environmental issues affecting road construction and maintenance. It was the first to publicize the potential value of verges as 'nature reserves'. In a booklet of 1967, one of its members, Clough Williams-Ellis, wrote, 'with the introduction of more intensive and cleaner systems of farming much of the British Flora is being ousted from meadow, pasture and hedgerow, and it seems logical that the roadside verge, particularly on the motorway where pedestrians are forbidden, should become a nature reserve and provide areas and secure habitat for our wild flowers'.[22]

The early planting schemes

In a book published in 1938 the author stressed that 'motor roads are made for use and not for ornament'. The motorist looked forward to the day when the whole country was covered by a network of straight 120-feet wide thorough-fares, with rounded corners at road junctions, and transparent wire fences instead of hedges. There would be no 'picturesque distractions', except for the milestones, direction posts and petrol pumps. Those in search of the picturesque and rural scenery would have to resort increasingly to footpaths and the open moorland.[23]

Not everyone shared this attitude. Bressey remarked in 1928 that the Roads Improvement Act had underlined 'the increased importance which public opinion in England attached to roadside amenities'. In a letter to *The Times*, Ashley asserted that the preservation of rural beauty was almost as important as directness and durability when laying out new roads. The highways were more then 'traffic conduits'. They had to impress foreign tourists and become 'one of the principal sources of pleasure for rich and poor alike', when going on outings and excursions.[24]

At first the Ministry encouraged authorities to plant not only the traditional hardy species, but also flowering species and those with variegated foliage, but, right from the start, there was criticism of the more formal and exotic plantings. By 1932 many authorities preferred to plant groups rather than lines of trees along the roadside. The Hampshire County Council tried to plant 'in a hap-hazard sort of way, as though the trees had sprung up by themselves', but it soon found that this was 'much more difficult than planting in a deliberately formal manner'. The Middlesex County Council regarded clumps as im-practicable where adjacent properties would be heavily shaded and room also had to be found for pavements and underground utilities.

Planting policies reflected differences in the perception of the roads. In some cases the highways were to be the centre-piece: some notes of the Roads Beautifying Association described how 'an arterial road sweeping over the brow of a hill or down from the summit often lends itself admirably to an avenue of trees which should form a feature of the landscape when seen from a distance'.

But the county surveyor for Hampshire warned of fierce local opposition if such a planting policy was adopted along the Winchester bypass. Instead, it was felt that the 'natural growth of the country' should be encouraged 'so that the road may fall as unobtrusively as possible into the landscape. Where the road passes through gaps of beech trees, we had thought of closing up the trees again . . . and where it goes through the beautiful meadows we would let the willows, rushes, and so forth, grow in upon it as far as may be possible'.

In an article published in the *Journal of the Institute of Landscape Architects* in 1939, Brenda Colvin wrote:

the object of roadside planting is not so much to 'beautify' the road as to link it satisfactorily to the other existing features of the countryside: so to knit the highway into the landscape that it no longer appears as a naked scar across the face of the earth but becomes an integral component part of the whole, blending happily into its surroundings from whatever point of view it may be seen

The blending of road and landscape was achieved not by planting 'pretty subjects' at more or less even distances apart, but by using 'massive tree forms in well defined groups, properly related to the curves of the road and to the surrounding contours'.[25]

It is impossible to measure the success of the 1925 Act in terms of the aggregate number of trees planted or lengths of verge sown, because the cost, and therefore details, were 'concealed' in the comprehensive estimates submitted by the highways authorities for new roads and widening programmes. It was very rare for an authority to apply for a grant from the Road Fund to cover only the cost of planting. Undoubtedly, the greatest contribution of the inter-war plantings was as a guideline for the post-war period, when the benefits of roadside planting were not only perceived, but the requisite resources and expertise became more readily available and effectively deployed. The powers of the 1925 Act were consolidated by the Highways Act of 1959.

In addition to providing the basis for contemporary legislation, the 1925 Act may have a wider significance. It provides an early example of a growing desire to enhance the environment: the advocacy of landscape improvement was taken up by voluntary and public bodies, and expressed through the media of roadside verges. And yet the Act indicated the difficulties of translating the perceived need into the accomplished fact: although the value of the Act was accepted and the Minister and Chief Engineer were personally interested in roadside amenities, the timing and content of the measure owed much to the contemporary situation. Although a 'minor non-controversial Bill', the Bill became 'embroiled' in wider political and economic considerations.

The aftermath of the Act provided a salutary reminder to the advocates of landscape improvement that it was not enough to acquire and designate a roadside verge: provision had to be made for its continued and adequate management. The Act was passed without any real appreciation of the difficulties of sustaining a planting programme and aftercare treatment where these activities were a low priority in the budgets of individual highway authorities. The abortive memorandum on grass verges in 1931, the use made of the Roads Beautifying Association, the temporary employment of W. J. Bean as a consultant, and the difficulties of appointing an official horticulturalist after the war, drew attention to the virtual absence of any expertise or experience in the management of extensive areas for amenity purposes. A completely new, interdisciplinary field of research and development had been identified, that was to have even greater significance following the eventual construction of motorways in the 1950s.

CONSERVATION   Historical pers.

What should be the guiding principles for the art and practice of landscape treatment? What form should enrichment take? In the search for the answer to these questions, a great deal of encouragement was provided by two comparatively new disciplines, landscape architecture and ecology. In the course of discussions on principles and land-use policies, the word *preservation* was gradually displaced by a more exciting and positive term, called *conservation*.

According to Thomas Adams, the careful planning of the countryside depended on the participation of the architect, the engineer, and the landscape architect, and it was because the landscape architect had usually been left out that rural planning was so often weak and negative. There had been a tendency to dwell on preservation to the extent that there was no professional or voluntary body explicitly dedicated to the enrichment and creation of new rural landscapes. To help redress the balance, and ensure that 'properly qualified' persons were employed, the Institute of Landscape Architects was founded in 1930.[26]

Adams might well have added a fourth member to the rural planning team—the ecologist. Vegetation was a vital component of the countryside. In order to preserve and enhance plant and animal life, there had to be a profound understanding of the distribution and habitat requirements of every species. Whereas farm crops and the plants used by the gardener and horticulturist had been closely studied over many centuries, the study of the infinitely more varied and complex natural environment of wild plants and animals was comparatively new, and associated with the science of ecology. In order to promote the young field of research, the British Ecological Society was founded in 1913 and, by the Second World War, its members had gained not only a more detailed knowledge of the wildlife of the countryside but also a deeper understanding of the changes taking place. In many cases, shifts in land use and management were causing a decline in the abundance and variety of plants and animals, to the detriment of amenity and scientific interest. On the other hand, ecologists were beginning to acquire the necessary scientific skills to formulate management programmes which would not only preserve, but actually enhance, the wildlife populations. The British Ecological Society was keen to ensure that this insight and experience should be fully utilized in the future planning of the countryside.[27]

In the same way as national parks might provide unprecedented opportunities for landscape design, so the designation of nature reserves could
provide the ecologist with the chance to carry out long-term investigations of
plant and animal life. He would be able to demonstrate the applicability of
ecological principles to wildlife conservation and to the wider aspects of land
husbandry. By studying the habitat requirements and behavioural patterns of
individual species and communities, it would be possible to maintain and
enhance wildlife. The sanctuaries would become not only outstanding
laboratories and classrooms, but vital components of the amenity of the
countryside.

The landscape architect and ecologist emphasized the need for a more
conscious and rigorous approach to the management of the countryside, using
the evidence of the landscape as the surest guide to its conservation. As Thomas
Adams wrote:

> the cultivated English landscape is not a fortuitous distribution of fields, parks, trees, hedges and
> roads, but is in a large degree, an artificial arrangement of natural features. Large landowners
> with skilled advisers in past generations have arranged and developed the pleasing features that
> are characteristic of this homely landscape of ours. They adapted the land and arranged its
> vegetation for different uses by more or less conscious design

Perhaps in no other country had man so skilfully adapted the landscape to his
varied needs and yet developed its natural beauty. Instead of falsely regarding
this creative achievement as 'nature's own doing', it was time planners recognized it as the outcome of an 'alliance between man and nature'. It should be
the task of planners to revive and develop the self-same creative abilities in the
form of landscape architecture.[28]

In the report advocating the concepts of nature conservation and nature
reserves, published in 1943, the British Ecological Society made a similar plea
for an alliance between man and nature. Wildlife was part of the national
heritage, and was to be cherished in the same way as ancient buildings and
monuments. Not everything could be preserved: the claims of new buildings,
agriculture, and forestry had to be recognized in any planning policy, but the
human need for 'a place for wildlife' should also be recognized. In the words of
the report:

> what we can do is to survey the whole problem with careful attention and then take steps to
> conserve, under proper control, more or less extensive samples of our natural vegetation and so
> much of our wild animal life as is reasonable and practicable, for our mental refreshment, for the
> enjoyment of its beauty and interest, and for purposes of study and education.[29]

The task of conservation—namely the preservation and enhancement of the
landscape—had to be undertaken in a disciplined manner. A discrete, un-
pretentious approach was required. As Thomas Sharp wrote in his book, *Town
and countryside*:

> we are the inheritors of a landscape that has already been almost fully developed. All that we have
> to do to conserve its beauty is to maintain the materials out of which it has been created, replacing

them as they decay. Here and there we may fell a corner that has never been developed, or we may modify existing scenes where we could create fresh beauty. But in the main our responsibility is of maintenance only.[30]

In a lecture to the Institute of Landscape Architects, John Dower warned against the uncritical adoption of the principles of the traditional British school of landscape design. The exponents of this school had converted farmland into parks around country houses, and had laid out town parks and ornamental gardens. A quite different approach was needed in the potential national park areas, where the origins and design of the landscape were 'almost entirely free from any conscious aesthetic purposes'. There was nothing fussily self-advertising, whether in the beauty of the 'intake' fields of a moorland farm, or the layout of gritstone and limestone walls striding over hills and through valleys. Even the farms, hamlets, and villages had been fitted into the scenery so that now they seemed 'a natural and essential punctuation'.[31]

The same restrained approach should be adopted in modifying the landscape to meet the needs of the holiday-maker. Road improvements, parking-places, camp-sites and hostels might be designed by engineers and architects, but their setting should be adjusted and clothed with vegetation by the landscape architect, so as to blend imperceptibly into the landscape. Buildings, walls, and fences should be constructed in local materials in the local tradition. Wherever possible, design should conform to local shapes, forms, and colour. Trees should be planted in irregular shapes and a variety of colours. Dower described the approach to landscape design as conservation. Far from being self-assertive, conservation called for 'a self-denying spirit', where the inspiration was derived entirely from what had been achieved by man and nature in the past. It called for the same kind of approach as that advocated by William Wordsworth, in his *Guide to the Lakes*.

In making these recommendations, Dower wanted to dispel any notion that conservation would put the countryside into a strait-jacket. A living architectural tradition could not stand still and, the greater its vitality, the more easily it would adjust itself to the changing needs and ways of those individuals and communities whose livelihood it supported and expressed. But the architectural tradition should retain throughout its evolution a core of basic characteristics corresponding to the enduring facts of its natural and human setting. In such areas as the Lake District, the changes 'should be of detail, not of essence'.

Neither did conservation mean 'the detailed and slavish imitation of Nature'. The opportunity should be taken to enhance Nature wherever she was not 'up to her best'. Not only had owners to recoup their investments in woodland, but there was considerable scope for new plantings. If undertaken in the right way in the appropriate places with the most suitable species, the results could provide a valuable and harmonious enrichment of the landscape. Dower compiled lists of tree and shrub species that were suitable for planting at various altitudes, situations, and densities in the Lake District. In addition to the various deciduous species, he recommended the planting of a few Scots pine and larch, but no spruce or other pryamidal evergreens. In order to enrich the colouring of the scenery, Dower suggested the planting of holly for winter-time, and of hawthorn and wild cherry for spring.[32]

Another aspect of landscape management was highlighted by what was happening on some of the commonlands during the inter-war period. This time the threat to the commons came not so much from the would-be encloser, who had to be fought off by litigation or legislation, but rather from changes taking place within the common itself. A member of the Estates Committee of the National Trust explained the problem to readers of the *Journal of the Commons, Open Spaces, and Footpaths Preservation Society* in the following manner. The variable beauty of most commons arose mainly from 'the picturesque distribution of grass, heather, bracken, or gorse, and perhaps small clumps of trees, over a wide open space'. This was the outcome of the way in which the commons had been exploited over many generations. The wood had been cut for building, fencing, and firing, the reeds, heather, and bracken for litter, the gorse for fuel, and the turf had been grazed by farmstock. Wherever the commoners' rights fell into disuse and the pressure on the vegetation was relaxed, the distribution and character of species changed, following 'definite laws of succession'.[33]

One of the first symptoms of change was the suppression of the grasses, heather, and other flowering plants by bracken. Previously, the commoners had cut the bracken as litter in the autumn, and the cropping and trampling effect of livestock in the following spring and summer had checked and damaged the young shoots. The underground stems had little opportunity to increase their food stores. Where both cutting and grazing had ceased, management committees had to find substitute forms of control if they wished to preserve the varied character of the vegetation. The only satisfactory programme was to cut, break, or bruise the fronds of the bracken in May when they had attained full height but before they had uncurled, and to repeat this on any second or third growths. Experience indicated that three cuttings or breakings in the first summer and two in the subsequent two years would exhaust food supplies sufficiently to leave the fronds short and feeble, thereby providing the grass and heather with a chance to reassert themselves. Treatment over three years was necessary because a bud forming on an underground stem took about that time to appear above ground as a frond. Such was the scientific theory, but experience had shown that the grass and heather did not always grow more vigorously, and management committees had to maintain constant vigilance, despite the consequent demands on resources. Cutting was usually done by a hook or stick, but the National Trust had begun to experiment with a Holt Bracken-breaker, consisting of a heavy, revolving metal bar drawn by a horse, which severely damaged the bracken. Power-driven machines were not only expensive but difficult to operate on the frequently rugged or steep-sided surface of the commons.

In her book, *Land and landscapes*, Brenda Colvin emphasized the close affinity between fine landscape and nature conservation. One of the most effective ways of conserving both scenery and wildlife was to introduce a system of rotational management. In ancient woodlands, for example, small sections might be felled as others reached maturity. The whole wood would be kept 'moving in a slow rotation'. In the words of Miss Colvin:

'this is a subject on which ecology can enlighten us, and although the subject presents a vast field, some elementary knowledge of it should be implanted in the minds of all who have to deal with country planning, since it forms a background essential to the proper understanding of all problems of land use in the countryside.'[34]

In 1942 a leading ecologist, A. G. Tansley, was asked to write a pamphlet expressly for local authorities, describing how areas of natural or semi-natural vegetation should be managed in order to conserve their vegetation cover. In his pamphlet Tansley warned that the appearance and interest of most open spaces and woodlands would change if the traditional forms of management such as grazing, mowing, and coppicing, ceased, and adequate substitutes were not found. Because vegetation communities were so dynamic, it was important to understand how plant and animal life had evolved and how it had been maintained in the past. Before deciding to acquire land for scenic purposes and outdoor recreation, local authorities should be certain that they could muster sufficient resources and expertise to manage the wildlife communities. In many cases, normal agricultural practices might suffice as a form of management, but a fundamental distinction had to be drawn between managing land for agriculture and the management of public open spaces and nature reserves. Whereas the farmer wanted the maximum yield from a comparatively few species, the visitor to the countryside looked for the maximum diversity of habitat and wildlife. This called for a fresh approach to planning the use and management of the countryside: one which the landscape architect and ecologist were just beginning to develop.[35]

CHAPTER XIII

The Historical Perspective

Every generation believes it is living through a turning point in history: the inter-war generation was no exception. According to Joad, it was the last to know 'England as it was before the flood gates were opened and the waters of change passed through'. Much of this book has been concerned with the way in which that generation perceived and responded to the changes taking place in the countryside over those twenty years. The book opened by describing the growing concern as to the effects of the movement of people and industries into the countryside, and the consequent destruction of rural amenity through building development and other, more subtle, forms of land-use change. Remedial action was taken first through *ad hoc* palliatives and later through more comprehensive measures. The book describes how voluntary bodies, local authorities, parliament, and governments became involved—and even the Prime Minister's office intervened at times.[1]

Achievements there were, but they were hardly on a breath-taking scale. A member of the Ministry of Health wrote in 1935 that 'a vast amount of paper and ink has been spent on town planning since 1909 with a very limited success', and the President of the Town Planning Institute reminisced in 1937 that, 'when we look back, it may seem that we have been a very long time engaged in accomplishing so little'. Despite the growing concern for the future use and management of town and country, the tangible achievements were so meagre as to confirm, in the minds of some commentators, that planning was just one more example of the missed opportunities and lost causes of the inter-war years.[2]

THE GRADUALIST APPROACH

Before passing judgement on the objectives and achievements of the rural preservation movement, it is salutary to take stock of the military conflict, economic depression, unemployment, and social deprivation that were such marked features of those twenty years. Not surprisingly, governments and local authorities, the wealthy and the poor, the active and inactive, were far more concerned with these issues than with the preservation of the countryside. It is instructive to discover that, in the Annual Report of the Ministry of Health in 1939, only thirteen of the 222 pages of text were devoted to planning issues. In his unpublished autobiography, Sir Edward Hilton-Young hardly mentions planning, in spite of his having been Minister of Health throughout the life of the National Government, under Ramsay MacDonald. He identified his chief preoccupations as housing, unemployment, and national insurance.[3]

The impact of the disastrous loss of life in the Great War cannot be overrated. The economic disruption of the early 1920s added to the trauma, and just as more permanent stability seemed within sight, the depression of 1929–33 dealt a further savage blow. Adversity acted as a stimulant for some. Harold Macmillan believed the crisis of 1931 had helped to liberate men's minds from the orthodoxies of the past but, for others, the way ahead seemed even more confusing: all the necessary assumptions and preconceptions for a planning policy were challenged and severely shaken. A fresh set of aspirations and plans was disrupted or destroyed by the prospect and eventual outbreak of the Second World War.[4]

Meanwhile changes in land use and management were taking place at what appeared to be an ever increasing rate. Over 4,000,000 houses were built, mostly before the Town and Country Planning Act of 1932 came into operation. Far from starting with a *tabula rasa*, the preservation movement had to take account of the many vested interests which had grown up so recently in badly located, ill-designed developments. As an internal minute of the Ministry of Health commented, 'thirty years ago, one could have bought long stretches of the north Cornish coast for a mere song, but the very extensive and spread-out bungalow development which has taken place since the war has no doubt put some sort of value on most of the coast land'. Instead of becoming easier, the task of acquiring land or regulating its use through statutory control was becoming harder. The course of the remedy was being outstripped by the disease.[5]

From a technical point of view, it would have been relatively easy if statutory planning and the voluntary bodies had been able to prohibit all further development in the countryside—to have stopped the clock of progress. But the total preservation of the countryside had become politically impossible in view of the otherwise tremendous benefits conferred by urban expansion into the countryside. Instead, the aim was to provide as many citizens as possible with a chance to live in a more rural setting. The challenge was somehow to accommodate greater numbers of people in the countryside and at the same time to preserve the countryside as *country*. This called for a much greater degree of skill, subtlety, and flexibility, and it is not altogether surprising that there were few local authorities of the calibre needed for such a new and delicate task.

Lessons are rarely learned overnight, and twenty years are a comparatively short time when it comes to perceiving and responding to social and economic trends. The inter-war years have been characterized as the time when open, suburban development was employed to provide an essentially urban population with houses in more rural surroundings. In a tribute to Sir Raymond Unwin, written in 1940, Barry Parker recalled the battles that had been waged to convince builders that high building densities did not lead to economies in costs. From a long process of trial and error, the optimal limit was found to be twelve houses per acre and, according to Parker, the general adoption of this limit had brought happiness and enjoyment to 'hundreds of thousands of people due to the spaciousness, openness and healthiness of their sur-roundings'.[6]

Unfortunately, the pendulum swung too sharply from a reaction against too *intensive* development toward the opposite extreme of *extensive* sprawl. In the eyes of many, planning and low-density development became inseparable, irrespective of whether it took the form of grouped or ribbon development. According to T. Alwyn Lloyd, the word 'planning' became a cliché. What was needed was 'real' planning, where the benefits of proper site-location, layout, and design were plain for all to see, and where attention was given not only to the suburbs but to town and country alike. The towns had to be rehabilitated and the country modernized, without destroying the essential character of each.[7]

Even if 'real' planning had been achieved, some observers were beginning to question the feasibility and value of the suburban ideal. In his book, *The Journey to work*, published in 1944, K. K. Liepmann described how it was almost impossible for 'the masses to work in the centres of large towns', enjoy such amenities as a large garden, *and* also live near their work. They were having to commute increasingly long distances. Meanwhile the deterrents to urban life were declining. Improvements in sanitation had removed many of the health hazards that had once made closely packed urban housing notorious. Accom-modation in town flats would make it much easier for people to live at high densities and also to be provided with light, air, and open space. For Liepmann, the inter-war years emphasized the value of 'nucleated development on a moderately compact plan'. This would lead to greater social cohesion, greater economies in the provision of utilities, shorter journeys to work and, perhaps, easier access for the townsman to the 'real' countryside.[8]

By the close of the inter-war period, it was clear that housing was not the only function to make increasing demands on 'space'. One of the most profound and detailed studies of those years was made by the Royal Commission on Popu-lation, appointed in 1944. The Economics Committee of that Commission drew attention to two important trends. First, the end of Britain's assured pre-eminence in manufacturing industry meant that there was a much greater need to produce home-grown food and, therefore, to conserve every acre of good farmland for that purpose. Secondly, outdoor recreation was exerting un-precedented demands on land resources. National parks, green belts, playing fields, recreation grounds, and private gardens were all consumers of land. Experience in the 1930s indicated that the peace and beauty of the countryside would 'be increasingly threatened by the wider enjoyment of regular holidays, by the spread among town-dwellers of the taste for rural outings, by improved transport facilities and by an increase in the numbers of those possessing motor-cars or motor-cycles'. Somehow these burgeoning demands would have to be reconciled with the more traditional users of space.[9]

It was sometimes suggested that the advocates of planning concentrated too exclusively on the non-economic aspects of land use and management. In his book of 1937 Sir Gwilym Gibbon explained how many people, perhaps most, regarded planning as primarily a matter of providing attractive housing, open spaces and other amenities, but Gibbon emphasized that a community has to earn its living before it could live well, and this meant that the overriding purpose of planning schemes should be the promotion of prosperity by helping to create the right conditions for economic progress and employment. Whilst none doubted the need to foster prosperity, it was not, however, easy to strike a fair balance. In a lecture of 1928 G. D. MacNiven described the kind of dilemma faced by the rural preservation movement. He observed: 'confronted as we are by economic and social problems of a pressing kind, it may seem to many that the attainment of what is after all an aesthetic ideal may await for better times. But when these better times arrive we may be too late'. Rural preservation was not a form of escapism, but a grim confrontation with reality—the realization that the developments which brought economic growth, prosperity, and happiness to many individual families and communities could also bring devastation and irreparable harm to the amenity of the countryside and coast. There could be no delay in finding ways of achieving one without the other.[10]

The town and country planner was often challenged to explain how his approach to planning differed from, and contributed to, those plans drawn up by the architect, engineer, farmer, and landscape designer in the normal course of their work. Whereas these other professions sought to discover how a piece of land should be used for a special purpose, W. G. Holford argued that the planner was unique in trying to find which purpose, out of the many possible contenders, was most appropriate to the piece of land and the general pattern of land use in the region. This did not imply that the planner was all-seeing and omnipotent. Holford warned that the surest way to make planning ineffectual was 'to blow it up to unmanageable size, or to regard it as a panacea for every social ill'. The town and country planner should simply base his information on the widest possible research and seek to provide those who would eventually take the land-use decisions with 'a flexible pattern of living and working, that will be a serviceable instrument to use, rather than a ready-made formula'. Holford expressed these sentiments at a meeting of the British Association in 1942, by which time he was in charge of the Research Section of the Ministry of Works and Planning, the department responsible for planning the physical reconstruction of post-war Britain.[11]

Land-use planning in Britain did not begin in the nineteenth century with a coherent set of ideas as to what had to be achieved. According to Cherry, it developed from a number of different points and as 'a pragmatic series of adjustments to ongoing events'. The government's Chief Town Planning Inspector throughout the inter-war years, George Pepler, believed the rise of planning bore out the contention that the English were not very logically minded. They preferred to work from the particular to the general, so that 'we began with the idea of planning the extension of towns (incidentally neglecting their cores), next we saw that even this requires regional planning, and now (in

1931) we realise that any sound system of planning must give equal weight to and provide a proper balance between the national, urban and rural points of view'. A year later, the Town and Country Planning Act was on the statute book.[12]

In his review of town and country planning in 1935, T. Alwyn Lloyd described how it would have been much more logical to have begun with a national survey in 1909 as a preliminary to the introduction of a series of national plans covering various aspects of land use and management, and then to have proceeded toward the more detailed planning of particular regions and localities. It was now too late to adopt such a course of action. Although lamentably slow, the mechanism set up by the legislation since 1909 was now in working order and many regional and local authorities were preparing schemes. They would resent interference from any new and inexperienced national survey/planning authority. Instead of introducing a belated revolution, ways had to be found of introducing the concepts of a national survey and a national plan into the existing machinery of statutory planning with the minimum of administrative disruption and delay.[13]

The fact that there was only one major change in planning law, namely the 1932 Act, should not be taken to suggest that thinking was completely at a standstill. On the contrary, the serious practical, and often theoretical problems, connected with planning were keenly debated. Every formula had its defects, which were identified by the case-work involving draft planning schemes and applications for Interim Development Orders. These difficulties gave rise to what some commentators have described as an experimental approach to planning. Nettlefold recalled in 1914 how the 'best informed town planners' regarded the Act of 1909 as only 'a sort of trial trip' and, writing in 1931, Thomas Adams described the period after 1909 'as an experimental era in town planning'. Adams looked forward to the next era when 'we can build on the foundations of past experience and accumulated knowledge'.[14]

In a sense the experiments continued. Far from being a dismal retreat, the eventual Act of 1932 contained a remarkable degree of administrative flexibility. In his letter to Ramsay MacDonald in 1932 Hilton-Young had emphasized the extent to which the Minister had retained extremely wide powers of discretion and initiative (see p. 74), and his contention was borne out by subsequent events. The Ministry encouraged local authorities to examine a wide range of planning procedures: conservative Ministers gave rulings on draft schemes and appeals against the refusal of Interim Development Orders which clearly gave warning that landowners should take account of the public interest when considering development. The fruits of this experience contributed to such concepts as the Rural Zone, introduced by the Ministry in 1938. War broke out before the results of this and other innovations could be assessed.

The experimental approach was welcomed by many planners. In his Presidential Address to the Town Planning Institute in 1937, E. C. Culpin claimed that 'it has been a very good thing to have a trying-out period during which things are more or less in a state of flux'. The experience would be invaluable when it came to implementing the individual planning schemes. It was entirely appropriate that the local authorities participated in this kind of experimentation. The first to be exposed to changes in social and economic conditions, the local authorities had a tradition of applying to parliament for Local Acts and Provisional Orders which might help them adapt to the new circumstances. In a debate of 1929 Aneurin Bevan described local administration as a political laboratory, where experiments were being carried out every day. Some of the new concepts put into operation were found to be so useful that they were later taken up as the basis for national legislation. In this context, statutory planning was an extension, and not a new departure, for the local authorities.[15]

To be fruitful and productive, an experimental approach needs a strong sense of purpose and direction—which central government failed to provide in the inter-war period. The times were perhaps against such a trend. Any move toward a more centralized form of planning immediately aroused fears lest this might reduce local autonomy. Many politicians from all parties served on county and district councils. Baroness Sharp must have represented most civil servants when she spoke of having been brought up to believe 'passionately that the foundations of our democracy were in local government'. Even in the field of housing, where the government made comparatively large sums available for slum clearance, the administration of the schemes was left in the hands of the local authorities.[16]

It was the role of central government to facilitate, and not to take over, the functions of local government, and this applied to planning as much as to any other sector of the government service. As a result, even the most innocuous grant-in-aid might be scrutinized to see whether it would lead to greater inspection, supervision, control, and criticism, and therefore reduce the right and capacity of local authorities to think and act for themselves. In any case, the inter-war period was hardly an appropriate time to turn local councils into receptacles for government policy, when the prestige of central government, especially after the Slump, was so low. Centralized forms of planning had to await the closing stages of the Second World War, when the credibility of central government was beyond doubt.[17]

The only previous occasion when an interventionist policy might have been practical was in the aftermath of the First World War, when the ministries of Labour, Health, and Transport had been established. A committee, appointed by the Prime Minister, warned of the large schemes proposed for housing, agriculture, forestry, electric power and commercial aviation in the post-war period. In order to ensure that each piece of land was put to the best use, private land should be expropriated without undue delay or expense, subject of course to the protection of the owner from injustice and award of fair compensation.[18]

The enthusiasm for reconstruction, and all it implied, soon waned. Although the ministries survived, the extension of the State's role in public life was modest. With respect to land-use planning, the post-war generation decided that new houses were so badly needed that planning had to take second place. According to Thomas Sharp, that generation cast aside all the virtues of a crisis. Periods of rapid change provide the greatest opportunities for achieving 'all those qualities that make a town good to live in'. It was much harder to impose order, organization and architectural cohesion when only one or two houses were being built at a time.[19]

The failure to sustain an interventionist role on the part of central government in the 1920s has been variously attributed to a loss of nerve on the part of governments and to a lack of resolution and policies on the part of the Treasury and the government departments. The obstructive role of the Treasury has already been noted with respect to ancient monuments and the promotion of outdoor recreation. Such instances highlighted the very considerable negative powers exerted by the Treasury, especially after 1924, when no new policy involving increased expenditure could be placed before the Cabinet without prior reference to the Treasury.

The effects of these constraints may have been compounded by the apathy and confusion on the part of the government departments. Faced with growing public concern as to the destruction of the countryside and extent of urban sprawl, the Ministry of Health extended statutory planning without, according to Baroness Sharp, any clear idea as to what was required and how it might be achieved. In her words, 'the whole thing evolved out of a modest extension of the building controls of local authorities', almost without any government noticing the implications of what was happening. The essentially permissive powers granted on an incremental basis had grown into something nationwide in its ramifications and significance.[20]

Whatever the merits of growth by default, one of the defects may be a lack of resources, and this became increasingly obvious with respect to statutory planning. According to the Deputy Secretary, Sir John Maude, planning was the Cinderella of the responsibilities of local government. Road-building might benefit from the Road Fund, and parliament had voted monies for slum clearance and house construction, but local councils were merely exhorted to undertake statutory planning. Clearly, there would have been considerable difficulties in deciding how, when and where Exchequer aid should have been awarded to planning, but such problems had been overcome with respect to other local government services. The lack of central funds for planning underlined its generally low priority. Planning had been introduced and extended almost incidentally—on the coat-tails of local government and housing legislation. Looking back over his years as Permanent Secretary in the Ministry of Health (1920–35), Sir Arthur Robinson is alleged to have regretted not having given planning the encouragement and resources which, with hindsight, it had so clearly deserved.[21]

In one fundamental respect, the arrangements made for planning were regarded as only an interim measure. The Labour Government had revived proposals for a tax on land values, and the Chancellor of the Exchequer, Philip

Snowden, introduced a Bill in 1930 for the valuation of land for this purpose. The proposals for land valuation and taxation were later incorporated in the Budget of 1931. These moves on the part of the Treasury naturally precluded the Minister of Health from concurrently making fundamental changes to the financial basis of planning. In a postscript to a letter of May 1931, a member of the Ministry wrote, 'the land tax is an infernal nuisance coming just at the moment'. It was expected that the existing arrangements for compensation and betterment would soon be overhauled and absorbed into a wider land-tax system. This did not happen. Following the change in government, the Land Valuation Clauses of the Finance Act of 1931 were suspended, and eventually repealed in 1934. This left the financial basis of the 1932 Act permanently unresolved and, because of the highly contentious nature of the subject, even within the respective political parties, no one was keen to grasp the nettle again.[22]

Because of these larger political issues, statutory planning was left in a state of limbo. The sanctity of property rights remained virtually untouched, and no Exchequer aid was forthcoming to offset the consequent costs of compensation or compulsory purchase. The Town and Country Planning Advisory Committee reminded the Minister in 1938 of the pressing need for decisions on such questions as the public ownership of land, a pooling of landownership, and the payment of compensation out of an increment fund. Until the government took the necessary decisions on how the value and ownership of land might be readjusted in the wider interests of the community, the existing methods of assessing and meeting the costs of compensation would deter local authorities from 'actively' intervening in land-use questions.[23]

The outcome was the appointment of another wartime committee to study the question of public control of land use, namely the Expert Committee on Compensation and Betterment under Mr Justice Uthwatt. In its report of 1942 the Committee attributed the lack of progress to the fact that the problems under study were so fundamental that they could not be resolved 'by a system of patchwork amendments of the existing code of law or piecemeal adaptation of the existing procedure' of, say, town planning. Existing legislation sought to preserve, in a highly developed economy, a purely individualistic approach to landownership. Whilst this might have been tenable in the past, it was no longer appropriate at a time when a premium had to be set on the proper and effective use of very limited national resources.[24]

The Uthwatt Committee emphasized that town and country planning was not an end in itself. It was an instrument by which land could be used to further the best interests of the community and, because the needs and outlook of the community were constantly changing, attitudes toward the use and ownership of land should also be modified to meet the new situations. The failure to reappraise the sanctity of property rights had arisen out of a failure to appreciate the full implications of the greater executive role conferred on local and central government. Until this was remedied, the conferment of further interventionist powers would merely compound the frustrations of the inter-war period.

In a review of the Uthwatt report, one writer drew attention to the wider implications of a drastic reappraisal of the rights of the landowner. If decisions as to the future development of land were to be transferred on an increasing scale from the individual to the State, as represented by the local authority, this would raise many questions about the competence of the new decision-makers. The reviewer believed that most of the criticisms of town and country planning in the past had sprung from doubts over the abilities of those whose job it was to administer planning. If local authorities were to be even more directly involved in questions of land use and management, they would have to be considerably overhauled.[25]

Not surprisingly, most attention in the early years of statutory planning was given to the promotion of the planning schemes. Abercrombie warned that there were simple people who thought that once an Act of Parliament was passed, its objectives were magically attained. In fact, the opposite was true: an Act or planning scheme was only the beginning. A scheme needed just as much skill and determination to administer as had gone into its preparation. In this context, Thomas Adams believed that statutory planning had been extraordinarily fortunate in the quality of its administrators.[26]

No one worked in watertight compartments: local authorities made generous acknowledgement to the advice given informally by inspectors from the Ministry. The kind of relationship that evolved between Pepler and the CPRE was suggested by a tribute made by its secretary, Herbert Griffin, who wrote, 'I cannot tell you how much I value the advice and assistance which you give me with such generosity. It is an enormous encouragement to me, and it would be quite impossible for me to get on without it'. Pepler also played an important role in helping to establish planning as a highly-esteemed and attractive career. As Honorary Secretary of the Town Planning Institute, he attended every meeting of Council and probably exerted more influence over the Institute than any other member.[27]

The traffic was not all one way. Abercrombie provides an example of how a leading academic figure in the planning profession and voluntary movement contributed to the work of both local and central government, acting as an expert consultant on many planning schemes and as an adviser to the Ministry on numerous occasions. Holford has written of how Abercrombie brought a uniquely synoptic view of physical planning problems to any discussion. He was a prominent member of the famous Royal Commission on the Distribution of Industrial Population, where 'his quick mind and wide experience helped to make the minutes of evidence illuminating' and the recommendations of more lasting value than usual. Abercrombie believed that it was the duty of all planners, in addition to their scientific and artistic work, to help promote their cause. While a university department might not feel that its first duty was to rouse public opinion, it should not err toward the opposite extreme by confining itself to abstruse speculations and purely theoretical solutions to human problems. At the summer schools of the Town Planning Institute, and in such gatherings as those of Political and Economic Planning (PEP), the interchange of ideas and experiences helped to establish a competence that ensured that town and country planning became an integral part of central and local government.[28]

The role of personalities in the decision-making process was often significant. At the regional scale, the contribution of J. Chuter Ede to the preservation of the rural landscape of Surrey is beyond doubt. Likewise, the initiatives and driving force of Sir Roy Robinson were critically important in the evolving relationship between afforestation and other forms of rural land use. On one occasion, Sir Warren Fisher, the Permanent Secretary of the Treasury, described Robinson as 'a vigorous, keen and active man—with the defects that often accompany these qualities, a tendency towards pushfulness and a liking to be "in the picture"'. Whatever his motives, Robinson used every opportunity to promote such initiatives as the National Forest Parks. The steps taken by Sir Lionel Earle to preserve the environs of ancient monuments, and by Charles Bressey to stimulate tree planting, serve to illustrate the scope for personal initiative within the government service of the inter-war years.[29]

According to a member of the Ministry of Health at the time, the 'real centre of power' in the Ministry was at the Principal level. With the possible exception of Pepler, the Principals and Inspectors were, however, so busy with casework that they hardly ever had an opportunity to exert a more general influence over policy in the planning field. Again, although two of the most senior civil servants, I. G. Gibbon and E. J. Maude, were personally interested in statutory planning, neither was able to give much time to the subject. The outstanding exception was in 1931/2, when Gibbon was engaged in drafting the Town and Country Planning Bills. His apparent fondness for conferences and his forcefulness in argument must have proved invaluable at that time.[30]

Among politicians, there was also scope for personal initiative, especially where the civil servants concerned were also found to be sympathetic. The deep-seated personal commitments of W. Ormsby-Gore and Col. W. Ashley as ministers helped to ensure progress in the preservation of ancient monuments and the planting of roadside verges respectively. Perhaps in response to strong pressure from Ramsay MacDonald, Sir Edward Hilton-Young decided to risk considerable unpopularity in the new parliament by reintroducing Labour's Town and Country Planning Bill. His son described him as a politician 'at home' in scholarship, administration, and debate, but never in party politics. His passionate interest in the countryside was widely recognized: he published a collection of essays on wild birds after his retirement.[31]

Perhaps the most enigmatic political figures were MacDonald and Chamberlain. Both were politicians who needed the countryside for inspiration and relaxation. Ramsay MacDonald continually yearned for Lossiemouth and the Highlands, and Chamberlain cherished the grounds of Chequers, for example, as much as any Prime Minister. A keen ornithologist, his personal papers contain many references to natural history subjects. MacDonald made many interventions on behalf of rural preservation, but rarely to any effect. There were so many demands on his time as Prime Minister that he was forced to admit, on more than one occasion, that 'I cannot be personally in charge of everything at home and abroad'. The result for MacDonald and rural preservation was a series of insights and initiatives which had to be left in mid-air, as hints rather than as policies. As for Chamberlain, his concern for planning seemed to diminish with personal promotion, so that by the time he had reached the highest office, he had almost disappeared from view on the planning scene.[32]

No one underestimated the difficulties that lay ahead in securing the wise use of land and its natural resources. Gwilym Gibbon wrote in 1921 that:

it is extremely important not to attempt too much at the beginning in the way of regulation, to watch carefully the results of measures which are taken, and to alter objectives and procedures accordingly, to conciliate public opinion and interests so far as is fairly possible, and to keep always in the forefront the gains of town planning for industrial and commercial efficiency.

The Ministry of Health was under no illusions as to the efficacy of this gradualist approach to improvements, or of the methods adopted under the 1932 Act and its predecessors. As Gibbon remarked, 'I do not expect much immediately . . . the most important matter, to begin with, is to have the principle [of statutory planning] established; its application can then be extended and modified.'[33]

In a lecture commemorating the twenty-first anniversary of statutory planning in 1931, Pepler asserted that:

there is still a long way to go before we shall be in sight of the realisation of our ideal, namely, that for every part of our country there shall be a plan, each plan being designed with the purpose of ensuring that every inch of our beloved land shall be put to its most productive use, with full regard to health, amenity, convenience and economy.

In discussion after the lecture, the Chief Engineer of the Ministry of Transport, C. H. Bressey, noted that the planners had already made a valuable start. Nowadays one could 'use the word amenity without being denounced as a highbrow or a long-haired artist'![34]

Even so, the stormy passage of the 1932 Bill was a timely reminder that progress, and indeed the existing status of planning, could not be taken for granted. In a speech to the Town Planning Institute in 1934, Neville Chamberlain stressed the need for everyone engaged in planning to prepare public opinion for the day when 'the whole country will come under control of some kind or another'. It would inevitably take a long time because of the way in which planning 'affected so closely personal interests and personal liberties'. In the meantime, there would be 'irreparable damage' to the towns and countryside. He concluded, 'We must all regret this delay, but at the same time, as practical people, I think we must recognise that if the pace was made too hot there would undoubtedly be reactions which might have even more disastrous results.' This was no doubt a wise and pragmatic view, borne out of years of hard-won experience as alderman and mayor of one of Britain's leading cities, Birmingham. Chamberlain had seen at first hand the unwavering hostility of many members of his own political party toward the concept of planning. But time was not on the side of Chamberlain and other advocates of the gradualist approach, whether on the home or international fronts.[35]

Before many of the statutory planning schemes and more general initiatives in land use and management had been realized, war broke out again. It had the effect of a late frost, striking just before harvest time. However, the most fundamental problems in securing a wise use of rural land resources had been recognized. How could a balance be struck between personal initiative and the needs of the community, or between local and regional or national interests? How could the financial implications of planning be resolved? How far should statutory planning cater for immediate needs? Was it better to allow national planning to evolve out of local and regional schemes, or should a centrally formulated plan be imposed? And, on a more general level, how could new uses of the countryside, such as large-scale tourism, be introduced with the minimum of disruption? What future was there for such concepts as multiple land use and the landscaping of old and new features in the countryside? The experiences of the 1930s would be highly relevant in the phase of recovery and reconstruction that would follow the new war.

THE POSITIVE APPROACH

Why was the pace so slow? Why were the policies for the optimal use and management of land regarded by many as premature—put forward before there was sufficient grass-roots support to ensure their acceptance and success? Perhaps the main reason was that it took time for people to appreciate the scale and effect of changes taking place in the countryside. From the vantage point of the 1970s, John Betjeman wrote of how it is now easy to forget how 'rich England was in undisturbed villages, where streets wandered into commons and woodland; how there were duckponds beside roads and horse-troughs beside highways'. There seemed to be so much unspoiled country and coast that some could be easily spared for building homes to accommodate those in search of fresh air.[36]

Dramatic changes were taking place in the quality of life. According to Glynn and Oxborrow, the inter-war years were something of a golden age when technology was clearly raising living standards without, as yet, many of the snags becoming apparent. There appeared to be 'no offsets to the better built, better heated houses or to running water or electric heating and lighting'. The roads were 'still fairly empty and the ownership of a motor car offered to many both technical interest and efficient and convenient transport'. The beaches were uncluttered and 'beauty spots were on the whole still beautiful'.[37]

How great was the demand for rural preservation? As late as 1937 a Member of Parliament warned that attempts to preserve the countryside in its natural state would come 'up against public opinion'. Most people regarded mountains with horror and hostility which, as in the case of Snowdon, could only be mitigated by building a railway. According to the member, 'it is no use pretending that beauty is in popular demand, because it just is not'. For most visitors to the countryside, the first priority was to introduce the essentials of urban life, beginning with Lyons tea-and-cake shops.[38] Others considered the main impediment to be one of ignorance and apathy, rather than belligerence. A leading figure in the garden city movement, F. J. Osborn, described how many urban areas were so devoid of visual beauty that man could hardly live there without his senses becoming dulled. Man nevertheless continued to love the countryside and greeted it with rapture whenever a visit was possible, but aesthetic starvation brought its retribution. His excursions often desecrated what he loved. By the same token, the speculators who built 'pink asbestos bungalows' in beautiful countryside, and those who lived in the visual outrages, were not vandals or social outcasts. In the words of Clough Williams-Ellis, they were 'decent, God-fearing, God-damning Englishmen', who lacked thought and imagination. In every man, there was an inherent love of nature and desire for amenity. The overriding need was to redevelop these attributes, and incorporate them more fully into the personal 'round of daily life'.[39]

Educative propaganda could take many forms. The child was 'the most promising pupil', and Sir Gwilym Gibbon, in his book of 1937, suggested that studies should be carried out to discover at what age children were 'likely to be most receptive to lessons leading to the love of nature and the beautiful'. As for adults, much could be achieved through 'general exhortation and instruction, as by books and pamphlets, addresses, exhibitions and the like', but the most effective education would come by encouraging people to visit the country and enjoy 'the amenities, with some gently insinuated instruction'.[40]

The task was not quite as daunting as appeared at first sight. Although 80 per cent of the population lived in towns, and a quarter was concentrated in thirteen towns, much of the growing concern for the preservation of nature and the countryside was coming from townspeople. The urban worker was showing just as much interest in the pleasures and beauties of the countryside as country folk. This was displayed not only by the growing popularity of such outdoor activities as camping and walking, but also in the contribution made by these urban dwellers to the work of the various projects and organizations concerned with amenity and nature protection.

Even the most sanguine observer had to concede that education was a long-term venture, and that the countryside was meanwhile being destroyed at an alarming rate. It was essential to take action while there was still something worth preserving and, on the premise that desperate situations called for desperate remedies, Clough Williams-Ellis wrote his book *England and the octopus*, in 'the hope of piercing the thick and often calloused skins of my countrymen'. As the author observed, 'the biological use and justification of pain is to give warning of damage or ill-health'. Perhaps the time had come to use the technique on the 'generously endowed English', so as to remind them that 'to go as you please is not always to arrive at what is pleasant'.[41]

Clough Williams-Ellis described his book of 1928 as the feelings of an 'angry young man', and many others wrote books and pamphlets, and gave talks and lectures, in a similar vein. A book edited by Williams-Ellis in 1937, *Britain and the beast*, drew together the outraged and indignant feelings of twenty writers, drawn from a wide literary and professional circle. The over-all effect was to arouse the interest of an unprecedented number of people, but there were serious defects in this almost total reliance on shock therapy. The effects soon worked off and many dismissed the dire warnings of rural demise as unduly melodramatic. Above all, it was a cheerless, negative kind of treatment, where fear was the main form of excitement and stimulation.[42]

On more than one occasion, the partisans of the rural preservation movement were criticized for their sentimental and obsessive concern for detail. W. A. Eden wrote in 1930 of how one local preservationist body had concentrated almost all its energies on saving a single row of old, half-timbered cottages. Not only did this enthusiasm ignore the more fundamental problems of the country-side, but it was likely to alienate those whose sympathies were essential for the movement. The time had come to look at rural preservation from a wider angle, to distinguish what was valuable, and to lay down some general principles for future development. Whereas previously, there had been a tendency to focus on the single building, street, or settlement, it was time to take the entire land-scape, with its ever-expanding borders, as a unit for study and treatment. This was one of the main attractions of the national parks movement of the 1930s. The proposed park areas were not only outstanding for their amenity and recreational potential, but their selection and administration would provide unprecedented opportunities for appraising, using and managing the country-side in its totality.[43]

In trying to arouse feelings and initiate action on behalf of amenity, it was easy for the various protagonists to appear arrogant and dogmatic. When a deputation met the Minister in 1933, the Ministry of Health took the oppor-tunity 'to interpolate a word as to the advantage of modesty among the advocates of amenities'. As a brief to the Minister stated:

there is in some quarters too great an inclination to think that their notion of what constitutes amenities is the one certain gospel. Taste is not a matter for dogmatism and, further, the most serious damage that the advocates of amenity can do to their cause is to give the general public any notion that there is something essentially incompatible between necessary development and amenity. The two have to be married, or amenity will be the one to suffer in the long-run.[44]

All too many writers dwelt on the troubles of the present, and gave little detailed consideration to realistic plans for the future. Many of the strident demands for a Ministry of Amenities, a system of national parks, and land nationalization, begged the question of how these concepts might be reconciled with all the other activities and aspirations of private and public life. Very few writers worked out in detail the ramifications of their proposals and how they would relate to the individual tracts of countryside and sectors of rural and urban life. It was as if they expected everything else to be cast aside for the sake of a revolution on behalf of rural amenity.

The recruits who joined the battle for the countryside did so mainly out of a sense of fear for the future. But fear alone is not a good recruiting officer: soldiers need something to fight *for*, as well as *against*. Other ways had to be found of stimulating and sustaining the battle—positive reasons which could make the future exciting and attractive for those who were repelled by the present and past. Fortunately, writers, who were capable of giving such a lead to individuals, organizations and eventually the government, were beginning to emerge during the 1930s.

Writing in the journal of the Institute of Landscape Architects, Thomas Adams criticized the rural preservation movement for failing to use more constructive methods of response to 'the widely expressed condemnation of vandalism'. There was too much reliance on public outcry and restrictive legislation. The only kind of positive response had been to imitate the past, rather than to create new landscapes 'to suit modern conditions'. According to Adams, 'if we are to save the beauty of England it must be done by design and planting that is adaptable to the new conditions, in addition to such preservation of good landscape as is possible'.[45]

Geoffrey Jellicoe was another writer to extol the need for a more positive attitude toward the landscape and the treatment of individual tracts of rural land. It was impossible to stop the march of progress and if it is accepted that conifer planting, for example, was required on a grand scale in the national interest, it was futile to oppose it. The aim should be to 'see how the best of the present English landscape can be preserved and absorbed into a new landscape that may not come to fruition for another hundred years'. In an editorial of 1938, Jellicoe described how the Sussex Downs might become afforested, or 'the Dorset meadows may give way to intensive cultivation, with all the accompanying indications of efficiency'. It was good that these changes should take place, because they proved that the nation was still 'virile', but their coming and impact had to be 'foreseen and designed', otherwise 'the beauty of the countryside will first become confused, as in fact it is to-day, and subsequently pass away'.[46]

One of the leading advocates of a more constructive and positive approach to rural preservation was John Dower, who played a considerable role in infusing this attitude of mind into the wider concern for town and country planning, especially during the Second World War when plans for post-war reconstruction were being laid. Although there was no chance of securing further safeguards for the countryside until the war ended, the delay might be put to good effect by using the delay to 'clear our minds for, and think out, future action'. The opportunity to pause for stock-taking and reappraisal was even more significant because of a profound shift that was taking place in public outlook.

In addition to winning the war, there was a growing public desire for radical improvements in the quality of life once peace returned. The mobilization of the nation's resources had brought military victory: now there were demands for post-war planning on a similarly all-embracing, far-reaching scale. The time was ripe for central government to make a further major bid for the governance of Britain.[47]

Dower's main concern was lest 'we should succeed in the more immediate and obviously negative tasks', such as banning sporadic and ribbon development in the countryside, 'but fail—or fail to get due credit—in the positive counterpart'. This would soon lead to defeat and chaos, because 'people would not tolerate indefinitely a system which seemed to do nothing but restrict and frustrate their desires and enterprises'. Ways had to be found of accommodating larger numbers of people in the countryside without impairing rural values and landscapes. Planners had to positively promote the development of overspill towns and the expansion of villages and hamlets, wherever this was in the wider interests of the community.

In a lecture on the preservation and development of rural Northumberland, Dower provided a case study of the scope for positive planning. In order to save the remarkable stock of stone-walled, slate-roofed cottages and farmhouses in the county, it was important to repair *and* adapt them to modern standards of living. Because it was generally too expensive to construct building extensions and replacement houses with traditional stone, alternative building materials had to be employed. It was now possible to render brickwork so that it resembled the colour of traditional stone-buildings. In addition to modernizing the homes of the people, the village communities also had to be equipped for modern life. Schools, village halls or community centres, playing-fields, piped water, and electricity were needed. Planners should conduct rapid but thorough surveys to identify these needs. In the upper valley of the North Tyne, there were exceptional opportunities to plan village communities *de novo*, where the vast planting programmes of the Forestry Commission were leading to a dramatic and permanent increase in rural population.[48]

Instead of opposing, or reluctantly conceding, every road construction and widening scheme, rural planners should help promote road improvement schemes where required, and ensure good design and harmony with the landscape. Negatively, they should prevent such out-of-place features as concrete kerbstones and tar-paved footpaths; positively, planners should encourage the planting of trees and shrubs, and careful shaping of the wayside banks and cuttings, and the establishment of a grass verge. A similar approach should be adopted with regard to mineral workings. Instead of waging a probably fruitless battle to prevent the extension of whinstone and limestone quarries, positive planning should aim to impose reasonable amenity standards. Not only should the amount of disruption and ugliness be kept to a minimum during the operational life of the quarry, but tidying-up, tree-planting and other forms of rehabilitation should be promoted after work had ceased.

Preservation should imply the management of the countryside in a positive sense—and nowhere was this clearer than in the protection of the remaining parkland and valley woods—'the chiefest jewel in Northumberland's crown'. With rare exceptions, it was far better to fell trees when they were mature, rather than to allow them to become stag-headed and decay with age. But for every tree cut down, it was essential that at least two were planted. Replanting and the revival of woodmanship were vital tasks in the planning of the future countryside.

Dower used the example of afforestation to emphasize the need to avoid a uniform approach to planning: each area had to be assessed on its own merits, using the skills and experience gained elsewhere. In Dower's view, the Keilder and Wark Forest would constitute a fine, if sombre, stretch of landscape, providing both timber and employment. The 'wide scale and easy slopes of the bulk of the upland country enables it to take extensive conifer plantations without the artificial and blanketing effects which they so patently and harmfully produce on the steep and delicately varied fellsides of the Lake District'. The potential for further planting in Northumberland was enormous, but Dower urged that the trees in some parts should be planted in scattered belts and patches, rather than as continuous forest. This would help to prevent the forest from dominating all areas and reduce the dislocation of sheep-farming.

After the war, the number of Tynesiders visiting the countryside for a day or longer was likely to increase substantially, and the Roman Wall, coastline, and other distinctive parts of the country would attract growing numbers of visitors from all over Britain and the world. It should be the aim of the planner to help provide holiday-makers with the greatest possible freedom in the countryside, 'subject only to such safeguards as will prevent consequent damage to its beauty, or to the well-being of those who inhabit and maintain it'. There should be 'ample sleeping and eating accommodation at reasonable prices, the right to ramble over uncultivated land, subject to a minimum of regulation, and the provision of adequate and convenient roads and footpaths to open the whole countryside to motoring, cycling and pedestrian enjoyment'.

During this period, John Dower was employed as a research officer in the Ministry of Town and Country Planning, preparing a report on the need for a series of national parks. When a draft of his report was circulated for comment at the end of 1943, another member of the Ministry used the opportunity to speculate on the administrative implications of a more positive approach to planning. Even if the government had the resources to take a more active part in deciding the optimal use and management of land, the writer was sceptical as to the feasibility of the exercise. How would the Ministry, for example, define amenity? What would be the criteria for implementing aesthetic controls? As the writer commented, 'pleasantness of physical environment is neither constant nor absolute, and different things pleased different people at the same time and the same people at different times'. For as long as planning was essentially negative, the Ministry and local authorities could avoid making judgements as to taste. If a distinguished architect applied for planning consent on a building, this could be given, not because the authority thought the design of the building was good but because it was inconspicuous and would not destroy any harmony of style in its neighbourhood. If planning became more positive, it would be very hard to avoid giving value-judgements as to whether a building were too modernistic or 'ye olde worlde'. Such judgements would take statutory planning into a completely new field of responsibility.[49]

THE ELUSIVE GOAL

During the inter-war period, a system of comprehensive town and country planning was evolving, designed to ensure the optimal use of each tract of land as appraised by the elected representatives of each locality and region. Some success was achieved, largely because the objectives of statutory planning were negative and the implementation of planning controls remained firmly in the hands of local and regional authorities. It was essentially a gradualistic approach and, not surprisingly, there were soon signs of impatience and frustration. More radical remedies were suggested for combating the speculative development of some regions and chronic decay of others. A greater sense of purpose was required in the form of positive and firm guidance at a national scale: the concept of a central planning authority was widely advocated.

As usual, the main difficulties were encountered in translating concepts into practice. How could the competence of a central planning authority be assured, and how could such an authority be introduced into the existing planning structure and the wider economic and social governance of the country? In spite of the unprecedented interest taken in planning during the Second World War, the chasm between good intentions and their implementation remained as wide as ever. Whether looking back at the previous twenty-five years of planning, or forward to the next quarter-century, it may be salutary to recall an exchange of letters that took place in 1945, shortly before the early death of John Dower.[50]

In 1945 the Ministry of Town and Country Planning asked him to comment on the draft of a circular to be sent to all local authorities, exhorting them to safeguard the natural beauty of the countryside and coast. The draft highlighted both the achievements and weaknesses of the early rural conservation movement. There was unequivocal support for conservation. The draft of the Minister's foreword began with the words: 'to conserve and cherish, and where practicable to restore or enhance, the natural beauty of our countryside and coastline is the concern of us all—holiday-visiting townsfolk no less than of resident countryfolk', and the foreword concluded with the sentence: 'the beauty of our country is one of the nation's greatest assets: it is for the planning authorities, as the nation's prime and statutory trustees, to safeguard this asset for the physical and spiritual refreshment of present and future generations'. But the remainder of the circular indicated that effective landscape planning was still some way off. The local authorities would still have to depend on their essentially negative powers, there was an acute shortage of technical, planning staff, the whole system of statutory planning was still under review, and the questions of new towns and national parks were unresolved. For some time yet, local authorities would have to defer positive action to ensure good development in the right place.

John Dower felt he had no alternative but to advise the abandonment of the circular. As he wrote, 'to say so little so cautiously, exposing so much indecision on key matters of policy, could only serve to depress and irritate the local authorities and to lower the Ministry's stock. Better to say nothing till we can say a good deal more, a good deal more confidently'. That occasion came in the Town and Country Planning Act of 1947, and the National Parks and Access to the Countryside Act of 1949.

NOTES

CHAPTER I

1 Dower MSS, lecture notes for a course at the London Polytechnic, 1937–9.
2 G. E. Cherry, 'The development of planning thought', in: *The spirit and purpose of planning*, ed. M. J. Bruton (Hutchinson), 1974, 66–84; A. J. P. Taylor, *English history, 1914–1945* (OUP), 1965, 298–320.
3 S. Glynn and J. Oxborrow, *Inter-war Britain: a social and economic history* (Allen & Unwin), 1976, 13–53.
4 Taylor, op. cit. 163–94.
5 N. Branson & M. Heinemann, *Britain in the nineteen thirties* (Panther), 1973, 156–7; J. Roebuck, *The making of modern English society from 1850* (Routledge & Kegan Paul), 1973, 108–39.
6 L. P. Abercrombie, 'The extension of the town planning spirit', *J. Tn Plann. Inst.* 12, 1925, 6; R. Graves & A. Hodge, *The long week-end: a social history of Great Britain 1918–1939* (Faber), 1940, 472 pp.; G. E. Cherry, 'Town planning and the motor car in twentieth century Britain', *High Speed Ground Transportation Journal*, 4, 1970, 69–79; H. Perkin, *The age of the automobile* (Quartet), 1976, 250 pp.; J. Burnett, *A social history of housing 1815–1970* (David & Charles), 1978, 246.
7 J. Stevenson, *Social conditions in Britain between the wars* (Penguin), 1977, 34–9; Glynn & Oxborrow, op. cit. 37; P. Mathias, *The first industrial nation* (Methuen), 1969, 438–44.
8 P. Hall, *Urban and regional planning* (Penguin), 1975, 83–4; D. E. Pitfield, 'The quest for an effective regional policy, 1934–7', *Regnl. Stud.* 12, 1978, 429–43.
9 Stevenson, op. cit. 11–27; W. Harrington & P. Young, *The 1945 revolution* (Davis-Poynter), 1978, 14; Perkin, op. cit. 99.
10 Glynn & Oxborrow, op. cit. 159–60; 'Next Five Years Group', *The next five years* (Macmillan), 1935, 7.
11 A. Marwick, 'Middle opinion in the thirties', *Eng. Hist. Rev.* 79, 1964, 285–98; A. Marwick, *Britain in the century of total war* (Bodley Head), 1968, 241–5; W. A. Robson (ed.), The Political Quarterly *in the thirties* (Allen Lane), 1971, 9–33.
12 G. M. Trevelyan, *Must England's beauty perish?* (Faber & Gwyer), 1929, 63 pp.; G. M. Trevelyan, *The call and claims of natural beauty: the third Rickman Godlee Lecture* (University College, London), 1931, 31 pp.; G. M. Trevelyan, *Autobiography* (Longmans, Green), 1949, 1–51.
13 R. W. Clark, *The Huxleys* (Heinemann), 1968, 283; R. G. Stapledon, *The land: now and to-morrow* (Faber), 1935, 4–8; V. Cornish, *The preservation of our scenery* (CUP), 1937, xi.

CHAPTER II

1 A. J. P. Taylor, *English history 1914–1945* (OUP), 1965, 167–8.
2 C. Hibbert (ed.), *An American in Regency England* (Maxwell), 1968, 142–3; J. M. Maidlow, *Six essays on commons preservation* (Sampson Low), 1867, 3; B. Kerr, *The dispossessed: an aspect of Victorian social history* (Baker), 1974, 37–8.
3 The *Standard*, 29/1/1914; N. Branson & M. Heinemann, *Britain in the nineteen thirties* (Panther), 1973, 220–1.
4 G. P. Wibberley, *Agriculture and urban growth* (Joseph), 1959, 54–5; Adams, Thompson & Fry, *North Middlesex regional planning scheme* (North Middlesex Joint Town Planning Committee), 1928, 15.
5 C. J. Cornish, *Wild England of today* (Seeley), 1895, 76–7.
6 East Sussex Record Office, Peacehaven Publicity Committee, *Peacehaven—the official guide*; V. Cornish, 'The cliff scenery of England and the preservation of amenities', *Geogrl. J.* 86, 1935, 505–11.
7 P. Abercrombie, 'The English countryside', in: The Political Quarterly *in the thirties*, ed. W. A. Robson (Allen Lane), 1971, 36–52.
8 A. Jackson, *Semi-detached London* (Allen & Unwin), 1973, 381 pp.; W. A. Robson, 'Minutes of evidence', *Royal Commission on the geographical distribution of the industrial population* (HMSO), 2, 1938, 778–94; J. Burnett, *A social history of housing 1815–1970* (David & Charles), 1978, 244.
9 Select Committees of the Houses of Lords and Commons, Minutes of Evidence on Surrey County Council

Bill, 1930–1; Surrey Record Office (SRO), TD 1084/3, and Law and Parliamentary Committee, minutes 1/10/1929.

10 SRO, TD 1084/3.

11 SRO, Town Planning Committee, minutes, 30/12/1929, 28/1/1930, and 23/1/1931.

12 Select Committees, op. cit.; SRO, Town Planning Committee, minutes, 28/5/1930, and 11/6/1930.

13 SRO, TD 1084/5.

14 P. Howarth, *Squire: most generous of men* (Hutchinson), 1963, 308 pp.; *Observer*, 22/9/1929, 17–18.

15 SRO, Law & Parliamentary Committee, minutes, 22/10/1929.

16 Epsom Rural District Council and Guildford Rural District Council Acts, 1930, 20 & 21 George 5, c. 115 and 116.

17 SRO, Law & Parliamentary Committee, minutes, 22/10/1929.

18 Select Committees, op. cit.

19 Surrey County Council Act, 1931, 21 & 22 George 5, c.101; SRO, Town Planning Committee, minutes, 20/1/1932.

20 SRO, Town Planning Committee, minutes, 3/5/1933, 4/7/1933, 30/11/1933, 16/12/1933, 20/12/1933, 11/4/1934, 10/10/1934, 5/7/1939, 6/9/1944.

21 SRO, Town Planning Committee, minutes, 17/1/1934 & 10/4/1935.

22 SRO, Town Planning Committee, minutes, 17/10/1934 & 1/1/1936.

23 SRO, Town Planning Committee, minutes, 6/2/1935.

24 SRO, Town Planning Committee, minutes, 11/4/1934.

25 SRO, Town Planning Committee, minutes, 31/3/1935, 10/4/1935, 7/10/1936, 11/11/1936, 2/12/1936, 13/1/1937, 23/2/1937, 2/2/1938.

26 Surrey County Council, leaflet on *Open spaces in Surrey*, 1969.

CHAPTER III

1 P. Abercrombie, 'The English countryside', in: The Political Quarterly *in the thirties*, ed. W. A. Robson (Allen Lane), 1971, 36–52.

2 Lord Phillimore, 'Agriculture and the preservation of the countryside', *J. Tn Plann. Inst.* 18, 1932, 171–4.

3 J. Sheail, 'Changes in the use and management of farmland in England and Wales, 1915–1919', *Trans. Inst. Br. Geogr.* 60, 1973, 17–32; E. H. Whetham, 'The Agricultural Act, 1920, and its repeal', *Agric. Hist. Rev.* 22, 1974, 36–49.

4 E. H. Whetham, *The agrarian history of England and Wales. Volume 8, 1914–1939* (CUP), 1978, 353 pp.; Public Record Office (PRO), MAF 38, 18 and 57.

5 D. Hall, *The pace of progress* (CUP), 1935, 25–26; K. A. H. Murray, *Agriculture* (HMSO), 1955, 17–39.

6 PRO, HLG 80, 1; Ministry of Works and Planning, *Report of the Committee on land utlization in rural areas*, Cmd. 6378, 1942, 138 pp.; C. S. Orwin for Agricultural Economics Research Institute, *Country planning* (OUP), 1944, 288 pp.

7 L. D. Stamp, 'The Scott report', *Geogrl. J.* 101, 1943, 16–30.

8 Anonymous, 'A new Stamp', *The Economist*, 143, 1942, 413; Anon., *Odi profanum vulgaris*, *The Economist*, 143, 1942, 263.

9 D. Hall, *Agricultural progress and agricultural depression during the last sixty years* (Kings College, Newcastle upon Tyne), 1939, 24–7.

10 PRO, MAF 38, 57.

11 Next Five Years Group, *The next five years* (Macmillan), 1935, 151–8.

12 PRO, MAF, 38, 71 and 641.

13 D. H. Smith, *The industries of Greater London* (King), 1933, 188 pp.

14 C. B. Purdom, *The building of the satellite towns* (Dent), 1949, 287.

15 R. E. Pahl, *Urbs in rure*, London School of Economics, Geography Papers, 2, 1964, 23.

16 A. M. Jones, *The rural industries of England and Wales: volume IV. Wales* (OUP), 1927, 42–3.

17 PRO, HLG 52, 547.

18 Malvern Hills Acts, 1909, 9 Edward 7, c. 37; and 1924, 14 & 15 George 5, c.36; Select Committee of the House of Lords, Minutes of Evidence on the Malvern Hills Bill, 1924; *Berrows Worcester Journal* & *Malvern News*; Cambridge University Library, Baldwin MSS, 64/D5, 2; Worcestershire Record Office, MSS 100.01, 288.1, and 233.18.

19 Parliamentary Debates, Commons, 310, 517–70.

20 Parliamentary Debates, Commons, 321, 1237–98.

21 Parliamentary Debates, Commons, 334, 422–83.

22 Parliamentary Debates, Commons, 374, 207–71.

23 Scottish Record Office (SRO), HH 1, 637
24 T. Johnston, *Memories* (Collins), 1952, 147–70.
25 Scottish Office, *Report of the Committee on hydro-electric development in Scotland*, Cmd.6406, 1942, 38 pp.
26 SRO, DD 11, 20; Parliamentary Debates, Commons, 387, 180–262; & 389, 1767–1818; Hydro-electric Development (Scotland) Act, 1943, 6 & 7 George 6, c.32.
27 SRO, HH 32, 231 & DD 11, 16.
28 J. Roebuck, *The making of modern English society from 1850* (Routledge & Kegan Paul), 1973, 108–39.
29 T. Sharp, *Town and countryside* (OUP), 1932, 11; T. Sharp, *Town planning* (Penguin), 1940, 152 pp.; S. D. Adshead, *A new England* (Muller), 1941, 66.

CHAPTER IV

1 G. D. MacNiven, 'Regional planning and rural preservation', *J. Tn Plann. Inst.* 15, 1928, 20–9.
2 C. Williams-Ellis, *England and the octopus* (Penrhyndeudraeth), reprinted 1975, 188 pp.
3 R. Fedden, *The continuing purpose* (Longmans), 1968, 226 pp.
4 O. G. S. Crawford, Editorial, *Antiquity*, 3, 1929, 1–4.
5 PRO, WORK 14, 213.
6 PRO, WORK 14, 488.
7 PRO, PRO 30/69, 1/56.
8 PRO, PRO 30/69, 2/25.
9 Parliamentary Debates, Lords, 79, 526–34; Ancient Monuments Preservation Act, 1931, 21 & 22 George 5, c.16.
10 PRO, WORK 14, 1124, 1259–61 & 1287.
11 PRO, WORK 14, 586–7.
12 Petroleum (Consolidation) Act, 1928, 18 & 19 George 5, c.32; Advertisements Regulation Act, 1907, 7 Edward 7, c.27; and 1925, 15 & 16 George 5, c.52.
13 C. E. M. Joad, *A charter for ramblers* (Hutchinson), 1934, 84–7.
14 PRO, PRO 30/69, 2/25.
15 PRO, HLG 52, 572.

CHAPTER V

1 P. Abercrombie, *The preservation of rural England* (Liverpool University Press and Hodder & Stoughton), 1926, 56 pp.
2 Scottish Record Office (SRO), HH 1, 633; P. Abercrombie, 'Planning in town and country', *Tn Plann. Rev.* 14, 1930, 1–12.
3 P. Abercrombie, *Country planning and landscape design* (Liverpool University Press and Hodder & Stoughton), 1934, 5–7.
4 J. B. Cullingworth, *Environmental planning. Volume I, Reconstruction and land use planning, 1939–1947* (HMSO), 1975, 283 pp.
5 W. Ashworth, *The genesis of modern British town planning* (Routledge & Kegan Paul), 1954, 167–237; G. E. Cherry, 'Influences on the development of town planning in Britain', *J. Contemp. Hist.* 4, 1969, 43–58; G. E. Cherry, 'The town planning movement and the late Victorian city', *Trans. Inst. Br. Geogr.* 4, 1979, 306–19.
6 R. Unwin, *Town planning in practice* (Fisher Unwin), 1909, 3–4.
7 J. S. Nettlefold, *Practical town planning* (St. Catherines Press), 1914, 493 pp.
8 Housing, Town Planning, &c., Act, 1909, 9 Edward 7, c.44; K. D. Brown, *John Burns* (Royal Historical Society), 1977, 138–51.
9 Ashworth, op.cit. 188–9.
10 T. Alwyn Lloyd, *Planning in town and country* (Routledge), 1935, 134; W. Kennet, *Preservation* (Temple Smith), 1972, 29.
11 J. B. Cullingworth, *Town and country planning* (Allen & Unwin), 1969, 18.
12 PRO, HLG 52, 552; SRO, HH 1, 635.
13 G. L. Pepler, 'Twenty-one years of town planning in England and Wales', *J. Tn Plann. Inst.* 17, 1931, 49–72; M. Bowley, *Housing and the State, 1919–1944* (Allen & Unwin), 1945, 288 pp.; Housing, Town Planning, &c., Act, 1919, 9 & 10 George 5, c.35; PRO, HLG 52, 688; Town Planning Act, 1925, 15 George 5, c.16.
14 PRO, HLG 52, 912.

15 SRO, DD 5, 721; Local Government (Scotland) Act, 1929, 19 and 20 George 5, c.25; Local Government Act, 1929, 19 George 5, c.17; K. B. Smellie, *A history of local government* (Allen & Unwin), 1946, 132.

16 Housing Act, 1923, 13 & 14 George 5, c.24.

17 P. Abercrombie and J. Archibald, *East Kent: regional planning scheme* (Liverpool University Press and Hodder & Stoughton), 1925, 113 pp.; G. Dix, 'Little plans and noble diagrams', *Tn. Plann. Rev.* 49, 1978, 337–8.

18 Rural Amenities Bill, 1929, 20 George 5, Bill 33; and 1930, 21 George 5, Bill 29; PRO, HLG 52, 552; SRO, HH 1, 635; Parliamentary Debates, Commons, 235, 1747–1831, and 247, 1931, 537–71.

19 PRO, HLG 52, 678–83 and 686.

20 Cambridge University Library (CUL), Kennet MSS, 16/10; Town and Country Planning Act, 1932, 22 & 23 George 5, c. 48.

21 PRO, PRO 30/69, 1/38.

22 Parliamentary Debates, Commons, 261, 39–51.

23 Parliamentary Debates, Commons, 251, 193–321.

24 C. F. A. Voysey, 'On town planning', *Archit. Rev.* 46, 1919, 25–6; T. Adams, 'The true meaning of town planning', *Archit. Rev.* 46, 1919, 75–7.

25 Parliamentary Debates, Commons, 266, 1859–68.

26 Local Government Board, *Report of Committee on building construction in connection with the provision of dwellings for the working classes*, Cmd. 9191, 1918, 97 pp.

27 E. G. Culpin, 'Notes and comments', *J. Tn Plann. Inst.* 17, 1931, 299–300; and 18, 1932, 227–9.

28 PRO, HLG 52, 686; CUL, Kennet MSS, 58/52a.

29 F. Longstreth Thompson, 'The new Act', *J. Tn Plann. Inst.* 19, 1932, 1–9.

30 J. Dower, 'Town planning and economics', *Weekend Rev.* 5, 1932, 420–1.

31 PRO, HLG 52, 686.

32 PRO, PRO 30/69, 1/38.

33 Cullingworth, 1975, op.cit. 168.

34 S. D. Adshead, 'Discussion', *J. Tn Plann. Inst.* 24, 1938, 191.

35 PRO, HLG 52, 548; Ministry of Health, *18th Annual Report, 1936–7*, Cmd. 5516, 1937, 144–5.

36 PRO, HLG 52, 686.

37 PRO, HLG 52, 548.

38 PRO, HLG 52, 678; East Sussex Record Office, Peacehaven Publicity Committee, *Peacehaven—the official guide*, and Accession Number 1275; E. H. W. Briault, 'Sussex', in: *The land of Britain*, ed. L. D. Stamp (Geographical Publications), 83–4, 1942, 552.

39 Poole Corporation Act, 1928, 18 & 19 George 5, c.94.

40 P. Abercrombie, 'Twenty years after', *Jl. R. Inst. Br. Archit.* 59, 1952, 156–61.

41 PRO, HLG 52, 548.

42 PRO, HLG 52, 678 and 682.

43 PRO, HLG 52, 679.

44 PRO, HLG 52, 681 and HLG 68, 21.

45 PRO, HLG 52, 747; Bowley, op.cit.

CHAPTER VI

1 Halifax Central Library, Archives, P 352, County Borough of Halifax, *Housing and town planning*, 1919–29, 34–7; Surrey Record Office, Surrey County Council, Town Planning Committee, minute books, 20/12/1933.

2 J. S. Nettlefold, *Practical town planning* (St. Catherine's Press), 1914, 147–53.

3 PRO, HLG 52, 912.

4 PRO, HLG 53, 269.

5 R. Unwin, *Town planning in practice* (Fisher Unwin), 1909, 416 pp.; Town Planning Committee, 'Suggestions to promoters of town planning schemes', *Jl. R. Inst. Br. Archit.* 18, 1911, 661–8.

6 G. E. Cherry, *The evolution of British town planning* (Leonard Hill), 1974, 275 pp.; M. P. Fogarty, *Town and country planning* (Hutchinson), 1948, 23.

7 J. D. Hulchanski, *Thomas Adams: a biographical and bibliographic guide* (Department of Urban & Regional Planning, Toronto University), 1978, 40 pp.; G. Dix, 'Little plans and noble diagrams', *Tn. Plann. Rev.* 49, 1978, 329–52; J. Sheail, 'The introduction of statutory planning in rural areas: the example of the North Riding of Yorkshire', *Tn. Plann. Rev.* 50, 1979, 71–83.

8 P. Hall, *Urban and regional planning* (Penguin), 1975, 64–7; P. Geddes, 'The influence of geographical conditions on social development', *Geogr. J.* 12, 1898, 580–7.

9 PRO, HLG 52, 912.

10 E. Sharp, *The Ministry of Housing and Local Government* (Allen & Unwin), 1969, 139–40.

11 PRO, HLG 52, 678.

12 F. B. Gillie, 'Problems of the historiography of British town and regional planning' (unpublished paper), 1978, 22 pp.

13 PRO, HLG 95, 92.

14 PRO, HLG 54, 176; Surrey County Council Act, 1936, 26 George 5 & 1 Edward 8, c.130.

15 Town Planning Institute, National planning and national survey, in: *Royal Commission on the geographical distribution of the industrial population* (HMSO), 2, 1938, 760–78; E. Sharp, 'Town and country planning', *Public Administration*, 26, 1948, 27–8.

16 PRO, MAF 48, 674.

17 S. Lee Vincent (personal communication).

18 Parliamentary Debates, Commons, 320, 419–81.

19 PRO, PRO 30/69, 1/38, & HLG 52, 678 and 708.

20 Town and Country Planning Advisory Committee, *Report on the preservation of the country* (HMSO), 1938, 36 pp.; Dower MSS, lecture notes for CPRE dinner, 1938; PRO, HLG 52, 709.

21 PRO, HLG 52, 547.

22 PRO, HLG 52, 550–1.

23 PRO, HLG 52, 549; J. Sheail, 'Coasts and planning in Great Britain before 1950', *Geogr. J.* 142, 1976, 257–73.

24 PRO, HLG 52, 545 and 549.

CHAPTER VII

1 Cumbria Record Office (CRO), CC4/7/36.

2 P. Abercrombie and S. H. Kelly, *Cumbrian regional planning scheme* (Liverpool University Press & Hodder & Stoughton), 1932, 220 pp.

3 CRO, CC4/7/30 & CC4/21/17.

4 PRO, HLG 52, 678.

5 PRO, HLG 53, 266 and 268.

6 Devon Record Office, Devon County Council, South Devon Regional Planning Committee, minutes.

7 P. Abercrombie, 'The extension of the town planning spirit', *J. Tn. Plann. Inst.* 12, 1925, 1–10.

8 P. Abercrombie, 'Administration of schemes prepared by joint committees', *J. Tn. Plann. Inst.* 23, 1937, 85–98.

9 East Sussex Record Office (ESRO), C/C2; Select Committee of the House of Lords, Minutes of evidence on the South Downs Preservation Bill, 1934; South Downs Preservation Bill, 1934, 24 & 25 George 5; Parliamentary Debates, Lords, 91, 907–23, & 96, 122–50; PRO, HLG 54, 59.

10 Parliamentary Debates, Commons, 235, 1747–1831.

11 PRO, HLG 29, 116 and 117.

12 T. Adams, *Recent advances in town planning* (Churchill), 1932, 73–4.

13 PRO, HLG 52, 716.

14 PRO, HLG 4, 60–1; West Sussex Record Office, OC/CM94/1/1–2 and OC/CM94/2/1.

15 ESRO, C/C2 and C/6.

16 PRO, HLG 52, 544.

17 G. E. Cherry, *Environmental planning. Volume II, National parks and recreation in the countryside* (HMSO), 1975, 173 pp.; J. Sheail, 'The concept of national parks in Great Britain, 1900–1950', *Trans. Inst. Br. Geogr.* 66, 1975, 41–56.

18 Cambridge University Library, Baldwin MSS, 64D, 5.3; PRO, F 19, 33.

19 PRO, HLG 52, 723 and F 18, 162; Financial Secretary to the Treasury, *Report of the National Park Committee*, Cmd. 3851, 1931, 131 pp.

20 F. Sandbach, 'The early campaign for a national park in the Lake District', *Trans. Inst. Br. Geogr.* 3, 1978, 498–514.

21 PRO, HLG 52, 716.

22 K. Spence, 'The Lakes', in: *Britain and the beast*, ed. C. Williams-Ellis (Dent), 1937, 251–2; PRO, HLG 52, 716.

23 PRO, HLG 52, 709.

24 PRO, HLG 52, 716.
25 PRO, T 161, 1183, S 34705.
26 PRO, HLG 52, 709.
27 PRO, HLG 68, 56.
28 PRO, T 161, 1183, S 34705.
29 PRO, HLG 52, 544.
30 Standing Committee on National Parks, *The case for national parks in Great Britain* (Council for the Preservation of Rural England), 1938, 16 pp.
31 J. Dower, *National parks in England and Wales*, Cmd. 6628, 1945, 57 pp.; National Parks and Access to the Countryside Act, 1949, c.97; H. C. Darby, 'British national parks', *Advmt. Sci.* 20, 1963, 307–18.

CHAPTER VIII

 1 P. Abercrombie, *Planning in town and country* (Liverpool University Press and Hodder & Stoughton), 1937, 11.
 2 J. Dower, 'Positive planning in Great Britain', *J. Tn. Plann. Inst.* 42, 1935, 961.
 3 Public Record Office (PRO), HLG 52, 532 and 715.
 4 PRO, PRO 30/69, 1/56; R. Fedden, *The continuing purpose* (Longman), 1968, 168–9.
 5 PRO, T 161, 293, S 34332.
 6 PRO, T 163, 70, G 3689/1 & 73, G 3870/1; C. B. Purdom, *Building of satellite towns* (Dent), 1949, 532 pp.
 7 PRO, HLG 52, 682; Parliamentary Debates, Commons, 251, 227–30.
 8 PRO, HLG 68, 21.
 9 PRO, HLG 52, 686.
10 PRO, PREM 1, 109 & HLG 68, 21; Ministry of Health, *Interim report of the Departmental Committee on regional development*, Cmd. 3915, 1931, 15 pp.
11 PRO, HLG 52, 678.
12 PRO, HLG 52, 531–2; Ministry of Health, *18th Annual Report, 1936–37*, Cmd. 5516, 1937, 129; F. B. Gillie, Privately circulated manuscript paper.
13 PRO, HLG 52, 686 and 747.
14 PRO, HLG 52, 1004 and 1006.
15 W. Ashworth, *The genesis of modern British town planning* (Routledge & Kegan Paul), 1954, 201–2; H. Warren and W. R. Davidge (eds.), *Decentralisation of population and industry* (King), 1930, 154 pp.
16 Dower, op. cit. 962–4.
17 G. Gibbon, *Problems of town and country planning* (Allen & Unwin), 1937, 54–9.
18 T. Adams, *Recent advances in town planning* (Churchill), 1932, 138–9.
19 L. Robbins, *Economic planning and international order* (Macmillan), 1937, 3.
20 Next Five Years Group, *The next five years* (Macmillan), 1935, 13.
21 PRO, PREM 1, 167; L. P. Abercrombie, 'Planning of town and country', *Tn. Plann. Rev.* 14, 1930, 1–12; J. Sheail, 'The Restriction of Ribbon Development Act: the character and perception of land-use control in inter-war Britain', *Regnl Stud.* 13, 1979, 501–12.
22 T. Adams, 'Landscape and road design', *J. London Soc.* 150, 1930, 117–28.
23 The Restriction of Ribbon Development Act, 1935, 25 & 26 George 5, c.47.
24 Parliamentary Debates, Commons, 305, 957–1070; Anonymous, 'The Ribbon Development Bill', *Justice of the Peace & Local Government Rev.* 99, 1935, 336–7.
25 Scottish Record Office (SRO), DD 15, 15; Scottish Economic Committee, *The highlands and islands of Scotland* (Scottish Economic Committee), 1938, 238 pp.; Parliamentary Debates, Commons, 350, 2171–7 and 2906–22.
26 SRO, DD 10, 302.
27 PRO, HLG 68, 50; Royal Commission on the Distribution of the Industrial Population, *Report*, Cmd. 6153, 1940, 320 pp.
28 PRO, HLG 68, 50.
29 A. Marwick, *The deluge* (Penguin), 1967, 261–2.
30 E. Simon, 'Town planning', *J. Tn. Plann. Inst.* 23, 1937, 381–9.
31 SRO, DD 10, 304; Parliamentary Debates, Commons, 359, 1026–94.
32 J. B. Cullingworth, *Environmental planning*, Volume I, *Reconstruction and land use planning, 1939–1947* (HMSO), 1975, 98–9.
33 B. Hackett, *Man, society and environment* (Percivall, Marshall), 1950, 236.

CHAPTER IX

1 L. P. Abercrombie, *Town and country planning* (OUP), 1933, 128–36.
2 J. B. Harley, *Ordnance Survey maps; a descriptive manual* (Ordnance Survey), 1975, 4; PRO, HLG 52, 541.
3 Departmental Committee on the Ordnance Survey, *Interim report* (HMSO), 1936, 16 pp., and *Final report* (HMSO), 1938, 39 pp.
4 J. B. Harley, *The Ordnance Survey and land-use mapping* (Geo Books), 1979, 58 pp.
5 Northamptonshire Record Office, Northamptonshire County Council, Education Committee minutes, volumes for 1927–30.
6 E. E. Field, 'The land utilization maps of Northampton', *Geography*, 87, 1930, 408–12.
7 L. D. Stamp, 'The land utilization survey of Britain', *Geogr. J.* 78, 1931, 40–53; L. D. Stamp, 'Planning the land for the future', *Town & Country Planning*, 5, 1937, 118; L. D. Stamp, *The land of Britain* (Longman), 1962, 3–19; C. Embleton and J. T. Coppock (eds.), *Land use and resources: studies in applied geography. A memorial volume to Sir Dudley Stamp* (Institute of British Geographers), 1968, 269 pp.
8 E. C. Willatts, 'Present land use as a basis for planning', *Geography*, 23, 1938, 95–106.
9 S. W. Wooldridge, 'Town and rural planning', *Geography*, 23, 1938, 90–3.
10 P. Abercrombie, 'Geography, the basis of planning', *Geography*, 23, 1938, 1–8.
11 L. P. Abercrombie, 'Planning of town and country', *Tn. Plann. Rev.* 14, 1930, 1–12.
12 J. Dower, 'The landscape and planning', *J. Tn. Plann. Inst.* 30, 1944, 92–102.
13 L. P. Abercrombie, *Country Planning and landscape design* (Liverpool University Press and Hodder & Stoughton), 1934, 7–14; T. Adams, 'Landscape and road design', *J. London Soc.* 150, 1930, 117–28.
14 J. Dower, 'Landscape in national parks', *Landscape & Garden*, 5, 1938, 91–3.
15 T. Sharp, *Town and countryside* (OUP), 1932, 29–30.
16 Dower, 1944, op. cit. 100–1.
17 A. E. Trueman, *The scenery of England and Wales* (Gollancz), 1938, 351 pp.
18 F. Younghusband, 'Natural beauty and geographical science', *Geogr. J.* 56, 1920, 1–13.
19 A. Goudie, 'Vaughan Cornish', *Trans. Inst. Br. Geogr.* 55, 1972, 1–16; V. Cornish, 'Harmonies of scenery', *Geography*, 14, 1928, 275–276.
20 V. Cornish, *The scenery of England* (Maclehose), 1937, 144 pp.; V. Cornish, *The beauties of scenery* (Muller), 1943, 128 pp.
21 O. J. R. Howarth, *The scenic heritage of England and Wales* (Pitman), 179 pp.
22 Dower, 1944 op.cit.; E. de Selincourt (ed.), *Wordsworth's Guide to the Lakes* (OUP), reprinted 1977, 212 pp.
23 A. Collett, *The changing face of England* (Cape), 1926, 289 pp.
24 Dower MSS, miscellaneous writings and lectures.
25 Abercrombie, 1934, op. cit.
26 Bristol Record Office, Bristol City Corporation MSS, 3245 and 3499B.
27 P. Abercrombie & B. F. Brueton, *Bristol and Bath regional planning scheme* (Liverpool University Press and Hodder & Stoughton), 1930, 167 pp. and also plan.
28 PRO, HLG 52, 1.
29 PRO, HLG 52, 2.
30 President of the Board of Trade, *Report of the Import Duties Advisory Committee*, Cmd. 5507, 1937, 75.
31 PRO, CAB 23, 89.
32 Ministry of Health, *Report of the Committee on the restoration of land affected by iron ore working* (HMSO), 1939, 117 pp.; PRO, HLG 52, 5.
33 PRO, HLG 52, 3–4.
34 PRO, HLG 52, 5.
35 P. Abercrombie, 'The basis of reconstruction', *Tn. Plann. Rev.* 17, 1919, 203–10.
36 G. Gibbon, *Problems of town and country planning* (Allen & Unwin), 1937, 68, 86–8, 183–5 and 188.
37 M. Nicholson, 'A factual basis for territorial planning', *J. Tn. Plann. Inst.* 22, 1936, 287–91.
38 PRO, T 161 844, S 41977 and HLG 52, 905; Scottish Record Office, DD 12, 44.
39 PRO, MAF 38, 432.
40 PRO, MAF 38, 57 and 432.
41 PRO, MAF 38, 868.
42 Ministry of Agriculture, *National farm survey of England and Wales, 1941–1943* (HMSO), 1946, 109 pp.

CHAPTER X

1 Dower MSS, 'The countryside after the war', and 'Planning for Britain's future in town and country'.
2 R. G. Stapledon, *The hill lands of Britain* (Faber), 1937, 138 pp.

3 Dower MSS, 'Afforestation and farming'.
4 G. Ryle, *Forest service* (David & Charles), 1969, 340 pp.
5 PRO, F 19, 21 and 22, and T 161, 1069, S 40641; H. H. Symonds, *Afforestation in the Lake District* (Dent), 1936, 97 pp.; F. R. Sandbach, 'The early campaign for a national park in the Lake District', *Trans. Inst. Br. Geogr.* 3, 1978, 498–514.
6 Parliamentary Debates, Lords, 100, 363–405.
7 PRO, T 161, 1069, S 40641.
8 Cambridge University Library, Baldwin MSS, 25D, 3.9.
9 PRO, F 18, 289.
10 Parliamentary Debates, Commons, 330, 525–9.
11 *The Times*, 23/12/1937.
12 PRO, F 19, 10.
13 *The Times*, 23/12/1937.
14 PRO, F 19, 21 and 22.
15 Forestry Commission, *Report by the Joint Informal Committee of the Forestry Commission and the Council for the Preservation of Rural England* (HMSO), 1936, 8 pp.
16 Parliamentary Debates, Commons, 330, 477–534.
17 *The Times*, 29/12/1937 and 16/12/1937.
18 PRO, T 161, 1069, S 40641.
19 PRO, MAF 50, 17.
20 PRO, F 19, 23.
21 Financial Secretary to the Treasury, *Report of the National Park Committee*, Cmd. 3851, 1931, 111–19; PRO, F 18, 162 and F 19, 9.
22 PRO, T 161, 628, S 38400.
23 PRO, F 18, 162 and F 19, 10; J. Walton (ed.), *Guide to the Argyll National Forest Park* (HMSO), 1938, 29 pp.
24 PRO, T 161, 1183, S 34705.
25 PRO, T 161, 1069, S 40641.
26 PRO, F 19, 37.
27 PRO, F 19, 11 and 38.
28 PRO, F 18, 217 and F 19, 23.
29 Forestry Commission, *Post-war forestry*, Cmd. 6447, 1943, 77–80.
30 J. Sheail, 'The concept of national parks in Great Britain, 1900–50', *Trans. Inst. Br. Geogr.* 66, 1975, 41–56.
31 PRO, T 161, 1183, S 34705.
32 Scottish Record Office (SRO), HH 1, 2587.
33 PRO, F 19, 10.
34 SRO, HH 1, 2587.
35 Forestry Commission, *British forestry* (HMSO), 1974, 30–6.

CHAPTER XI

1 Lord Eversley, *Commons, forests and footpaths* (Cassell), 1910, 356 pp.
2 B. Ward, *The retreats of Epping Forest* (Epping Forest Conservators), 1978, 31 pp.
3 J. B. Priestley, *English journey* (Heinemann & Gollancz), 1934, 173–5.
4 Malvern Hills Act, 1930, 20 & 21 George 5, c.72; *Berrows Worcester Journal*, 3/5/1930.
5 C. E. M. Joad, *The untutored townsman's invasion of the country* (Faber), 1946, 116–17.
6 W. H. Williams, *A short history of the Society and its work* (Commons, Open Spaces and Footpaths Preservation Society), 1965, 30 pp.
7 Access to Mountains Act, 1939, 2 & 3 George 6, c.30; G. E. Cherry, *Environmental planning. Volume II, National parks and recreation in the countryside* (HMSO), 1975, 16–25.
8 J. Dower, 'Holiday use of countryside and coastline', *Jl. R. Inst. Br. Archit.* 50, 1943, 181–4; J. Sheail, 'Coasts and planning in Great Britain before 1950', *Geogr. J.* 142, 1976, 257–73.
9 R. Graves and A. Hodge, *The long week-end* (Faber), 1940, 244–7; Scottish Record Office (SRO), DD 13, 226.
10 Camping Club of Great Britain, *Sites list and year book* (Camping Club of Great Britain), 1975, 384–8.
11 Public Health Act, 1875, 38 & 39 Victoria, c.55; Housing of the Working Classes Act, 1885, 48 & 49 Victoria, c.72; Public Health (Scotland) Act, 1897, 60 & 61 Victoria, c.38.
12 Public Record Office (PRO), HLG 52, 393, 399–400.
13 Public Health Acts Amendment Act, 1907, 7 Edward 7, c.53.

14 Select Committee of the House of Lords, *Minutes of Evidence on Surrey County Council Bill*, 1931, 4.
15 PRO, HLG 52, 394.
16 PRO, HLG 52, 399.
17 Select Committee of the House of Commons, *Minutes of Evidence on Surrey County Council Bill*, 1931, 1.
18 PRO, HLG 52, 393–4 and 411.
19 Surrey County Council Act, 1931, 21 and 22 George 5, c.101.; Surrey Record Office, TD 1084; PRO, HLG 54, 174–5.
20 Lincolnshire Archives Office, Lindsey County Council, 1517–18; J. Sheail, 'The impact of recreation on the coast: the Lindsey County Council (Sandhills) Act, 1932', *Landscape Plann.* 4, 1977, 53–72.
21 Essex County Council Act, 1933, 23 & 24 George 5, c.45; PRO, HLG 52, 394.
22 Plympton St. Mary Rural District Council Act, 1933, 23 & 24 George 5, c.78.
23 SRO, DD 13, 226; PRO, HLG 52, 395–6.
24 PRO, HLG 52, 393–4 and 398–9.
25 PRO, HLG 52, 395.
26 SRO, DD 13, 226 and, for example, DD 13, 1540; Bridlington Corporation Act, 1933, 23 & 24 George 5, c.73.
27 Camping Club of Great Britain & Ireland, *Year book, with list of camp sites* (Camping Club of Great Britain), 1935.
28 *Surveyor and Municipal and County Engineer*, 18/8/1933.
29 PRO, HLG 52, 395.
30 PRO, HLG 52, 399 and HLG 54, 466.
31 Rhyl Urban District Council Act, 1935, 25 & 26 George 5, c.50; Flintshire Record Office, Hawarden, Clwyd, Rhyl Urban District Council MSS, 230–3; *Rhyl Journal*, 1934–5; Sheail, 1976, op. cit. 261–2.
32 *Camping: official organ of the Camping Club of Great Britain*, 24, 1928, 139, and 29, 1933, 206–7.
33 PRO, HLG 52, 397; Local Government and Public Health Consolidation Committee, *Second Interim Report*, Cmd. 5059, 1936, 118; Parliamentary Debates, Lords, 100, 1936, 413–30.
34 Parliamentary Debates, Lords, 101, 274–8; Public Health Act, 1936, 26 George 5 & 1 Edward 8, c.49.
35 PRO, HLG 52, 407; *Camping*, 34, 1938, 132 and 135; 35, 1939, 185.
36 Parliamentary Papers, Proceedings of the Joint Committee of the House of Lords and the House of Commons on the Public Health Bill, 1936, *Minutes of Evidence* (Reports from Committees), 1935–6, 135–40.
37 Town and Country Planning Act, 1947, 10 & 11 George 6, c.51.
38 SRO, DD 13, 226.
39 Joad, op. cit. 218–19.

CHAPTER XII

1 Ministry of Works & Planning, *Report of the Committee on land utilisation in rural areas*, Cmd. 6378, 1942, 138 pp.
2 D. Hall, *Reconstruction and the land* (Macmillan), 1941, 171–200.
3 Public Record Office (PRO), MAF 48, 241; J. Sheail, *Nature in trust: the history of nature conservation in Britain* (Blackie), 1976, 58–67.
4 PRO, MAF 48, 665.
5 Dower MSS.
6 A. G. Street, 'The countryman's view', in: *Britain and the beast*, edited by C. Williams-Ellis (Dent), 1938, 130.
7 G. Gibbon, *Reconstruction and town and country planning* (Architect & Building News), 1942, 23–8.
8 R. G. Stapledon, *The land: now and to-morrow* (Faber), 1935, 323 pp.; R. G. Stapledon, *The hill lands of Britain* (Faber), 1937, 65–6.; L. D. Stamp, 'Nationalism and land utilisation in Britain', *Geogr. Rev.* 27, 1937, 1–18.
9 Sheail, op.cit. 141–3.
10 J. Sheail, 'Documentary evidence of the changes in the use, management and appreciation of the grass-heaths of Breckland', *J. Biogeogr.* 6, 1979, 277–92.
11 PRO, MT 39, 43; CAB 35, 24; CAB 40, 24; CAB 41, 24; CAB 49, 25; CAB 24, 167 and 171; CAB 26, 6 and 7; Parliamentary Debates, Commons, 182, 992–1037; Lords, 62, 53–7 and 267–91; Roads Improvement Act, 1925, 15 & 16 George 5, c.68.
12 Middlesex County Council Act, 1914, 4 & 5 George 5, c.98.

13   Public Health Acts Amendment Act, 1890, 53 & 54 Victoria, c.59; PRO, F 18, 81.
14   Road Improvements (Blind Corners Prevention) Bill, 1924–5, 15 George 5, Bill 99.
15   PRO, MT 39, 54.
16   PRO, MT 39, 70.
17   PRO, MT 39, 60.
18   Roads Beautifying Association, *Roadside planting* (Country Life), 1930, 170 pp.
19   PRO, MT 39, 63 and 45, 32.
20   PRO, MT 39, 119, 459–60.
21   Parliamentary Debates, Lords, 160, 1005–20, Commons, 489, 1883–4.
22   C. Williams-Ellis, *Roads in the landscape* (HMSO), 1967, 22 pp.
23   J. W. Gregory, *The story of the road* (Black), 1938, 273–4.
24   *The Times*, 10/2/1926.
25   B. Colvin, 'Roadside planting in country districts', *Landscape & Garden*, 6, 1939, 86–9.
26   T. Adams, 'Landscape design and preservation', *Landscape & Garden*, 4, 1937, 232–4.
27   Sheail, 1976, op. cit. 270 pp.
28   Adams, op. cit., 232–4.
29   British Ecological Society, 'Nature conservation and nature reserves', *J. Ecol.* 32, 1944, 45–82.
30   T. Sharp, *Town and countryside* (OUP), 1932, 33.
31   Dower MSS, lecture notes: a national policy for rural areas.
32   Dower MSS, list of trees and shrubs for Lake District planting.
     H. M. Heyder, 'The control of bracken on commons', *Journal of the Commons Open Spaces, Footpaths Preservation Society*, 5, 1937, 9–13.
34   B. Colvin, *Land and landscapes* (Murray), 1948, 266 pp.
35   A. G. Tansley, *The maintenance of natural vegetation in open spaces and woods acquired by public authorities* (Geographical Publications), 1943, 6 pp.

CHAPTER XIII

1   C. E. M. Joad, *The untutored townsman's invasion of the country* (Faber), 1946, 218–19.
2   Public Record Office (PRO), HLG 52, 747; E. C. Culpin, 'Presidential address', *J. Tn. Plann. Inst.* 24, 1937, 1–7.
3   Ministry of Health, *20th Annual report, 1938–39*, Cmd. 6089, 1939, 222 pp.; Cambridge University Libirary (CUL), Kennet MSS, 82/1.
4   J. Roebuck, *The making of modern English society from 1850* (Routledge & Kegan Paul), 1973, 108–13; H. Macmillan, *The middle way* (Macmillan), 1938, 7–8.
5   PRO, HLG, 52, 544.
6   B. Parker, 'The life and work of Sir Raymond Unwin', *J. Tn. Plann. Inst.* 26, 1940, 159–62.
7   T. Alwyn Lloyd, *Planning in town and country* (Routledge), 1935, 1–2.
8   K. K. Liepmann, *The journey to work* (Kegan Paul, Trench & Trubner) 1944, 107–8.
9   Economics Committee, Report, in: *Papers*, Royal Commission on Population (HMSO), 3, 1950, 64 pp.
10   G. Gibbon, *Problems of town and country planning* (Allen & Unwin), 1937, 38–9; G. D. MacNiven, 'Regional planning and rural preservation', *J. Tn. Plann. Inst.*, 15, 1928, 20–9.
11   W. G. Holford, 'The use of land in town and country', *Advmt Sci.* 2, 1942, 35–7.
12   G. E. Cherry, 'The town planning movement and the late Victorian city', *Trans Inst. Br. Geogr.* 4, 1979, 316–18; G. L. Pepler, 'Twenty-one years of town planning in England and Wales', *J. Tn. Plann. Inst.* 17, 1931, 49–72.
13   Alwyn Lloyd, op. cit. 134.
14   J. S. Nettlefold, *Practical town planning* (St. Catherines Press), 1914, 147–8; T. Adams, *Recent advances in town planning* (Churchill), 1932, 73–4.
15   Culpin, op. cit., 1–7; Parliamentary Debates, Commons, 231, 2125–38.
16   E. Sharp, 'What's wrong with local government', *Municipal Rev.* 31, 1960, 712–17.
17   W. A. Robson, 'The central domination of local government', *Political Quarterly*, 4, 1933, 85–104; P. Addison, *The road to 1945* (Quartet), 1977, 334 pp.
18   R. Lowe, 'The erosion of state intervention in Britain, 1917–24', *Econ. Hist. Rev.*, 31, 1978, 270–86; Ministry of Reconstruction, *First report of the Committee dealing with the law and practice relating to the acquisition and valuation of land for public purposes*, Cmd. 8998, 1918, 9–10.
19   T. Sharp, *Town planning* (Penguin), 1940, 34.
20   E. Sharp, 'How are we governed: logic or chance', *Struct. Engr.* 49, 1971, 3–9.

21 PRO, HLG 52, 709.

22 PRO, HLG 52, 572; R. Douglas, *Land, people and politics* (Allison & Busby), 1976, 198–226.

23 Town and Country Planning Advisory Committee, *Report on the preservation of the countryside* (HMSO), 1938, 36 pp.

24 Ministry of Works & Planning, *Expert Committee on compensation and betterment: final report*, Cmd. 6386, 1942, 4, 6, and 12.

25 A. Robinson, 'The Scott and Uthwatt reports on land utilisation', *Econ. J.* 53, 1943, 37.

26 P. Abercrombie, 'Administration of schemes prepared by joint committees', *J. Tn. Plann. Inst.* 23, 1937, 85–98; Adams, op. cit. 353.

27 CPRE archive, Pepler file; G. E. Cherry, *The evolution of British town planning* (Leonard Hill), 1974, 113; A. Mackrell, *Register of the papers of Sir George L. Pepler* (University of Strathclyde), 1969. 72 pp.

28 W. G. Holford, 'Sir (Leslie) Patrick Abercrombie 1879–1957', in: *Dictionary of national biography*, 1951–1960, ed. E. T. Williams and H. M. Palmer (OUP), 1971, 1–3; P. Abercrombie, *Planning in town and country* (Liverpool University Press and Hodder & Stoughton), 1937, 9–12.

29 PRO, T 161, 628, S 38400.

30 W. A. Ross, 'Local Government Board and after: retrospect', *Public Admin.*, 34, 1956, 17–25; 'I. F. Armer, Sir (Ioan) Gwilym Gibbon', in: *Dictionary of national biography*, 1941–50, ed. L. G. Wickham-Legg and E. T. Williams (OUP), 1959, 297; Anonymous, 'Sir John Maude', *The Times*, 7/2/1963.

31 CUL, Kennet MSS. 16/10; Wayland Young, Edward Hilton Young, in: *Dictionary of national biography*, ed. E. T. Williams and H. M. Palmer (OUP), 1971, 1088–90; E. Hilton-Young, *A bird in the bush* (Country Life), 1936, 146 pp.

32 D. Marquand, *Ramsay MacDonald* (Cape), 1977, 87, 401–3 and 733; Birmingham University Library, Chamberlain MSS; G. E. Cherry, 'The place of Neville Chamberlain in British town planning', in: *Shaping an urban world: planning in the twentieth century*, ed. G. E. Cherry (Mansell), 1980, pp. 161–79.

33 PRO, HLG 52, 912.

34 Pepler, op. cit. 49–72.

35 N. Chamberlain, 'The twenty-first anniversary dinner', *J. Tn. Plann. Inst.* 21, 1934, 20–1.

36 J. Betjeman, 'A preservationist's progress', in: *The future of the past*, ed. J. Fawcett (Thames & Hudson), 1976, 58–9.

37 S. Glynn and J. Oxborrow, *Inter-war Britain* (Allen & Unwin), 1976, 49–50.

38 Parliamentary Debates, Commons, 320, 459–66.

39 F. J. Osborn, 'Introduction', in: *The beauties of scenery*, by V. Cornish (Muller), 1943, 9–14; C. Williams-Ellis, *England and the octopus* (Penrhyndeudraeth), reprinted 1975, 9–16 and 97.

40 Gibbon, op. cit. 153–82.

41 C. Williams-Ellis, op. cit. 9–10; C. Williams-Ellis, *Architect errant* (Constable), 1971, 179–81.

42 C. Williams-Ellis (ed.), *Britain and the beast* (Dent), 1937, 332 pp.

43 W. A. Eden, 'Order in the countryside', *Tn. Plann. Rev.* 14, 1930, 95–103.

44 PRO, HLG 52, 714.

45 T. Adams, 'Preserving and developing the beauties of the English landscape', *Landscape & Garden*, 3, 1936, 148.

46 G. Jellicoe, 'National forestry', *Landscape & Garden*, 3, 1936, 14–15; G. Jellicoe, Editorial, *Landscape & Garden*, 5, 1938, 139.

47 Dower MSS, 'The countryside after the war', and 'Planning for Britain's future in town and country'.

48 Dower MSS, 'Rural Northumberland: its preservation and development'.

49 Dower MSS, 'National parks'.

50 Dower MSS, 'Interim safeguarding and local authority housing'.

INDEX